The Third Asiatic Invasion

NATION OF NEWCOMERS
Immigrant History as American History

General Editors: Matthew Jacobson and Werner Sollors

Beyond the Shadow of Camptown: Korean Military Brides in America
Ji-Yeon Yuh

Feeling Italian: The Art of Ethnicity in America
Thomas J. Ferraro

Constructing Black Selves:
Caribbean American Narratives and the Second Generation
Lisa D. McGill

Transnational Adoption: A Cultural Economy of Race, Gender, and Kinship
Sara K. Dorow

Immigration and American Popular Culture: An Introduction
Jeffrey Melnick and Rachel Rubin

From Arrival to Incorporation: Migrants to the U.S. in a Global Era
Edited by Elliott R. Barkan, Hasia Diner, and Alan M. Kraut

Migrant Imaginaries: Latino Cultural Politics in the U.S.-Mexico Borderlands
Alicia Schmidt Camacho

The Force of Domesticity: Filipina Migrants and Globalization
Rhacel Salazar Parreñas

Immigrant Rights in the Shadows of Citizenship
Edited by Rachel Ida Buff

Rough Writing: Ethnic Authorship in Theodore Roosevelt's America
Aviva F. Taubenfeld

The Third Asiatic Invasion:
Empire and Migration in Filipino America, 1898–1946
Rick Baldoz

The Third
Asiatic Invasion

*Empire and Migration in
Filipino America, 1898–1946*

Rick Baldoz

NEW YORK UNIVERSITY PRESS
New York and London

NEW YORK UNIVERSITY PRESS
New York and London
www.nyupress.org

References to Internet websites (URLs) were accurate at the time of writing.
Neither the author nor New York University Press is responsible for URLs
that may have expired or changed since the manuscript was prepared.

Library of Congress Cataloging-in-Publication Data

Baldoz, Rick, 1969–
The third Asiatic invasion : migration and empire in
Filipino America, 1898–1946 / Rick Baldoz.
p. cm. — (Nation of newcomers: immigrant history as American history)
Includes bibliographical references and index.
ISBN 978-0-8147-9108-0 (cl : alk. paper) — ISBN 978-0-8147-9109-7
(pb : alk. paper) — ISBN 978-0-8147-0921-4 (e-book : alk. paper)
1. Filipino Americans—History—20th century. 2. Philippines—Emigration and
immigration—History—20th century. 3. United States—Emigration and immigration—
History—20th century. 4. Immigrants—United States—History—20th century.
5. United States—Foreign relations—Philippines. 6. Philippines—Foreign relations—
United States. I. Title.
E184.F4B35   2011
973'.049921—dc22   2010041365

New York University Press books are printed on acid-free paper,
and their binding materials are chosen for strength and durability.
We strive to use environmentally responsible suppliers and materials
o the greatest extent possible in publishing our books.

Manufactured in the United States of America

c 10 9 8 7 6 5 4 3 2 1
p 10 9 8 7 6 5 4 3 2 1

Contents

Acknowledgments

Although the current incarnation of this book began in graduate school, the roots of this project go back much further. I got my first lessons in Filipino American history from family and friends who lived and worked in and around Yakima Indian Reservation in Washington State. My grandfather Roy Baldoz was part of the first wave of Filipinos to migrate to the mainland United States in the mid-1920s and later became a prominent civil rights activist in the Pacific Northwest. I grew up on the farms, canneries, and warehouses of eastern Washington and listening to my grandfather and other manongs telling remarkable tales of labor strife, race riots, and political struggle. One of my uncles, Gene Viernes, was particularly vocal about the struggles of Filipinos in American society and framed his political activism in the 1970s as a continuation of the work of the manong generation. His murder in 1981 at the hands of agents of Ferdinand Marcos in Seattle was a formative event in my youth and later served as an inspiration for me to write this book. I own a large debt of gratitude to the Filipino community of the Yakima Valley for giving me my first and best education.

I have accumulated a number of intellectual debts over the course of this project. A few people merit special attention: Evelyn Nakano Glenn has been a great mentor and friend over the years, offering unflinching support and good humor at critical moments. Rhacel Parreñas has been a source of wisdom and inspiration, and my work has benefited greatly from her interventions. Jonathan Okamura shared ideas and offered careful readings of the manuscript that helped to clarify the book's argument.

A vibrant group of Filipino and Filipino American scholars provided encouragement and advice over the years: Steve McKay, Celine Parreñas Shimizu, Anna Guevarra, E. San Juan Jr., August Espiritu, Nerissa Balce, Victor Bascara, Martin Manalansan, Catherine Ceniza Choy, Robyn Rodriguez, Rick Bonus, Theo Gonzalves, Allan Isaac, Emily Ignacio, Joe Ponce, Sunny Vergara, Linda España-Maram, Anthony Ocampo, Denise Cruz, Sarita See,

Dylan Rodriguez, and Emily Lawsin. Others that deserve mention for their constructive feedback on my work include Martin Murray, Michael Omi, Judy Tzu-Chun Wu, Moon-Kie Jung, Roger Waldinger, David Johnson, Eiichiro Azuma, and Shelley Streeby.

I was lucky to spend a year as a Faculty Fellow at Stanford University's Center for the Comparative Study of Race and Ethnicity. While at Stanford, I benefited from conversations and counsel with Larry Bobo, Gordon Chang, David Palumbo-Liu, Tom Guglielmo, Lori Flores, and Hazel Markus. I was invited to test run various parts of my project with audiences at UC Berkeley's Department of Ethnic Studies, UCLA's Department of Sociology, the Library of Congress, Ohio State University, the University of Illinois's Asian American Studies Program, and Stanford University's Faculty Fellows Forum, and I profited from these exchanges.

My experience with NYU Press has been a rewarding one. One would be hard-pressed to find a more supportive editor than Eric Zinner. His enthusiasm for the project provided extra incentive to finish things up. Ciara McLaughlin has shepherded the book through the editorial and production process with great patience and care. I would also like to thank copyeditor Andrew Katz for his meticulous work on the manuscript. A special shout-out goes to Matthew Frye Jacobson for soliciting the monograph for the "Nation of Newcomers" series he coedits with Werner Sollors. Matt's work has been a major inspiration over the years, so it is an honor to be part of this series. Thanks also to the anonymous readers for their constructive feedback and suggestions that helped to strengthen the final product. I am grateful to Dawn Mabalon and Stockton FANHS for granting permission to use one of their photographs for the book jacket. An early version of chapter 1 as "The Racial Vectors of Empire: Classification an Competing Master Narratives in the Colonial Philippines," *Du Bois Review* 5(1): 69–94.

I owe my biggest debts to my family for love and support through the years. They showed an unshakable faith that I would eventually finish the book, even as the project dragged on. My dad has been there for me at every turn, offering encouragement and inspiration whenever needed. My brother Ryan and sister Aimee opened up their homes to me while I was conducting research in the Pacific Northwest and made my life far richer in the process. My last note of recognition goes to Shelley Lee, who has played a pivotal role in my life. She has read and critiqued the whole manuscript, offering constructive insights that have improved the book in innumerable ways. Her faith in me throughout this journey has enriched my life in ways big and small.

Introduction

On October 22, 1934, a young couple, Rafael Lopez de Onate and Eleanor (Ellen) Wilson McAdoo, appeared at the Riverside County Clerk's Office in California to apply for a marriage license. They did not actually get married that day, as California law required prospective partners to file a three-day "notice of intention to marry," so their visit to the clerk's office was the first step in a multipart process.[1] The couple's decision to file their application in Riverside was curious, as both De Onate and Wilson McAdoo resided in West Hollywood, California, about seventy miles away. The pair likely wanted to proceed with their marriage plans away from the media spotlight of Los Angeles because De Onate was Filipino and Wilson McAdoo was white. The prospective bridegroom was a light-skinned mestizo and might have escaped scrutiny had he not listed the Philippines as his place of birth on the application. This piece of information, however, raised a red flag with Riverside County Clerk D. G. Clayton, who reminded the couple of the state's antimiscegenation statute that proscribed intermarriage between whites and "Malays." De Onate and Wilson McAdoo would certainly have been aware that Los Angeles had been the site of a prolonged legal struggle around the issue of whether the state's prohibition on interracial wedlock applied to Filipinos. In 1933, just a year before De Onate and Wilson McAdoo applied for their marriage license, the California State Supreme Court had ruled in the highly publicized *Roldan v. Los Angeles County* case that Filipinos, unlike Chinese and Japanese, were eligible to intermarry with whites based on a technical issue related to their racial classification as "Malays." This state of affairs was short-lived, as the legislature amended the state's antimiscegenation statute a few weeks later, adding Filipinos to the list of the groups legally barred from intermarrying with whites, and thus settled legal questions surrounding the issue (see chapter 3).

The pair's attempt to circumvent the state's bar on intermarriage might have gone unnoticed if it were not for the distinguished lineage and social standing of De Onate's fiancée. Ellen Wilson McAdoo was the granddaughter of former president Woodrow Wilson and the daughter of William Gibbs McAdoo, a powerful U.S. senator from California. If the couple believed that they could avoid scrutiny by traveling to Riverside, they were wrong. News of the pair's impending nuptials caused a media frenzy, generating sensational headlines across the country. Scrutiny of relationships between Filipino men and white women was not new in California, and in fact, anxieties about such pairings had provoked a series of violent race riots and vigilante campaigns on the West Coast during the late 1920s and early 1930s.

The romance between De Onate and Wilson McAdoo struck many observers as a novelty because it flouted conventional thinking about the character of interracial intimacy. Why, after all, would an attractive white woman such as Ellen Wilson McAdoo, just nineteen years old, want to marry a Filipino man, knowing that such a union violated both legal and social conventions? Her upper-class background and patrician pedigree flew in the face of popular explanations of interracial attraction, which held that only lower-class or morally debased women were attracted to Filipino men (see chapter 4). News accounts described the bride-to-be as a "statuesque blonde" who lived on a ten-thousand-dollar-a-year allowance provided by her wealthy parents. The thirty-eight-year-old De Onate, on the other hand, was a struggling Hollywood actor eking out a modest living through part-time work in Spanish-language films.[2]

Media coverage of the case centered on two main themes: the vocal opposition to the marriage raised by the Wilson McAdoo family and the contested racial status of Rafael De Onate, who claimed to be of Spanish rather than Filipino descent. When news of the impending nuptials reached Senator McAdoo in Washington, DC, he immediately asked his friend and law partner in California, Colonel William H. Neblett, to intercede. Neblett served as the family spokesman during the affair, marshaling the Wilson McAdoo clan's political resources to prevent the marriage from taking place. The family applied personal pressure on Ellen, asking her to rethink her "wild plans" to marry De Onate. Senator McAdoo claimed that his vehement opposition was due in part to the fact that he had never met the prospective bridegroom, yet there was clearly more to the story.

The family issued a public threat to "disown" and "disinherit" Ellen if she were to follow through with her marriage plans, and her car was seized by Colonel Neblett to prevent her from meeting with her fiancé. The bride-to-be, according to media accounts, was a well-heeled "debutante," accustomed to a life of bourgeois privilege and excess. This stood in stark contrast to the social milieu of her potential husband, who labored on the margins of the Hollywood film industry. An investigation of Rafael De Onate's finances conducted by Neblett discovered that De Onate's annual income for the previous five years had averaged less than one thousand dollars per year.[3] Observers wondered if the threat of disinheritance would convince the couple to alter their plans knowing the potential financial consequences. Would Ellen McAdoo come to her senses when her lavish lifestyle was jeopardized? In light of the media scrutiny of their relationship and pressure from the Wilson McAdoo family, the couple decided to postpone their betrothal. There were conflicting accounts, however, of what the delay meant. The spokesman for the McAdoo Wilson family claimed that the wedding plans had been called off permanently. Rafael and Ellen, however, insisted that they still intended to get married once the media attention died down, and it soon became clear to all involved that the pair were moving forward with their matrimonial plans despite threats of familial and financial alienation.[4]

Legal obstacles proved to be a more serious roadblock to the couple's plans than family pressure was. State officials in California had made it clear from the very beginning of the process that they had no intention of granting a marriage license to the pair until questions surrounding Mr. De Onate's racial background were settled. Senator McAdoo and Colonel Neblett contacted Riverside officials, expressing their opinion that the bridegroom was subject to the state's antimiscegenation statute. D. G. Clayton of the Riverside County Clerk's Office was adamant that no license would be issued to the couple until De Onate provided evidence that he had "no Filipino or Malay blood in his veins."[5] When asked by reporters if a copy of the bridegroom's birth certificate would be sufficient verification of his ancestry, Clayton tersely replied, "No it would not. . . . I want proof of the racial blood of his parents."[6] The Wilson McAdoo family applied political pressure to officials outside of California as well, issuing a public appeal to government authorities in the neighboring states of Arizona and Nevada warning them of De Onate's Filipino heritage, in order to thwart the couple's rumored elopement plans to other jurisdictions.[7]

William McAdoo's apprehension about the racial status of his potential son-in-law was not surprising, given that the senator had grown up in the American South with strong family ties to the Confederacy. Interracial marriage was quite rare in the 1930s, and the practice was held in disrepute among the nation's white population. The senator was no stranger to the nation's contentious racial politics, having been a central player in the infamous Democratic "Klanbake" Convention in New York in 1924.[8] Race mixing between

Filipino men and white women was a particularly sensitive topic in California, where nativist forces had seized on anxieties about interracial sex and labor competition to advance a national campaign aimed at forestalling immigration from the Philippines (see chapter 5).

Throughout the controversy, Rafael De Onate maintained that he was of "pure Spanish blood" and therefore not subject to the state's prohibition on intermarriage. His embrace of the European part of his heritage is not surprising, considering the obvious material advantages that redounded to the white population as a result of its privileged position in the social order. The taint of Filipino blood, moreover, brought with it a social stigma that De Onate almost certainly wanted to avoid in the nativist climate of 1930s California. He condemned media speculation about his suspect ancestry, calling questions about racial background "ridiculous." De Onate proclaimed, "I am Spanish—most certainly I am not Filipino. I cannot understand why such a fuss is being made, just because Ellen and I are in love." His public statements about his background did little to clarify matters, offering vague and sometimes contradictory claims about his personal history. In interviews he claimed that he had been "educated" in the United States, but according to authorities, he had migrated to the country as an adult. He also told reporters that he "considered himself" an American citizen, but he offered no explanation about how he circumvented U.S. nationality law that debarred Filipinos from naturalized citizenship. The notoriety surrounding the case prompted federal authorities to look into the issue. An inspector from the Los Angeles branch of the U.S. Immigration and Naturalization Service (INS) questioned the actor at the Fox Film Studios lot in Los Angeles about his background and citizenship status but found nothing to contradict his public accounts of his family history.[9]

Official documentation from the Philippines did little to clarify matters since public records offered conflicting evidence about the De Onate family's Spanish bloodlines. The lack of uniform standards or criteria for determining racial boundaries added another layer of confusion to the story. The various parties involved in the case frequently conflated color and nationality in their efforts to prove or disprove the family's racial pedigree. Rafael De Onate repeatedly declared that both his parents were natives of "Basque Country" who had migrated to the Philippines during the Spanish colonial period. Rafael's sister, Mercedes Lopez De Onate West, offered a slightly different version of the family's history, claiming that their father was from Barcelona and that their mother, Isabel Novarro, was a full-blooded Spanish subject born in the Philippines.[10] Philippine officials provided documentation that seemed to back up these claims, verifying that both parents were recognized as nationals of Spain. Indicia of the family's Spanish nationality, however, did not resolve questions about the bridegroom's racial bona fides after it was established that Rafael's mother, Isabel Novarro, had indeed been born in the Philippines. This piece of information raised immediate suspicions about the "purity" of her bloodlines, since racial admixture was commonplace under the Spanish colonial regime. Phillip Whitaker, Rafael and Mercedes's stepfather, added fuel to this speculation, claiming that the late Ms. Novarro was in fact of mestiza extraction. Whitaker told reporters in Manila that prior to her passing, Isabel Novarro-Whitaker had confided to him that she was of "1/4 or 1/8 Filipino blood." This assertion raised the possibility that Rafael De Onate was of one-eighth or one-sixteenth Filipino ancestry, though Phillip Whitaker's claims about his late wife's miscegenous bloodlines could not be verified.[11]

The story took an unexpected turn just two weeks later, when the Wilson McAdoo family abruptly dropped its opposition to the couple's marital plans. The reason for the family's change of heart is unclear, but Senator McAdoo did eventually meet his daughter's fiancé, giving him the opportunity to question De Onate about his background. With the family's blessing, Rafael Lopez De Onate and Ellen Wilson McAdoo refiled a declaration of intention to be married, this time at the Los Angeles County Clerk's office on November 8, 1934. To their dismay, they discovered that Rosamond Rice, chief of the Los Angeles Marriage License Bureau (and ardent opponent of interracial marriage), had no intention of issuing the couple a license until De Onate could "produce proof he is of the Caucasian race." Though it was not readily clear what constituted "proof" of membership in the Caucasian race, Rice suggested that she wanted documentary evidence of the applicant's unalloyed whiteness before she would sign off on the couple's nuptials.[12] It was unlikely that Rafael De Onate could meet the Los Angeles Marriage Bureau's purity threshold even though he was likely seven-eighths or fifteen-sixteenths white and probably passed as a white man in his everyday interactions. Whether Rosamond Rice's narrow interpretation of the state's proscription on interracial marriage would hold up under scrutiny from the courts was an open question. California's antimiscegenation law was vague on the blood quantum required to qualify an individual as a white person, and the application of the statute often differed by jurisdiction.

The California attorney general's office soon weighed in on the case, acknowledging that state law lacked an operative definition of legal whiteness. Nonetheless James Howie, deputy attorney general of California, advocated a narrow metric for determining the boundaries of whiteness: "if a person has at least one-quarter Malay blood, he is not white." According to the attorney general's office, a person of three-quarters white blood and one-quarter Malay blood would be legally classed as a member of the Filipino race and therefore barred by state law from marrying a Caucasian person. This interpretation did not settle the issue of Rafael De Onate's eligibility, since he was only one-eighth or one-sixteenth Filipino. Howie floated the possibility that the "one-drop rule" might apply to the state's intermarriage ban, suggesting that a "person with any Malay blood whatever" might be prevented from marrying a Caucasian in California.[13] Deliberations among state officials about De Onate's "true" racial identity underscore the fluid nature of social classification and highlight some of the difficulties in maintaining categorical distinctions between population groups. It also reminds us that race is not a fixed or settled category, but rather a social construct that has been wielded by dominant-group members to valorize ascriptive boundaries and monopolize access to material resources and civic status.

Lingering (and likely embarrassing) questions about Rafael De Onate's racial legitimacy finally convinced the couple to look for friendlier environs in moving forward with their nuptials. On November 10, 1934, the pair flew to New Mexico and were married in Albuquerque at the home of local attorney William Keleher, a former associate of William Gibbs McAdoo. Married at long last, the bride and groom expressed relief that their vexing ordeal was over. Rather than dwell on the imbroglio that had surrounded their relationship, Ellen Lopez De Onate preferred instead to focus on her impending honeymoon. Senator McAdoo also seemed reconciled to the couple's actions, telling reporters, "love laughs at locksmiths, . . . and that is all there is to it." He told reporters that he gave the pair his blessing after meeting with De Onate and determining that he was indeed of "Spanish parentage." He had little to say about his previous objections to their relationship and said that he knew nothing of the couple's future plans.[14] McAdoo's statements of support later came under scrutiny when the pair went through a contentious divorce a few years later, in 1937.

In Ellen Lopez De Onate's filing for dissolution of the marriage, she cited a lack of spousal support as precipitating the couple's estrangement. She stated that her husband had failed to provide financially for her and the couple's young son, Ricardo, even though he had the means to do so. Rafael De Onate told reporters he was surprised by the divorce suit and claimed that his financial difficulties were a result of the Wilson McAdoo family's interference. During the contentious divorce proceedings, he told the court that

Senator McAdoo paid the couple to leave the country after their wedding to "avoid unfavorable publicity" due to his racial heritage. Moreover, the senator footed the bill for the pair to stay in Europe for two years after their nuptials to evade further media scrutiny of their controversial relationship. The couple's two-year "honeymoon" in Europe, it seemed, was less romantic adventure than a voluntary exile carried out to protect the Wilson McAdoo family's public image.

Upon returning to the United States, Rafael De Onate found it difficult to secure film work in Hollywood, and he blamed this situation on his two-year exile from the movie industry. Senator McAdoo and his ex-wife, Eleanor Wilson, both testified at the divorce proceedings and denied that they had meddled in the couple's marriage or that he had ever opposed the coupling on racial grounds. Ellen McAdoo was granted an interlocutory divorce on April 2, 1937, as well as sole custody of Ricardo.[15] She was remarried a year later, in 1938, to musician William Hinshaw. Though Ellen held legal custody of Ricardo after her divorce, the boy actually lived with Senator McAdoo and his wife in Santa Barbara, California. In May 1940, the case reappeared in the news as the McAdoos filed court papers to formally adopt their four-year-old grandson, Ricardo Lopez De Onate. Rafael De Onate appeared unexpectedly at the adoption proceedings to seek custody of his son and to challenge the revocation of his paternal rights. Judge Atwell Westwick dismissed De Onate's custodial claims to his son and granted a decree approving the adoption. The McAdoos immediately rechristened their "son" with a new Anglo name, Richard Floyd McAdoo, expunging outward evidence of the boy's suspicious racial pedigree.[16]

Though the curious chronicle of Rafael Lopez De Onate and Ellen Wilson McAdoo was a major scandal at the time, it is likely unfamiliar to most Americans today. It is not difficult to see why the couple's unlikely romance received so much media attention at the time, since it featured high-profile social actors (Senator William McAdoo, Ellen Wilson) and controversial themes (interracial romance, crossing of class lines, family interference). More important than the human drama surrounding the events are the social and political themes that it brings to light. Rafael Lopez De Onate is hardly a well-known figure in Filipino American history, and considering his public statements at the time, he would probably express ambivalence about being included as part of that historical narrative.[17] His story is instructive, nonetheless, in that it highlights the contentious politics surrounding Filipinos' immigration to the United States and the ways in which their arrival confounded authorities charged with enforcing racial and national boundaries.

Although it might seem odd to begin a book about Filipino Americans with a story involving a man who publicly denied that he was Filipino, I believe that Rafael De Onate and the events that unfolded around him provide a useful point of entry to analyze themes of race, immigration, and American empire. Take, for instance, the issue of De Onate's racial identification, which was so central to the marriage controversy. Race, we are often reminded, is a social construction, a human contrivance that has been used to frame and rationalize hierarchical divisions between population groups in the modern world. In racially stratified societies, people are assigned into discrete, hierarchically organized social categories, which subsequently become the basis for collective identification and action. This begs the question, who is doing the assigning, and to what end? In the case at hand, the primary racializers included a gauntlet of local and state officials tasked with policing the color line in matters of interracial association and family relations.

Private citizens (family members, media observers) also played an important role in policing ascriptive hierarchies, recognizing that the monopoly on power and privilege held by whites in American society was contingent and required vigilant adherence to norms of racial propriety. This task was easier said than done, since group boundaries were often fluid and contested, held together by a disjointed system of public and private sanctions. Rafael De Onate's identification was particularly vexing, since the tall, light-skinned actor likely passed as white in most of his social interactions and might have done so again in Riverside had he not listed his place of birth as the Philippines on the marriage application. Other social actors also weighed in on the issue, especially when the high-powered Wilson McAdoo's family expressed objections to Ellen's suitor. The case received an elevated level of scrutiny from local authorities, who were wary of letting a "colored" infiltrator circumvent the race line in such a high-profile case. The operative assumption of public officials and media observers was that De Onate was Filipino, unless he could offer "proof" that he was of pure Spanish blood. Simple resolution of the case, however, proved problematic in this situation because California state law was ambiguous on the issue of blood quantum as it pertained to the eligibility of mixed-race individuals. Adding to the drama was the fact the Rafael De Onate emphatically rejected his assignment into the Malay race category and claimed, instead, to be white.

The contentious debate surrounding the disposition of the De Onate case recalls the observations of sociologist Herbert Blumer regarding the labyrinthine character of the American racial hierarchy. Blumer astutely noted that the color line in the United States is best represented not as a "single, sharply drawn line" but rather "as a series of ramparts," tenuously held together through a patchwork system of legal barriers, cultural routines, and social conventions.[18] The absence of clear-cut, consistent definitions about racial classification gave local bureaucrats and state officials wide latitude in determining the boundaries of exclusion, since they were free to interpret statutory meanings in line with prevailing community prejudices. Fluid definitions of race also opened up the potential opportunities to challenge the criteria of exclusion. Countless individuals, De Onate included, tested the system and, in doing so, highlighted cracks in the racial order. The structure of white domination, however, proved remarkably resilient despite its contradictions and inconsistencies, due in no small part to the vigilance of public and private gatekeepers who held the line against rival claimants.

The scandal surrounding the case also serves as a springboard into other key themes taken up in this book, namely, the entanglement of immigration, empire, and citizenship. Recall that INS officials intervened in the case, interrogating De Onate about his personal history and legal status in the United States. Why was such an intervention necessary? Why did officials not simply look up his immigration records to ascertain when he entered the country? The answer to these questions lies in the unique historical relationship between the United States and the Philippines, a political attachment that dates back to 1898, when the United States seized the islands in the aftermath of the Spanish-American War. As a result, Filipinos became U.S. "nationals," an anomalous political designation that placed them in a political twilight zone between citizenship and alienage. Their unique sociolegal status accorded them certain rights, including the freedom to move across and within the borders of the United States. Since Filipinos were not classified as aliens, they were not subject to U.S. immigration laws and were essentially treated the same as citizens when it came to entering or exiting the country. Consequently, American immigration authorities kept no official records on arrivals from the Philippines and did little to track their movements once they arrived. When an inspector from the INS interrogated Rafael De Onate about his history in the United States, it was likely a perfunctory exercise, since the INS held no authority over his standing as a legal resident.[19]

Filipinos' special status did not extend into the arena of naturalization law. Like other Asian immigrant groups, they were racially ineligible for naturalized U.S. citizenship (except for a small group of men who had served in the U.S. armed forces during World War I). This makes Rafael De Onate's claim that he was an American citizen suspect. He told the *San Francisco Chronicle* that when he reached a certain age, he was "given the choice" of becoming an American or a Spanish subject and chose the former. The assertion that he "considered himself" an American citizen leaves open the question of whether he really held officially recognized national membership or whether he was referring to his own self-definition. It is possible that he convinced a naturalization examiner in the United States that he was Spanish, which would have made him eligible for citizenship as a "white person," but public accounts offer no evidence of a naturalization certificate. De Oñate's status, like that of many other Filipinos, confounded authorities tasked with managing the nation's internal and external border controls, since the newcomers did not fit neatly into the extant classificatory system. The De Onate affair, and the notoriety that surrounded it, offers a brief glimpse into the complex and contentious history of Filipino America. I now want to lay out the aims of the book to put the case into perspective.

The Making of Filipino America

The Third Asiatic Invasion: Empire and Migration in Filipino America, is a work of historical sociology that examines the interlocking politics of race, immigration, and empire. Its central argument is that the incorporation of Filipinos into American society played an important role in shaping the politics of citizenship and race during an important period in U.S. history. This study places a series of questions at the forefront: (1) How did Filipinos' status as American colonial subjects affect their standing in the United States? (2) How were racial boundaries organized in American society, what did they mean to different social constituencies, how did they evolve over time, and under what conditions did they intersect or diverge from other sources of social and political action? And (3) How and why did Filipino immigration to the United States come to be defined as a "social problem," and what public resources were mobilized to remedy the putative problem? To answer these questions we must situate the Filipino experience within the larger political and economic transformations sweeping across the globe during the late nineteenth and early twentieth centuries. This book employs a composite analysis, which takes place at two levels: internationally, through an audit of the sociolegal architecture of American empire, and domestically, through an examination of the formation of Filipino communities in the United States. I reveal how American practices of racial exclusion repeatedly collided with the imperatives of U.S. overseas expansion.

The triumph of the United States in the Spanish-American War of 1898 (and later the Philippine-American war) inaugurated the nation's ascendance as global imperial power. The spoils of victory included the acquisition of former Spanish colonies including the Philippines, Puerto Rico, Cuba, and Guam. The United States had acquired millions of new political subjects in these territories (and in the separately annexed territory of Hawaii), subjects whose status vis-à-vis the American polity had to be resolved.[20] Public debate centered on the question of whether inhabitants of colonial possessions were granted U.S. citizenship by virtue of treaty, or if not, whether they were eligible for naturalization under American law. The U.S. Congress, backed by the Supreme Court, declared that the political status of inhabitants of "unincorporated territories" such as the Philippines and Puerto Rico was to be determined by Congress on a case-by-case basis (see chapter 1).[21]

An influential bloc of U.S. congressmen and public figures opposed extending American sovereignty over the Philippines, warning that such an act would automatically confer U.S. citizenship to all residents of the islands. Previous territorial annexations by the United States had included provisions collectively naturalizing inhabitants of those jurisdictions. The prospect that Filipinos might be integrated into the U.S. polity with the same political rights enjoyed by white citizens set off alarm bells, as a broad cross-section of the populace questioned the capacity of the nation's democratic institutions to absorb millions of newcomers of suspect racial stock. Advocates of annexation, on the other hand, drew on a different vein of Progressive Era racial thinking to bolster their case for extraterritorial expansion. This paternalistic worldview held that the Anglo-Saxons had demonstrated a singular capacity for civilizational development, a talent that might be imparted to premodern peoples inhabiting the dark corners of the globe. According to the imperialists, the United States was duty bound to rescue the Filipinos from their debased condition, a project that would require holding the islands in subjection for an indefinite period of colonial apprenticeship. Spokesmen on both sides of the "Philippine question" agreed that Filipinos were unfit for citizenship and set about fashioning a new national policy that allowed the United States to attach its sovereignty to overseas territories without necessarily incorporating the undesirable inhabitants of those possessions into the American polity (at least not as full members).

The contentious politics surrounding the Philippine issue echoed contemporaneous debates about the changing sociolegal status of blacks and the putative threat posed by unrestricted immigration from Asia and southern and eastern Europe. The acquisition of overseas colonies heightened anxieties about race and nationality in a Progressive Era political culture dominated by a virulent strain of civic protectionism. Debates about immigration and nationality policy became increasingly racialized during this period, as the "science" of eugenics was deployed to explain the inevitability of racial hierarchies and the dangers of amalgamation. The ascendance of the United States as a global power was attributed to superior intellectual and physical traits of the nation's Anglo-Saxon ruling bloc, whose socio-cultural hegemony was evidenced by the ease with which they conquered the continent and by the country's decisive victory over Spain and Filipino insurgents at the turn of the century. Many observers, however, cautioned that the very source of America's rise to power (its Anglo-Saxon cultural base) was being weakened by an influx of undesirables and lesser peoples who were either unable or unwilling to assimilate into the national culture.[22]

The passage of the Chinese Exclusion Act of 1882 was the first in a series of legislative enactments that evinced both the political will and the administrative capacity of the federal government to manage population flows based on racially selective criteria. Chinese exclusion set an important statutory precedent that explicitly welded together external (national border controls) and internal (racial dividing lines) boundary processes. Restrictionist sentiment gained momentum in subsequent decades as nativists warned of an impending crisis triggered by the unfettered influx of inferior population groups. The increasing presence of Asian and southern and eastern European immigrants in the United States, along with the enhanced mobility of African Americans, was, according to nativist spokesmen, slowly enervating the Anglo-Saxon character of the national culture. Anxieties about unrestricted immigration and the shifting contours of the American racial hierarchy led federal officials to assert greater control over both who could legally enter the physical borders of the United States and who could be admitted within the political boundaries of the national community. As a result, the U.S. Congress passed the Naturalization Act of 1906, which consolidated previously separate immigration and naturalization functions of the government into a single federal agency, the Bureau of Immigration and Naturalization.[23] Growing concerns about the demographic composition of U.S. society reflected a marked shift in how Americans (to borrow a phrase from Benedict Anderson) "imagined" the nation, which by the early decades of the twentieth century was increasingly envisioned as a gated community whose survival depended on the vigilant enforcement of immigration and nationality controls.[24]

Extraterritorial expansion complicated efforts to shore up the nation's external and internal ramparts. Filipinos and other U.S. nationals were not citizens, yet they were officially recognized as fractional members of the American polity, with certain narrowly defined rights and protections. Boundary lines ran between metropole and colony but at the same time encircled them, a fact that confounded gatekeepers tasked with policing the shifting and uncertain borders of the national community. The most significant privilege accorded Filipinos was immunity from restrictive immigration quotas imposed by the federal government during the early twentieth century. American policymakers were wary of allowing the unfettered entry of Filipinos into the United States but were bound by international convention, which held that imperial subjects be granted free admittance to the "mother country."

Hawaii sugar planters were the first to recruit labor from the Philippines, beginning in 1906, and by the early 1920s, Filipinos made up the largest segment of the plantation workforce in the islands. The burgeoning canned-salmon industry in Alaska soon followed, enlisting Filipinos in the early 1920s to meet the industry's growing labor needs, and by the end of the decade Filipinos made up the bulk of the cannery workforce. By the mid-1920s, emigration from the Philippines had gained internal momentum, fueled by a series of factors: the evolution of the transpacific imperial zone as a major political-economic hub, the steady flow of remittances from nationals working abroad, and targeted recruitment by global steamship companies eager to profit from the transpacific traffic of steerage passengers. Filipino migration to the U.S. mainland, which is the primary focus of this book, increased in both scale and velocity during the mid- to late 1920s as western U.S. agricultural interests strained to meet labor needs in an industry experiencing unprecedented growth. Agribusiness leaders expressed consternation about the increasingly restrictive character of the federal immigration apparatus, which obstructed traditional channels of labor and drove up the cost of doing business. Ironically, it was the passage of the 1924 Johnson-Reed Act and the introduction of subsequent legislative proposals seeking to place Mexican immigrants under restrictive quotas that spurred the recruitment of Filipinos, who were excepted from limitative regulation.

The influx of Filipinos to the U.S. mainland during the 1920s riled nativist leaders who viewed the newcomers' special status as U.S. nationals as an affront to the restrictive spirit of the 1917 and 1924 immigration acts. Although gatekeepers could not control Filipinos' movement across national borders, they made a concerted effort to delimit Filipinos' standing within the United States by demanding the newcomers adhere to a staunch observance of extant racial hierarchies in American society. That Filipinos did not fit neatly into the preexisting classificatory schema generated a good deal of confusion for authorities tasked with enforcing a patchwork structure of racial regulations enacted at the federal, state, and local levels.

One example of this problem was evident in early disputes over whether Filipinos were eligible for citizenship in the United States. Clear resolution of this issue proved elusive because American naturalization law only applied to "aliens" and contained no procedure for naturalizing the newly invented class of persons known as "nationals." Filipinos, moreover, claimed that their compulsory allegiance to the United States entitled them to civic recognition from their political sovereign. Efforts to bring them under the purview of legal proscriptions regulating citizenship, family rights, employment, and property rights produced a series of conflicting and idiosyncratic rulings that reveal the contingent character of the nation's ascriptive hierarchy. Filipinos took advantage of the uncertainty surrounding their administrative status to challenge their subordination, exploiting loopholes in statutory language to claim rights and creating headaches for authorities. These issues are important because they highlight tensions between various state actors, most notably between high-level officials in national or state legislatures, who designed exclusionary laws, and intermediary authorities tasked with interpreting and enforcing statutory prohibitions at the local level.

Attempts to keep Filipinos "in their place" proved more difficult than expected because of their anomalous political status and because they frequently circumvented racial checkpoints. Uncertainty about the administrative status of Filipinos in the United States reflected an appreciable tension between prevailing nativist/racist attitudes, on the one hand, and the race-neutral legal tenets enumerated in the U.S. Constitution, on the other. Lawmakers had to make some effort to abide by Fourteenth Amendment protections, which often blunted the effectiveness of discriminatory measures. By the late 1920s, nativist leaders had become increasingly frustrated by what they saw as state officials' ineffectiveness in containing the Filipino population on the West Coast. A host of actors in civil society also contributed to the problem: employers seeking cheap labor, taxi-dance-hall proprietors, and white women who socialized across the color line. All these individuals allegedly put self-interest ahead of the public good by allowing Filipinos to infiltrate white society. This prompted nativist spokesmen to launch an intensive campaign aimed at raising societal awareness about the dangers posed by Filipino migration and settlement and the need for public interdiction. California had, since the late nineteenth century, served as a political center of the American nativist movement, and its leaders took pride in the vanguard role that the state played in pressing for federal restrictions barring the entry of Asian immigrants. Movement partisans characterized the influx of Filipinos into the United States as the "third Asiatic invasion," a rhetorical frame linking the phenomenon to previous waves of Chinese and Japanese immigrants.

Exclusionists, however, faced an uphill battle in their efforts to restrict Filipinos, since national lawmakers were concerned about the diplomatic fallout that would result from barring the nation's doors to its own political subjects. Enacting such a ban, as Philippine leaders pointed out, would have created a rather dubious international precedent whereby Filipinos were free to travel anywhere in the world under an American passport except to the United States. Nonetheless, nativists and their political allies remained undaunted and mobilized their ample resources to fashion a new societal consensus about the issue. Although nativists were a powerful constituency, the enactment of exclusionary legislation aimed at Filipinos was far from a forgone conclusion. Other powerful sectors of society, including western agribusiness interests, often opposed the passage of new immigration restrictions since their industry relied on transborder labor to bolster profits.

In a bid to rally public support, movement crusaders ratcheted up their rhetoric, employing a "social problem" narrative to frame Filipino immigration and settlement as serious threats to American society. This is a common rhetorical strategy used by social movements seeking to drum up support for their agenda and mobilize public resources to remedy the putative problem. Identifying an issue or phenomenon as a "social problem," as sociologist Joseph Gusfield has argued, is a "rhetorical device, . . . a claim that some condition, set of events, or group of persons constitutes a troublesome situation that needs to be changed or ameliorated." He adds that "those who define the problem, do so from a standard which involves them in the role of legitimate spokespersons for the society or public interest. Having defined the condition as a 'social problem,' there is then a legitimate basis for bringing public resources to bear on it in the manner defined."[25] Nativist leaders cast themselves as defenders of the public interest, animating anxieties about unfettered immigration, interracial intimacy, and downward social mobility to label Filipinos a problem population whose continued presence posed a danger to the white community. Movement partisans were drawn from influential sectors of American society, and the media treated them as legitimate authorities on issues of immigration and race relations. The nativist lobby was led by a powerful network of public figures and powerbrokers, which included Paul Scharrenberg, the de facto head of the California State Federation of Labor; V. S. McClatchy, media baron and president of the American Coalition of Patriotic Societies; California attorney general Ulysses S. Webb; and Charles M. Goethe, renowned California banker and eugenicist. These activists linked their efforts through several important organizations, including the California Joint Immigration Committee, a kind of nativist supergroup that brought together prominent political officials, social reformers, and leaders of allied organizations such as the American Legion, Native Sons of the Golden West, the Commonwealth Club, and the Grange.

By 1930, nativists were describing the "Filipino problem" in increasingly hyperbolic terms, reasoning that the more acute the problem, the more legitimate their calls for public action. Movement spokespersons claimed that the issue had reached a crisis point on the West Coast and would soon spread to other parts of the country. Nativists and social reformers alike traded in the politics of racial rescue, positioning themselves as the guardians of the social order, out to protect the white community from racial retrogression and moral decline. The negative consequences of Filipino immigration were, they claimed, serious and far-reaching: they stole jobs from native whites, exhibited high rates of criminality, depended on public assistance, practiced substandard hygiene, and were susceptible to diseases that jeopardized the well-being of the larger society. Partisans were particularly outraged by the perceived brazenness with which Filipinos defied conventional codes of racial propriety, especially when it came to matters of interracial sex and marriage. The Filipino population on the West Coast was largely made up of young men recruited to work in agriculture, with a male-to-female ratio of fourteen to one (a rate that was even more disproportionate in some rural communities). That these young men believed it was within their rights to interact socially with whomever they pleased, including white women, provoked a strong negative reaction from the larger society. This issue attracted sensational media attention, which depicted Filipino men as a problem population instinctively drawn into deviant associations with white women that inevitably led to social conflict. The emphasis on the dangers of race mixing was part of a deliberate strategy of western U.S. nativists, who believed the issue would attract the support of southern congressmen, whom they saw as natural allies on public policy relating to breaches of the color line.

Escalating tensions about race mixing and labor competition soon became front-page news on the West Coast, with stories featuring alarmist statements by public officials and moral entrepreneurs. The failure of the federal government to curtail immigration from the Philippines and the ineffectiveness of formal legal obstacles in containing the Filipino population on the West Coast spurred nativists to assert local sovereignty over the issue. Exclusionists took up the mantle of popular direct action to confront the putative problem, advocating racialized collective action aimed at taking back their country from the unwelcome outsiders. This revanchist campaign took an increasingly volatile character by the late 1920s, marked by extralegal violence and local initiatives to "deport" or expel the unwelcome newcomers from West Coast communities. A series of race riots and vigilante attacks targeting Filipinos swept across the region and attracted nationwide media attention, providing an outsize platform for exclusionists to mobilize public support for their crusade. Though wary not to explicitly endorse extralegal reprisals, nativist leaders exploited the racial discord, blaming the persecuted Filipino community for the turmoil and claiming that they had brought the violence on themselves with their provocative behavior. The white community, according to these claims makers, had been abandoned by the federal government and was, thus, forced to take the law into its own hands to defend the nation against another "Asiatic invasion."

Movement leaders played a decisive role in shaping how these conflicts were interpreted and represented in the media and in public culture. They cast the riots as regrettable but inevitable responses to shortsighted government policies that allowed an unassimilable racial group to overrun the nation's borders. Nativist arguments were couched in the aggrieved discourse of white victimhood, a rhetorical strategy that both explained and legitimated racialized collective action. Claims makers appealed to white Americans' "sense of group position," suggesting that their hegemonic standing in U.S. society was imperiled by the newcomers, who threatened to upend the social order. Framed in this way, direct-action campaigns targeting Filipinos were forceful expressions of the popular will, which lent an aura of righteousness to the exclusionists' crusade. Nativists' ultimate goal was to fix responsibility for the Filipino issue on the federal government, believing that it was best positioned to remedy the problem through its legislative powers.

Political pressure from nativists and the notoriety of western race riots increased national attention on the issue, but many lawmakers still balked at the idea of barring the nation's doors to Filipinos while they remained under U.S. dominion. It was not until nativist forces switched tactics and aligned themselves with other key interest groups lobbying for Philippine independence (midwestern agribusiness and Filipino nationalists) that they were able to muster enough support in Congress to advance their political goals.

Nativists believed that relinquishing sovereignty over the islands would, by definition, forestall the entry of Filipinos, since they would be stripped of their status as U.S. nationals and therefore be subject to the restrictive provisions of the 1924 Immigration Act. The domestic independence lobby was led by midwestern agribusiness interests (primarily sugar-beet concerns and dairy producers) anxious about competition from inexpensive, duty-free Philippine imports (cane sugar and coconut oil). Filipino nationalists were also key players in the eclectic alliance of constituencies lobbying for an independence bill, albeit for very different reasons than the other pressure groups they were aligned with. This loose coalition eventually helped secure passage of the Tydings-McDuffie Act in 1934, which granted the Philippines its independence after a ten-year probation period. A key provision of the bill mandated that Filipinos were immediately subject the 1924 Immigration Act and placed the Philippines under the lowest immigration quota for any country in the world (fifty persons per year).

Though exclusionists celebrated the curtailment of further immigration from the islands enacted by Tydings-McDuffie, they quickly recognized that the "Filipino problem" was far from solved, since the new quota restrictions did nothing to address the population already living in the United States. Consequently, movement leaders took up an ancillary campaign aimed at sending resident Filipinos back to the Philippines. In a key section of the book, I track this evolution of nativist objectives beyond the initial goal of exclusion to their subsequent focus on immigrant expulsion. Efforts by the federal government to repatriate Filipinos underscore the continuing hostility they faced in the United States as well as the conviction held by nativist leaders that immigration quotas alone could not solve the problem. The repatriation campaign, which lasted from 1936 to 1940, was ultimately deemed a failure, since very few individuals took part in the program, which was viewed by the Filipino community as a not-so-subtle form of voluntary deportation. Though the campaign did not produce the desired results (mass exodus back to the islands), it highlights once again how the specter of empire continued to shape Philippine-American relations, since the U.S. government was politically averse to carrying out compulsory repatriations against Filipinos, as it did with persons of Mexican ancestry during this same period.

The final section of the book looks at the political transformations ushered in by World War II and the inauguration of Philippine sovereignty. The Tydings-McDuffie Act stipulated that independence be granted only after the successful completion of a ten-year probationary period beginning in 1936.[26] The United States had justified its continued presence in the islands, in part, as a protective measure designed to safeguard the Philippines from foreign intervention as it made the transition to self-rule. But midway through the probation period (December 8, 1941), Japan invaded the islands, routing American defense forces, who retreated and left Filipinos to wage a sustained guerrilla campaign against Japanese occupation forces, while the United States focused its military resources elsewhere. The U.S. government eventually inducted between one hundred thousand and two hundred thousand Filipinos into the U.S. military command in the Pacific. Filipino fighters served under the authority of General Douglas MacArthur, who issued orders remotely from the U.S. base of operations in Australia. Filipino nationals and Filipino Americans both played a significant role in the Allied war effort. My discussion of the World War II era reveals how racial boundaries were recalibrated during this period, when other forms of collective identity, particularly patriotic nationalism, became more salient. The contours of the American racial order shifted in important ways during this period, partly to meet the prerogatives of a wartime state and partly in response to civil rights activists, who pressed the federal government to live up to its rhetoric of inclusiveness and ethnic tolerance. Filipino veterans, emboldened by their war service, demanded a greater stake in America's democratic institutions, which they had been called on to defend overseas during the war. The liminal political status of Filipinos during the Commonwealth period reveals how the entanglement of race and empire continued to shape Philippine-American relations both during and after the war.

Throughout the book I have tried to remain attentive to the ways in which the Filipino experience has intersected with that of other racialized groups in the United States. Filipinos clearly share much in common with earlier waves of Asian immigration. Anti-imperialist politicians warned that annexing the Philippines would extend American citizenship to Chinese-Filipino "half-breeds," and West Coast nativists invoked the specter of the Chinese coolie laborer to mobilize support for Filipino exclusion. The Filipino story is also entangled with the history of Puerto Ricans in important ways. Both territories were acquired in the aftermath of the Spanish-American War, and U.S. policymakers saw the political fate of the two colonies as closely linked. American officials, though, quickly put the two territories on divergent political paths, due in large part to fears about another influx of Asian laborers and concerns about the racial makeup of the Philippine population. The Filipino saga has also been enmeshed with the experience of Mexicans for much of the twentieth century. The two groups shared a common position in the agricultural labor market and often found themselves on the same side of political struggles aimed at bettering the working conditions for immigrant laborers. Both populations, moreover, were subject to exclusion and repatriation campaigns in the 1920s and 1930s, a movement that produced mixed results. By highlighting the ways in which the experience of Filipinos paralleled with and diverged from other groups, I hope to shed light on how racial and national boundaries were constructed and reconstructed at different times and for different ends.

1

The Racial Vectors of Empire

*Classification and Competing Master
Narratives in the Colonial Philippines*

The late nineteenth century was a time of rapid political transformation in the Philippines. A national independence movement had taken hold, putting three centuries of Spanish colonial rule on the verge of collapse. This struggle was quickly derailed, however, as the Philippines were dragged into the American imperial orbit during the Spanish-American War. Under the terms of the Treaty of Paris in 1898, Spain ceded the Philippines to the United States. Meanwhile, the American drive for an extraterritorial empire created problems at home as lawmakers struggled to justify the nation's acquisition of overseas territories. The United States itself was a product of anticolonial struggle, with a political culture that rested in part on universalist principles of natural rights and government by consent. It was not immediately clear, for instance, how the campaign to "liberate" the Philippines, Puerto Rico, Cuba, and Guam from Spanish tyranny could be reconciled with American plans to exercise dominion over these territories. As a result, U.S. officials were careful to highlight the benevolent and paternal aims of overseas expansion, suggesting that American imperium was different from the kind of rapacious colonialism practiced by European powers, which was focused solely on commercial and territorial aggrandizement.[1]

The question of how to absorb overseas territories into the U.S. polity triggered an intense ideological debate about the social and political consequences of global expansion. Territories previously annexed by the United States, such as Louisiana, Mexico, and Florida, had been treated as "incorporated territories," whose inhabitants were collectively naturalized into the American Union.[2] The idea of incorporating the Philippines and by extension Filipinos into the body politic of the United States provoked a protracted debate about whether it was in the nation's best interest to retain the islands permanently or to grant them their sovereignty. Advocates of U.S.

expansionism argued that the acquisition of overseas territories was benefi-
cial both to Americans and to the residents of newly enchained colonies. The
United States, they claimed, was uniquely positioned to bring the light of civilization and economic development to populations who had fallen behind
the rest of the world while under centuries of Spanish misrule. The acquisition of colonies did not, according to expansionists, pose any threat to the
political integrity of the United States, since the U.S. Congress had plenary
power to determine who was included or excluded from the boundaries of
American citizenship. Opponents of overseas expansion, on the other hand,
equated annexation with incorporation and worried that the inhabitants
of overseas colonies would be integrated into the U.S. polity as fully vested
members. They also raised the prospect that these newly minted American
subjects would migrate in large numbers to the imperial center, where they
would compete with whites for scarce economic resources.

Proponents and opponents of extraterritorial expansion both employed
the language of race to advance their political agendas, but they drew on different strands of American racial thinking. Imperialists justified the conquest
and seizure of the Philippines through a paternalistic racism that stressed the
social and cultural inferiority of Filipinos, while at the same time emphasizing their potential for advancement under a program of corrective colonialism. They viewed American intervention in the Philippines as both an
opportunity and an obligation. The most obvious opportunities were political and economic, as the United States attempted to bolster its position vis-à-
vis other core capitalist states competing for access to emerging commercial
markets in the Asia-Pacific region.[3] Installing a U.S. colonial outpost in the
Philippines was not simply a matter of reaping economic rewards and geostrategic advantage. It was also, proclaimed the imperialists, the duty and
destiny of the United States to share its talent for democratic development
and save the Filipinos from civilizational ruin. Colonialism, then, was not
simply a political choice but also a moral and racial obligation to be carried
out by "Anglo-Saxons" for the benefit of the world's "lower races."[4]

The anti-imperialists also traded in the politics of race, but they employed
an ideology of aversive racism that drew on scientific theories of ethnological
difference and fears about racial retrogression. They amplified the potential
dangers posed by incorporating the Philippines into the U.S. polity, painting the alarmist scenario of millions of Filipinos flooding across America's
borders to compete for jobs and to intermarry with whites. Anti-imperialists
also warned that formally annexing the Philippines would result in the collective naturalization of all inhabitants of the islands, putting them on equal

footing with white citizens. Elected officials from southern and western states were particularly vocal in stoking fears about the racial consequences of imperial expansion, since they represented regions of the country where anxieties about economic competition and integration with blacks and Chinese ran deep.

As congressional leaders worked to resolve the political status of the Philippines, President McKinley set about establishing the machinery of colonial rule in the archipelago. One of his first acts was the creation of the Philippine Commission in 1899 to survey and report on conditions in the islands. The commission was charged with investigating the islands' material resources, inhabitants, and commercial potential to evaluate their economic and geopolitical value to the United States. The commissioners conducted an ethnological study that cataloged the various "races" and "tribes" of the archipelago for purposes of scientific classification and colonial administration. Other population surveys quickly followed, and this initiative reached its zenith with the completion of an official territory-wide census of the islands in 1903. The publication of the territorial census was important because it registered as social fact the intention of colonial administrators to use race as an organizing principle of the new Philippine social structure.[5]

This chapter examines how racial knowledge about Filipinos was produced and institutionalized as a mode of rule during the early years of American dominion in the islands. More specifically, it examines how American officials reconciled two seemingly contradictory objectives: the drive to enlarge the territorial borders of the United States through overseas imperial conquest and the simultaneous desire to delimit the boundaries of the American polity to exclude those populations deemed unfit for national citizenship. The first section looks at the congressional debates about overseas expansion, focusing on how the language of race and class was deployed by proponents and opponents of annexation. Imperialists, I argue, used paternalistic racism to undercut Filipino demands for national self-determination in the aftermath of the war and to justify claims about the need for a protracted period of Anglo-Saxon discipline and tutelage in the islands. Anti-imperialists drew on a very different strand of racial ideology to frame their case. American society, they argued, was already beset by racial conflicts, and the annexation of the Philippines would only add to the nation's intractable "race problem." Though the imperialists ultimately triumphed, the anti-imperialists had an important influence on the direction of U.S. colonial policy, especially when it came to determining the civic status of subject populations.

The second section explores the impact of early colonial population surveys in the Philippines, revealing how the very practice of enumeration and classification produced new lines of division in Philippine society. These initiatives, as Benedict Anderson has argued, allowed the colonial state to quantify and "serialize" all those under its jurisdiction, making it easier to carry out governmental functions such as taxation, public education, military conscription, and the like across diverse and dispersed territories. The surveys were both descriptive and prescriptive, assigning names and meanings to social collectivities and placing them into taxonomic grids that demarcated boundaries and relationships between population groups.[6]

The racial knowledge generated by American surveyors in the islands soon came full circle, as colonial officials arranged for representatives of different Filipino "races" to be displayed at world's fairs and expositions across the United States during the first decade of the twentieth century. Filipino ethnological exhibits quickly became a national sensation and were among the most popular draws at expositions in St. Louis, Portland, and Seattle, providing a powerful visual representation of imperial hegemony and America's global ascendancy. The final section of the chapter examines the ideological functions of these ethnological displays, revealing how these showcases encouraged vicarious identification with U.S. imperial mastery and reinforced popular attitudes about global racial hierarchies.

The Burdens of Empire

Territorial expansion had long been a guiding principle of American national development, even before the United States made its bid for a transoceanic empire during the final decade of the nineteenth century. The Treaty of Paris, signed in 1898, formally ended the Spanish-American War and resulted in the cession of the Philippines, Puerto Rico, Guam, and Cuba to the United States. Congress ratified the treaty in 1899, but this did not put an end to the debate on the issue of territorial expansion.[7] Opponents of annexation argued that it was in the best interests of both Americans and Filipinos for the United States to relinquish its claim of sovereignty over the Philippines. Anti-imperialists initially couched their agenda in humanitarian terms, highlighting the incompatibility of colonial subjection and democratic governance, but their arguments took on a more explicitly racial tone as the debate wore on. Chief among their concerns was the political status of America's newly acquired subjects. Precedents regarding the acquisition of territories (e.g., Florida, Louisiana, northern Mexico) had contained some treaty provision for granting citizenship to the "civilized" inhabitants of annexed lands.[8] Whether this custom would apply to America's new insular possessions became the source of intense contestation in the U.S. Congress. Annexationists argued that the acquisition of overseas dependencies simply continued the nation's tradition of frontier expansion beyond its contiguous borders. Anti-imperialists saw America's bid for a global empire as violating the sacred principle of "government by consent" found in the Declaration of Independence, and they argued that the United States could not annex territories without also incorporating their inhabitants into the nation's body politic. Easy resolution of this issue was complicated by the fact that lawmakers wanted to disaggregate the political status of the Philippines and Puerto Rico to assure that the course of action taken in one territory did not bind them to apply the same policy in the other dependency.

The Philippines stood apart from the other insular possessions in a number of ways. The local population had vociferously opposed the imposition of American colonial rule in the islands and quickly took up a protracted insurgency against the United States. Its geographic location in "the Orient" and its large population (relative to the other Spanish holdings) also distinguished the Philippines from the other territories.[9] Yet for many U.S. lawmakers the potential rewards that might be reaped from a colonial outpost in the Asia-Pacific region outweighed the risks. An influential group of American politicians and industrialists had long expressed interest in expanding its influence in the Far East. A series of economic depressions during the last decades of the nineteenth century amplified anxieties in the American business community about a glut of industrial capacity and the inability of the national market to absorb surplus goods produced by domestic manufacturers. Increasing commercial ties with foreign markets offered one potential solution to this problem, and U.S. trade with Asia had been on a rapid upward trajectory, growing from $5.7 million in 1870 to nearly $45 million in 1898.[10] The imperialist lobby viewed the Philippines as a potential boon to American business interests as well as a strategic vantage point from which they could launch their economic and geopolitical ambitions on a global scale. U.S. and European industrialists jockeyed for position during this period, hoping to gain some sort of strategic advantage with regard to the vast consumer markets in China.[11]

Imperialists readily acknowledged that their primary interests in the Philippines centered on commercial and geostrategic opportunities in the Asia-Pacific region. They regularly touted the potential for new market outlets in Asia. Senator Albert Beveridge, the staunch imperialist from Indiana, advanced this sentiment in bold terms:

American factories are making more than the American people can use; American soil is producing more than they can consume. Fate has written our policy for us; the trade of the world must and shall be ours. And we will get it as our mother [England] has told us how. We will establish trading posts throughout the world as distributing points for American products. We will soon cover the ocean with our merchant marine. We will build a navy to the measure of our greatness. Great colonies governing themselves, flying our flag, and trading with us, will grow about our posts of trade. Our institutions will follow our flag on the wings of commerce. And American law, American order, American civilization, and the American flag will plant themselves on shores hitherto bloody and benighted, but those agencies of God henceforth to be made beautiful and bright. . . . The Philippines are logically our first target.[12]

Senator Henry Cabot Lodge described the Pacific as "the ocean of the future" and extolled the prospects for American investors by citing a recently conducted survey of the islands: "There are many opportunities for the investment of capital, Hemp, tobacco, coffee, cacao and rice are assured products. Cattle do well. Timber, gold, copper and iron are found in the mountains. . . . A steam or electric railway is needed to connect with the northern districts, which are rich, but undeveloped. It could be easily built and would yield large results to the investor."[13] Senator Chauncey Depew, a former Wall Street banker, highlighted the value of a transoceanic commercial empire during his address to the 1900 Republican national convention:

The American people now produce 2,000,000,000 worth more than they can consume, and we have met the emergency and by the providence of God, by the statesmanship of William McKinley, and the valor of Theodore Roosevelt and his associates, we have markets in Cuba, in Puerto Rico, in the Philippines, and we stand in the presence of 800,000,000 people, with the Pacific an American lake. . . . The world is ours."[14]

Political and economic benefits notwithstanding, public opinion remained divided when it came to the probity of colonial conquest. "Liberating" the Philippines and other colonies from Spanish autocracy had support across the political spectrum, but holding the archipelago and its people in subjection for commercial gain raised some difficult moral questions. That Filipino leaders continued to press their demands for national independence, even after formal annexation, kept the debate about the ethics of empire alive. Consequently, imperialists modified their message to emphasize the moral and paternalistic aims of U.S. empire. Filipinos, they argued, lacked the capacity for self-government and required a lengthy period of American colonial supervision before they would be ready to join the family of modern nations. Seen from this point of view, imperial conquest was not so much about the global scramble for territory and markets but a moral duty required of Anglo-Saxons for the betterment of the world's "lower races." Imperialists drew heavily on the doctrine of racial paternalism that gained popularity during the Progressive Era and linked America's program of "benevolent assimilation" with the reformist impulses that characterized this period. For example, they frequently drew parallels between the pacification of the Philippines and the subjugation of Native Americans during the "Indian Wars." Filipinos were regularly compared to Native Americans, and expansionists looked to federal Indian policy as a model for colonial education and governance in the Philippines.[15] Secretary of State John Hay, for example, advised American envoys surveying the islands to consider inserting a provision in the treaty with Spain that would affix to Filipinos a status similar to the "uncivilized native tribes" in the Alaska territory.[16]

That Filipinos so publicly and vociferously rejected America's gift of armed benevolence did not deter the expansionists. Imperialists derided Filipino demands for national self-determination as the petulant utterances of a childlike population who did not know what was good for them. Senator Samuel McEnery of Louisiana declared that only one-quarter of Filipinos were "semi-civilized," and "the rest of the population is as ignorant and savage as the aboriginal Indians."[17] Albert Beveridge agreed, warning that "self-government is no cheap boon, to be bestowed on . . . liberty's infant class, which has not yet mastered the alphabet of freedom. Savage blood, oriental blood, Malay blood, Spanish example—in these do we find the elements of self-government? . . . We must never forget that in dealing with the Filipinos we deal with children."[18] By fusing narratives of Anglo-Saxon hegemony and Filipino backwardness, imperialists sought to bring closure to the question of "the natives'" state of civilization and thus their entitlement to self-determination.

Race and Region

Anti-imperialists faced an uphill battle in their campaign to derail annexation. Their early efforts focused on the incompatibility of long-distance colonial rule with U.S. traditions of "government by consent." This strategy was a tough sell, insofar as Americans did not have to look very far to see examples (e.g., Native Americans) where the consensual governance principle had been conveniently disregarded. In a bid to drum up support for their campaign, anti-imperialists in Congress, especially those from southern and western states, shifted tactics and began highlighting the potential racial and class consequences of overseas expansion. Annexation, they argued, would result in the collective naturalization of eight to ten million "dark-skinned" Filipinos who would be incorporated into the national polity as fully enfranchised members.[19]

Southern congressmen invoked the "failed" experiment of Reconstruction to make the case against annexation. They claimed that black advancement during Reconstruction had come at the expense of Southern whites and warned that incorporating Filipinos into the Union would produce similarly disastrous results. Senator James Berry of Arkansas likened the imperialists to the misguided northerners who elevated the status of African Americans in the South after the Civil War. Recalling the experience of Reconstruction, Berry told fellow lawmakers that he would "never vote to force upon the inhabitants of the Philippine Islands, Malays, Negroes, and savages though they may be, the curse of a carpetbag government."[20] Other southern spokesmen admonished their northern colleagues, whose lack of firsthand experience living alongside "inferior" non-white races hampered their ability to understand the racial implications tied up in the Philippine question. Senator Benjamin Tillman of South Carolina, who represented a state "where the race question has been the cause of untold misery and woe," claimed expertise on the real dangers of race mixing and chastised annexationists from the North, pointing out that "hitherto the South has enjoyed a monopoly in the odium of shooting and hanging men of the colored race. Have the Northern people grown envious and do they seek to emulate our example?" Tillman warned imperialist leaders that the projection of American power in the Pacific would invite social conflict, "We inherited our race problem. You are going out wantonly in search of yours and the nation's. . . . Have we not enough debased and ignoble people in our midst that we should seek by conquest . . . to incorporate 10,000,000 more colored people?"[21]

Opponents of annexation also expressed doubts about the capacity of the United States to actually carry out a civilizing mission in a place such as the Philippines, considering the racial makeup of the population. Senator John Daniel of Virginia declared, "Not in a hundred years, nay, not in a thousand years can we lift the Philippine Islands and the mixed races that there inhabit to the level of civilization which this land, God-blessed, possesses."[22] In a similar vein, Representative George Gilbert of Kentucky observed, "No empire has ever civilized any people in the world's history." European imperial powers, according to Gilbert, had failed to deliver on their promises of colonial progress in Africa and Asia, so he implored his fellow congressmen to rethink their expansionist agenda: "Let this wild march of imperialism stop now before it is too late. England has not civilized the Egyptian, the Australian, nor the Hindoo. We have not civilized the Indian, the negro, nor the Eskimo, and we will not civilize either the negroes of Puerto Rico or the Malays on the other side of the earth."[23]

A vocal bloc of anti-imperialists from the western states echoed similar concerns but drew on their experience with another group of racial undesirables, the Chinese, to make their case. Western representatives maintained that Asians could not be civilized and were impervious to America's assimilative institutions. Annexation of the Philippines, they argued, would result in a flood of cheap labor across the nation's Pacific border, a phenomenon that was sure to arouse racial and class conflict in the United States, as white workers were displaced by "the cheap half-slave labor, savage labor, of the Philippine Archipelago."[24] Representative Francis Newlands of Nevada warned that Filipinos would "be invited here in swarms by speculators of labor, as were the Chinese," if annexation was ratified by the Congress.[25] In this same vein, Senator George Turner of Washington likened Filipino immigration to a foreign invasion in which "10,000,000 Filipinos now, or 20,000,000 or 40,000,000 in the indefinite future," would stream into the United States and pit "underpaid and underfed Filipinos against the mechanic, the artisan and the laboring man of this country." Annexation would, according to Turner, "be the beginning of the end of the American Republic," since whites would be forced to adapt themselves to Filipino customs and habits of living.[26]

Other opponents of annexation suggested that the imperialists' plan to carry out a civilizing project in the tropics was a fool's errand, since "Asiatics" were impervious to Anglo-Saxon cultural influence. Even more absurd was the prospect that Filipino students would travel to the United States to experience American institutions as part of their colonial education. Representative George Gilbert said, "I say keep them out. We cannot even civilize the Chinese within our borders and who have been here for fifty years. These Chinese . . . wear pigtails, eat rats, and worship Confucius . . . in spite of all the churches and schools around and about them." He warned that annexation would generate a new flood of immigration to the United States, "open[ing] wide the door by which . . . Asiatics can pour like the locusts of Egypt into this country."[27] The sizeable Chinese settler population in the Philippines added another troubling dimension to the debate over annexation, since that raised the possibility that Chinese "half-breeds" might be allowed to enter the United States by virtue of their residency in the islands.

The imperialists ultimately prevailed in the debate over the annexation and retention of the Philippines. The paternalistic racism espoused by the expansionists played an important role in pushing their agenda through Congress and marshaling public support for extraterritorial acquisition. Imperialist lawmakers successfully argued that Filipinos were unfit for self-government due to their racial and cultural backwardness. The United States, they claimed, was duty bound to take possession of the islands and remake Philippine society in America's image. Anti-imperialists, however, did not come away from the debate empty-handed, securing assurances from their opponents that Filipinos would not be granted U.S. citizenship by virtue of annexation. Though the anti-imperialists were not able to muster up the votes to prevent annexation and retention of the islands, they were able to shape the direction of U.S. colonial policy as American lawmakers took up the task of determining the political status of colonial wards.

The Philippines, but Not Filipinos

Congress acted quickly to enact legislation preventing Chinese residents in the islands from surreptitiously circumventing legal barriers restricting their entry into the United States. Specifically, federal officials declared that all U.S. immigration laws, including the Chinese Exclusion Act, would be put into force in the insular territories.[28] Resolving the political status of native Filipinos proved to be a far more complex task, since lawmakers had different assessments of the civic potential of the residents of the Philippines and Puerto Rico.[29] Congressional leaders devoted their energies to crafting legislation that would establish a new framework for dealing with insular subjects. Lawmakers wanted to avoid precedent applied in previous cases of domestic territorial acquisition which extended citizenship rights to the "civilized" inhabitants of those lands. The projection of U.S. power overseas prompted lawmakers to exercise more discretion over exactly which rights would be extended to newly acquired subjects. While there was support in Congress for extending U.S. citizenship to Puerto Ricans, the idea of granting the same privileges to Filipinos was universally scorned. As a result, lawmakers set about devising legislation that would give them flexibility to selectively draw the boundaries of inclusion and exclusion on a case-by-case basis.

Racial politics played an important role in shaping the direction of insular policy as congressional leaders sought to limit America's political liabilities. A key rationale for treating the Philippines and Puerto Rico differently was the alleged racial and cultural differences found in the two territories. American officials described Puerto Ricans as a "friendly and peaceful" people who were "orderly, law abiding, and anxious for development" under American rule.[30] This characterization starkly contrasted with the "unruly and disobedient" inhabitants of the Philippines, who had launched an armed insurrection against the U.S. occupation. The people of Puerto Rico were portrayed as more racially palatable than those inhabiting the Philippines, who were said to be an admixture of African and Asian blood strains. Representative Sereno Payne of New York claimed that the Puerto Rican population consisted of "generally full-blooded white people, descended of the Spaniards, possibly mixed with some Indian blood." He added reassuringly, "none of them" are of "negro extraction."[31] Ohio's Jacob Bromwell proclaimed that Puerto Rico had "as a whole a higher grade of civilization" than the Philippines. Puerto Ricans, moreover, had "professed themselves ready to become . . . loyal citizens of this country."[32]

These self-serving depictions of Puerto Ricans eagerly embracing American colonial dominion were contrasted with the more ominous situation in the "Orient." Representative Thomas Spight of Mississippi underlined the importance of disaggregating U.S. policy in the two territories, stating, "How different the case of the Philippines. . . . The inhabitants are of wholly different races of people from ours—Asiatics Malays, negroes and mixed blood. They have nothing in common with us and centuries can not assimilate them."[33] Concerns about the racial composition of the Philippines led many lawmakers to express fear that legislative efforts aimed at granting citizenship to Puerto Ricans "would be used against us" by Filipinos, who would in turn demand equal treatment.[34] Expansionists maintained that Congress held plenary power to determine the political status of territorial subjects and assured skeptical colleagues that Filipinos were not entitled to any civic rights or constitutional protections not explicitly approved by Congress. They pointed to federal policy governing the political status of Native Americans as a case in point. The United States, they argued, had long ruled over Native Americans and their ceded lands without bestowing citizenship or full constitutional protections to them.[35] This example was cited as evidence that the U.S. government was free to extend or deny political rights to subject populations on a case-by-case basis, and lawmakers proceeded with plans to establish formal administrative custody in Puerto Rico and the Philippines.

Whether this new doctrine of territorial conquest and subjection stood up to constitutional scrutiny was quickly taken up by the Supreme Court beginning in 1901. In a series of rulings known as the Insular Cases, the Court clarified the constitutional relationship between the United States and its outlying colonies. The rulings handed down in two of the early Insular Cases (*Downes v. Bidwell* and *Dorr v. United States*) affirmed broad congressional authority over matters pertaining to the status of imperial wards and established the important legal distinction between incorporated and unincorporated territories. The act of territorial annexation, according to the Court, was separate from the act of territorial incorporation, a distinction that held the key to the new doctrine of American empire. The U.S. Constitution, the justices explained, had indeed "followed the flag" to incorporated territories such as Louisiana and Florida and to the lands annexed from Mexico via the Treaty of Guadalupe Hidalgo. Consequently, the inhabitants of these domains were entitled to constitutional rights and protections. The Court clarified, however, that these populations were incorporated in the American polity not because of the consent doctrine, but because of language in the treaties of cession between the United States and the former "owners" of the territories (i.e., Spain, France, and Mexico) providing for the collective naturalization of the residents of these jurisdictions. These incorporated territories were projected to be fully integrated into the Union through eventual statehood, so the residents of annexed lands were absorbed into the national polity in anticipation of this process. The situation in the unincorporated territories, such as Puerto Rico and the Philippines, departed from those earlier instances of territorial acquisition. The Treaty of Paris, the justices pointed out, promised neither citizenship for Filipinos or Puerto Ricans nor a pledge of eventual statehood for the former Spanish colonies. The Supreme Court's rulings in the Insular Cases gave Congress a free hand to decide the political status of insular subjects however it saw fit.

Racial considerations weighed heavily in the Court's interpretation of congressional authority over matters relating to the status of newly procured colonial wards. Justice Henry Billings Brown cautioned that extending constitutional protections to the "alien races" in the unincorporated zones and placing them on equal footing with U.S. citizens would be a "fatal" step for the republic.[36] Residents of the colonial zones, argued Brown, could not be readily assimilated via "Anglo-Saxon principles" and were best held in subjection while American officials evaluated their capacity for development. Justice Edward White, in a concurring opinion, affirmed that Filipinos and Puerto Ricans would remain outside the boundaries of the national community until they could prove that they were ready to "enter into and form part of the American family." The determination that the U.S. Constitution did not follow the flag into the unincorporated territories did not mean that they were not part of the American polity. Justice White, in an act of dexterous judicial reasoning, declared Puerto Rico, the Philippines, and other outlying possessions to be part of the United States in the sense that they "belonged" to the United States and were subject to its sovereignty. At the same time, they were "foreign," in the sense that territories "peopled by savages" were unfit for full, coequal integration into American society.[37] Insular subjects, according to this legal doctrine, had a status similar to that of aliens in the United States, who were also guaranteed certain baseline civic protections such as freedom of religion and safeguards against the deprivation of life, liberty, and property. Whether Filipinos or Puerto Ricans might be entitled to other rights or immunities beyond those available to aliens was to be determined by Congress on a piecemeal basis.

The Insular Cases provided Congress with a powerful constitutional endorsement of its claim of plenary power in matters of imperial statecraft. In essence, the Supreme Court sanctioned the right of the United States to seize overseas territories without having to worry that the Constitution followed the flag into the newly annexed territories. The Court's rulings silenced anti-imperialist critics who had warned that claiming title over the Philippines or Puerto Rico would put newly acquired subjects on equal political footing with white citizens of the republic. Congress had a free hand to determine the status of the inhabitants of these jurisdictions on a piecemeal basis by whatever criteria it saw fit.

Colonial Taxonomies

Although the Insular Cases clarified what Filipinos *were not* (U.S. citizens), their precise standing within the American polity remained unsettled. President McKinley appointed a commission to sort out the political future of the islands. The first Philippine Commission was tasked with surveying social and economic conditions in the islands and appraising the fitness of Filipinos for self-government and their potential for socio-economic development. Not surprisingly, the first commission determined that Filipinos were not ready for self-government, nor were they fit for U.S. citizenship. A second group of commissioners was appointed a few years later and was charged with managing a U.S.-controlled civil government in the Philippines that would guide Filipinos in the art of republican statecraft.

The ethnological makeup in the islands was a major preoccupation of American officials during these years. The first of these ethnological surveys was conducted in 1899 by the first Philippine Commission and was quickly followed by another study carried out by the Department of War in 1901. This surveying project reached its apex with the publication of a territory-wide census in 1903, which employed the latest scientific methods to assign the Philippine population into official identity categories recognized by the colonial state. *The Census of the Philippine Islands* drew together much of the previous ethnological data collected in the studies carried out by the Philippine Commission and the Department of War but sought to move beyond some of the more speculative and politicized claims of the earlier studies. Borrowing personnel and methods used in recent U.S. surveys of Cuba and Puerto Rico, census enumerators scrutinized data on race, occupation, sex, age, mortality, disease, household structure, and a range of related subjects. David Barrows, University of California at Berkeley professor and director of the Philippine Bureau of Non-Christian Tribes, headed the census's demographic unit.

All three of these survey projects devoted considerable attention to the "race question" and placed the sections dealing with racial matters at the front of their reports. The race work carried out by colonial surveyors proved to be a powerful ideological tool that legitimated the U.S. expansionism. The surveys bolstered the imperialists' claims that Filipinos were incapable of self-government because of their racial backwardness. The ethnological findings of the surveyors were also used to explain why Filipinos were unfit for U.S. citizenship, inasmuch as their racial unassimilability was corroborated by the data. The surveys, moreover, show how Progressive Era racial thinking served as a blueprint for colonial officials tasked with managing the new and unfamiliar peoples who inhabited America's imperial frontier.

The first Philippine Commission in 1899 was led by Cornell University president Jacob Schurman. The other members of the commission, Charles Denby, Elwell Otis, George Dewey, and Dean Worcester, were appointed because of their respective expertise in the areas of political, scientific, and military affairs. The commissioners were charged with investigating the "political, social, and racial questions" relating to the islands and gathering information on demographic characteristics, natural resources, climatic conditions, and commercial opportunities.[38] The commission's preliminary report was sent to Congress in November 1899, and a four-volume anthology detailing its findings was published in 1900. The following year, the secretary of war's office submitted its own study, titled "The People of the Philippines," which took up many of the same questions as the commission's report. Secretary of War Elihu Root explained that his department had carried out its ethnological survey to meet the "constantly growing demand for information on this subject" from Congress and the American people.[39]

The data collected in the surveys provided the first official source of information detailing the population characteristics of the archipelago. The Philippine Commission's study collected secondary source materials on the history of the islands and supplemented this information with testimony from a host of individuals claiming to have specialized knowledge of the islands. Dean Worcester, a zoologist from the University of Michigan, headed the commission's ethnological survey team. Colonial officials set out to catalog all the inhabitants of the archipelago and assign them into a comprehensive taxonomic grid that could be used to monitor the "traffic habits" of the population through an array of institutions (public schools, courts, prisons, etc.) administered by the central state. One important feature of this project was the establishment of a "registration law" in the Philippines that transferred the authority of marriage, birth, and death registrations from local church parishes to the colonial authorities.[40]

The first substantive section of the commission's four-volume report was titled "The Native People of the Philippines," which identified perceived lines of racial and political hierarchy in the islands. Volume 2 contained a more exhaustive discussion of Filipino "tribes" and their "physical characteristics," "manners," and "customs." The report divided Filipinos into both "tribal" and "racial" groups, although these two typologies were often used interchangeably. The inhabitants of the Philippines were placed into "three sharply distinct races—the Negrito race, the Indonesian race, and the Malayan race." These "races" were further subdivided into eighty-four tribal groups, whose language, customs, and "degree of civilization" were listed in a series of tables and graphs that charted the vertical interfaces between different identity groups.[41]

The commissioners identified the Negritos as the original inhabitants of the Philippines and considered them to be the most "backward" population group in the islands. Prevailing ethnological opinion during this period posited that the Negritos had migrated to the area from Africa during the sixteenth century. This theory was endorsed by the commissioners, who sometimes referred to the Negritos as "blacks."[42] Their report described the Negritos as "weaklings of low stature, with black skin, closely curling hair, flat noses, thick lips, and large, clumsy feet." The commission's description of their physical shortcomings was matched by an equally dismissive valuation of their mental capacities. The report noted that "in the matter of intelligence," the Negritos stood "at or near the bottom of the human series, . . . incapable of any considerable degree of civilization."[43]

The Philippine Commission's evaluation of the two other "races" on the islands, the Indonesians and Malays, served a different function, insofar as these groups were deemed capable of social advancement through remedial intervention. The commissioners described Indonesians as physically superior to the Negritos, with a greater potential for mental development. The commission's survey approvingly noted their European features such as light-colored skin and "high foreheads, aquiline noses, [and] wavy hair." The Malays, the archipelago's largest ethnological group, were said to be short of stature, with dark-brown skin. Because Malays had the most sustained interaction with Europeans, they stood at the top of the Philippine caste order. Consequently, American officials set about making alliances with leading Malay political figures who could assist them with implementing a new colonial order in the islands.[44]

Alongside these three "pure races" were the mestizos, a mixed-race population whom the surveyors singled out for special scrutiny. Mestizos fell into two classes: those of European-Filipino extraction and the offspring of Chinese-Filipino parentage. The first group traced their origins to Spanish and British settlement in the islands and made up a small but influential segment of the population. The commissioners attentuated the privileged position of this group in Philippine society by pointing out that the European mestizo "is usually the most important and noble, because it has, if one may say so, in its blood the nature and culture of the superior race."[45]

The surveys conducted by the Philippine Commission and the secretary of war showed a strong interest in miscegenation, both among indigenous ethnic groups and between Filipinos and other "Asiatics." The corruption of blood resulting from the admixture of Filipinos and Chinese was linked to political instability in the islands. This group, according to the commissioners, exhibited superior mental traits, which placed them in a intermediate stratum of the population. This in-between status also explained their purportedly aggressive aspirations for upward mobility. The "Chinese half breeds" were said to be "shrewder than the natives of pure extraction," but also possessed some of the nefarious traits attributed to "Chinamen," such as dishonesty, clannishness, and conceit. The Chinese mestizos, resentful of their ethnic outsider status, often resorted to subterfuge to gain advantage over native Filipinos. Americans officials accused members of the Chinese mestizo population of fomenting local opposition to American rule to advance their own malicious political agenda. Mestizo insurgent leader Emilio Aguinaldo and his "Chinese half-breed" lieutenants were held up by the commissioners as prime examples of the political dangers of this population.[46]

Moral Makeup

Colonial surveyors also highlighted alleged deficiencies in the "moral makeup" of the native population as further evidence of their unfitness for self-government. The most alarming of these cultural defects was Filipinos' inability to control their savage instincts. The surveyors claimed that Filipinos lacked normal "sentiment" and showed little capacity to feel pain or empathy. The commissioners linked this problem to the tropical climate of the islands. The tropical conditions and other environmental factors produced a "relative enervation of the cerebral mass" that manifested itself in bipolar displays of rage and docility. One side of the Filipino personality was evidenced in their tendency to "run amok," a condition defined as an uncontrollable frenzy of indiscriminate homicidal violence. This propensity for running amok helped to explain why Filipinos had taken up arms against American military occupation, since guerrilla resistance to U.S. rule was, in the minds of surveyors, "irrational." Claims such as these bolstered the legitimacy of the American colonial project insofar as Filipino insurgents could be dismissed as fanatical and lawless bandits who delighted in random violence.[47]

The flipside to Filipinos' bipolar personality was their alleged laziness and frivolity. Surveyors debated whether the native population could be cured of their indolent lifestyle and taught to embrace a protestant work ethic. U.S. officials regularly expressed concerns about the "lazy habits and the worthless character of [the Filipinos'] manual labor."[48] The natives, according to the commission's report, were "disinclined to work," because they preferred to spend their time on wasteful leisure activities. American surveyors worried about the ability of the indigenous population to participate in plans to transform the islands into a modern capitalist export economy. Expert witnesses testifying before the Philippine Commission's hearings expressed similar doubt about the natives' suitability as wage laborers. According to one expert, Filipinos would only work for a couple days before telling their employer, "I am going on a holiday, you had better look out for someone else."[49]

Surveyors theorized that the Filipinos' childlike love of leisure played a large part in their poor work habits. Filipino men were happy to "demoralize themselves and others" by living on the "earnings of their wives," a practice that stood in stark contrast to Western gender roles and familial norms.[50] Instead of engaging in regularized wage labor, local men were "content to lounge around, indulge in cockfighting and other sports, and let their wives do all the work."[51] This weakness for impulsive, pleasure-seeking behavior manifested itself in other ways as well. Surveyors identified gambling, especially cockfighting, as a rampant vice. For the Filipino, gambling was not a simple "pastime" but a "means for obtaining a living."[52]

Although the native population's cultural deficiencies were daunting, U.S. officials expressed confidence that the natives could be cured of their racial debilities after a prolonged period of Anglo-Saxon tutelage. Surveyors highlighted Filipinos' talent for mimicry and imitation as a positive trait that could be exploited by colonial administrators. As a census official observed, "The Filipino, as a general thing, is very fond of imitating the people whom he believes to be his superiors in culture; and as they are fond of culture, they are desirous of obtaining it."[53] The secretary of war's report made this same point in a different way, stressing the native population's compliant character: "Under the eye of his master he is the most tractable of all beings. He never (like the Chinese) insists on doing things his own way, but tries to do things just as he is told, whether it be right or wrong. . . . If not pressed too hard he will follow his superior like a faithful dog."[54]

·Empire at Home

While colonial authorities expressed confidence in the ability of Anglo-Saxon institutions to remake Philippine society, many Americans remained ambivalent about the costs and benefits of long-distance imperialism. Federal officials, in a bid to drum up support for expansionist policies, arranged for an ethnological exhibit of native Filipinos to travel to the United States for the 1904 world's fair in St. Louis. This initiative turned out to be a public-relations triumph for colonial statesmen looking to sell their imperial vision to a wary citizenry. Streams of visitors flocked to the colonial pavilions, where they were treated to a powerful visual representation of the new global racial hierarchy and white Americans' place at the top of the world's pecking order. The St. Louis fair and subsequent expositions in Seattle and Portland provided a unique opportunity for American citizens to bask in the glory of overseas imperial triumph without having to leave the nation's continental borders.[55]

The Louisiana Purchase Exposition, held in St. Louis in 1904, offered a particularly timely platform for U.S. officials to communicate doctrines of imperial expansion and racial hegemony to American consumers. Philippine civil governor William Howard Taft instructed the Philippine Commission to form an exposition board to organize a Filipino exhibit. The commission named William P. Wilson of the Philadelphia Commercial Museum to manage the project with the assistance of other well-known ethnologists Ales Hrdlicka of the Smithsonian's Museum of Natural History and Gustavo Niederlein. The "Philippine Reservation" was a large and expensive display that covered forty-seven acres of prime midway real estate. The federal government allotted one million dollars for the exhibit, which featured over eleven hundred Filipinos, more than one hundred structures, and seventy-five thousand supplementary artifacts. U.S. officials believed that the large expenditures were necessary to "bring together the personnel and the material that make up a splendidly complete and strikingly picturesque representation of life in its varied phases on those troublous isles of the East which are now Uncle Sam's particular share of the white man's burden."[56] Governor Taft saw the exposition as an opportunity for his administration to present a "vivid outline picture" of the Filipino population and "all the gradations of civilization in the islands" for the education of American consumers.[57] The Philippine reservation featured a range of "tribes," which included "70 Igorottes, 39 Negritos, 79 Malayans, 350 Filipino Scouts, 250 Constabulary, 150 Moros, 18 Tinguanes, 16 Monguanes, and others too numerous to mention." The Igorotte and Negrito villages were the most popular attractions on the midway, as fairgoers could observe "outright savages" walking around unashamedly in "g-string" breechclouts.[58] For many observers, the monetary expense and "scientific" detail of the Philippine exhibit bolstered its legitimacy as a truly accurate depiction of life in the islands. The civilizing institutions of American empire were also an important part of the exhibit, most notably the "Manila Normal School," which showed white teachers instructing Filipino students in a simulated classroom setting.

The Philippine exhibit quickly became the most popular attraction at the St. Louis fair and received extensive national media attention. Most of the attention focused on the Negrito and Igorotte villages, reflecting their popularity at the fair. The Negritos, following the suspect claims of colonial ethnologists, were displayed as an aboriginal race of dwarves "resembling the African negro." The initial Negrito exhibit even had the villagers "dressed up like plantation nigger[s]," until the Negritos objected to these clothes and switched to their own traditional apparel.[59] The Igorottes were almost always referred to in popular accounts as "headhunters" or "dogeaters," to emphasize the spectacular and exotic nature of America's imperial wards. Racialized descriptions of the Filipinos dominated media coverage of the exhibit, perhaps best captured in a *Washington Post* story describing how a monkey accidentally made its way into the Filipino village. The article detailed how St. Louis exposition inspectors mistook the animal for a native baby, because the monkey's visage "looked so much like the face of an Igorotte infant."[60] Although much of the public discussion of the exhibits focused on the racially exotic character of the Philippine population, the educational features of the colonial pavilions also attracted positive attention. Media accounts praised exhibit organizers for striking the right balance between scientific authenticity and commercial showmanship and more importantly for making "white man's burden" legible to the general public. A reporter from the *Portland Oregonian* declared that any informed people who studied the Filipino habitat would immediately "disabuse themselves of any impression that the natives could take care of themselves." The *Los Angeles Times* echoed this sentiment, remarking that the "Filipino reservation is a most excellent place for the benevolent assimilation of ideas regarding the subjects of our first experiments in colonial government."[61]

Some of those who witnessed the backward condition of Filipinos offered to assist with the nation's civilizing mission on the domestic front, believing that imperial beneficence began at home. One popular news account described how wealthy families in St. Louis and Baltimore had offered their homes to the "Little Savages at the Fair." According to the story, the U.S. War Department had granted permission to two families, Will Campbell of St. Louis and Mrs. Charles Wentz of Baltimore, to adopt children from the Filipino exhibit. The Campbell family was interested in an Igorotte boy named Antaero, described as a "full blooded head hunter," and the Wentzes expressed their desire to adopt a "little Moro girl" named Tabae. The War Department endorsed adoptions, seeing them as a warm-hearted example of benevolent assimilation whereby patriotic white families had volunteered to "take the little Filipinos in their homes and teach them American ways."[62]

In July 1904, a delegation of Filipino "chiefs" from the exposition traveled from St. Louis to Washington, DC, to meet with President Theodore Roosevelt at the White House. The trip was organized as a public-relations event aimed at promoting the Roosevelt administration's commitment to training Philippine political leaders in the nuances of U.S. democracy. The delegation's visit caused a brief national controversy when American officials voiced concerns that the Filipino "chiefs" would show up at the White House sans pants.[63] This potentially embarrassing scenario was averted when the "little naked savages" arrived fully clothed for their engagement with the president. The event was compared to previous ceremonies hosted at the White House with Native American leaders, with the *New York Times* commenting that Filipino chiefs displayed a similar childlike reverence for "the Great White Father." President Roosevelt used the meeting as an opportunity to reaffirm his administration's commitment to imperial uplift, though the wardrobe controversy provided a stark reminder of just how much "civilizing" remained to be done in the Philippines.[64]

The national notoriety of the Philippine reservation at the 1904 St. Louis exposition made Filipinos a highly sought-after attraction for organizers of the Lewis and Clark International Exposition in Portland the next year. T. K. Hunt, who had managed the Igorotte and Negrito villages in St. Louis, was initially tapped to organize the Philippine concession in Portland. He had some familiarity with these populations, having previously served as a high-ranking colonial official in the Bontoc Province. His bid to manage the exhibit at the Portland exposition was rejected in favor of a rival company run by Edmund Felder and Richard Schneidewind. The agreement for a Philippine exhibit came as a relief to Portland organizers, since colonial administrators had expressed reservations about sponsoring another high-priced ethnological display, after spending $1.2 million on the St. Louis concession.[65]

The Filipinos did not arrive until the final months of the Lewis and Clark Exposition, but they made an enormous impact. The *Washington Post* described the euphoric mood of the city surrounding the Igorottes' arrival: "The dog-eaters have come, and Portland is glad." The article noted that the Filipino exhibit was the "most-talked-of feature of the fair," with eager throngs of visitors streaming to the midway hoping to catch a glimpse of a "savage feast."[66] The spectacle of the dog-eating Igorottes again garnered national media attention and further reinforced imperial narratives depicting Filipinos as a primitive people "2000 years behind" Anglo-Saxon civilization."[67] The *Portland Oregonian* jokingly warned the city's residents to lock up their dogs once the Filipinos arrived for the exposition and ran stories featuring blow-by-blow accounts of Igorotte villagers slaughtering a "fat juicy puppy" as part of their daily scheduled performance.[68] The spectacle of the Igorotte dog-eaters did not appeal to everyone in the city, and the Portland Humane Society even organized a campaign to have the practice stopped. Humane Society spokesman W. T. Shanahan characterized the exhibit as a "disgusting and sickening spectacle" and questioned why American consumers desired to see Igorotte "heathens" engage in such cruel practices.[69] As in St. Louis, the exotic features of the Igorotte village received disproportionate attention. Efforts by exhibit organizers to emphasize the civilizational progress being made in the islands also garnered some public notice. Observers stressed that the natives on display at the Portland fair showed signs they were finally reconciling themselves to the fact that they were incapable of self-government. The *Portland Oregonian* praised colonial initiatives in the islands but was careful to note that native resistance to Anglo-Saxon discipline had not been fully extinguished. The paper remarked that Filipinos still "pout[ed] and act[ed] like unruly children" when they had a grievance against their American overseers, a sign that obstacles to progress in the islands remained.[70]

The success of the Philippine exhibits inspired private commercial interests to develop a traveling showcase of natives to be displayed as a sideshow attraction at various amusement parks and venues across the nation. Spurned by Portland officials, T. K. Hunt organized his own traveling exhibit of Filipinos around the time of the Lewis and Clark Exposition to cash in on the notoriety. Felder and Schneidewind followed suit shortly after the Portland expo with their own commercial sideshow. The exhibits crisscrossed the country, including stops in Los Angeles (Chutes Park), New Orleans (Mardi Gras), Chicago (Riverside Park), and New York (Coney Island), bringing the shows to audiences across the nation. The traveling exhibitions received mixed reviews in different cities and were marked by problems. Hunt's show featured only Igorottes, as he saw little value in displaying "civilized" Filipinos alongside the "headhunters." His "Philippine Wild Men" show generated sensationalist news stories wherever it went. In 1905, for example, during a stop in Los Angeles, the *Los Angeles Times* ran a story about a meeting at City Hall between three of the "Bow-wow Chiefs" and the city's mayor, Owen McAleer, in which the Filipinos appeared "Sans Pants." The article noted that Filipinos offered McAleer advice about how to deal with his political opponents on the Los Angeles City Council. According to the *Times*, one of the chiefs bragged that he had once threatened to chop the head off the "hostile chairman of the Committee on Dogmeat in the village of Bontoc" and reportedly gave the mayor an ax from the Philippines to use against his political rivals.[71]

The treatment of Filipinos at these privately organized traveling exhibitions was poor compared with what they received at government-sponsored displays. Hunt, Felder, and Schneidewind were only interested in reaping maximum profits from their acts, so they spent little money on working conditions. The men were later accused of embezzling the wages of their native charges. Some of the Filipino performers demanded to be returned home to the Philippines, complaining of neglect and graft by their overseers. Their grievances, however, also became the source of racial condescension and caricature. The *New York Times*, for instance, reported on a dispute at Luna Park on Coney Island, where Igorottes had gone on a "genuine American labor strike." The Filipino protest, the paper reported, was not about wages or working hours but about their "right" to eat dogs. The *Times* further remarked that the Igorottes had been fed "watermelon [and] wienerwurst done in the choicest Coney Island style" but that they rejected these American delicacies in favor of dog meat. When the fair management ignored the Filipinos' requests, they went on strike and refused to dance or sing for their masters until their demands were recognized. When the Luna Park management refused to capitulate, the exhibit was shut down and relocated to the neighboring Dreamland amusement park.[72]

Hunt, Felder, and Schneidewind eventually crossed paths again, operating the Igorotte concession at the Alaska-Yukon-Pacific (A-Y-P) Exposition in Seattle in 1909. The Seattle organizers advertised their city as the "Gateway to the Pacific" and emphasized its commercial ties to the "Orient." They also promoted the fair as a "Laboratory for the Study of Races" and included a strong cast of scientific authorities to assist in the creation of the ethnological exhibits.[73] The displays in Seattle offered a broader cross-section of the Filipino population than previously seen in the United States. The organizers of the Philippine reservation at the A-Y-P placed great emphasis on progress made in the islands after a decade of U.S. rule. American officials hoped that A-Y-P visitors would be able to see the natives' state of civilization "both before and after the white man changed ideas and methods of living."[74] James G. Smith, governor general of the Philippines, traveled to Seattle for the opening of the Igorotte Village at the Alaska Yukon Exposition in June 1909 and praised the exhibit for accurately depicting the progress made during his tenure. Smith's efforts in the islands were extolled by exhibition visitors, who commended him for having done a "fair share of carrying the 'white man's burden'" during his many years of imperial service.[75] The progressive effects of colonial programming in the Philippines was evidenced, according to one local newspaper, not only by the presence of "civilized" natives at the A-Y-P but also by the fact that "headhunting" was on the decline in the islands.[76] The U.S. government stopped sponsoring Philippine exhibits after the 1909 Seattle exposition, but by that time popular perceptions about Filipinos' backwardness and their need for imperial tutelage were firmly established in American national culture.

Conclusion

The establishment of a U.S. colonial outpost in the Philippines had far-reaching consequences, affecting both Filipinos and Americans. The "migration" of American personnel, cultural practices, and institutions to the Philippines set changes into motion that profoundly altered the character of both societies. Domestic anxieties about racial and class conflict shaped debates about the direction of extraterritorial expansion, especially as it pertained to integrating Filipinos into the U.S. polity. Imperial statesmen responded to these concerns by asserting the unqualified authority of Congress to nationalize newly acquired territories without naturalizing the inhabitants of U.S. dependencies. American officials were quickly dispatched to the Philippines to evaluate conditions in the islands and implement a colonial infrastructure. A series of ethnological surveys carried out by American authorities helped to establish the legitimacy of U.S. rule, deeming the local population racially unfit for self-rule. The Roosevelt administration attempted to boost public support for its imperialist initiatives in the Philippines by sponsoring a series of ethnological exhibits that would highlight the need for American guardianship over the natives. Whether these colonial exhibits (and their sideshow spinoffs) were effective in mobilizing genuine enthusiasm for expansionist policies is difficult to gauge. It seems abundantly clear, however, that these showcases resonated with the American public in two important ways. First, they bolstered a collective sense of mastery among the white citizenry, who could take satisfaction in their place at the top of the world's racial hierarchy. Second, the colonial displays reverberated with paternalistic impulses of the Progressive Era, insofar as Filipinos were seen as needy targets of social reform.

These early imperial encounters created new material and cultural linkages between the United States and its outlying possessions. A small legion of Americans was dispatched to the Philippines during this initial period to assist with the buildup of a colonial infrastructure in the islands. By the end of the first decade of U.S. rule, however, the flow of traffic between metropole and colony was redirected toward the imperial center. The demand for agricultural labor in the United States sparked the recruitment of Filipino migrants to Hawaii, Alaska, and the U.S. mainland, further cementing structural and ideological links with the "mother country." The politics of race and empire continued to play a decisive role in the lives of Filipinos entering the United States during the early decades of the twentieth century.

2

Transpacific Traffic

Migration, Labor, and Settlement

Empire and migration go together, inasmuch as industrial development and growth of international trade networks spurred large movements of people across national borders and made it cheaper and simpler for individuals to traverse the globe. New transportation and communications networks collapsed the spatial and ideological distance separating metropole and colony, facilitating the two-way flow of people back and forth across the Philippine-American divide. Despite hyperbolic claims made by nativists and anti-imperialists, most American statesmen did not expect the Philippines to become a major source of immigration to the United States. This turned out to be a serious miscalculation, though the attention given to the topic of Philippine migration far exceeded the actual demographic presence of Filipinos in the country. That Filipinos and other insular subjects could enter and exit the borders of the United States without restriction took on great consequence during this period, as the transpacific imperial zone increased in economic and geopolitical importance. Securing a steady supply of cheap, flexible labor for this region's burgeoning agri-industrial sector was a major challenge during the early decades of the twentieth century, as previous streams of labor from Asia were cut off by a series of restrictive legislative initiatives. The special status of Filipinos proved fortuitous, insofar as it opened up a new channel of labor at a time when exclusionist policies threatened to raise the costs of doing business for American firms competing for market share in the dynamic global economy.

The first clusters of Filipino immigrants began arriving during the first decade of the twentieth century. These newcomers fell into three main groups, drawn from very different sectors of Philippine society. One notable group was made up of college students coming under the auspices of the Pensionado Act of 1903. The pensionado program was developed by Civil Governor William Howard Taft as part of a larger policy of "Americanization" in the islands. The Pensionado Act established an exchange program for Filipino students, who, through government sponsorship, would study in the United States, with the expectation that they would promptly return home to take up leadership positions in the colonial government. The 289 students who were part of this program were predominantly young men from elite backgrounds, and they attended American colleges and universities from 1903 to 1911.[1] A second group of migrants included Filipino veterans of the U.S. Navy who settled in the United States. This population was also a product of colonial programming in the islands and stemmed from an Executive Order issued by President McKinley in 1901 authorizing the admission of Filipinos into the U.S. Navy. McKinley and other American policymakers believed that Western-style military training and service was an important part of the civilizing process, which over time would create a loyal class of native protégés. Some of these men settled in American port cities upon completion of their service, often finding work in naval shipyards or as merchant seamen on the West Coast. The final group of early denizens was the first cohort of Filipino plantation laborers recruited to work on sugar plantations in Hawaii.[2]

Imperial Border Crossing

The arrival of Filipinos in the United States during the early twentieth century took place against a larger set of political and economic developments connected to U.S expansionism. Colonial acquisition, by its very nature, entails border crossing, as imperial powers seize territory previously outside their geographic jurisdiction. Cross-border traffic moves at first in the direction of the colony, since newly enchained territories have property and resources that need to be protected and populations that require supervision.[3] In the case of the Philippines, a small legion of officials, soldiers, and auxiliary agents was dispatched to the islands to administer colonial policy. Their arrival in the islands set the stage for a sustained interchange of people back and forth across the imperial borderlands. The thousands of U.S. citizens who migrated to the Philippines included not only colonial administrators and military personnel, but also an array of other individuals, such as businessmen, teachers, medical professionals, academics, and social reformers. The Republican presidential administrations that governed the Philippines during the early years of U.S. rule launched an "Americanization" program aimed at imparting Anglo-Saxon values and institutions to the local population. Local political and economic structures were overhauled to mirror the U.S. system, and English was made the official language of the administrative and educational bureaucracy in the Philippines.

Developing an American-style democracy in the tropics was a massive undertaking, but there was no shortage of volunteers willing to advance the cause of progressive uplift. An estimated ten to twelve thousand Americans, eager to remake Philippine society and culture, were living in the islands by 1904.[4] A key area of colonial intervention was the establishment of a nationwide public education system in the islands organized around English-language instruction. This triggered a wave of U.S. educators and reformers into the Philippines to overhaul the country's patchwork school system. The most renowned cohort of teachers who joined this mission were known as the "Thomasites," who began arriving in 1901 and eventually numbered over one thousand. Many of these young instructors came from prestigious U.S. colleges and universities and were eager to edify the native population through American-style teaching methods. Filipino students were taught with American textbooks that extolled the virtues of historical figures such as George Washington, Thomas Jefferson, and Abraham Lincoln. Importantly, they learned that the United States was an open democratic society with unlimited prospects for social mobility if one seized the opportunity.[5] The colonial school system also fostered a kind of imperial nationalism among Filipinos, who were taught to identify with, and form an adherence to, the United States and its ruling system. Students pledged allegiance to the American flag at school, a daily reminder of their connection to and membership in the larger imperial polity. These practices reinforced ideological and cultural ties between metropole and colony and laid the groundwork for an increase in transpacific traffic during the early decades of U.S. rule.[6]

An influx of American consumer products accompanied this first wave of migrants into the islands, which also had a profound effect on Philippine civil society. The popularity of American magazines and movies, along with the proliferation of English-language newspapers, painted a romantic and enticing portrait of life in the United States. American cultural hegemony quickly took hold through the absorption of consumer goods and services imported from the United States. Traditional Philippine norms of reciprocity and mutual aid were disrupted as new values of individualism, materialism, and social mobility took hold. These changes were accompanied by colonial economic policies that focused on the export of cash crops to international commodity markets. The subsequent social dislocations engendered by these economic transformations uprooted large sectors of the population, providing the backdrop for emigration.

Pacific Development

Momentous social changes taking place in the Philippines during the first years of colonial rule were matched by equally important developments in the United States. Chief among these was the growing importance of the transpacific imperial zone as a commercial powerhouse and a global center of agribusiness, mining, and oil production. Demand for agricultural commodities from this region—sugar from Hawaii, canned salmon in Alaska, and fruits and vegetables in California—grew precipitously, as did the need for laborers to bring these products to market. Filipinos played a central role in the development of these industries, providing a much-needed stream of workers for American employers. The largest and most significant bloc of migrants to arrive during the early 1900s was made up of laborers recruited to work in Hawaii's booming sugar industry. The overwhelming majority were young men who came from the impoverished Ilocos and Visayas regions of the Philippines.

The demand for Filipino workers in Hawaii was fueled by two factors. One impetus was anxieties among sugar planters worried about new federal regulations curbing the entry of immigrants from China and Japan. The second factor was the increasing militancy of the Japanese, who were the largest group in the plantation workforce. Sugar barons believed that Filipinos might solve both problems, because, as American nationals, they were exempted from federal immigration restrictions and because they could serve as a potential ethnic buffer to the Japanese. Hawaii's sugar industry had imported various ethnic groups over the decades seeking an ideal workforce that exhibited the right mix of industriousness and obedience. Experimentation with various immigrant groups from Europe, Asia, and Latin America led planters to conclude that Asians made the best fieldworkers, so they focused their recruitment on that part of the world. The exact attributes that the sugar industry found so appealing were summarized bluntly by a U.S. labor commissioner investigating economic conditions in the islands. Filipinos and other "Asiatics" were favored by planters, he explained, because they "did not object as much as white men to living perpetually under the shadow of a master."[7]

The escalating demand for sugar in world markets rapidly transformed Hawaii into an economic juggernaut. Sugar exports from the islands increased exponentially during this period, due largely to the Reciprocity Treaty of 1875 between Hawaii and the United States, which allowed island sugar to enter the United States duty-free. Hawaiian sugar production doubled from 129,899 tons in 1890 to 298,544 tons in 1900 and then increased again to 518,127 tons in 1910 and 646,445 tons in 1915, which, in turn, intensified the demand for labor on the plantations. Securing and maintaining a steady workforce in a geographically remote location such as Hawaii was a recurring problem for planters, an issue made more acute with the enactment of restrictive legislation targeting Asian immigrants during the late nineteenth and early twentieth centuries. Industry leaders quickly recognized that the Philippines might provide a solution to their predicament.[8]

The arrival of Filipinos in Hawaii in the first two decades of the twentieth century was followed by secondary migrations to the West Coast and Alaska during the 1920s. Each of these regions featured booming agricultural sectors that required a steady flow of low-cost seasonal labor. Filipinos were sought after because of their unique political status and their reputation as tractable workers. By the mid-1920s, a regularized migration network linking the Philippines and the United States had taken root that would shape relations between the two nations for the rest of the century.

Hawaiian Sugar and Filipino Migration

The growth of the plantation economy in Hawaii was fueled by the ascendancy of sugar as a staple commodity in the industrializing economies of western Europe and the United States.[9] The emergence of pineapple as another burgeoning industry at the turn of the century further extended commercial ties between the territory and global markets. The U.S. mainland was the primary destination of Hawaii cane sugar following the Reciprocity Treaty of 1875, which eliminated tariffs between the two nations. This process was accelerated when the United States overthrew the native government and annexed the Hawaiian Islands in 1898. Annexation was directly tied to the political machinations of American plantation interests in the islands, who wanted to prevent members of the Hawaiian monarchy from interfering in their business affairs.[10]

The first group of Filipino laborers arrived in Hawaii in 1906 under the auspices of the Hawaiian Sugar Planters' Association (HSPA). The HSPA was a powerful agribusiness federation that represented all sectors of the sugar industry, from labor recruitment and cultivation to industrial processing and shipping. The association dominated the territory's economic system and held a viselike grip over island politics. Albert Judd, a Honolulu lawyer acting as a business agent for the HSPA, traveled to Manila in 1906 to secure an agreement with American colonial officials for the importation of Filipino labor to Hawaii. Judd's early recruiting efforts were disappointing, as he was only able to bring 15 workers in 1906 and another 150 in 1907. The recruitment campaign was intensified in 1909 in response to Japanese strike activity in the islands. Planters were especially concerned about the increasing organizational capacity of Japanese workers, who in 1909 made up approximately 75 percent of the plantation workforce. The HSPA thus lobbied officials at the Bureau of Insular Affairs in Washington, DC, to secure workers from the Philippines in partnership with U.S. colonial authorities by setting up a recruiting office in Manila.[11]

The reason behind the sudden enthusiasm for Filipino laborers among the planters was no secret: they admitted both publicly and privately that an alternative pool of workers was needed to offset the growing political organization of Japanese workers. This divide-and-rule strategy reflected the desire of the HSPA to "break up the race solidarity" of the Japanese and "simplify the problem of plantation discipline and plantation management."[12] From the planters' perspective, the perfect workforce would be a population "accustomed to subordination" and holding "modest expectations in regard to a livelihood." They believed that Filipinos, with their extended history of colonial subjection and economic privation, might be the answer to their prayers.[13] Interest in Filipino workers took on new urgency in 1909 in response to the emergence in Hawaii of a Japanese labor advocacy organization known as the Higher Wages Association. The association sought across-the-board wage increases along with improved working and living conditions at the plantation camps. In spring 1909, some seven thousand workers on the island of Oahu walked off the job after their demands were ignored.

In response to the strike action, the HSPA's agent in the Philippines arranged for the transport of 639 Filipinos in 1909, followed by another 2,915 in 1910. In what became an established pattern, almost all these early immigrants were young men from the underdeveloped rural regions of Ilocos in northwestern Luzon and from the Visayas. Most were signed up under three-year labor contracts that stipulated wages, living arrangements, and certain transportation costs. Though the 1885 Foran Act outlawed contract labor in the United States, Filipinos were exempted from that law, which only applied to "alien" contract labor. Some Philippine leaders expressed trepidation about large-scale emigration and exploitative conditions in Hawaii but hoped that formal labor contracts would protect workers. More important, the large licensing fees paid to the Philippine government by the HSPA and its labor recruiters overrode concerns about the treatment of its nationals abroad.[14]

While the HSPA celebrated the flow of Filipino labor into Hawaii, other sectors of the population expressed reservations about the new arrivals. The Japanese-language press, which backed the 1909 strike, made no secret of its disdain for Filipinos, seeing the newcomers' presence as a threat to Japanese organizing efforts. Daniel Keefe, commissioner general of the Bureau of Immigration and Naturalization, railed against the importation of Filipino labor in a report on economic conditions in the islands. Keefe described the newcomers as "lazy and shiftless" with an innate predisposition toward criminality.[15] Scrutiny of the newcomers was intensified when a small group of Filipino recruits was quarantined in 1910 after taking ill on the sea voyage from Asia to Hawaii. Some local officials called for a moratorium on further immigration from the Philippines, citing the potential public health threat posed to the general population. Keefe expressed support for such a ban and lamented that there was nothing that the Bureau of Immigration and Naturalization could do to "prevent these very undesirable Asiatics" from coming to the United States or Hawaii, because of their status as American "nationals." Keefe's call for a federal immigration prohibition provoked a sharp reaction from Manuel Quezon and Benito Legarda, the Philippine resident commissioners in Washington, DC, who told officials at the Bureau of Insular Affairs that exclusionary legislation would be seen by the Filipino people as an affront. In the end, no change to the immigration status of Filipinos was enacted, as the HSPA promised better medical scrutiny of potential laborers from the Philippines.[16]

Anxieties about the social consequences of unrestricted Filipino immigration to Hawaii continued into the 1920s. The ever-increasing demographic majority of Asians in the territory led some nativist leaders on the U.S. mainland to question the sustainability of white settler control in the islands. Hawaii sugar barons, however, argued that their political and economic hegemony was actually dependent on a steady flow of Filipino immigrants. HSPA officials claimed that white rule of the islands required a regular influx of new populations into the territory, so that plantation managers could play different Asian/Pacific Islander groups against one another. Efforts by nativists on the U.S. mainland to cut off immigration from the Philippines, according to the planters, would actually endanger white hegemony and might very well lead to "Oriental" control of the sugar industry.

The recruitment of Filipinos therefore continued unabated, and by 1916, more than twenty thousand laborers had made their way to Hawaii, making up more than 20 percent of the plantation workforce. Few of these migrants had any kind of experience with the type of highly routinized labor regime that they encountered in Hawaii. The HSPA by this time was a large, scientifically managed business organization that controlled almost every aspect of the industry, from labor and cultivation to processing and shipping. The association, acting as the official labor broker of the sugar industry, distributed Filipino workers to various plantations on the islands of Oahu, Maui, Kauai, and Hawaii. As newcomers, the Filipinos were assigned to "unskilled" jobs at the bottom of the plantation hierarchy, which primarily involved the most labor-intensive types of fieldwork such as planting, cane cutting, hoeing, fertilizing, hauling, and fluming. Almost all Filipinos came on three-year labor contracts that stipulated they be paid eighteen dollars for twenty-six days of work per month, making them the lowest paid group in the racially stratified plantation system. Failing to complete all twenty-six days negatively affected the terms of the contract, and the worker received penalties and often a loss of wages. Filipinos' overrepresentation in these types of jobs gave rise to the stereotype that they were naturally drawn to low-paying stoop labor and were therefore contented with their place in the social hierarchy. Such thinking reinforced planters' paternalistic view of Filipinos as a compliant, and complacent, alternative to an increasingly disgruntled Japanese workforce.

Complaints from Filipino workers about exploitative conditions on the plantations in the 1910s attracted attention from Philippine officials, who threatened to halt immigration to Hawaii unless new protections for their nationals were enacted. A bill was eventually passed by the insular government that mandated some basic rights and protections for Filipino workers brought to Hawaii, most notably a guarantee of return passage back to the Philippines at the end of their labor contract. More important, the bill imposed a tax on labor recruiters (i.e., the HSPA), putting much-needed money into the coffers of the insular government.[17] The increasing flow of remittances sent back home by laborers in Hawaii (reaching an estimated three million dollars a year by 1920)[18] gave overseas employment an added cachet and quelled further attempts by Philippine officials to restrict emigration.[19] The global flow of remittances sent back home by Filipinos during this period elevated the profile of overseas workers and set the stage for even more outmigration. The Philippine state's role in brokering and profiting from its overseas migrants during this period represented an early incarnation of a national development strategy that continued for the next century.

Popular stereotypes of contented and obedient Filipino laborers were reinforced in no small part by the repressive and coercive structure of

Hawaii's plantocracy. As total institutions, plantations were designed to maximize managerial control over the day-to-day lives and behavior of those under company dominion. Most of Hawaii's plantations were located in isolated, rural areas, an environment that allowed managers to carry out nearly unbroken surveillance of their workers. Filipinos and other laborers worked under the territory's infamous "perquisite system," in which they received a portion of their earnings in the form of "free" housing and medical care. The perquisite system, often cited by managers as an example of their paternal beneficence, constituted a key element of the planters' command and control structure. Workers lived in segregated company housing and were subject to constant supervision by camp authorities. Residents found to be engaging in labor-organizing activity faced immediate eviction, and supervisors maintained an elaborate network of spies who reported all suspicious activity to company management. The free medical care provided under the perquisite system was also a means of disciplining workers. Plantation medical personnel were constantly on the lookout for "lazy" employees and reported those who they suspected of trying to evade work by claiming injury or illness. Medical officers also kept detailed records of recalcitrant laborers as part of an information-sharing network with other plantations to warn other HSPA members about potential problem employees.[20] Moreover, the spatial isolation of the plantations meant that poorly paid workers relied on company stores for basic goods such as food and living supplies. These stores charged high markups on basic necessities, effectively returning workers' meager earnings right back to their employers and further extending planters' dominion over their employees.

Although the command and control system of the Hawaii plantocracy placed severe constraints on workers' lives, it did not extinguish completely the capacity of rank-and-file laborers to challenge exploitative conditions. By the early 1920s, the popular stereotype of the docile and contented Filipino was tested by a series of disruptive strikes, forcing plantation managers to recalibrate their methods of labor discipline. The evolving class-consciousness of Filipino fieldworkers paralleled rising political militancy among their Japanese co-workers. Relations between the two groups were often marked by tension, since plantation managers deliberately played them against one another through racially differentiated pay scales, occupational segregation, and ethnically partitioned living quarters. Shared class interests and a mutual disdain for the repressive methods of the plantation lunas (field foremen), however, fostered a communal solidarity among fieldworkers. Conditions on Hawaii's plantations had deteriorated during the late 1910s, due in large part to the volatile world sugar market, which affected the fortunes of the local economy. This downturn hit workers particularly hard, with wages remaining frozen from 1912 to 1920, during a period that saw the cost of living in the islands increase by 50 percent.[21]

Mobilizations

Growing economic hardship, combined with collective resentment about the harsh and often violent methods of labor discipline on the plantations, led Filipino and Japanese workers to join forces in Hawaii's first large-scale interracial labor strike in 1920. The strike temporarily merged two separate organizations: the Filipino Labor Union (FLU), led by Pablo Manlapit, and the Federation of Japanese Labor (FJL), an umbrella group of workers, civic leaders, and businessmen.[22] Prior to 1920, the two groups had run parallel campaigns aimed at improving conditions for their own coethnics. Beginning in late 1919, Manlapit aggressively pursued a cooperative alliance with the FJL but found the Japanese leaders hesitant to commit to the more militant demands of the FLU. The planters' divide-and-conquer tactics that had long pitted different ethnonational groups against each other proved a difficult barrier to overcome, and the coalition between the two unions was often marked by suspicion and apprehension.

FLU president Manlapit was a charismatic yet inexperienced labor leader who lacked the organizational structure of his Japanese counterparts. Additionally, the FLU leadership did not have clear lines of authority and communication with rank-and-file workers, and Manlapit's impulsive leadership style sometimes hampered the effectiveness of the Filipino organizing efforts. Despite differences in structure and organization, the FLU and the FJL shared many of the same demands. These included appeals for a significant wage increase to offset the rising cost of living, the expansion of recreational and medical services, and reform of the bonus system, which penalized workers during downturns in the global sugar market regardless of rates of labor productivity.

The FLU and the FJC formed a temporary alliance in 1920, though the groups submitted their demands to the HSPA separately. The planters rejected both of the organizations' demands out of hand, believing that the Filipinos and Japanese were too divided to carry out a coordinated action in response. In the wake of the HSPA's dismissal, Manlapit called for an immediate strike vote, but Japanese leaders were divided about whether to partner with the Filipinos or to move forward separately. A number of key FJL leaders were ethnic nationalists who were skeptical about joining forces with Filipinos, whom they generally considered their inferiors. FJL representatives decided to cut off ties with the FLU but left open the possibility of Filipinos' joining their union if they promised to "obey" Japanese leaders. Rank-and-file workers on Oahu, frustrated by the indecisiveness of Manlapit and the FJL, voted to strike on January 18, 1920, and two days later twenty-six hundred Filipino workers (along with three hundred Puerto Ricans) staged a walkout at selected Oahu sugar plantations, staging mass pickets that disrupted cultivation. Japanese workers were initially hesitant to join the strike but were also worried about crossing picket lines and facing confrontations with their co-workers.[23] Tensions grew quickly between strikers and the Japanese workers who crossed the picket lines. The two groups reconciled, however, when the FJL belatedly voted to join the walkout.

The HSPA saw the multiethnic labor action as a serious threat to its hegemony and refused to negotiate with the strikers. The intransigent stance of plantation management forced the workers to dig in for a prolonged campaign that eventually exposed the coalition's strategic vulnerabilities. Pablo Manlapit, whose control over the rank-and-file Filipinos was tenuous at best, strove to advance union demands, but his anarchic organizational style and lack of logistical preparation for a sustained strike impaired the FLU's cause. When, for example, Filipino workers were evicted from camp housing at various plantations on Oahu, he had no contingency plan or strike fund to house or feed destitute strikers. A serious influenza outbreak during the winter months added to the turmoil, as scores of homeless, hungry Filipinos took ill with no access to medical care. By the beginning of February, Manlapit had lost influence over the rank-and-file Filipinos and had been effectively marginalized by FJL leaders who viewed him as a reckless liability. His credibility was further damaged when the HSPA launched a propaganda scheme publicly accusing him of soliciting a fifty-thousand-dollar bribe from the planters to call off the strike. Though the story was false, it injured Manlapit's reputation and raised doubts about his leadership.[24] As the strike moved into the spring months, the morale of workers started to decline, with little evidence of a settlement forthcoming. The death of ninety-five Filipino and fifty-five Japanese workers from the influenza outbreak also took a toll on strikers' resolve. The strike finally ended after six months in July 1920, with none of the workers demands being met and both unions in disarray.

Although the dual union strike did not produce tangible concessions for the FLU or the FJL, it did result in significant financial losses for the struck Oahu plantations. The federated structure of the HSPA, however, spread the losses across all Hawaii's plantations, which greatly enhanced the ability of individual firms to collectively outlast strikers. Although the planters ultimately prevailed in the 1920 strike, the specter of interracial unionism forced them to rethink some of their management tactics. And while the tenuous political coalition between Filipinos and Japanese proved especially brittle during the 1920 campaign, it did not take much imagination for planters to envision a more formidable alliance emerging between the two groups in the future. As a result, the HSPA redoubled its efforts to keep workers divided and distracted. The HSPA launched a recruiting effort in the Philippines to bring in more women, hoping that a more stable family life would have a calming effect on young male Filipino workers. From 1920 to 1929, sixty-five thousand Filipinos were brought to Hawaii. The HSPA specifically recruited workers from the Ilocos region in the wake of the strike, believing Visayans had been the prime instigators of the labor uprising. In addition, the planters and their political allies lobbied Congress in 1921 to grant Hawaii an exemption from the Chinese Exclusion Act. They hoped that reintroducing workers from China would act as counterweight against Filipino and Japanese cooperation. Though this effort ultimately failed, it offers insight into the strategic mindset of the planters in the wake of the 1920 strike.[25]

Plantation workers faced an uphill battle in rallying public support for their cause in the wake of the 1920 campaign. The establishment press in Hawaii (the *Pacific Commercial Advertiser* and the *Honolulu Star-Bulletin*) stepped up its public criticism of labor activists in the aftermath of the conflict, characterizing strikers as alien agitators seeking to take over the sugar industry. The 1920 walkout was portrayed as the handiwork of foreign radicals who had used Bolshevik methods to arouse an otherwise contented plantation workforce. Wallace Farrington, the editor of the *Star-Bulletin* and a Hawaii gubernatorial candidate, condemned the catalytic role of Filipino workers in the Oahu strike, calling them the "most un-American specimens of humanity in the Territory." Farrington claimed that Filipino labor leaders were bent on radically altering the island's political-economic system by leading the islands' brown-skinned majority into power.[26] The aftermath of the 1920 strike witnessed the proliferation of new regulations on the plantations aimed at ferreting out potential agitators. For instance, an HSPA blacklist identifying the names of known activists was disseminated to all company managers on the islands. Being on the blacklist rendered a person unemployable in the sugar industry and barred him or her from entering the grounds of HSPA plantations. Moreover, the period following the 1920 strike saw an increase in criminal prosecutions of union organizers, an initiative aimed at crippling the labor movement. Authorities frequently arrested labor leaders on trumped-up conspiracy charges, which treated almost any kind of union activity as unlawful subversion. Adding to the planters' already well-stocked arsenal of political tools was the passage of new laws that proscribed union activities, including antipicketing ordinances, trespassing laws that prohibited access of organizers to plantations, and restrictions on freedom of the press aimed at criminalizing the publication of union literature deemed by authorities (i.e., the HSPA and their allies) to be antibusiness.[27]

Despite all the legal obstacles labor leaders faced, they continued unionization efforts on the plantations in the wake of the 1920 strike. This campaign was carried out under the banner of the newly formed United Workers of Hawaii (UWH). The UWH had the backing of the Honolulu labor establishment, which until that point had shown little interest in organizing plantation workers. Pablo Manlapit was a key figure in the organization and partnered with members of the Honolulu Central Labor Council and the Higher Wages Association to press for union recognition on the plantations. By 1922, Filipinos made up the largest percentage of Hawaii's plantation workforce (41 percent of the total plantation labor force), and they were especially active in the UWH. Early stereotypes about their tractability and naiveté slowly gave way to new narratives that emphasized their inborn militancy and political solidarity. Efforts by labor leaders to draw attention to abysmal conditions on the plantations worried HSPA officials concerned about the industry's popular image. The HSPA waged a public-relations campaign to counter public sympathy for the plight of workers, portraying Filipino labor leaders as aggressive, knife-wielding thugs who "ran amok" at the slightest provocation.

Wage cuts implemented during the early 1920s continued to squeeze workers to the breaking point but also created an opportunity for organizers to win rank-and-file support, and the UWH issued a new set of pay and benefit demands to the HSPA in early 1923. After more than a year of fruitless negotiations, Manlapit called for a strike in April 1924. The action began at a handful of worksites on Oahu and eventually spread to twenty-three of Hawaii's forty-five plantations. The strike was poorly planned and reflected Manlapit's impulsive top-down organizing strategy. To disrupt production, workers used targeted walkouts at key plantations, using tactics such as pickets and slowdowns. In June, Manlapit was arrested by Hilo authorities on conspiracy charges as part of an HSPA strategy to silence him. The arrest backfired, however, firming up the resolve of workers who saw the harassment and intimidation of Manlapit and other union leaders as more evidence that the island's legal system was controlled by the plantation bosses.

The situation grew more volatile over the course of the summer, with the HSPA relentlessly portraying strikers as subversives and thugs who would stop at nothing to cripple the sugar industry.[28]

Things came to a head on September 6, when a group of Filipino strikers at the Hanapepe plantation on Kauai detained two strikebreakers. The Kauai sheriff, William H. Rice, who worked closely with the HSPA and whose brother Charles Rice was an influential sugar planter and politician, appointed a special squad of civilian deputies to secure the release of the two strikebreakers. When the workers ignored the sheriff's demands, police sharpshooters opened fire on the crowd. The results were tragic, with sixteen strikers and four policemen killed in the melee. Another 143 laborers were arrested in the aftermath of the massacre, and most faced felony charges. Local authorities quickly dumped the bodies of the Filipinos victims into a mass grave overlooking Hanapepe Bay, so that they could not be given a martyr's funeral that might spur on more labor activism. Not surprisingly, the HSPA and its political surrogates in the local media blamed the whole affair on the radical orientation of the strikers. The *Star-Bulletin* singled out the alleged role of "professional agitators" and "reds" who were doing their "bolshevik best" to stir up dissension among the Filipinos. These labor leaders, according to the newspaper, preached "class warfare" as part of a communistic scheme to take over the sugar industry. The public branding of union organizers as radicals reinforced the HSPA's grip on power, by blaming the turmoil on subversives within labor's ranks and therefore justifying the exercise of repressive authority against those deemed a threat to good order.[29]

The HSPA used the territorial legal system to punish strike participants jailed in the aftermath of the Hanapepe massacre. Planters subsidized the prosecution of activists, providing financial aid to county law enforcement and supplying extra legal counsel to the local district attorney's offices to assist with the trials. Public sentiment against the Hanapepe workers ran high, as local politicians and the press labeled them as violent troublemakers. Although there was little local sympathy for the Hanapepe strikers, they did receive some support from concerned political leaders back home. Members of the Philippine legislature passed a resolution demanding an official investigation of labor conditions in Hawaii in response to the Hanapepe massacre, but American colonial officials ultimately derailed these efforts.[30]

The 1924 strike crippled the UWH and the Higher Wages Movement. Dozens of labor leaders were in jail awaiting trial, and the hundreds of rank-and-file workers across the territory also faced criminal charges for their political activities. Seventy-two Filipinos were charged with rioting for their role in the Hanapepe affair (another fifty-seven pleaded guilty to other charges before going to trial). The HSPA capitalized on the trails to make an example of the strikers, hoping to send a strong message to other potential partisans. The limitless resources, both financial and political, of the HSPA made the outcome of the trial a forgone conclusion. The strikers never had a chance for a fair hearing on Kauai, and in fact, they were not even granted legal counsel until after the trial had already begun. Sixty of the defendants were eventually found guilty of various charges (e.g., assault, vagrancy, rioting) in connection with the Hanapepe incident, receiving sentences ranging from four to ten years in prison. The trial judge, parroting the HSPA party line on the 1924 strike, blamed the massacre on the violent and "anti-American" ideology of Filipino labor leaders.[31]

Meanwhile, Manlapit's conspiracy trial on Oahu began a week after the Hanapepe incident. He and his colleague Cecilio Basan faced charges of suborning perjury in a case involving the publication of a controversial article in the Filipino union newspaper *Ang-Batay* in April 1924. The article accused the HSPA of denying emergency medical care to the infant son of plantation worker Pantaleon Inayuda. The child eventually died, and the *Ang-Batay* article suggested that indifferent HSPA officials were partly to blame. The defendants were accused of coaching Inayuda to lie during a libel trial earlier that same year. Local authorities had been gunning for Manlapit for years and saw the conspiracy trial as a chance both to silence him and to cripple the union. Manlapit and Basan were found guilty in a show trial that featured a barrage of preposterous and contradictory testimony from prosecution witnesses, most of whom were paid off by the HSPA. The defendants received sentences of two to ten years in jail for their crime, effectively sidelining the union's two most visible leaders. The crackdown on the union did not stop there, as Filipino labor activists on all four major Hawaii islands were jailed by authorities and charged with a variety of offenses related to their political organizing.[32]

The 1924 strike, like the one carried out in 1920, produced bitter disappointment among rank-and-file workers and their families and left the labor movement fragmented and demoralized. Fed up with the low pay and onerous conditions in the sugar fields, many Filipinos started moving into other sectors of the Hawaii economy. A significant number found employment in the fast-growing pineapple industry, which took off during the 1910s and 1920s. In addition to fieldwork, significant numbers of Filipinos, including women, took jobs at pineapple canneries in the islands. This work paid better than jobs in many other industries, since Hawaii held a near monopoly on the lucrative world market for canned pineapple. Moreover, the canneries' location in urban centers made the industry more desirable than jobs on isolated rural sugar plantations. Filipinos also started moving into the burgeoning tourism industry, which by the 1920s had become the third-largest sector of Hawaii's economy (behind sugar and pineapple). The tourism economy, however, comprised a highly segmented labor market, and Filipinos were routinely channeled into the lowest paying, unskilled jobs, such as dishwashers, pantry helpers, and busboys. A smaller number found work as bellboys in hotels.[33]

The mid- to late 1920s also witnessed the first large-scale movement of Filipinos to the Pacific coast of the United States and Alaska. The passage of the 1924 Immigration Act severely curtailed the flow of foreign-born labor, a development that left western U.S. agribusiness interests searching for new sources of workers to fill labor shortages in the booming agricultural and fish-canning industries. The movement of Filipinos to North America was aided by the growth of the transpacific shipping industry, which aggressively advertised in the Philippines. The Dollar Steamship Company (known as the Dollar Line) was a dominant player in this global business, winning federal-government contracts for the transport of mail from the United States to the Asia-Pacific region. The company, however, sought additional ways to make money on its return voyages to the United States. Passenger travel was one logical method to bring in revenue, but American immigration laws restricted the entry of Asian nationals. Filipinos, however, were exempted from the 1924 act, so the Philippines became a major focus of the Dollar Line's marketing.[34]

By the mid-1920s, it did not take much inducement to find a large base of potential passengers eager to travel abroad in search of economic opportunities—so much so that the HSPA had stopped subsidizing the transport of laborers from the Philippines in 1926, since the flow of labor to Hawaii was self-sustaining by that point. Private agents took over the business of recruiting workers for the HSPA and other American agricultural interests on a commission basis. The agents pointed to examples of former overseas workers who settled back in the Philippines with the plentiful savings they had accumulated in Hawaii or on the U.S. mainland. The returnees offered fantastic tales of cosmopolitan life overseas and the riches that could be earned abroad. The steady flow of remittances from overseas workers served to reinforce the popular perception that economic opportunities in the metropole were more lucrative than those at home.[35]

Alaska Canned Salmon and Filipino Labor

The development of the Alaska canned-salmon industry, like other Pacific agri-industrial enterprises, had long relied on Asian immigrants to fill unskilled and semiskilled labor slots.[36] The seasonal nature of the industry and the remoteness of the territory provided challenges for employers, who sought large numbers of workers willing to relocate to Alaska to work grueling three-month stints. The canneries used a flexible hiring system that allowed plant owners to farm out the recruitment of labor to independent contractors who supplied work gangs to companies on a piece-rate system. Demand for canned salmon grew exponentially in the 1910s and 1920s at the same time that federal immigration policies curbed the entry of Chinese and Japanese into the United States.[37] With traditional sources of labor drying up, the industry turned to Filipinos. The Alaska canners first explored the idea of using Filipinos in the 1910s, sending labor agents to Hawaii to enlist recruits from the plantations. This endeavor was not well received by the HSPA, which, in an ironic twist, tried to get a law passed by the territorial legislature to prevent rival recruiters in Alaska or on the U.S. mainland from soliciting immigrant workers whom it had recruited to Hawaii. Territorial legislators acted quickly to protect the HSPA's interests, imposing exorbitant fees on outside labor agents to discourage them from tapping into Hawaii's exclusive preserve of Asian labor.[38]

Filipino cannery workers, popularly referred to as "Alaskeros," quickly became the principal labor force in the canned-salmon industry. By the early 1920s, the canneries were a regular stop on the seasonal labor circuit that stretched from Southern California to Alaska. Contractors in West Coast port cities such as Seattle, Portland, and San Francisco enlisted Filipino crews during the fruit and vegetable off-season, with Seattle serving as the primary recruitment and departure hub. By 1921, nearly one thousand Filipinos were working in Alaska, outnumbering the Chinese and Japanese who had previously made up the majority of laborers in the fish-processing plants. By 1928, 3,916 Filipinos toiled in the canneries, more than the combined total of Japanese and Chinese workers.[39]

The life and work routines in Alaska bore some striking similarities to those on the sugar plantations of Hawaii. Most of the canneries were in isolated rural areas and, like plantations, operated as total institutions. Workers lived in racially segregated housing owned by the company or in rudimentary bunkhouses leased out by the contractors. As the last large group to arrive in Alaska, Filipinos entered at the bottom of the cannery hierarchy. Most of the labor contractors were the more established Chinese or Japanese, who had long-term relationships with cannery owners. To sustain profitability in the unpredictable world market for canned foods, plant managers sought to maximize production outputs while at the same time keeping their labor costs down, which put pressure on labor contractors to do the same. Contractors negotiated numeric benchmarks with plant owners, guaranteeing delivery of a set number of cases of canned salmon on a seasonal basis for a fixed fee. Labor suppliers sought to hire tractable workers who could meet variable salmon-pack targets and adapt to the capricious demands of cannery managers without complaining. Contractors' profits came out of the difference between the fixed amount they received from the canners for production yields and the aggregate wages they paid to their work crew. This system led to exploitative conditions for workers, who faced relentless pressure from both contractors and plant managers to increase their productivity in order to increase company profit margins.[40]

Contractors or their subagents enlisted new recruits with promises of stable work and better wages than could be earned in segmented labor markets open to Filipinos in Hawaii or on the West Coast. The promised wages, however, were not what they seemed, since the contractors deducted costs for things such as clothing, food, and housing out of the workers' pay. Potential employees were typically required to pay a finder's fee (payoff) to the contractor who hired them, which became a frequent source of abuse since cannery positions were highly coveted. Most of the contractors had little concern for the conditions of work in the canneries, since their interests were aligned with management. The role of Chinese and Japanese as labor brokers often made them the focus of antagonism from their Filipino workers, who frequently saw the ethnic middlemen as the source of their exploitation.

Opportunities for social mobility in Alaska were limited, and Filipinos were relegated to the lowest paying, least desirable jobs at the canneries, working as cutters, slimers, scalers, gutters, and lidders.[41] The adverse conditions on the cannery floor were made even worse by poor living conditions and limited leisure opportunities. Contractors covered the costs of crew food out of the brokering fee they received from the company, so the cafeteria offerings were minimal, with meals of gruel and rice serving as dietary staples. Workers had the "option" to buy supplementary provisions such as fruits, vegetables, meat, or alcohol at company stores run by the contractors, which charged exorbitant prices. The purchase of these extras made cannery life more bearable, but it also quickly chipped away at workers' savings. The drudgery of work and the geographic isolation of processing plants compelled workers to make the most of the little free time they had. The most ubiquitous leisure activity at the worksites was gambling, and contractors ran illicit betting operations at labor camps. Contractors actively promoted gaming, and some even hired professional gamblers to work their rackets. Gambling losses left many workers in debt at the end of the salmon season and became a highly effective means for contractors to repossess the wages they paid to laborers.[42]

The contracting system in Alaska came under increasing challenge in the 1930s from Filipinos who remained at the bottom rungs of the industry. Contractors had long assumed that the newcomers were too pliable and disorganized to contest their authority, and the seasonal nature of cannery employment was an impediment to sustained political solidarity. Filipino workers launched a unionization campaign during the 1930s in which they sought better wages, improved working conditions, and reforms to the exploitative contractor system. In 1932, they formed the Cannery Workers and Farm Laborers Union (CWFLU), a labor organization affiliated with the American Federation of Labor. All of the CWFLU's leadership positions were held by Filipinos, who also made up the majority of the rank-and-file membership. The union faced significant hurdles in its organizing efforts, as contractors still controlled all the hiring at the canneries and were able to co-opt a number of workers with preferential treatment. Ethnic divisions among Filipinos also proved to be a barrier, as Ilocano, Visayan, and Tagalog workers competed with one another for power and prestige in the union.

Despite these challenges, by the mid-1930s the CWFLU was able to force some major reforms in the industry, aided in part by federal officials seeking to reform industrial conditions in the canneries during the New Deal era. The union won some significant victories including the abolition of the contracting system and a closed-shop agreement that established a CWFLU hiring hall in Seattle. As the union's membership and influence grew, so too did the political agenda of its Seattle-based leadership. The CWFLU actively supported the Philippine independence movement and lobbied state legislators to oppose discriminatory measures such as alien land laws and a proposed antimiscegenation statute in Washington State. Few Filipinos lived in Alaska year-round, and most cannery workers also toiled in the fruit and vegetable fields of the West Coast, where they encountered a very different set of political challenges.[43]

Imperial Valleys: Pacific Coast Agriculture

The 1920 U.S. census estimated the population of Filipinos in the continental United States to be just 5,603. This group was made up primarily of students, former pensionados who remained in the country after their schooling, veterans of the U.S. Navy who remained stateside after completing their service, and merchant seamen who settled in or around various port cities across the United States where economic opportunities were available. The presence of Filipinos in the United States did not register much attention until the mid-1920s, when the character and scale of immigration changed. These demographic changes were spurred by major economic transformations in California during the early decades of the twentieth century, a period that saw the region become the nation's principal producer of fruits and vegetables. The introduction of intensive agriculture in the region, a production regime characterized by high capital investment and flexible labor inputs that combined to generate large yields of produce for the national market, took off during this period. This modern form of corporatized farming required large supplies of inexpensive seasonal labor for both planting and harvesting and soon came to dominate the West Coast's agricultural sector. The shift to intensive agriculture was aided by technological advances; refrigerated railroad cars, the spread of cheap hydroelectricity, and the expansion of a modern irrigation infrastructure in California. The development of new water supplies, in particular, transformed the region into an agricultural powerhouse as the amount of irrigated farmland in the state grew from one million acres in 1890 to five million acres in 1930.[44] Public irrigation projects facilitated agricultural expansion into previously underdeveloped parts of the state, particularly the Central Coast (Ventura, Santa Barbara, Monterrey, and Santa Cruz counties) and the inland Central Valley (Sacramento and San Joaquin) regions.[45] Moreover, the climatic conditions in the state allowed the industry to maintain a nearly year-round production schedule for popular crops, giving California agriculture an advantage over rival states. Farm exports from the state increased by leaps and bounds during the early twentieth century, with gross revenues increasing 800 percent, from $100 million in 1899 to an estimated $800 million in 1929.[46] This revenue growth was fueled by a steady increase in the number of farms and orchards devoted to labor-intensive fruit and vegetable crops, and by the 1920s California was the nation's largest producer of these commodities.

This commercial development would not have been possible without a large supply of tractable labor willing to work under harsh conditions for modest remuneration. Attracting a steady stream of workers to western agriculture was a longstanding dilemma for growers, who like employers in Hawaii and Alaska, saw previous labor streams from Asia evaporate during the exclusion era. Growers on the West Coast claimed that native white workers were not a practical option for industrial agriculture because of the seasonal nature of employment and these workers' access to higher-paying jobs in the primary sector of the labor market. Mexican immigrants provided a logical answer to labor needs in the industry, though agribusiness leaders regularly expressed reservations about the suitability of Mexicans for intensive agricultural work. Nevertheless, recruitment of workers from Mexico accelerated in the 1910s, and by World War I, Mexicans made up the bulk of the workforce in the California fields.

The continuing availability of labor from Mexico, however, was called into question in the 1920s, as West Coast nativists pressed Congress to pass new legislation that would place individuals from Latin America under limitative quotas similar to those established under the 1924 Immigration Act. Lawmakers John Box of Texas and William Harris of Georgia introduced a series of bills in the mid-1920s to place the Western Hemisphere under immigration quota restrictions (see chapter 5). Though Mexicans were not, at this time, subject to formal exclusion, they still faced a variety of impediments that limited their movement across the American border. In order to be admitted into the United States, they were required to pass a literacy test and pay an exorbitant ten-dollar visa fee and eight-dollar head tax at the border crossing, onerous prerequisites that spurred an increase in "illegal" immigration in this period. The newly created Border Patrol (mandated by the 1924 Immigration Act) added another obstacle that threatened to disrupt the flow of labor from Mexico, especially as U.S. authorities launched a series of high-profile roundups and deportations of Mexicans during the late 1920s.[47]

Concerns about the long-term availability of Mexican labor led growers to turn to Filipinos as one of the few viable alternatives for agricultural labor in the West. As American nationals, Filipinos were not classified as immigrants by the federal government, a status that made them particularly attractive to growers. The majority (56 percent) of Filipino arrivals during the 1920s migrated from Hawaii to the West Coast. The exodus from Hawaii to the U.S. mainland was the product of both economic and political factors. Exploitative conditions on the sugar plantations led many Filipinos to leave for the mainland after completing their employment contracts, in search of better job opportunities. The violent labor conflicts that swept across Hawaii in 1924 also propelled Filipinos to relocate to the West Coast for work, and many of those who departed for the mainland had been blacklisted from employment by the HSPA for participation in strikes.[48]

A marked increase in Filipino migration to the West Coast occurred in the mid-1920s, with the vast majority of Filipinos disembarking in California. The number of arrivals in the Golden State swelled from an average of 618 per year from 1920 to 1922 to 5,408 per year from 1926 to 1929. The majority of these newcomers (82.3 percent) arrived at the port of San Francisco, with the other 17.7 percent entering through Los Angeles. Seattle was another key port of entry because of its proximity to the Alaskan canneries. Filipinos on the West Coast faced a very different demographic and work environment than they had encountered in Hawaii and Alaska. A key difference was the presence of a large white, working-class population against whom they might compete in the labor market. The geographic isolation that Filipinos experienced in Hawaii and Alaska was replaced by the more densely settled communities of the American West, where anti-Asian racism was a deeply entrenched part of the political culture.

New arrivals at West Coast ports were often greeted by labor agents waiting at the docks ready to sign them up for farm work. Most Filipinos worked under labor contractors who coordinated work crews specializing in certain crops. Farm operators preferred this hiring system since it allowed them to externalize most of their traditional obligations, including transportation, food, and housing, to the contractors who bore all responsibility for the care of workers. Filipinos regularly worked alongside Mexican work crews, and growers characterized both groups as naturally suited for the so-called stoop labor necessary in fieldwork. Filipinos developed a reputation for their dexterity with crops such as asparagus, lettuce, and celery that required workers to stoop their backs close to the ground. They dominated the cultivating and harvesting of these crops in California's Coastal and Delta regions, especially in areas such as Salinas, Watsonville, Stockton, Sacramento, and Fresno. Though especially renowned in the West for their skill in harvesting fickle products such as lettuce and asparagus, their reputation as proficient field laborers found them coveted by growers of all types of cash crops across the region. By the end of the 1920s, Filipinos were traversing the West Coast picking melons and tomatoes in the Imperial Valley, carrots and sugar beets in Santa Maria, apricots and peaches in Merced, pears in San Jose, and cherries in Solano County.[49]

The Filipino labor circuit extended well beyond California's boundaries, stretching north into Washington State and Oregon, states that also featured burgeoning agricultural sectors. The expansion of the Pacific Highway in

1923 created a modern road network that stretched from Southern California to the Canadian border, greatly facilitating automobile travel along the Pacific coast.[50] Enhanced transportation routes now directly linked cities such as Salinas and Stockton to Portland and Seattle, and it became commonplace to see carloads of Filipino work crews following seasonal harvests up and down the West Coast.

Washington State was a regular node on the migratory labor circuit and boasted the second-largest population of Filipinos on the U.S. mainland. The State had a large agricultural industry dependent on migrant labor. By 1930, there were 3,480 Filipinos living in Washington, with the population evenly split between the urban hub of Seattle and the rich agricultural regions of the Yakima and Wenatchee valleys in the central and eastern parts of the state.[51] Filipinos were a major presence in the apple and cherry orchards in Yakima and Wenatchee as well as in the hop and potato fields in the eastern section of the state. Oregon witnessed a similar pattern of immigrant employment, but on a smaller scale, with Filipinos working primarily in the hop-growing areas of the Hood River and Willamette Valley regions and the salmon canneries located on the Columbia River.[52]

Farm operators were said to favor Filipinos because they were "steadier, more tractable and more willing to put up with longer hours, poorer board, and worse lodging facilities" than other ethnic groups.[53] These traits were contrasted with the work ethic of native whites, whom employers characterized as inefficient, unreliable, and insolent. White workers, according to growers, often left their jobs before the harvest was completed, leaving crops to spoil in the fields or orchards. One grower in Exeter declared Filipinos to be "100 percent better" than white laborers, a sentiment common among farm owners during the period.[54] The alleged political subservience of Filipinos was also cited by growers as an attractive trait. An investigator from the California Department of Industrial Relations acknowledged that this sentiment was popular among farm operators, observing, "Where a white worker may feel restive and disgruntled because of bad working conditions, the Filipino newcomer is satisfied to stay on the job 'without kicking.'"[55] The suggestion that Filipinos were "satisfied" with their place at the bottom of the economic hierarchy echoed similar stereotypes repeated in Hawaii and Alaska about their natural passivity and contentedness with their place in the socioeconomic hierarchy.

Agribusiness defended the importation of immigrant labor, claiming that the industry could not survive without the continued flow of labor from the Philippines and Mexico. Growers saw both groups as a distinctive category of the national labor supply that embodied the two attributes they desired most: namely, they were cheaper than native workers and were racially and politically disenfranchised. Growers wanted their workers to come as cheaply as possible since intensive fruit and vegetable cultivation was a high-risk business that relied on provisional labor to harvest perishable crops during a narrow harvest window. Profits could easily evaporate if workers walked out for higher wages, leaving crops to spoil in the fields. Moreover, concerns about fluctuating national market prices for agricultural products, the costs of shipping commodities via railroad car across the country, and the constant threat of crop losses (from weather, pest infestation, strikes, etc.) compelled western growers to take a hard line on wages, since it was one of the few production costs they could control. Farm operators were not shy about acknowledging their dependence on Filipino and Mexican labor and viewed the strident nativist movement of the 1920s as a threat to their economic prosperity. Growers allied with other powerful business interests that employed foreign labor to lobby sympathetic lawmakers to oppose restrictionist legislation being considered by Congress during this period. Powerful western agribusiness interests even lobbied Congress to overturn the Chinese Exclusion Act(s) from 1906 through the end of World War I, in the hope that a new influx of "Chinamen" would help to solve labor shortages.[56]

While western employers embraced the arrival of Filipinos, other sectors of American society were far less welcoming. Leaders of the West Coast nativist movement in particular were outraged by what they saw as the latest invasion of unassimilable foreigners across the Pacific border. Nativist leaders and trade-union spokesmen decried the influx of Filipinos, claiming that they stole jobs from white citizens and undermined the American standard of living. Accusations of job displacement and declining wages masked the more complex realities underpinning industrial agriculture in the region. Growers and the migrant workers themselves frequently pointed out that their presence actually created jobs and bolstered the overall commercial infrastructure of the West Coast. The availability of Filipino field labor helped to create jobs in related industries as well as in other sectors of the economy. Higher-paying jobs in the packing sheds, warehouses, and fruit and vegetable canneries on the West Coast were monopolized by white workers and were directly tied to the labor performed by Filipinos and Mexicans in the fields. Moreover, the rise of California's fruit and vegetable industry sparked job growth in commercial transportation industries, such as road building, trucking, and railroad services that linked western agricultural commodities to the national market. Agribusiness and nativists remained at odds over the issue of Filipino immigration during the 1920s and the early part of the 1930s. By the mid-1930s, however, growers' toleration of Filipino workers, which was always conditional, started to shift as the costs, both economic and political, of employing them escalated. The self-serving stereotypes of the contented Filipino stoop laborers toiling away in the fields began to give way to a more ominous reputation. Following the same pattern as in Hawaii and Alaska, Filipinos developed a potent class-consciousness that became the basis for collective action and political organization. They engaged in scores of large agricultural strikes up and down the coast that earned the ire of business interests and authorities. As a result, they lost favor with the growers who just a few years before had held them up as model workers, leaving them with few supporters in the larger society.

The early decades of the twentieth century witnessed dramatic economic transformations across the Pacific frontier of the United States. Burgeoning agricultural industries in Hawaii, Alaska, and the American West required large supplies of foreign labor to meet new market demands. The Philippines emerged as a popular source of labor, since residents of the islands could migrate to the United States and its territories without restriction. While Filipinos experienced no physical barriers to their admission into the United States, they encountered a wide array of legal obstacles that delimited their social and political mobility in American society. The following chapter analyzes debates about the sociolegal status of Filipinos in the United States, focusing on struggles over citizenship, interracial marriage, and property rights.

3

"It Is the Fight of This Nation against the Filipinos"

Redrawing Boundaries of Race and Nation

The growing visibility of Filipinos in the American West during the 1920s drew considerable public attention in a region that had long been the locus of anti-Asian sentiment in the United States. Discriminatory measures restricting the socioeconomic mobility of Chinese and Japanese immigrants in the late nineteenth and early twentieth centuries evolved into a more generalized campaign to curb the entry and settlement of all Asian groups in the United States, a movement that reached its apex with the passage of the 1924 Immigration Act.[1] As U.S. nationals, Filipinos were exempted from the restrictive quotas established by the law, a situation that frustrated nativists and their congressional allies. Unable to prevent the physical movement of Filipinos across U.S. borders, nativist leaders shifted their focus on erecting legal barriers designed to inhibit their social and political entry into American society. The porousness of the nation's Pacific borderlands was a longstanding preoccupation of nativists, who worried about the so-called peaceful penetration of Asian and Mexican immigrants into West Coast communities. California state assemblyman E. G. Adams voiced this sentiment in a 1929 address: "California, because of its location on the western rim of this continent, always has had the duty, unpleasant perhaps, of leading the fight to stem the tides from the Orient." He continued, "First it was the fight for Chinese exclusion, won in 1882; then, forty years later, it was the Japanese undertaking; and now beginning in 1929, it is the fight of this nation against the Filipinos."[2] The "fight" that Assemblyman Adams spoke of called for the deployment of state power to shore up the integrity of racial and civic boundaries, which exclusionists saw as under threat by Filipino immigrants.

Enforcing discriminatory legislation against America's colonial wards proved easier said than done. Filipinos invoked the tenets of social equality that they had been taught in the American-run public schools in the Philippines to challenge their disfranchisement in the United States. They pointed to the troubling divide between the rhetoric of benevolent assimilation espoused by American statesmen and the iniquitous system of racial subordination they encountered once they arrived in the metropole. Filipinos reminded U.S. officials that American citizens residing in the Philippines were granted naturalization, property, and intermarriage rights and asked why the same privileges were not accorded to Filipino nationals living in the "mother country."

Debates over the political standing of Filipinos and uncertainty about where they fit into the nation's ascriptive hierarchy proved contentious and led to a series of legal battles during the early decades of the twentieth century. On one side of this conflict were the gatekeepers: judges, state officials, and local bureaucrats who served as the first line of defense against the latest wave of Asian "invaders" flooding across the Pacific border. On the other side were Filipinos who contested their assignment into disadvantaged social categories, often using the federal government's own bureaucratic machinery against itself. They appropriated American rhetoric of imperial allegiance and republican beneficence to protest discriminatory legislation and to put forward alternative definitions of civic belonging.

This chapter focuses on struggles over citizenship, interracial marriage, and property rights, highlighting the ways in which the arrival of Filipinos exposed the shifting and uncertain boundaries of the nation's ascriptive hierarchy. Filipinos' distinctive national and racial status created dilemmas for American lawmakers, who had to reconcile official proclamations of imperial liberality on the international front with established traditions of racial subordination and exclusion on the domestic front. Filipinos were officially recognized as "nationals" of the United States, but what this meant in concrete political terms was ambiguous. Were they eligible for admission to naturalized citizenship in the United States if they met the requisite criteria? Were they on equal footing with citizens when it came to eligibility for employment with the federal government or access to welfare benefits provided by the state? The outlier racial status of Filipinos confounded authorities charged with policing categorical distinctions between population groups. The fact that Filipinos did not fit neatly into the nation's preexisting system of racial classification was a source of great confusion. Recall that leading ethnologists of the period had identified "Malays" as the dominant racial group in the Philippines, a separate and distinct category from Chinese and Japanese, who were legally classed as "Mongolians." The Malay designation placed them outside the prevailing racial taxonomy and forced state officials to recalibrate the normative criteria for determining the boundaries of exclusion. Filipinos seized on the ambiguities regarding their sociolegal status to claim rights and recognition in the United States with some success. Yet these victories were usually temporary, since whenever they successfully challenged one set of discriminatory practices, gatekeepers developed new, more dexterous mechanisms to sustain white privilege. The ever-changing rationales used by American officials to enact social closure against Filipino immigrants highlight the contingent and contested nature of racial and national boundaries and the tenacity with which ascriptive hierarchies were challenged by marginalized populations.[3]

Beyond a Boundary

While Filipinos' status as imperial subjects afforded them the right to travel freely within the territorial borders of the United States, their standing vis-à-vis the political boundaries of American nationality was far less clear. This issue took on new urgency during the first two decades of the twentieth century as small numbers of Filipino immigrants began petitioning for naturalization. Congress had previously determined that the acquisition of overseas territories did not *automatically* confer U.S. citizenship to colonial subjects residing in those territories, yet the question of Filipinos' eligibility through the regular naturalization procedures available to other immigrants was left unresolved.[4] The racial disqualification of Asians from naturalized citizenship in the United States was, by the early decades of the twentieth century, a matter of settled law, but Filipinos' distinctive political status as American nationals raised new questions that had not been addressed in previous judicial rulings.[5] Were they, as U.S. dependents, entitled to special consideration with respect to nationality law? Did alien disability statutes, such as those restricting land ownership or barring noncitizens from employment in public works or from occupations requiring official state licensing (attorneys, nurses, etc.) apply to Filipino nationals? What role did their prescribed allegiance to the United States play in determining the political obligations between state and subject?

Racial considerations have longed played a role in American immigration and nationality policy. The first U.S. naturalization law, enacted in 1790, limited citizenship to "free white persons." The racial prerequisites for naturalization were amended to include "persons of African nativity" following the Civil War.[6] The passage of the Chinese Exclusion Act in 1882 ushered in a new phase of federal policy regarding immigration and naturalization controls, characterized by what Erika Lee has called the "gatekeeping" approach to American nationality.[7] The gatekeeping metaphor astutely captures the restrictive ethos of American policymakers during the late nineteenth and early twentieth centuries, as they aggressively moved to forestall the entry of immigrant populations deemed unfit for membership in the national community.

Effective control was hindered until the early twentieth century by a lack of uniform procedures for naturalization, since courts in different states required varying forms and fees for the application process. Scandals and corruption involving both immigration agents and local naturalization officers prompted the federal government to impose greater administrative control over national borders. Congress passed the Immigration and Naturalization Act of 1906, which for the first time interfused the immigration and naturalization functions of the federal government into a single agency, the Bureau of Immigration and Naturalization. Lawmakers believed that this legislation would allow greater supervision over naturalization courts and aid in the fashioning of a comprehensive population-management policy directed by federal authorities.[8]

The nation's unwieldy immigration and naturalization apparatus complicated efforts to delineate clear and consistent rules about who was eligible for national citizenship. Lawmakers in the U.S. Congress were responsible for the design of the nation's immigration and naturalization system, while the task of interpreting and enforcing these laws was left to intermediary authorities such as judges or local-level officials. The ambiguity of congressional enactments regarding the status of Filipinos meant that these mid- or low-level functionaries wielded tremendous latitude in interpreting and applying citizenship controls. The absence of uniform criteria for determining racial eligibility exacerbated the problem for officials entrusted with enforcing categorical distinctions between population groups. The issue was confused even more when those called on to interpret the law cited inconsistent criteria to determine group boundaries. Judges and government officials sometimes employed "scientific" definitions of race to maintain social closure and at other times relied on popular/folk understandings of racial identification to police the boundaries of exclusion. Erratic and contradictory rulings about the legal properties of race, however, did not diminish the power of the nation's ascriptive hierarchy and in some ways actually bolstered the capacity of gatekeepers to sustain the institutionalized system of white advantage, despite constant challenges.

The political status of newly acquired Filipino subjects, as discussed in chapter 1, was a key concern of American lawmakers when they were crafting early imperial policy. Beyond the determination that Filipinos had not been collectively naturalized by virtue of annexation, not much else had been decided about their status until the passage of the Philippine Government Act in 1902, an organic law that established the terms of civilian rule in the islands. The act provided that all residents of the territory would be classified as "citizens" of the Philippine Islands but not of the United States.[9] This political designation meant that Filipinos were "citizens" of an American dependency but not of a nation-state. The term "U.S. nationals" was used to describe the status of Filipinos and other insular subjects who were neither citizens nor aliens. Filipinos, as a result, occupied an anomalous political space, inside the borders of American empire but outside the boundaries of the national citizenry. American nationals were formally entitled to "protection" from the United States in matters of international or diplomatic affairs, but they were not extended the political rights enumerated in the U.S. Constitution unless explicitly granted by Congress.[10]

Early test cases on the issue of Filipino naturalization eligibility generated a series of conflicting legal rulings that highlight the paradoxical standing of U.S. nationals. Congress had not explicitly addressed the issue of citizenship eligibility, opening the way for a series of legal battles over the boundaries of the imperial polity. The language of contemporaneous American nationality law was the first hurdle, since it was not clear whether Filipinos could even apply for citizenship under the existing system. The rules established by Congress to regulate eligibility for citizenship were designed for the naturalization of "aliens" and contained no provisions to deal with individuals under the newly invented category of "nationals." The taxonomic liminality of Filipinos led to other problems when it came to processing the standard application paperwork required of naturalization candidates. The application document, for example, required a "Declaration of Intention" form, which involved two steps. The first part required that a petitioner formally declare his or her intention to apply for U.S. citizenship at a local naturalization court. The second step entailed signing an "oath of renunciation" in which the applicant renounced allegiance to his or her former sovereign nation-state. This created a predicament for Filipinos, since as American nationals, they "owed permanent allegiance" to the United States, making the renunciation requirement illogical.[11] Early petitioners cited their prescribed political attachment to the United States to claim citizenship, arguing that they were already members of the American polity by virtue of annexation. Whether their distinctive political status qualified them for U.S. citizenship became a key source of legal contention as gatekeepers tried to determine whether racial or political criteria would prevail in determining the eligibility of Filipinos.

The Legal Labyrinth

The first set of Filipino naturalization cases in the 1910s raised difficult questions about the political consequences of extraterritorial expansion. The petitioners argued that their status as U.S. nationals entitled them to special consideration regarding their eligibility for citizenship. This strategy arose, in part, from Filipinos' expectations that the republican principles that had been inculcated in them as colonial subjects would match the policies practiced in the United States. American officials had always framed their ambitions in the Philippines as benevolent and assimilatory, so newly arrived Filipinos in the United States were often surprised to discover they were considered racial undesirables. They were particularly insulted by the lack of reciprocity between metropole and colony when it came to political rights and obligations. The fact that U.S. officials had ruled that Americans living in the islands were eligible for "Philippine citizenship" led the initial group of petitioners to believe that they were entitled to similar rights in the United States.[12]

Many of the early test cases involved Filipino veterans who filed their citizenship papers while stationed at military bases in the continental United States. Some petitioners applied for naturalization based on special provisions in federal immigration law granting citizenship to aliens who had served honorably in the U.S. military. This strategy was especially popular during World War I, when the federal government hailed military service as the ultimate expression of national fidelity. Another set of petitioners cited their mixed Filipino-white ancestry, recognizing the obvious institutional advantages of legal whiteness. By invoking their part-European lineage, these individuals attempted to exploit definitional ambiguities in officially recognized race categories. The boundaries of American citizenship proved remarkably fluid in the face of these new challenges, expanding and contracting in response to changing political exigencies.

Two early attempts to petition for U.S. citizenship submitted by Filipino residents in Ohio and California were rejected in 1907 without formal hearings, though local naturalization officers expressed uncertainty about the legal standing of the newcomers.[13] The first federal ruling on the issue of Filipino eligibility was handed down in a Pennsylvania district court in 1912. The case involved Eugenio Alverto, a native Filipino who had served two enlistments in the U.S. Navy. His petition for citizenship advanced three claims. The first was that he was qualified under Section 30 of the Naturalization Act of 1906, which authorized "the admission to citizenship of all persons not citizens who owe permanent allegiance to the United States, and who may become residents of any state or organized territory of the United States."[14] This provision seemed directly aimed at Filipinos and other noncitizen nationals (Puerto Ricans, Chamorros), who were previously outside of the statutory language on U.S. naturalization law.[15] Alverto's second line of argument was that he was eligible under the Naturalization Act of 1894, which provided special provisions for aliens who had served honorably in the U.S. military. And finally, as a person of mixed-race ancestry, he invoked his partial whiteness to claim fitness for American citizenship. Government attorneys opposed Alverto's application, maintaining that Filipinos were precluded from naturalization on racial grounds. The government's case rested on the exclusionary clause established in the U.S. Revised Statutes as Section 2169, which limited naturalization to "free white persons, and to aliens of African nativity and to persons of African descent."[16]

Eugenio Alverto was the first in a long line of Filipino petitioners who argued that his status as a U.S. national provided immunity from racial bars to naturalization. Government lawyers rejected his argument, citing established legal precedent that disqualified Asians from naturalization in the United States. The novel question before the court in this particular case was whether the amended provisions found in the Naturalization Act of 1894 or the Naturalization Act of 1906 superseded the racial prerequisites found in Section 2169. Government attorneys pointed out that racial limitations to citizenship had repeatedly been upheld against challenges brought by Asian servicemen.[17] Rulings in all these previous cases affirmed that service in the U.S. military "did not extend the right of naturalization to those who are beyond the provision under section 2169." The court did acknowledge Alverto's record of "commendable service" in the U.S. Navy but nevertheless found that citizenship could not be granted to "those not coming within the racial qualifications" prescribed in the Revised Statutes.[18] The court also dismissed the "permanent allegiance" of Filipinos to the United States as a material factor in determining their eligibility for American citizenship.

The final issue taken up by the court was Alverto's invocation of his partial European ancestry as a qualifying criterion. The judge acknowledged that Alverto's grandfather was a "Spaniard" who had married a "Philippino woman." This, according to the court, made the petitioner, "ethnologically speaking, one-fourth of the white or Caucasian race and three-fourths of the brown or Malay race." In the eyes of the court, Alverto's particular ratio of nonwhite blood (three-quarters Filipino) undercut any claim to membership in the white race. Judge Thompson's ruling maintained that congressional intent was clear regarding unalloyed racial purity as precondition for legal whiteness, citing previous case law barring mixed-race petitioners from citizenship. The court declared, "The use of the words 'white persons' clearly indicates the intention of Congress to maintain a line of demarcation between races and to extend the privilege of naturalization only to those races named."[19] In the judge's opinion, the legal category "white" was meant to be interpreted in the narrowest possible terms and excluded individuals with any discernable presence of nonwhite blood. The court also dismissed Alverto's claim that the 1906 Naturalization Act extended citizenship rights to American nationals, such as Filipinos, who owed allegiance to the United States. The 1906 act, in the court's opinion, simply accorded naturalization rights to racially eligible individuals (whites and persons of African descent) living in the Philippines but left existing racial bars intact. This interpretation of the 1906 act meant that "white" Spaniards, including those who had fought against the United States during the Spanish-American War, were eligible for citizenship, while Filipino nationals were not.[20]

Although Eugenio Alverto's application for citizenship was denied, the matter of Filipino eligibility was far from resolved, and the issues raised in his case were revisited in future legal challenges.[21] Questions about the rights and duties of colonial subjects residing within the domestic borders of the United States, as well as uncertainties about the racial classification of Filipinos, remained unsettled. The *Alverto* case and those that followed unfolded as part of a larger debate about the boundaries of the national community during a tumultuous historical conjuncture marked by large-scale international migration and global wars between rival states in the world system. Nationalist sentiment ran high during this period and fueled calls for tighter immigration and naturalization controls. The political crises brought on by America's entanglement in these global conflicts, in particular, forced American policymakers to modify the nation's boundaries of inclusion/exclusion to meet the manpower needs of the wartime state. Consequently, Filipino activists pushed the issue of their compulsory U.S. allegiance and their martial service to the "mother country" to challenge their disqualification from citizenship.

The Impermanence of Permanent Allegiance

The question of whether Filipinos' prescribed allegiance to the United States entitled them to special consideration vis-à-vis nationality law generated significant disagreement among public officials. This issue struck at the heart of American naturalization law, which placed great emphasis on the principle of undivided political fidelity to the U.S. government as a fundamental qualifying condition for admission to national citizenship. That Filipinos met this particular criterion was not in question. The Treaty of Paris established that the "permanent allegiance" of Filipinos to Spain had been "dissolved" and transferred to the United States upon ratification of the treaty.[22] In the cases that followed *Alverto,* the courts directly addressed the question of Filipinos' "allegiance" in a more substantive way, as they tried to determine whether their imperial attachment to the United States and its democratic institutions overrode the exclusionary racial provisions of Section 2169.

In addition, petitioners continued to test the boundaries of legal whiteness as part of a larger effort to gain civic recognition from the state. The strategic deployment of partial European ancestry by Filipino mestizos is not surprising since the institutional advantages accorded to those deemed legally white were so great. These petitioners recognized that the matter of where one was assigned into the American racial taxonomy was a verdict on future entitlements and adjusted their claims to meet this system of incentives. Claiming whiteness, however, for the most part proved to be a fruitless enterprise, since the government officials who made the determinations about racial assignment had a vested interest in excluding those who threatened the material advantages and individual prestige of whites as a status group. A series of naturalization cases filed between 1916 and 1917 illustrate some of the complexities surrounding the question of Filipinos' civic and racial categorization and the evolving rationales used to ascertain their place in the American social hierarchy.

In 1916, Francisco Mallari filed a naturalization petition in a Massachusetts district court. At the time of his application, he was a veteran of the U.S. Navy and had been recommended for reenlistment by his commanding officer. Both of Mallari's parents were natives of the Philippine Islands, making him a "full-blooded" Filipino. The question before the court was whether Filipinos' eligibility for citizenship was authorized by Section 30 of the 1906 Naturalization Act or whether racial restrictions remained in effect. Judge James Morton noted that the 1906 act authorized "the admission to citizenship of *all persons* not citizens, who owe permanent allegiance to the United States." By italicizing the words "all persons," he highlighted the inclusive, seemingly all-encompassing language in the statute. Morton acknowledged the racial limitations to naturalization established in Section 2169 but injected the historical context of extraterritorial acquisition as the prism through which to interpret legislative intent with the 1906 act. He further noted that the congressional debate on the 1906 Naturalization Act had made specific reference to the situation of the noncitizen nationals, and he cited contemporaneous opinions by other federal agencies suggesting that Filipinos were eligible for naturalization.[23]

The court stressed that the liminal status of Filipinos as neither citizens nor aliens placed them at a serious disadvantage in the United States. Denying naturalization rights to U.S. nationals effectively meant that immigrants from America's colonial possessions were "more unfavorably treated by our laws" than aliens from foreign nations. In Morton's estimation, it would be impolitic for the United States to subject residents of its dependencies to the same racial limitations used to deny the franchise to aliens from other Asian nations. Mallari's petition for citizenship was eventually denied on a technicality, unrelated to racial prohibitions, but the ruling in this case offered hope that Filipinos might be exempt from Section 2169. Subsequent cases, however, demonstrated that the eligibility issue was far from settled.[24]

The question of whether Filipinos were subject to racially restrictive citizenship laws received a very different interpretation later that same year. This case, filed in Southern District Court in New York State, involved a U.S. Navy veteran, Ricardo Lampitoe. Lampitoe's petition for naturalization was rejected in a terse three-sentence opinion by renowned American jurist Billings "Learned" Hand. Judge Hand asserted that the petitioner fell within the exclusionary legal precedent established in the *Alverto* case. The court's ruling made no reference to the petitioner's military service, nor to the unique political status of Filipinos. For Judge Hand, the racial proscriptions established in Section 2169 of the Revised Statutes were sacrosanct and rendered all other issues related to the civic qualifications of the petitioner moot.

Lampitoe, like Alverto, was a mestizo, with a Spanish father and a Filipino mother. He cited his European ancestry as well as his military service as grounds for naturalization. The court, however, summarily rejected his claim, holding to a narrow interpretation of legal whiteness. Judge Hand allowed that an applicant's white ancestry might theoretically merit consideration in certain instances, but an applicant would have to meet some undefined blood quantum before he or she could be accepted as a member of the white race. Although the judge did not quantify what that threshold of legal whiteness was, he made it clear that it had not been met in Lampitoe's case because "where the Malay blood predominates it would be a perversion of language to say that the descendant is a 'white person.'" Judge Hand ridiculed the notion that someone like Lampitoe could claim whiteness based on having a "remote" white relative in his family tree.[25] The court glossed over the fact that it was the applicant's father, not some "remote" ancestor, who was of European extraction. This was one of many cases in which mestizo petitioners were denied citizenship based on arbitrary racial criteria. Because the precise properties of the category "white" were elastic, gatekeepers had wide latitude in determining who was included or excluded from this social classification. In this case, Judge Hand relied on a biological definition of race, suggesting that the presence of "Malay blood" abrogated Lampitoe's claim to whiteness and the entitlements that came along with that legal designation. In other cases, the courts employed popular or folk definitions to discern whom the state would recognize as white. This lack of consistency among naturalization courts about the statutory properties of whiteness and the vagueness of congressional intent regarding the 1906 Naturalization Act continued to produce contradictory, and at times capricious, interpretations of Filipinos' civic status. This point was plainly illustrated in two 1916 cases, heard just a few months apart in Hawaii, that yielded opposing rulings on the issue of naturalization eligibility in the same district court.[26]

The issue was taken up again in two 1917 cases that generated even more confusion. The case of Penaro Rallos, deliberated in the Eastern District Court of New York, yielded a ruling that Filipinos were ineligible for naturalization. The petitioner was the son of a Spanish father and a "Philippino" mother, making him "half white" biologically speaking. Rallos argued that his European ancestry exempted him from racial bars to naturalization. This claim was dismissed by the court, which declared that even though the petitioner was half white, he was not "a 'white' person as the term is used in the Naturalization Law."[27] Judge Thomas Chatfield dismissed the legal reasoning used previously in the *Mallari* case that had declared Filipinos eligible for citizenship, in particular that court's literal interpretation of the term "all persons" as used in the 1906 Naturalization Act. Judge Chatfield declared this reading of the law to be misguided, since it would make "Chinese [and] Japanese" residents of the Philippines eligible for naturalization. This interpretation of the 1906 law was counterintuitive, in light of longstanding federal policies mandating racial limitations on American nationality. The court concluded that the 1906 act was aimed at extending naturalization rights to "all persons" residing in the Philippine Islands who met the racial criteria laid out in Section 2169, in other words, only those persons of "white or African ancestry."[28]

A case heard later that year in the Northern District Court of California offered yet another twist on the Filipino naturalization question. The ruling handed down in the case of Engracio Bautista offered a much more thoroughgoing exploration of the legal issues taken up in previous suits. Bautista fit the same profile as many of the previous petitioners, having been identified by the court as a mestizo and a veteran of the U.S. Navy. His case was complicated by the fact that he had not filed a "declaration of intention" to become a citizen, as required by the 1906 Naturalization Act. Bautista, however, claimed eligibility via the Naturalization Act of June 30, 1914, which made special provisions for aliens who had served in the U.S. military.[29] Government attorneys objected to Bautista's application, arguing that he "belonged to the brown or Malay race." This designation disqualified from citizenship because he was "not an alien of the white race, nor . . . an alien of African nativity."[30]

William Morrow, the presiding judge in the *Bautista* case, took it upon himself to carefully scrutinize governmental interpretations of the 1906 Naturalization Act. He examined congressional debates surrounding the passage of the 1906 act and concluded that Congress had intended to grant Filipinos and Puerto Ricans special consideration concerning naturalization. Morrow also examined opinions from federal agencies that construed the law as extending citizenship eligibility to noncitizen nationals. The judge cited U.S. Attorney General Charles J. Bonaparte, who in 1908 issued an opinion to the secretary of interior on the matter, stating that Filipinos were eligible under the 1906 Naturalization Act. Bonaparte explained that Section 30 of the 1906 act described "exactly the status of the Philippine Islands." He added that Filipinos were "not aliens, for they are not subjects of and do not owe allegiance to any foreign sovereignty. They are not citizens but they owe permanent allegiance to the United States, since they owe it and can owe it to no other sovereignty." Judge Morrow also cited a memo issued by the U.S. State Department in 1916 that suggested support for Filipinos' qualification, highlighting the fact that Filipinos "owed permanent allegiance" to the United States, a designation that placed them squarely within the boundaries of the national polity.[31]

Taken together these considerations led Judge Morrow to conclude that Congress had expressly amended the 1906 act to admit Filipinos and Puerto Ricans to citizenship in recognition of their status as American subjects. He noted that U.S. officials had made this decision "with full knowledge that the Filipino belonged to the Malay or Brown race," making clear their intention to relax as to them the racial limitations found in Section 2169. The court was careful to point out that this exemption did not overturn the restrictive language of Section 30 of the 1906 act but rather created a special category for those residents of the Philippines, who owed *permanent allegiance* to the United States. This distinction was important since this requirement explicitly excluded Chinese and Japanese residents of the islands, who owed only "temporary allegiance" to the United States. The interpretation of the statute undercut the legal reasoning offered in the *Rallos* case that admitting Filipinos to citizenship would, by extension, open up citizenship to previously debarred Asian groups. The court granted Engracio Bautista his petition for naturalization.[32]

The naturalization cases heard from 1912 to 1917 yielded a series contradictory rulings on the civic standing of noncitizen nationals residing in the United States. The courts had weighed in on the issue multiple times, yet a precedent-setting decision on the matter remained elusive. Filipinos were held eligible for naturalization in *Mallari, Bautista,* and *Solis,* but they were ruled ineligible in *Alverto, Lampitoe, Rallos,* and *Ocampo.*[33] These cases reveal some of the difficulties that plagued authorities trying to manage racial and national boundaries in the age of American empire. Foremost among these was the disconnect between federal lawmakers who crafted immigration and naturalization statutes and intermediary officials charged with interpreting and enforcing nationality controls. Federal policymakers were tasked with reconciling expansionist foreign-policy initiatives, including the nation's imperial obligations in the Philippines, with domestic pressure for tighter immigration and nationality controls. Consequently, national-level officials made some effort to recognize the distinctive political status of Filipinos, seeing the issue as a reflection on the U.S. reputation as a principled global power. Intermediary authorities, on the other hand, were operating at the local scale, where the real prospect of interacting with Filipinos as social equals prompted a very different set of concerns. As a result, local-level officials were often hostile to any efforts that might upset the racial status quo. Filipinos in the United States remained in limbo until the political exigencies of World War I forced American policymakers to address the status of noncitizen nationals in a more unequivocal way.

Citizenship in Wartime

Changes in American naturalization policy initiated by the federal government during the World War I era changed the political terrain for Filipinos seeking American nationality. Not surprisingly, definitions of citizenship emphasizing patriotic service and national allegiance took on increasing significance during this time. The federal government launched a series of public campaigns aimed at strengthening links between patriotic sacrifice, civic obligation, and national membership to mobilize support for the war effort. The intensive nationalism and militarism of this period gave rise to important modifications in naturalization law, including policies that expedited admission to citizenship for aliens who enlisted in the military. Efforts to recruit noncitizens into the armed forces took on particular urgency during the World War I period, when one out of every six draft-age men in the United States was an alien.[34] Though these efforts were primarily aimed at European immigrants, Filipino servicepersons demanded the same entitlements for their patriotic war service.

As discussed in the preceding section, Filipinos had long contended that their compulsory allegiance to the United States entitled them to special consideration vis-à-vis American naturalization law—an argument that produced decidedly mixed results. The war, however, provided an opportunity to actually demonstrate their unqualified allegiance to the nation through martial sacrifice. The 1914 Naturalization Act (discussed earlier with regard to the *Bautista* case) was one of the early legislative initiatives aimed at rewarding foreign enlistees with citizenship, but it remained unclear whether Filipinos were actually eligible under this provision, since they were not technically classified as "aliens." A more propitious piece of legislation was the Act of May 9, 1918, passed during the height of American involvement in World War I. The bill offered expedited naturalization to "any alien" who served in the U.S. armed forces during the war. Importantly, the 1918 act contained a specific provision aimed a clarifying the status of Filipinos and Puerto Ricans. Specifically, the seventh subdivision of Section 4 of the statute permitted Filipinos who had served "in this present war" to petition for naturalization.[35]

In practical terms, this provision meant that Filipinos who had rendered the requisite military service would be eligible for citizenship, while those who had not served in the U.S. armed forces remained disqualified "based on color or race."[36] The geopolitical exigencies of the war led the federal government to temporarily ease some of its restrictions against the naturalization of noncitizen soldiers of Asian descent. After some initial confusion about the issue, naturalization courts across the nation and in the territory of Hawaii started granting citizenship to soldiers of Asian descent with the blessing of the Bureau of Immigration and Naturalization.[37] Although wartime policy aimed at encouraging the military enlistment of aliens provided a brief window of opportunity for soldiers of Asian descent to obtain naturalized citizenship, this opening was quickly closed after the war as nativist forces regained prominence and began challenging the legitimacy of the naturalization certificates granted to Asian veterans under the 1918 act. A number of legal challenges filed during the interwar period tested just how far the boundaries of nationality had extended during the war and whether Section 2169 was still in force. Any hopes held by Asian American activists that they might use war service to demonstrate their racial fitness for U.S. citizenship were quickly dashed. The decisions handed down by the Supreme Court in the *Ozawa* and *Thind* cases in 1922 and 1923 reaffirmed the prewar norm of Asian exclusion from national membership.[38] Neither case, however, directly engaged the issue of whether Asian veterans had correctly been granted citizenship under the 1918 act.[39]

The Supreme Court finally took up the issue of the eligibility of Asian veterans in 1925 in the case of *Hidemitsu Toyota v. United States*. The case involved a Japanese immigrant, Hidemitsu Toyota, who applied for naturalization after serving for ten years in the U.S. Coast Guard.[40] Though the case involved a Japanese petitioner, the Court also weighed in on the status of Filipinos, primarily to distinguish their situation from that of other persons of Asian descent. The Court ruled that Asian veterans, including Toyota, were not eligible for citizenship under the 1918 Naturalization Act, because that law did not explicitly overturn the racial prerequisites found in Section 2169 of the Revised Statutes. The court, however, was careful to separate the status of Filipinos from other Asians because of their compulsory allegiance to the United States.[41] The justices traced the history of legal precedents regarding the status of Filipinos and concluded that they had been made eligible for naturalization by the 1918 act but *not* before the enactment of that legislation.[42] The Court reviewed previous lower court rulings and found that the judges in the *Mallari* and *Bautista* cases had erred in ruling that Filipino petitioners were eligible under the 1906 Naturalization Act. That legislation effectively abolished the requirement of alienage as a prerequisite in American nationality law, while leaving the racial limitations established by Section 2169 in place. The effect of the 1918 act, however, "was to make eligible, and to authorize the naturalization of native-born Filipinos of whatever color or race," if they met the prescribed military obligations. The justices emphasized that their ruling in no way abolished the racial barriers to citizenship previously established in Section 2169; it simply created a narrow exemption for noncitizen nationals who had served in the U.S. military during wartime.

The Court's opinion was careful to note that "it has long been the national policy to maintain the distinction of color and race, [and] radical change is not is not lightly deemed to have been intended. . . . As Filipinos are not aliens and owe allegiance to the United States, there are strong reasons for relaxing as to them the restrictions, which do not exist in favor of aliens who are barred because of their color and race."[43]

The Supreme Court's ruling in *Toyota* reaffirmed the racial boundaries of U.S. nationality and made it clear that all other Asian immigrants were still excluded from naturalized citizenship. This decision stymied the efforts of Asian veterans to assert an alternative definition of national membership based on patriotic sacrifice and military service. Yet the Court's ruling also acknowledged the unique place of Filipinos in the American polity and affirmed the eligibility of U.S. nationals who met the prescribed qualifications of the 1918 act. The decision handed down in the *Toyota* case led some observers to wonder if the Court had established a new precedent, adding Filipinos to the list of "races" eligible for national citizenship in the United States. After all, Filipinos had, according to the Supreme Court, demonstrated their fitness for citizenship during the war, and as a result Filipino veterans were granted naturalization rights. The ruling in the *Toyota* case, however, begged the question, how could some Filipinos (war veterans) be racially qualified, while all others were not? And, what criteria, civic or racial, did the U.S. government use as the decisive factor in determining an individual's fitness for national membership?

Citizenship as a Moving Target

The issue of how far the color line had been extended was tested two years after the *Toyota* decision in a Washington, DC, appeals court in 1927. In this case, government attorneys sought to cancel the naturalization certificate of a Filipino named Ambrosio Javier who had been granted naturalization papers in the District of Columbia. Javier, a "native-born Filipino," had been granted a certificate of naturalization by the Supreme Court of Washington, DC, in 1924 (not to be confused with the U.S. Supreme Court). Government attorneys sought to have his citizenship revoked, claiming that he was racially ineligible for naturalization under Section 2169. Javier, according to the court, had not served in the U.S. military, nor was he of white or African descent. A representative from the U.S. Bureau of Naturalization had appeared at his original hearing in 1924 and objected to his petition on racial grounds, but the court issued a certificate anyway. During the appeals court hearing three years later, neither Javier nor his attorney appeared to challenge the revocation of his citizenship. Drawing on the interpretation handed down in the *Toyota* case, the appeals court asserted that the 1918 act was not intended to "authorize the naturalization of native-born Filipinos," except those who had met prescribed military obligations. Since Javier had not met those requirements, he was subject to the racial limitations laid out in Section 2169 that debarred Asians from national membership. The appeals court voided Javier's certificate of naturalization.[44]

The ruling in the *Javier* case again highlighted the paradoxical status of Filipinos in the United States during the interwar period. The appeals court's decision reiterated the civic fitness of Filipino veterans who had "proven" their allegiance to the United States through wartime military service. Yet the courts also declared that Filipinos who had not served in the U.S. armed forces remained racially excluded from national membership, even though they too owed allegiance to the United States. Though Filipino veterans' eligibility was seemingly affirmed by the *Javier* decision, they continued to face hostility from the courts when they tried to claim their hard-earned citizenship rights. U.S. attorneys continued efforts to derail the citizenship petitions of Filipinos veterans through the 1930s. In these cases, government attorneys raised specious technical issues to collaterally challenge the eligibility of Filipino veterans, claiming, for example, that the appellants had failed to submit their petitions for citizenship within the prescribed six-month time frame required by the statute. The two most notable cases occurred in 1931, the first in the Eastern District Court in Michigan, involving a Filipino named Sixto Cariaga, and the other in the Eastern District Court of New York, involving a petitioner named Mariano Rena. In both cases, U.S. district attorneys (with the support of the Department of Commerce) opposed granting naturalization certificates, claiming that the applicants had failed to file their petitions in a timely manner. The 1918 Naturalization Act required alien soldiers to submit their paperwork within six months of their honorable discharge from military service to be eligible for the special provision. Rena, however, cleverly exploited a loophole in the naturalization law, noting that the statutory language of the six-month filing requirement referred to "aliens" but made no mention of nationals. Since Filipinos were not aliens, he argued, they were not subject to the six-month filing requirement.

The judges in both the *Rena* and *Cariaga* cases acknowledged that the law in question was confusing and suffered from poor grammatical construction. And while they might have been sympathetic to the government's position regarding the limited eligibility of Filipinos, the judges in the two cases said they were bound by the statute's capacious language to grant certificates of naturalization in the cases at hand. Although the rulings might seem to be of minor importance at first glance (simply affirming previous precedent), the cases merit attention because they reveal how dramatically the government's attitude toward Filipino veterans had shifted since World War I. During the war, American officials had hailed the loyalty and sacrifice of colonial soldiers. This public posture, in turn, compelled the federal government and naturalization courts to grant Filipinos naturalization rights as a just reward for their military service. Yet this inclusive sentiment only went so far, and the vast majority of Filipinos remained racially outside the boundaries of the American polity. By the 1930s, as these two cases demonstrate, even Filipino veterans encountered hostility from U.S. officials as memories of their contributions to the war effort started to fade.[45]

As the Filipino population in the United States grew dramatically during the interwar period, the consequences of their civic disenfranchisement became more far-reaching. The economic disabilities that stemmed from their outlier political status were particularly noteworthy. States regularly enacted laws that barred noncitizens from select professions for which the employment of "undesirable aliens" might pose a threat to the public welfare. Western states with large Asian populations were particularly aggressive in delimiting access to the labor market. These statutes were designed to limit competition from Asian immigrants and, more generally, to make it as difficult as possible for them to make a living in the jurisdiction where they lived. State lawmakers were careful to craft legislation that achieved the discriminatory effects but did not violate the equal protection clause of the U.S. Constitution. Consequently, these laws often targeted "aliens ineligible to citizenship," a seemingly race-neutral idiom used to enforce social closure against persons of Asian descent. Among the occupations in various western states that required one to be a citizen were attorney, registered nurse, public school teacher, accountant, liquor sales, and pharmacist, all livelihoods which required licensing from the state. Many states also had statutory provisions barring noncitizens from public employment and restricted their eligibility for state welfare provisions.[46] As a result, Asian immigrants were largely confined to agricultural and service occupations, sectors of the economy exempted from federal laws regulating labor conditions and work hours. These economic disabilities compounded the effects of Filipinos' political marginalization in the United States in the 1920s and 1930s and contributed to their growing sense of indignation about their subordinate status in the "mother country." Efforts to contain and control the mobility of Filipino immigrants in the United States extended to other areas of social life as well, especially as their numbers grew. State legislatures played a vital role in buttressing the color line, since they could more efficiently enact laws that reflected community prejudices and local customs of segregation. The "failure" of the federal government to prevent the entry of Filipinos into the United States put extra pressure on officials in western states to aggressively enforce rules of racial caste.

Malays, Mongolians, and Miscegenation

No arena of race relations attracted more attention and intervention from state authorities than the issues of interracial sex and marriage. Race mixing was viewed as a dangerous practice in a social order predicated on the immutability of racial difference, for it called into question the legitimacy of biologically determined social boundaries. Interracial unions, moreover, raised vexing questions about where mixed-race offspring fit in an ascriptive hierarchy premised on the legal fiction of racial purity. Interracial marriage was rare in the early twentieth century, largely due to social conventions that held such couplings to be subversive of good order. And when private discrimination and moral sanction failed to prevent such relationships, state power was deployed to reinforce norms of social and sexual propriety.

Statutory prohibitions against interracial intimacy in the United States date back to the seventeenth century, but they took on new urgency after the Civil War, when fear of black political empowerment heightened concerns about maintenance of the color line. The laws had two main functions. One was largely symbolic, aimed at policing and "protecting" white women's sexuality and the fictive purity of the white race. White women quite literally, bore the biological burden of reproducing the race but could not always be trusted to keep their amorous desires on the "right side" of the color line. Antimiscegenation laws also had a more material function, which was to restrict the transfer of assets and property rights to nonwhite spouses and their mixed-race children.[47]

The rise of the eugenics movement in the early twentieth century only amplified anxieties about the putative "race degeneration" that resulted from interracial couplings. Opposition to intermarriage in the western states often focused on the threat posed by Asian-white pairings. California congressman Charles Curry voiced these concerns in candid terms: "The miscegenation of the white with the yellow race always results in production of a hybrid mongrel mentally, morally, and physically inferior to either race. . . . It does not elevate the yellow race and does deteriorate the white race." He added, "The very thought of intermarriage is revolting. It shatters the very keystone of occidental civilization. It is demoralizing in morality and menacing in problems of mongrel racial degeneracy. It brings into being dangers of manifest evil to American homes and institutions. I conceive that we would be unworthy of our heritage if we gave countenance to the prostitution of what we honor as the most sacred contract under law."[48] Eugenicists also lent scientific credibility to the contention that the "mongrel" children born of racial admixture were biologically and morally inferior and, as a result, disposed to criminality and dependence on public welfare. Claims such as these served to bolster the case against intermarriage, since they reinforced the notion that seemingly private intimate choices had serious public consequences for the larger society.[49]

Filipinos, however, did not passively accept legal restrictions on their freedom of association, nor did they sit idly by while nativists characterized them as racial inferiors. They waged an aggressive campaign to contest the miscegenation laws, which they saw as unwarranted intrusion into their private lives.[50] Filipinos regarded themselves as "Americanized" because of their colonial education and took the egalitarian rhetoric propagated by U.S. officials and teachers in the islands at face value. Moreover, they saw nothing wrong with seeking the companionship of whites, since amorous relationships (including marriage) between American men and Filipina women were openly practiced in the Philippines without legal or social sanction. Interracial couplings were so common, in fact, that by the mid-1920s the issue attracted attention from U.S. social reformers concerned about the islands' large population of mestizo children living in destitution after their American fathers had abandoned them.[51] The permissive practices allowed in the colonies, though, did not translate to the metropole where interracial relationships remained taboo.

A statutory ban on intermarriage between Asians and whites was first instituted in California as part of the raucous anti-Chinese movement that was sweeping the state during the 1870s. Section 69 of the California State Civil Code was amended in 1880 to add "Mongolians" to the list of races barred from intermarrying with whites. The state's civil code was amended again in 1905 to retroactively invalidate marriages between whites and "Mongolians" that had taken place before the passage of the 1880 law. That lawmakers targeted "Mongolians" proved to be significant, since this ethnological classification referred to a specific population group with recognized definitional boundaries. Efforts to bring Filipinos under the purview of the state's antimiscegenation laws proved more difficult than expected. In this case, it was their outlier racial status, rather than their imperial attachment, that confounded authorities. Problems of social classification again came to the fore, creating quandaries for those on both sides of the color line.[52]

The Filipino immigrant population on the West Coast was overwhelmingly made up of single young men (a male-to-female ratio of fourteen to one), following a demographic pattern established by Chinese and Japanese immigrants in earlier periods. The character and frequency of interaction between Filipinos and whites differed from previous customs of social intercourse in important ways. Intimate relationships between Chinese and Japanese men and white women on the West Coast were uncommon, and those that did occur were rarely visible to the larger society.[53] Filipinos, however, were different, eschewing normative conventions that mandated a certain measure of social distance between Asian men and white women in public spaces. This defiant attitude earned them a controversial reputation and attracted considerable attention from western authorities worried about the potential domino effect that might result from breaches in the race line. The brazenness with which Filipino immigrants flouted proscriptions on interracial association took authorities by surprise. The effectiveness of the American system of racial segregation relied to a significant degree on the "voluntary" compliance of minorities with customary practices of social distance and deference. Fear of violent reprisal and/or private sanction went a long way in ensuring that minorities abided by certain well-understood ground rules about public observance of the color line. Filipinos' open defiance of the race line put extra pressure on authorities to vigilantly enforce legal prohibitions that sustained white advantage—including restrictions on intermarriage and family rights.

Many western states already had antimiscegenation statutes barring intermarriage between Asians and whites by the time Filipinos began arriving in large numbers in the 1920s.[54] Filipino aggressively challenged antimiscegenation statutes, both through litigation and through collective protest. The issue attracted a lot of attention in California, which had the largest population of Filipinos on the U.S. mainland. Activists challenged the applicability of the state's miscegenation ban in court, arguing that Filipinos fell outside the statutory language of the law. Sections 60 and 69 of the California civil code specifically outlawed all marriages between "white persons" and members of the "negro" and "Mongolian" races.[55] Filipinos, however, disputed their assignment into the "Mongolian" racial category, asserting instead that prevailing scientific opinion held them to be "Malays." This categorical distinction, they argued, exempted them from California's antimiscegenation code, since legislators had not included Malays within the scope of the original statute. Legal opinions on this matter varied, with officials in different jurisdictions issuing contradictory interpretations of the state's antimiscegenation law. As with the debates about naturalization eligibility discussed earlier, the intermarriage question pivoted on the question of legislative intent. The issue generated a steady stream of legal challenges focusing on rules of statutory construction and the fuzziness of racial boundaries.

Edward Bishop, assistant county counsel in Los Angeles, issued an early ruling on the statutory scope of the state's antimiscegenation statute in 1920. The case involved Leonardo Antony, a Filipino war veteran, and his Mexican American fiancée, Luciana Brovencio (legally classified as white), who were denied a license to wed by the Los Angeles County marriage bureau based on Antony's purported racial disqualification. Bishop's office looked into the matter and ordered that the bureau issue the couple a license, after determining that Filipinos (as Malays) fell outside the purview of the California miscegenation prohibition.[56] He clarified his ruling a year later to L. E. Lampton, Los Angeles County clerk, informing him that that Filipinos were not subject to the state's intermarriage ban:

> While there are scientists who would classify the Malayans as an offshoot of the Mongolian race, nevertheless, ordinarily when speaking of the "Mongolians" reference is had to the yellow and not the brown people and we believe that the legislature in Section 69 did not intend to prohibit the marriage of the Malay race with white persons. We are further convinced of the correctness of our conclusion when we regard the history of the situation. In 1880 Section 69 was amended so as to prevent the marriage of a white person with a . . . Mongolian. It was about this time that there was a Chinese problem in California. . . . At that time the question of the marriage of white persons with members of the brown or Malayan race was not a live one, and there was no call for a solution. We do not believe that members of the Malayan race are "Mongolians" as that word is used in Section 69 of the Civil Code.[57]

The intermarriage issue produced a very different outcome a few years later, by way of a shocking murder trial in 1925. The case involved a Filipino immigrant named Timothy Yatko who was accused of murdering another man in a jealous rage. The trial received considerable media attention in Southern California and was held up as a cautionary tale about the putative perils of interracial relationships. Yatko was a restaurant worker at a Los Angeles eatery and was married to a white nightclub entertainer named Lola Butler Yatko. The crime was committed when Yatko followed his wife to the apartment of another man, Harry Kidder. When he looked through the window of the apartment, he saw Kidder in bed with his wife in a state of undress. Yatko burst into the apartment to confront the couple and a struggle ensued that resulted in the death of Kidder. Yatko was depicted in news accounts as a "Filipino Sheik" who had viciously killed the "man who stole his pretty white wife away from him."[58] Lola Butler Yatko, on the other hand, was described by the *Los Angeles Times* as a "beautiful 21-year-old café dancer" who had lost her moral compass after drifting into the city's dangerous vice world. The victim, Harry Kidder, was no angel either, as it was revealed that he was married and that his wife was pregnant at the time he took up his affair with Mrs. Yatko. Timothy Yatko argued that the assault was carried out in self-defense after Kidder attacked him with a chair during the confrontation at the apartment. Fearing that his own life was in danger, Yatko said he pulled out a knife and stabbed Kidder. In addition to Yatko's claim of self-defense, his attorney attempted to invoke an "unwritten law" defense, arguing that his actions were justified as an honor killing—a crime of passion carried out by a jealous husband who found his wife betraying their marriage vows.

Prosecutors attempted to combat the defense's case by attacking the validity of Timothy and Lola Butler Yatko's marriage. The prosecution argued that state law prohibited "marriages between persons of opposing races," a "fact" that rendered the defense's honor-killing strategy invalid. The couple's marital status was central to the prosecution's case, which hinged on the testimony of Lola Yatko, who was expected to contradict her husband's claim of self-defense. Defense attorneys sought to prevent Mrs. Yatko (who was the state's chief witness) from testifying at the trial, arguing that she could not be compelled to testify against her husband in court. Furthermore, even if the couple was not legally married at the time of the incident, the defense asserted that Mrs. Yatko "was under the belief that they were, and should not have been allowed to testify."[59] The prosecution's case hinged on its ability to convince the court that the California legislature had intended to include Filipinos under the state's antimiscegenation law when it was drafted in 1880. There was no evidence that California lawmakers had ever meant to include Filipinos under the original statute, but prosecutors dismissed this fact as a mere technicality. The real aim of the law, they argued, was to insulate white families from racial contamination, and Filipinos, whatever their ethnological origins, fell within the racist intent of the original statute.

The court accepted the prosecutor's entreaty to uphold the color line against any and all trespassers and ruled that the Yatkos' marriage was invalid on racial grounds. As a result, Timothy Yatko was convicted of first-degree murder. Judge C. S. Hardy explained his ruling in stark racial logic: "the dominant race of the country has a perfect right to exclude other races from equal rights with its own people and to prescribe such rights as they may possess." The issue of whether Filipinos should be allowed to "intermarry with our American girls" was, the judge claimed, a matter of "far-reaching importance." Judge Hardy expressed skepticism about the large body of scientific opinion presented by Yatko's defense team supporting their contention that Filipinos were classified (ethnologically speaking) as Malays. The judge relied instead on his own personal "observation" to settle the question of Filipinos' racial identification: "I am quite satisfied in my own mind . . . that the Filipino is a Malay and that the Malay is a Mongolian, just as much as the white American is of the Teutonic race . . . or of the Nordic family, carrying it back to the Aryan family. . . . Hence, it is my view that under the code of California as it now exists, intermarriage between a Filipino and a Caucasian would be void."[60] California's attorney general, Ulysses S. Webb, himself an outspoken advocate of Asian exclusion and a prominent member of the nativist organization the Native Sons of the Golden West, quickly endorsed the ruling in the case. Attorney General Webb ignored prevailing scholarly thought on the topic, claiming disingenuously, "there seems to be no difference of the opinion that Malays belong to the Mongoloid Race, and therefore come under the classification of Mongolians."[61]

The opinion in the *Yatko* case failed to set a precedent on the matter because of the dubious legal reasoning employed by the court. Filipino mutual-aid organizations such as the Filipino Civic League in Northern California and Pablo Manlapit's Filipino Labor Union in Los Angeles, along with various community newspapers in the state, vigorously protested efforts to reclassify Filipinos as Mongolians, arguing that doing so arbitrarily assigned them into a disadvantaged legal category without justification.[62] Judicial officers in Southern California also expressed unease about the court's ruling, since there was no evidence that California legislators had meant to include Filipinos under the original law and the ex post facto arguments cited by prosecutors did not hold up to scrutiny. Judge Hardy and Attorney General Webb's activist stance on the issue also raised some red flags, since their intervention seemed to place themselves above the law, superimposing their own attitudes and prejudices onto the issue to achieve a particular political outcome. As a result, Los Angeles County clerks continued to grant marriage licenses to Filipino-white couples, relying on County Counsel Bishop's 1921 directive up through the late 1920s. The issue got a fresh look from the courts in 1930, in large part because of the sensationalist media attention paid to Filipino interactions with white women on the West Coast. Opponents of intermarriage continued to press the courts to interpret the law broadly to maintain lines of racial separation. Most of the Filipino miscegenation cases were decided in the late 1920s and early 1930s, a period when the scientific definitions of race were being supplanted in the courts by more flexible criteria based on "common understanding."[63] This definitional shift empowered the courts to construe the legal boundaries of race through the popular prejudices of the "common man" (i.e., the white majority), rather than relying on the increasingly unpredictable definitions provided by scientists and scholars.[64]

The intermarriage question was revisited again in 1930 in the case *Robinson v. Los Angeles County*. The notoriety surrounding the issue had gathered momentum in the late 1920s as the Filipino population in California grew. There were fifty-five applications submitted by Filipino-white couples in 1929 in Los Angeles County, a notable increase over previous years.[65] Nativists expressed their displeasure about the phenomenon and pushed for a new test case that might set a binding precedent. The *Robinson* case involved a couple, Ruby F. Robinson, a white woman, and her Filipino fiancé, Tony V. Moreno. Stella Robinson, the mother of the bride-to-be, filed for an injunction in Los Angeles District Court to prevent the issuance of a marriage license on grounds that Moreno was racially disqualified from marrying her daughter. The court ruled in the mother's favor, declaring that Filipinos were subject to the state's intermarriage prohibition. Superior Court Judge J. A. Smith's injunction employed the same rationale offered a few years earlier in the *Yatko* case, favoring personal observation over prevailing scholarly opinion on the matter of racial classification: "There are only three main races of people. These are the white, yellow, and black. I hold that a Filipino is of the yellow or Mongolian race."[66] The court also speculated that Filipinos might be disqualified for other reasons, citing the Negrito origins of the Philippine population as a relevant factor in considering whether they should be allowed to intermarry with whites.

Dr. Walter S. Hertzog, director of historical research for the Los Angeles public schools, testified in favor of the injunction, positing that there were only three races in the world (black, white, and yellow), a theory that departed from the classic five-race theory (black, white, yellow, brown, and red) proposed by earlier ethnologists. Hertzog opined that Filipinos were an admixture of the black and yellow groups, a claim that made them doubly ineligible for intermarriage with whites, as a result of their Negro and Mongolian ancestry. The *Los Angeles Times* concurred with the court's legal rationale in the *Robinson* case, remarking that there was "no question" that Filipinos have "negrito . . . [and] Chinese blood in their veins," a fact that underscored the need to safeguard the white community from racial defilement.[67]

The decision in the *Robinson* case was handed down against a backdrop of rising racial antipathy aimed at Filipinos, whose social interactions with white women were subject to growing scrutiny from public officials and the media. The *Stockton Record* newspaper endorsed Judge Smith's blunt legal reasoning in the *Robinson* case: "While the consensus is that [the ruling] may not have been entirely correct from an ethnological viewpoint it was right sociologically." The *Record* noted, "Authorities on racial origins are not agreed upon ethnic divisions. . . . But that the Filipinos are not Caucasians and therefore ineligible to inter-marry with whites is obvious." The newspaper claimed that white Californians' opposition to intermarriage was motivated not by racist sentiments but by concerns about cultural incompatibility: "As has been our attitude toward the Japanese, the distinction between white and yellow does not carry any inference of inferiority. It is merely the immutable barrier between East and West." The outcome of the *Robinson* case had some broader consequences, as Rosamond Rice, head of the Los Angeles County Marriage Bureau, had placed a hold on twelve Filipino-white marriage applications, which were subsequently denied after Judge Smith's decision.[68]

The ruling handed down in the *Robinson* suit was not well received by other judges in the Los Angeles Superior Court system, who did not appreciate having established precedent capriciously overturned by J.A. Smith, a visiting justice from Calaveras County. Some officers of the Los Angeles court system also expressed skepticism about the shifting criteria of racial classification employed by opponents of intermarriage, who substituted the three-races theory for the five-races taxonomy. Two marriage-annulment cases decided in Los Angeles in 1931 reveal some of the internal fault lines on both sides of the Filipino question. In one case, a petitioner, Estanislao Laddaran, sought an annulment from his wife, Emma, on the grounds that his marriage violated the state's antimiscegenation statute. Superior Court Judge Myron Westover declined to annul the couple's marriage, "because no proof had been offered that a Filipino is of the Mongolian Race and due to the fact that the question has not been determined by the higher courts." This decision did not sit well with Rosamond Rice. Rice had long held that Filipinos were "of the Malay race [and] that the Malay is of the Mongolian race and that therefore a Filipino is a Mongolian." Judge Westover, however, broke ranks with Rice and denied Laddaran's annulment petition. Westover declared that Filipinos were exempt from the state's intermarriage ban until a higher court settled the "Mongolian Blood Question."[69]

A few months later, in *Murillo v. Murillo*, it was Ilona Murillo, a "white girl," who petitioned the Los Angeles Superior Court to annul her marriage to her Filipino husband, Tony Murillo, because he was a "Mongolian." In her suit, Mrs. Murillo claimed that she was unaware of the prohibition against Asian-white unions when she married Tony and requested that the court retroactively invalidate her marriage. Judge Thomas Gould denied Mrs. Murillo's petition, citing legislative intent as the basis of his ruling: "To hold this marriage void it is necessary to hold that, ethnologically, Filipinos are Mongolians, and that the Legislature in adopting Section 60 of the civil code had in mind the prohibition of marriages between Filipinos and whites." In the absence of such evidence, the court saw little choice but to accept the ethnological classification of Filipinos as Malays that prevailed at the time of the statute's passage in 1880. Judge Gould argued that retroactively placing Filipinos into the "Mongolian" category to mollify racial animus against them set an imprudent legal precedent that violated norms of statutory interpretation. He also warned California officials of the potential legal turmoil that could result from the state's adopting the three-races theory to reclassify Filipinos as Mongolians. As Gould astutely pointed out, the three-races typology endorsed by opponents of intermarriage employed a remarkably broad definition of the Mongolian race, which included peoples from Finland, Turkey, Hungary, and the Americas. This sweeping classificatory shift would bring groups such as "Laplanders, Hawaiians, Esthonians, Huns, Finns, Turks, Eskimos, . . . and American Indians" under the purview of the California antimiscegenation code. The result, according to Judge Gould, would be mayhem, since the marital status of these "Mongolians" would also be subject to legal challenge in the courts.[70]

Questions about the legal status of Filipino intermarriage also vexed officials in other parts of California. Take for instance the case of Michael Madriaga and his wife, Dorcia Wilson Madriaga, who resided in San Francisco. The couple was married in Tijuana, Mexico, in 1929 with the blessing of Dorcia's parents. Mr. Madriaga worked as a restaurant cook and had been supporting his wife's family with his wages. When the couple temporarily relocated to Bremerton, Washington, Dorcia's father reported the pair to local authorities for violating California's antimiscegenation statutes. The couple was arrested in Washington and interrogated by a Department of Justice agent at the request of San Francisco police. Dorcia Madriaga issued a sharp rebuke against her father for his meddling, telling the *San Francisco Chronicle* that he was simply angry for having lost his "meal ticket." She explained the situation further: "As long as he [Michael Madriaga] was turning his wages over to support the family in San Francisco everything was lovely, but as soon as we determined to come to Bremerton and visit my cousin, who is also married to a Filipino, my father started raising a howl." Washington authorities eventually released the Madriagas since they had not violated any laws, having been legally wed in Mexico.[71]

The continuing dispute between the different branches of Los Angeles County government over the issue prompted Rosamond Rice and L. E. Lampton to contest interracial marriage applications with extra vigor, in an effort to isolate Filipinos socially and to prevent them from planting family roots in the state. The County Clerk's Office began turning away Filipino-Mexican couples on racial grounds, claiming that Mexicans were "white" and therefore debarred from intermarrying with persons of the Mongolian race. This intervention was unusual, since authorities rarely bothered to enforce antimiscegenation laws against Mexicans seeking to marry Asians. It reveals, moreover, the contingent character of racial order, as local officials capriciously wielded state power to effectuate social closure against a group (Filipinos) who defied de facto and de jure rules of segregation. One of these cases involved a Filipino man, Gavino Visco, and a Mexican American woman named Ruth Salas. The case hinged on the question of whether Visco was eligible to marry Salas, who was technically classified (like other persons of Mexican descent) as "white." The Los Angeles County Clerk's Office initially denied the couple a license, based on a strict interpretation of Salas's legal whiteness. The couple did not back down in the face of bureaucratic harassment, filing for a writ of mandate to compel the court to issue them a license. The couple employed a novel strategy in their petition, emphasizing Salas's "Indian" ancestry (i.e., the indigenous peoples of Mexico) over her conditional whiteness. Judge Thomas Gould granted their writ, though his decision did not directly take up the issue of Salas's contested racial identification. Judge Gould, like many of his colleagues on the Los Angeles bench believed that Filipinos were exempted from California's intermarriage law as members of the Malay race. Lampton and Rice vowed to appeal Gould's ruling, hoping to get the writ overturned, but they were not successful.[72]

Two days later, a similar case came up, involving another Filipino-Mexican couple, Caterno de la Cerna and Phyllis Eagen. Following a similar strategy to that used in the Visco-Salas case, the couple tried to exploit soft spots in the state's classificatory system to circumvent the law. Eagen, a mixed-race Mexican American, sought to disavow her whiteness (or at least obfuscate it) by listing her race as "Irish Indian" on their marriage application. Like Ruth Salas, she stressed the indigenous "Indian" character of her Mexican ancestry, believing that the intermarriage prohibition only applied to Caucasians. This strategic identity claim made sense, inasmuch as nativist leaders on the West Coast, such as California attorney general U. S. Webb, had publicly declared Mexicans to be "Indians" as part of a campaign to challenge their eligibility for U.S. citizenship and to force them to attend segregated Mexican-only schools. The County Clerk's Office expressed skepticism about the couple's identity claim, seeing it as a ruse to sidestep the law. Lampton demanded an affidavit from Eagen to prove that her mother was a Mexican, as she claimed.[73]

Variations of this strategy also popped up frequently among women who fit a more conventional definition of whiteness. In these cases, women would sometimes identify themselves as "Filipino" to evade segregationist policies. A woman in Santa Ana, California, for example, claimed to be an American-born Filipina in order to marry her Filipino sweetheart, but local officials expressed skepticism about her self-identification. The Orange County clerk refused to grant the couple a marriage license because the bride-to-be could not provide "proper proof that she was a Filipino."[74] Similarly, white women who worked as taxi dancers in California would sometimes claim to be Filipino when they were arrested and faced charges for violating local ordinances prohibiting mixed-race dancing (see chapter 4). That white women went to such lengths to circumvent racial checkpoints is striking considering the intense community disapproval they faced for engaging in interracial relationships. In addition to private sanction, white women also faced potentially serious legal consequences for entering into relationships with Filipino men, including the loss of political rights. A 1930 ruling issued by Paul Armstrong, the federal district director of naturalization in San Francisco, declared that even though Filipinos were U.S. nationals, white women who married them would be stripped of their American citizenship.[75]

The Roldan Case

The California State Court of Appeals finally took up the Filipino-intermarriage question in 1933, handing down a precedent-setting decision for the lower courts to follow. The case, *Roldan v. Los Angeles County and the State of California*, involved a Filipino, Salvador Roldan, and his British fiancée,

Marjorie Rogers, whose application for marriage had been rejected by the county clerk in August 1931. The couple petitioned for a writ of mandate soon after, which was eventually granted by Superior Court Judge Walter Gates. Not surprisingly county counsels L. E. Lampton and Everett Mattoon filed an injunction with the state appeals court, hoping to get Gates's decision reversed. U. S. Webb and Associate Attorney General Frank English also filed an amicus curiae brief on behalf of the appellants, supporting the county clerk's contention that Filipinos were members of the Mongolian race. The legal maneuvering in this case centered on two interrelated issues: the contested racial status of Filipinos and the statutory intent of the California legislature regarding Sections 60 and 69 of the state civil code.[76]

To determine the first question, the court reviewed scientific and popular opinion pertaining to the racial identification of Filipinos. The justices surveyed the racial classification schemas provided by the leading scholarly sources of the day, including the New American Cyclopedia and various dictionaries (e.g., *Webster's, Standard,* and *Ogilvie's Imperial Dictionary of the English Language*), with a particular focus on the racial taxonomies that prevailed at the time of the law's passage in 1880. The court came to the conclusion that although there was some variation of opinion about the racial assignment of Filipinos, the five-race taxonomy (white, black, yellow, brown, red) developed by renowned ethnologist Johann Blumenbach was the most widely accepted at the time of the addition of "Mongolians" to the state's miscegenation prohibition. Importantly, the court also noted that the U.S. Congress's own widely referenced publication the *Dictionary of Race or Peoples* listed Filipinos under the "Brown or Malay" race. These sources tended to support Roldan and Rogers's contention that Filipinos fell outside the purview of the California prohibition.[77]

County and state officials sought to contravene the petitioner's argument by citing the work of Ales Hrdlicka, a contemporary anthropologist who claimed that Filipinos belonged to the "yellow-brown race or Mongoloid race." The court determined that the issue of Filipinos' ethnological classification was irresolvable since there was a range of contradictory opinions on the matter. The ever-changing racial assignment of Filipinos was not an issue the court felt qualified to resolve. Justice T. Archbald, who wrote the *Roldan* opinion, declared that the "sole question" before the justices was whether the California legislature meant to include Filipinos under the term "Mongolian" in 1880 (or in 1905, when the law was amended again). On that issue, the justices accepted that Blumenbach's theory was the dominant classification schema through the first decade of the twentieth century, an interpretation that bolstered the petitioners' case.

The justices also examined the intermarriage question from a "common understanding" approach to assess whether Filipinos had been included under the term "Mongolian" in popular discourse in the late nineteenth and early twentieth centuries. The court noted that the history of California was "replete with legislation to curb the so-called Chinese invasion," so there was a voluminous public record that documented the statutory intent of nativist lawmakers. Justice Archbald averred that it was clear from reviewing the long history of California's nativist policies (including the miscegenation ban) that the legal category "Mongolian" had explicitly been used "to designate the class of residents whose presence caused the problem at which all the [exclusionist] legislation was directed, . . . the Chinese, and possibly contiguous people of like characteristics." The court added, "there was no thought of applying the name Mongolian to a Malay" in any of the debates or discussions relating to the enactment of the original legislation. Filipinos, as a result, were exempted from the state's intermarriage ban since lawmakers had never explicitly intended to include them under legal prohibitions targeting Mongolians. The justices in the Roldan case were quick to point out that their ruling was in no way an endorsement of interracial unions between Filipinos and whites. Judge Archbald's ruling reminded all involved that the role of the courts was to interpret the law, not to manufacture it. If California lawmakers wanted to add Filipinos to the state's intermarriage ban, the court noted, then they needed to do so explicitly through the legislative process.[78]

Although Filipinos in California were technically eligible to intermarry with whites as a result of the Roldan decision, they still faced hostility from local officials who refused to recognize the appellate court's ruling. County clerks across the state refused to issue licenses to Filipinos while Los Angeles County officials and Attorney General Webb appealed the Roldan ruling to the California Supreme Court. In San Francisco, for instance, Harry I. Mulcrevy, the city's county clerk, spurned the state appellate court's ruling, declaring, "no such marriage applications would be issued here" until the Roldan appeal was heard by the California Supreme Court. State legislators, in the meantime, were working on a bill to add Filipinos to the list of races proscribed from intermarrying with whites, offering even more incentive for belligerent officials to stall issuing licenses to mixed-race couples.[79] Nativist efforts to have the Roldan decision overturned by a higher court were dashed on March 27, 1933, when the California Supreme Court upheld the appellate justices' ruling by refusing to grant Lampton and Webb's appeal for a rehearing. Salvador Roldan and Marjorie Rogers were given the green light to move forward with their marriage and they applied for a license soon after, on

April 3, 1933, in Los Angeles County, where their long and expensive legal ordeal had begun back in August 1931.[80]

Although the verdict in the *Roldan* appeal signaled a legal victory for California's Filipino community, only a few individuals got to take advantage of the ruling. State lawmakers had already begun crafting a legislative remedy in the event that the appeal failed. Senator Herbert C. Jones of San Jose introduced two bills (Resolutions 175 and 176) in the state legislature in March 1933. The first measure explicitly outlawed marriages between whites and "members of the Malay race," and the second one prohibited county clerks from issuing licenses to mixed-race couples. The bills were quickly ratified in the state senate and assembly and were then passed on to Governor James Rolph on April 5, 1933, to sign into law.[81] The new law barred Filipinos from intermarriage with whites until 1948, when the California Supreme Court ruled the state's antimiscegenation statute unconstitutional because it violated the due process and equal protection clauses of the Fourteenth Amendment.[82]

The amended antimiscegenation statue implemented an important legal roadblock in the way of Filipino-white couples, but its effectiveness was blunted by the jurisdictional limits of state laws. By the early 1930s, Filipinos had developed a web of social networks that pooled information (about how and where they could be legally married) and resources (sharing automobiles and pooling money for coethnics to travel to other states to obtain a marriage license). Western states including Oregon, Wyoming, Nevada, Idaho, South Dakota, and Arizona amended their antimiscegenation laws to target "Malays," but Filipino-white intermarriage remained legal in adjacent jurisdictions, such as New Mexico and Washington (and in Tijuana, Mexico).[83] The few western states that did not prohibit Filipino-white unions faced pressure to enact like provisions to prevent Filipinos from obtaining legal marriages in their jurisdictions. California legislators, for example, sent a resolution to officials in Utah, imploring them to promptly update their statutory prohibition on intermarriage to "stop the practice whereby citizens of the State of California and members of a non-assimilable alien race have been defeating California marriage laws by resorting to a subterfuge of transient residence in the State of Utah."[84] California lawmakers' obtrusive intervention into the civil affairs of another state demonstrates the increasing sense of frustration expressed by western nativists, aggravated by Filipinos' aptitude for subverting traditional racial checkpoints. Filipinos' success in circumventing California's amended antimiscegenation law eventually prompted state legislators to introduce a bill that would void Filipino-white marriages contracted legally in other jurisdictions.[85]

That antimiscegenation laws were often ineffective in containing interracial intimacy does not diminish their importance as instruments of social control. Efforts to cut off access routes to public life continued unabated, as gatekeepers hoped that the relentless legal harassment and institutional exclusion of Filipinos would discourage them from settling permanently in the United States. The controversy generated by interracial relationships, moreover, provided added ammunition for nativists who cited the deviant sociality of Filipino men as proof of their unassimilability and the need to shore up racial and national boundaries.[86]

Prohibitions on Property

The wielding of state power to effect social closure against Filipino immigrants also extended into the area of property rights. Lawmakers in western states with sizeable Asian immigrant populations worked in concert with one another to implement a series of legislative enactments barring the outsiders from owning "real property," in the hope that restrictive property controls would push them back to the margins of the agricultural labor market. By the early 1920s, the land laws had become an effective tool in the restrictionists' arsenal, delimiting the socioeconomic mobility of Asians in the United States. Efforts to enforce alien land laws against Filipinos in the American West in the 1920s and 1930s offer yet another lesson in how the impulse to maintain hard and fast racial boundaries was confounded by the newcomers' paradoxical political status as well as by the resolve of Filipino activists who refused to accept their subordinate station in American society.

Japanese immigrants in California were the initial targets of the alien land legislation. The Japanese had by the early 1900s supplanted the Chinese as the main bogeyman of the exclusionist movement. During this period, California lawmakers sponsored and/or ratified scores of bills aimed at imposing legal disabilities against Japanese immigrants, including an "alien poll tax," measures seeking to deny birthright citizenship to American-born children of Asian ancestry, and forcing resident Japanese into segregated public schools. Calls for restrictive legislation came from the usual suspects: urban-based commercial concerns that competed with Asian small business and western trade-union spokesmen, whose commitment to yellow perilism was unshakable.

Restrictionists, however, ran up against powerful competing forces, including the state's powerful farm bloc and federal officials who opposed anti-Japanese legislation. By the early 1900s California farm operators relied heavily on Japanese workers to cultivate and harvest crops and worried that restrictionist legislation would dry up their main labor supply and drive up wages. Representatives from the federal government also opposed the enactment of discriminatory policies, worried about the fallout that racialist legislation would have on diplomatic relations with Japan. Interventions from the Roosevelt and Taft administrations helped to delay the passage of a number of discriminatory measures for a brief period, but political currents began to shift in the 1910s as the Japanese population on the West Coast continued to grow, despite the so-called Gentlemen's Agreement, an accord negotiated by the Roosevelt administration under which the Japanese government agreed to voluntarily limit the emigration of its citizens to the United States.[87]

Support for the anti-Japanese campaign gathered momentum when the spokesmen from the farm bloc switched sides and threw their support behind restrictive legislation. By 1910, established agribusiness concerns faced increasing competition from the Japanese who started purchasing their own plots of agricultural land and began siphoning labor (mostly their coethnics) away from white farm operators. White farmers hoped that the passage of an alien land law would thwart the upward mobility of Japanese eager to transition from wage laborer to independent freeholder. The remarkable success of Japanese truck farmers in niche produce markets provoked a new sense of urgency in the California legislature, fueled by hysterical claims that western agriculture was being rapidly "Orientalized." In May 1913, state lawmakers passed the Webb-Heney Alien Land Law, which prohibited all "aliens ineligible to citizenship" from purchasing "real property," except as guaranteed by international treaty.[88] The novel statutory language employed by the law reflected the changing sociolegal landscape of the early twentieth century. State lawmakers had to be mindful of constitutional prohibitions against overt racial discrimination and worked to square restrictions on property rights with federal guarantees of equal protection and due process enumerated in the Fourteenth Amendment. Rather than explicitly targeting specific racial groups, officials used the putatively neutral classification "aliens ineligible to citizenship," a clever euphemism that permitted state legislators to implement discriminatory regulations without violating the Constitution. Though Japanese were the immediate target of the legislation, the statutory language also encompassed Filipinos and all other Asian immigrants, since they too were "ineligible to citizenship."[89]

California attorney general Ulysses S. Webb, who coauthored the bill, acknowledged that the "race undesirability" of Asians was the primary motivation behind the measure. He explained that the new land legislation was an attempt to "limit their presence by *curtailing their privileges* which they may enjoy here; for they will not come in large numbers and long abide with us if they may not acquire land. And it [the 1913 law] seeks to limit the numbers who will come by *limiting the opportunities* for their activity here when they arrive" (emphasis added). The bill passed despite appeals from Woodrow Wilson's administration, which lobbied California lawmakers to quash the measure to avoid an "international incident" with a rival imperial power. Federal intervention on issues related to anti-Japanese measures was less persuasive than it had been in previous years, especially since Wilson was a Democrat trying to exert influence over the state's Republican powerbrokers. California legislators framed the passage of the land law as a forceful expression of "states' rights" that was designed to serve as a stop-gap measure aimed at deterring Japanese immigration while state officials continued to pressure Congress to enact comprehensive Asian exclusion at the national level.[90]

Nativist agitation accelerated in the ensuing years when it became clear that the law had failed to achieve the desired effects of curtailing immigration or forcing Japanese back into their previous role as low-wage peons. A 1911 commercial treaty between the United States and Japan guaranteed the right of Japanese residents to own property for commercial, residential, and manufacturing purposes, so the 1913 land act only barred them from purchasing agricultural land. Japanese immigrants, moreover, frequently circumvented the law by purchasing land in the names of their American-born children or buying property through front corporations nominally controlled by citizens, or devising trust arrangements that gave them effective ownership. As a result, the agricultural acreage owned or leased by Japanese actually increased markedly between 1913 and 1920.[91] By the late 1910s, state legislators moved to close up loopholes in the alien land law and successfully ratified a much more stringent measure in 1920 that effectively closed most of the flaws in the earlier statute.[92]

State leaders also took their campaign nationwide, establishing ties with other western lawmakers in an attempt to create a united front on the "Oriental" question, believing that their crusade would be more effective if likeminded laws were adopted uniformly across the region. Using California as a model, several other western states including Washington, Oregon, Idaho, Montana, Wyoming, and New Mexico adopted restrictive land laws that targeted Asian immigrants. Western nativists also kept up pressure on the federal government to enact comprehensive legislation that would bar all immigration from Asia once and for all. To this end, California congressional leaders in Washington, DC, launched a national organization composed of senators and representatives from thirteen states to "present the viewpoint of the people of the West to the people of several States of the Union on Oriental immigration and land ownership." One of the main aims of the coalition was to explain and defend the legality of the land statutes in anticipation of looming constitutional challenges in the federal courts. Coalition spokesman Representative Charles Curry explained, "It is the duty of our Government to protect itself and its citizens from foreign invasion and commercial and industrial exploitation, whether they come in the shape of bombarding men-of-war . . . or in the shape of passenger and freight ships carrying cheap labor and cheap goods. . . . Hence we must exclude them from our shores as settlers and prohibit them from owning land." The coalition claimed that land laws were "essential to the national welfare," warning that without restrictive legislation "the richest section of the United States will gradually come into complete control of an alien race. They will outnumber us in population; they will control the pulse of commerce."[93]

Western nativists hoped that this type of alarmist "invasion" rhetoric would stir up political support for restrictionist legislation by framing the land laws as defensive measures designed to protect the nation from being overrun by Asian colonists. The national-security argument took center stage when a series of test cases weighing in on the constitutionality of the alien land laws were argued before the U.S. Supreme Court in 1923. The cases addressed different aspects of the land laws, such as whether the statutes violated the equal protection and due process guarantees stipulated by the Fourteenth Amendment, whether the prohibitions illegitimately restricted Asians' right to earn a livelihood or violated the 1911 commercial treaty between Japan and the United States, and whether sharecropping agreements constituted a form of illicit tenancy.[94] The Court upheld the constitutionality of alien land laws in *Terrace v. Thompson* (concerning Washington State's land law), dismissing claims that they violated the due process or equal protection clauses and contending that the statutory discrimination based on "alienage" was different from that based on "race or color."[95] Justice Pierce Butler acknowledged that alien land laws had an inequitable effect since they only applied to "Japanese, Chinese, and Malays" but declared this type of discrimination to be a valid exercise of state police power. In a shrewd example of legal cross-referencing, the Court cited the fact that Congress debarred Asian immigrants from U.S. citizenship as evidence that certain types of categorical discrimination were legitimate if they served a vital public interest (e.g., preventing Asian control of agriculture, denying them the franchise, etc.).[96]

Alien land laws were firmly entrenched in the American West by the time Filipinos started arriving in large numbers in the mid- to late 1920s. As instruments of social closure, the property restrictions reinforced occupational and residential segregation and placed serious constraints on the newcomers' life chances. Their status as American colonial subjects placed them at a distinct disadvantage when it came to the burdens imposed by the land laws. The Philippines, unlike Japan, had no commercial treaty with the United States guaranteeing its emigrants certain immunities from the land laws, which meant that Filipinos, unlike the Japanese, were potentially barred from owning or leasing commercial and residential property in addition to agricultural land. Western lawmakers' claims that restrictive land laws were necessary to protect U.S. soil from alien control came off as disingenuous to Filipino immigrants, since American citizens and corporations owned large swathes of property in the Philippines and never expressed any concern about the nefarious effects of foreign land tenure in the islands. Arguments about mutual reciprocity did not garner much sympathy in the nativist political climate of the 1920s, especially with the memory of Japanese socioeconomic mobility still fresh in people's minds. Restrictionists cited Filipinos' controversial reputation for mixing with white women as an added justification for proscriptions on property, since the laws would discourage them from settling in West Coast communities and intermarrying with local women.[97]

Filipinos again took to the courts to challenge the alien land statutes, contesting the laws on multiple fronts. Filipinos in Washington State employed a novel strategy to evade that state's bar on alien land ownership, forming an alliance with local Native Americans to exploit jurisdictional loopholes in the law. Filipino leaders, moreover, argued that their status as U.S. nationals placed them outside the statutory definition of the term "alien." Exclusionists dismissed this "technicality," contending that Filipinos were still subject to the property prohibition because of their ineligibility to citizenship. The statutory language used by Washington lawmakers added to the uncertainty, since it barred "non-declarant aliens" rather than "aliens ineligible" from owning property. This neologism provided the state extra insulation from constitutional challenge since it put the onus on aliens for not having declared their intention to become a citizen. Asian immigrants, of course, could not declare their intent to be naturalized (at least not in "good faith," as required by law), so the discriminatory effect was the same.[98] The battle over property prohibitions in Washington once again illustrates the complex and often contradictory role played by federal, state, and local officials in enforcing categorical boundaries.

"Orientalizing the Reservation"

The settlement of Filipinos on the Yakima Indian Reservation in eastern Washington State in the mid-1920s created problems for officials charged with enforcing the state's alien land statute. The newcomers had been recruited to the Yakima Valley to labor in the region's booming agricultural sector, which specialized in apples, hops, cherries, pears, and a variety of other fresh fruits and vegetables that required a mobile and disciplined labor force to cultivate and harvest the highly perishable crops. Their arrival quickly generated a backlash from local white residents who saw them as a social and economic threat, especially when Filipinos started leasing land on the reservation to take up independent truck farming. Authorities faced increasing pressure to intervene after a series of vigilante attacks and bombings targeting Filipinos leaders. Aggressive enforcement of the alien land law seemed like the most obvious way to put the newcomers back in their place. State officials, however, faced a jurisdictional problem since the Yakima tribe held nominal sovereignty over reservation land. Tribal leaders had no stake in abiding by the alien land act and had their own longstanding conflicts with local whites and state officials. And to the degree that the law interfered with their ability to get the best lease price for reservation holdings, their interests were at odds with the state, insofar as it restricted their ability to negotiate the best price for their land with Filipino lessees who were often willing to pay premium rates for marginal farm land.

In 1926, a small number of Filipinos applied for land leases on the reservation, which prompted Yakima Reservation Superintendent Evan Estep to seek guidance from the Bureau of Indian Affairs (BIA) about their eligibility. No clear ruling on the matter was issued, so Estep took it upon himself to declare that Filipinos were subject to the state land law. The applicability of the state property prohibitions on a federally administered reservation, however, was uncharted legal territory. Estep noted that it had long been federal policy to respect individual states' property laws "as a matter of comity."[99] The case at hand, though, raised more complex issues about the ability of Washington State officials to exercise authority over land that was technically outside their domain. Yakima tribal members saw Estep's intervention as a breach of their sovereignty and believed they were within their rights to lease reservation land to whomever they pleased.

Tensions continued to simmer as Filipinos increased their social and economic presence in the Yakima Valley in the late 1920s. A few years later, the reservation's new superintendent, C. R. Whitlock, again sought clarification from federal authorities on the issue of Filipinos' eligibility for land ownership on Yakima lands. In 1932, the state's assistant commissioner of Indian affairs offered another ambiguous response but suggested that the unique status of Filipinos as American nationals gave "strong reasons for relaxing as to them [Filipinos] the restrictions which do not exist in favor of aliens who are barred because of their color or race."[100] Superintendent Whitlock opposed relaxing the alien land laws for Filipinos, and federal authorities took no action to stop his decision to prohibit Filipinos from land ownership. Unable to obtain land through traditional channels, Filipinos began the practice of subleasing land either through white intermediaries or through covert labor agreements with Native American owners in which Filipino farmers were listed as "employees" of the Yakima tribal allottee. These arrangements and the continuing cooperation between the Yakima tribe and the Filipinos raised the ire of white officials who saw these alliances as a threat to their dominion over both populations. Superintendent Whitlock, in particular, vehemently opposed these labor agreements, arguing that they were in practice "alien subterfuge" that allowed Filipinos to surreptitiously circumvent the law.

Racial tensions in the Yakima Valley grew among white residents who feared competition from Filipino farmers and laborers. The growing presence of the newcomers in the region led to fears that "the colonization of a large number of Filipinos on these lands might easily create moral equities and political pressures that would be hard to overcome."[101] Local white residents organized a vigilante campaign aimed at pressuring local white and Japanese agriculturalists to forsake Filipino laborers. Farmers and landowners who employed Filipinos were subjected to a series of arson attacks and dynamite bombings for cooperating with the "barbaric black natives." Superintendent Whitlock, frustrated by Filipinos' ingenuity in circumventing the law, pushed for an amendment to the alien land law "to prohibit alien employment as well as ownership, leasing, renting, and sharecropping." He received the backing of the local white Grange organization as well as support from Governor Clarence Martin and U.S. congressional representatives Marion Zioncheck and Knute Hill. Reservation officials increased surveillance of Filipinos who were suspected of subverting the alien land laws. Officials observed what they characterized as alien subterfuge through which Filipino men were surreptitiously accessing land through intermarriage with female members of the Yakima tribe. Agents noted that Filipinos had mixed "sexually with the Indian girls and women, corrupt[ed] their morals" and that their "presence on the reservation is a constant menace to our Indian population."[102]

State officials, frustrated by the lack of federal intervention, decided to take matters into their own hands and set about crafting legislation explicitly targeting Filipinos. In 1935, the governor ordered the state attorney general to bring charges against individuals who violated the alien land law by subleasing property to Filipinos. The legality of the prosecutions hinged on competing interpretations of Filipinos' racial and political status in the United States. Lloyd Wiehl, deputy prosecutor of Yakima County, believed that Filipinos' distinctive status as American subjects might possibly exempt them from being defined as "aliens" with regard to the land laws. He called on state legislators to amend the law to include "non-citizens, or persons incapable of becoming citizens" to the land statute to resolve this potential problem. Until that time, the district attorney placed a moratorium on prosecutions until the state could make a definitive ruling on the newcomers' legal status. In 1937, the state legislature amended the alien land legislation to include Filipinos. The amendment barred "non-citizens of the United States and who are ineligible to citizenship by naturalization" from land ownership in the state.[103] Labor and cropping agreements between the Yakima tribe and Filipinos were also declared illegal, and local authorities shut down a farmers' cooperative on the reservation organized by local activist Roy Baldoz. Government officials stepped up efforts to prosecute those who were accused of defying the statutes, and eighteen Filipinos were arrested and charged with conspiring to violate the state's alien land law. They were all convicted and received six-month sentences for their activities, though they were eventually freed after a lengthy and expensive process of appeals.[104]

The constant harassment from local authorities was intended to force Filipinos out of the region, yet it had the opposite effect. Activists intensified their efforts to challenge the discriminatory land laws. Filipinos in the Yakima Valley merged their struggle with community organizations on the western side of the state that were confronting similar legal obstacles. The groups united around the case of Pio De Cano, a Seattle community leader involved in a legal challenge testing the constitutionality of the 1937 amendment to the state's alien land law. The case involved both political and technical issues related to the amended act, including De Cano's eligibility for citizenship, the racial status of Filipinos, and the constitutionality of the statute. De Cano employed a clever strategy to circumvent the Washington land law; he filed a "declaration of intention" for naturalization, even though he was racially ineligible for citizenship. As discussed earlier, the Washington statute allowed aliens who had filed a "declaration of intent" to purchase land, but it did not stipulate that the declaration had to be approved. De Cano used his declaration form to acquire a tract of fee-simple land in Seattle in 1939. Upon learning of this situation, the King County prosecuting attorney, B. Gray Warner, filed a complaint against De Cano, charging him with violating the state's alien land law and demanded that his property be forfeited to the state. A King County judge, however, dismissed the complaint, stating that the 1937 amendment adding Filipinos to Washington's land law violated the state's constitution. B. Gray Warner and the Washington State attorney general, John Belcher, appealed the decision to the state supreme court. The Seattle Filipino Community Clubhouse, a fraternal organization that wished to acquire land on which to build a clubhouse, joined De Cano in his legal challenge.[105]

The Washington State Supreme Court's ruling revisited, once again, the issue of Filipinos' political standing, noting that federal courts had consistently held that they were nationals and not aliens. Both sides acknowledged that the 1937 amendment to the state's land law had been written to restrict Filipinos from land ownership, but they differed as to whether the new law was enforceable. The plaintiffs challenged the constitutionality of the amended land law, arguing that it used an overly expansive definition of the term "alien" that was not consistent with accepted legal definition of that category. The state countered that De Cano had acted in "bad faith" with his declaration of intention and held that Filipinos were racially ineligible for land ownership in Washington State. In adjudicating the case the justices scrutinized De Cano's racial background, noting that he was of Filipino ancestry and had migrated to the United States at the age of seventeen. He had not served in the U.S. armed forces, so according to the justices, he had not "removed his racial disqualification" from naturalization, rendering his petition for citizenship null and void. The justices also dismissed the legal standing of the Seattle Filipino Community Club to join in the suit because it had not yet actually submitted payment to buy a parcel of land.

The constitutionality of the 1937 amendment, however, was a source of judicial concern. The plaintiffs argued that the state's amended statute had imposed an arbitrary and unusual meaning on the term "alien" which usurped the power of Congress to classify aliens and nationals. The justices concurred with this characterization, noting that the title of the legislation characterized it as "an act relating to the rights and disabilities of aliens with respect to land, and amending [the] Laws of 1921," yet the aim of the amendment clearly went beyond the accepted meaning of the term "alien." Justice

Driver's ruling remarked that the 1937 act's title stated that it pertained "to the rights of aliens with respect to land," but it did not explicitly state that it contained an "amended definition of the word 'alien' which brings within its purview a whole new class of persons who are not in fact aliens in common understanding, by judicial construction, or under the express definition contained in prior law." A declaratory judgment was issued stating that the 1937 amendment as written was unconstitutional, rendering the issue of De Cano's declaration of intention moot.[106]

Bolstered by the Seattle community's victory and the support of the Philippine resident commissioner in Washington, DC, Filipinos on the east side of the state forged ahead with their campaign. After years of developing alliances with members of the Yakima tribe, community leaders Roy Baldoz and Paul Tabayoyon entered into an agreement with tribal leaders in 1941 to lease farmland on the reservation. These arrangements were opposed by both state and federal officials, even after the decision handed down in the *De Cano* case. Hoping that the legislature would pass a new land statute explicitly barring Filipinos, the state attorney general's office asked reservation officials to refrain from leasing land to them pending legislative action. Hostility toward Filipinos remained strong and Washington legislators acted quickly to again bring them under the purview of the state's alien land laws. House Bill 592 was introduced the day after the ruling in the *De Cano* case was delivered and was designed to resolve the constitutional problems of the 1937 amendment. The bill, however, did not pass the 1941 legislative session and its reintroduction was put on indefinite hold as the United States entered into World War II later that year. The role of the Philippines as allies in World War II compelled federal officials to make some concessions to Filipinos in the Yakima Valley on a provisional basis, even though opposition remained strong from nativist forces, most notably the local chapter of the Grange. As Filipinos' role in the war became more widely known, their continued exclusion from property rights on the reservation became far less tenable, and they were slowly granted access to small tracts of land under the oversight of federal authorities.[107]

Alien land laws barring land ownership and leasing agreements in the western states restricted Filipino immigrants from gaining a foothold in small-scale commercial farming from the early 1920s to the 1940s. This left them particularly vulnerable to discriminatory practices in the labor market at the hands of unscrupulous employers. The prohibition on land ownership was yet another barrier that limited the social mobility of Filipino immigrants. Taken together with racial proscriptions on citizenship and bars on interracial marriage, the land legislation was another powerful political tool employed by state officials to relegate Filipinos to a disadvantaged position in the social order. Efforts to enforce the color line against the newcomers, however, proved more difficult than expected, and they continued to challenge norms of racial segregation and subordination. Their intransigence led many whites to view legal prohibitions against Filipinos as ineffective and, therefore, inadequate. Consequently, as the following chapter shows, nativist leaders stepped up campaigns to enforce racial boundaries through extralegal means to defend the white communities from the Filipino menace.

4

"Get Rid of All Filipinos or We'll Burn This Town Down"

Racial Revanchism and the Contested Color Line in the Interwar West

Early efforts by lawmakers and nativists to control the Filipino immigrant population and keep them "in their place" using conventional methods achieved mixed results. While these legal measures severely restricted the social and economic mobility of Filipinos, immigration from the islands grew steadily during the late 1920s, with an estimated population of around forty-five thousand living in the U.S. mainland by 1930. Western nativists had warned of an impending Filipino "invasion" dating back to the mid-1920s, but their calls for legislative action on the issue failed to generate much national attention. The failure of the federal government to curtail immigration from the Philippines and the inability of state and local officials to effectively contain the Filipino population in the United States compelled exclusionists to take ownership of the issue. Nativist leaders wielded heavy sway over immigration and nationality policy and played a leading role in framing public debate about the "Filipino problem." When they made claims about the dangers of unrestricted immigration or racial admixture, they were treated as legitimate authorities acting on behalf of the public interest. Movement spokesmen used their cultural authority to define Filipino immigration and settlement as social problems and to propose potential remedies. Nativist groups such as the Native Sons of the Golden West, the California Joint Immigration Committee, and the American Coalition of Patriotic Societies and allied organizations such as the American Legion, the Commonwealth Club, the Grange, and western labor unions all mobilized their resources to position and keep the Filipino issue on the public agenda.[1]

In nativists' bid to mobilize popular support, they frequently indulged in fear mongering to exaggerate the prevalence of the putative problem.

Movement spokesmen hoped to catalyze or reactivate anti-Asian sentiment by broadcasting alarmist messages about the consequences of the Filipino "invasion." The issue, according to nativists, had reached a crisis point that threatened to enervate the Anglo-Saxon character of American society. Claims makers invoked the language of crisis to galvanize support, calculating that the more critical the social problem, the more urgent their call to action. Alarmist rhetoric about labor conflict, race mixing, and public health threats spurred new public awareness of the issue and bolstered nativist demands for exclusion. Mustering support in civil society did not, however, yield the desired results. Nativists tried to fix responsibility for the Filipino problem on the federal government, which held plenary authority over immigration policy. Federal officials were slow to act on the issue because they were bound by international convention to allow imperial wards to enter the country. They also faced pressure from western agribusiness interests, which favored lax immigration laws that maximized their access to tractable Filipino and Mexican labor.

The failure of national lawmakers to take ownership of the Filipino problem compelled nativists to assert local sovereignty over the issue. This took a variety of forms, ranging from public resolutions imploring the federal government to bar immigration from the Philippines to boycotts of employers who hired Filipino labor and vigilante campaigns aimed at driving the newcomers out of western communities. Nativists defended their actions, claiming that they were carrying out the popular will, safeguarding the white community from dangerous interlopers who threatened to destroy their way of life. In most civil societies, extralegal coercion and violence is considered to be outside the bounds of legitimate authority. In the case of the anti-Filipino movement, extralegal compulsion was incorporated into the repertoire of normal politics and used by claims makers to launch their crusade onto the national stage. Nativist leaders successfully employed a discourse of racial victimhood to defend vigilante sentiment and mobilize collective action.

Alarmist messages about unrestricted immigration, interracial sex, and labor competition constituted the social-psychological underpinning that fueled an intensive and often violent campaign to vanquish the "Filipino problem." Nativists and their allies were careful to frame their movement in defensive terms, characterizing vigilantism as a regrettable but necessary response from besieged communities that were simply trying to protect themselves from swarms of alien invaders. Appeals to racial self-defense were common currency among nativist leaders, who characterized the anti-

Filipino campaigns as purging rituals aimed at cleansing the American body politic of dangerous contaminants before they spread to the vital organs of the social system.[2]

The construction of Filipino immigration as a social problem revolved around four key themes: the putative public heath hazard posed by the newcomers, anxieties about interracial sex and deviant sociality, labor competition, and the threat of political radicalism. This chapter examines how these concerns were articulated and acted on during the 1920s and 1930s, focusing on the link between alarmist messages, collective action, and the policing of racial and class boundaries. Nativist leaders and western elites argued that the Anglo-Saxon character of American society was in peril unless state resources were brought to bear against Filipino immigration and settlement. These public figures played a catalytic role in the upsurge of revanchist sentiment that swept across the West Coast during this period. These same social actors were recognized as legitimate spokespersons on immigration issues and were accorded privileged access to the media, which allowed them to frame how events such as violent confrontations between Filipinos and whites were interpreted and represented in the public sphere. The proliferation of anti-Filipino attitudes and vigilante violence was held up by nativists as evidence of the incompatibility of whites and Asians, which, in turn, legitimated their calls for coercive state-building policies aimed at shoring up the nation's immigration and nationality controls.

"He Is a Disease Carrier"

The biological and hygienic fitness of Filipinos had been subject to critical scrutiny dating back to the advent of American rule in the islands. U.S. officials had drawn attention to the premodern public health conditions in the Philippines and the lack of civilized hygienic practices among the native population to justify colonial reform of the public health system. Much of the initial work conducted by U.S.-based scientists focused on the medical threats faced by white Americans in the Philippines, with a special focus on tropical disease ecologies and the unsuitability of the islands as a settler colony. Colonial hygiene programs later undergirded governmental initiatives aimed at transforming health practices among the local population through the establishment of a U.S.-run public education system that would impart modern health techniques to the natives to contain the spread of germs and disease.[3] Concerns about the normative deficiencies of the Filipino population took on a new urgency when they began migrating to Hawaii and the

U.S. mainland in significant numbers, potentially exposing vulnerable white Americans to tropical diseases and foreign pathogens. Exclusionists had long associated unregulated immigration with the outbreak of disease epidemics, and popular perceptions of Filipinos as unhygienic and uncivilized made them easy targets for scrutiny.[4] To make matters worse, Filipinos were not technically classified as "immigrants" (entering the country freely as U.S. nationals), meaning they were not subject to the same level of medical inspection that other newcomers faced when entering the country. Claims makers elaborated on racial distinctions in the hygiene practices of Filipinos to stigmatize them as a public health threat that warranted greater surveillance from state authorities.

Nativists framed their message in defensive terms, emphasizing how the well-being of white citizens was jeopardized by the proliferation of Filipino "colonies" scattered up and down the West Coast. According to exclusionists, Filipinos defied and/or disregarded middle-class health and sanitary habits and therefore willfully endangered the communities they settled in. Their alleged health deficiencies were characterized as a product of inborn racial differences that were incompatible with the hygienic conventions adhered to by white citizens. The public health menace posed by the newcomers was magnified by the fact that many Filipinos lived in squalid housing in rural labor camps and in segregated boardinghouses in urban Chinatowns where substandard sanitary conditions were a fact of life. According to public officials, the abysmal hygiene practices found in Filipino enclaves made these places a potential breeding ground for disease and contagion that could spread to the larger society if not held in check.[5]

Claims makers also argued that Filipinos were ill suited for the climatic differences they encountered in the United States, making them especially vulnerable to diseases such as tuberculosis, pneumonia, and influenza. This charge was central to the communicative message of the nativist lobby, since Filipinos' susceptibility to disease combined with their precarious economic standing meant that they were likely to become "public charges" of the U.S. government, draining social welfare resources from white taxpayers. Efforts to raise awareness about the issue gathered momentum in the late 1920s as nativists searched for an issue that might galvanize public support for exclusion. The influential Commonwealth Club commissioned a "study" of the Filipino question in 1929, highlighting a host of social problems associated with Filipino immigration in the United States. The Commonwealth Club was a leading Progressive Era men's club that described itself as "the nation's oldest and largest public affairs forum," with a membership drawn from powerful business, civic, and political leaders in western society. They held a symposium on Filipino immigration in 1929 aimed at highlighting Filipinos' undesirability and unassimilability. The club commissioned an investigation of the issue and shared its initial findings at a community forum. The Commonwealth Club's report described the newcomers as a "decided liability from the standpoint of public health. Physically [the Filipino] is not a very good specimen; [he] is under-sized and frequently under-nourished. Employers in Hawaii have found it necessary to instruct the Filipinos in the ordinary rules of health, to show him how to eat and how to live."[6] One of the club's featured speakers was David Barrows, chairman of the political science department at the University of California at Berkeley, who had previously served as an ethnological surveyor in the Philippines (see chapter 1). Barrows declared that the Filipino's "low standard of life" made him prone to "intestinal parasitism . . . including hookworm, amoebiasis, tuberculosis, venereal diseases," asserting that this susceptibility was "undeniable." He warned that Filipinos were carriers "of infectious diseases," a condition that exacerbated the "complexities of our problems of health and sanitation."[7] Vaughn McCaughey, another club associate, used his presentation to condemn the swarms of "human stuff" that the Philippines was sending to the United States. The Filipinos that had settled on the West Coast, according to McCaughey, were drawn from the worst segments of the Philippine population and could not be assimilated into American institutions because of their mental and physical inferiority. These charges were seconded by R. W. Kearney, attorney chief of the California Division of Sanitation and Housing, whose agency had conducted an inquiry into the living conditions of the state's agricultural workers. Kearney told the club's audience that Filipino residences were incubators of disease, alleging that his investigators had discovered 125 Filipinos living in a small house meant to accommodate a family of four. This high housing density was attributed to the unwillingness of Filipinos to adapt to modern habits of healthy living.[8]

The American Federation of Labor (AFL) also weighed in on the putative health menace posed by Filipino immigrants. An article published in the *American Federationist* claimed that Filipinos contracted deadly diseases on passenger ships originating in Asia and carried dangerous foreign viruses with them across the Pacific Ocean. According to the AFL, "scores" of Filipinos had been afflicted with "spinal meningitis and other diseases" en route to the United States.[9] The "meningitis menace" was said to have originated in the "Orient," although the exact source location was unclear. Newspaper accounts reported that a significant number of Filipinos recruited to work on sugar plantations in Hawaii had been stricken by the disease. American medical officials conducted an investigation of the outbreak and concluded that the disease had not originated in the Philippines but was likely contracted as a result of unsanitary conditions on commercial liners that brought Filipinos to the United States. They had likely contracted the infection while traveling in the steerage sections of passenger ships after stopping at ports in China and Japan. The fact that large numbers of the newcomers worked in agriculture and in the service sector made the hygiene issue a recurring theme among exclusionists, even though no cases of disease outbreaks among the white population were ever attributed to the presence of Filipinos.[10]

Dr. William Hobdy, who served as a public health official and chief quarantine officer in Hawaii, contributed to the anti-Filipino rancor at a public health forum in San Francisco in 1928:

> When transplanted from their native islands, the Filipinos commonly develop tuberculosis. Pneumonia is also common; sometimes twenty Filipinos will die of pneumonia en route from the Philippine Islands to the Hawaiian Islands. . . . The Filipinos of both sexes smoke. The women smoke cigars and even small children of three years of age are seen toddling around smoking cigars as long as their forearm. . . . The typical Filipino child is short of stature, underweight, malnourished, bandy-shanked and afflicted with intestinal parasites. I can hardly conceive of my son or daughter or any of my grandchildren intermarrying with these people. I believe that they should be excluded from this country.[11]

Officials from the California State Board of Health bolstered claims that the Filipino population on the West Coast represented a ticking time bomb for municipal authorities. According to one California State Board of Health official, the Filipinos "constitute one of our worst problems at the present time," a predicament exacerbated by the fact that many of them were "working as food handlers, either working in fields with fresh fruits or vegetables or working in kitchens and restaurants."[12] Edythe Thompson of the California Bureau of Tuberculosis added to the chorus of public health figures calling for exclusion:

> As in many of the other general hospitals, the beds on the tuberculosis service were nearly all filled with Filipinos. These people seem to have more complications than other races. Rarely do I see a Filipino with just a pulmonary involvement. They require very much more nursing than a white

patient, and since they are so often disturbed mentally . . . it makes life very miserable for white patients around them.[13]

California authorities took an increasingly active role in lobbying the federal government to take action on the Filipino issue. With the backing of the state board of health, Thompson submitted a resolution to Congress calling for the exclusion and repatriation of Filipinos, citing the likelihood that they would become "public charges" of local relief agencies. The resolution emphasized that Filipinos' susceptibility to tuberculosis and other diseases constituted a looming governmental burden since "these people must occupy beds in county hospitals and be cared for at public expense." To assist with their removal, California authorities suggested that federal immigration officials use American military transports to deport "these unfortunate dependent people" back to the Philippines "at the earliest possible moment."[14] The prospect that American taxpayers might be burdened with providing for the welfare of these parasitic immigrants struck a chord during the late 1920s and early 1930s, when public resources were already stretched thin.

D. W. Rohrback, an influential judge in Northern California and a leading figure in the anti-Filipino movement on the West Coast, conducted a series of interviews with local newspapers during January 1930 highlighting the health dangers presented by Filipinos on the West Coast. He argued that the Filipinos'

customs, habits, and standard of living are dangerous to our social condition. . . . Unrestricted immigration [of Filipinos] is viewed with alarm both from a moral and sanitary standpoint, while constituting a menace to white labor. . . . We adopt such methods and means to prevent further immigration of this class of people.[15]

In a widely publicized interview published a few weeks later, Rohrback criticized the newcomers for their "clannish, low standard mode of housing and feeding," in which "fifteen Filipinos will live in a room or two . . . contenting themselves with squatting on the floors and eating fish and rice." He added that the "unsanitary living habits" of the Filipino worker rendered him a "disease carrier" and "spreader of meningitis germs among the products he handles causing innocent persons to suffer through their consumption."[16] Highlighting the health risks of eating fruits and vegetables harvested by Filipinos was part of a conscious strategy to pressure the agricultural industry to employ white labor exclusively. Characterizations of Filipinos as a public

health menace were part of a larger campaign aimed at raising public apprehension about the dangers of unrestricted immigration. Nativist spokesmen
amplified anxieties about disease, portraying Filipinos as unhygienic and
sickly and as posing a risk to the white population.

Even more disconcerting than the prospect of living in the same community as the new arrivals or consuming products handled by "Orientals" was
the prospect of intimate physical or sexual contact between whites and Filipinos. Most immigrants from the Philippines had grown up under a political and educational system designed by Americans, a system that fostered
principles of social equality and individual rights. When Filipino immigrants
tried to exercise these rights and freedoms in the United States, however,
they discovered a wide gulf between rhetoric and reality.

The "Boy Crisis"

No other dimension of the "Filipino problem" received more attention than
Filipinos' so-called "social maladjustment." This term was employed by soci-
ologists and social reformers on the West Coast in the 1920s to describe the
failure of Filipinos to "adjust" to norms of racial subordination and social
distance in American society. Filipino men were characterized as having a
pathological attraction to white women that could not be contained by conventional modes of enforcement.[17] Antimiscegenation laws, as discussed in
the preceding chapter, were generally ineffective and were more of a nuisance than a comprehensive legal deterrent. Statutory prohibitions on intermarriage, moreover, did nothing to prevent dating and casual sexual relationships, a fact that frustrated reformers.[18]

Efforts to frame interracial relationships between Filipinos and whites as
an urgent social problem revolved around three key themes: moral degeneracy, eugenic decline, and racial rescue. Interracial intimacy was characterized as a type of high-stakes deviance that undermined the sanctity of the
white family. White women who engaged in sexual relations with Filipinos
were portrayed either as young girls preyed upon by dark-skinned predators
or as low-class fallen women who placed personal aggrandizement or sexual
gratification ahead of community standards of decency. One challenge faced
by nativists seeking to exploit this issue was explaining why white women
were so attracted to Filipinos in the first place. The most common explanation held that Filipinos appealed to white women through a false front of
flashy attire and ostentatious behavior that belied their true status as uneducated menial laborers. They spent lavishly on consumer goods such as styl-

ish clothing and sporty automobiles that conned white women into thinking they were socializing with "made men" instead of working-class outsiders. White women usually realized too late that these showy displays were a ruse to win their affections, eventually discovering that these men were con artists looking to take advantage of them. This sentiment was articulated by San Francisco municipal court judge George Steiger, who described the "typical" Filipino as a public nuisance "walk[ing] our streets clad in the extreme loud pearl-buttoned suits, wearing spats, light hats, brightly colored ties, who follow our high school girls" around the city, seducing them and living off the earnings of their white paramours.[19]

Interracial relationships were also said to produce inferior hybrid offspring that degraded the integrity of the white community. By the late 1920s, the American eugenics movement was in full swing, and its cautionary claims about white racial decline attracted serious attention from social reformers. Nativists stoked fears about blood contamination and downward mobility for whites who traversed the color line. This problem was depicted as having potential consequences for the larger community because Filipinos often mixed socially with poor white women, whose genetic credentials were already suspect. Such pairings posed a risk to American society insofar as eugenic theory claimed that the progeny of mixed-race couples inherited the worst traits of both parents, making the children more likely to become public charges or juvenile delinquents.

Nativists frequently portrayed sexual relationships between Filipinos and whites as an invitation to violence and conflict because of white men's inherent antipathy to perceived trespasses of white womanhood by dark-skinned suitors. White women who crossed the color line were in dire need of racial rescue, and forceful measures were often required to enforce social distance. This argument both explained and rationalized white vigilantism, framing anti-Filipino racism as a natural and inevitable response to violations of white racial honor. The sexual brazenness and public swagger of Filipino men was seen as a challenge to the social order, a threat that if left unchecked, might embolden other men of color to defy racial conventions. Exclusionists cited a series of violent assaults and race riots targeting Filipinos during the late 1920s and early 1930s as evidence that they had aroused "race feeling" among whites, leading to a wave of violent confrontations.

Nativists and social reformers alike recognized that the uneven sex ratio in the Filipino American population, in which men far outnumbered women, was a key source of the "Filipino problem." Some observers even expressed empathy for the predicament of young Filipino men who found themselves in a new social milieu with a different set of cultural rules than their home society. Unlike previous Asian immigrant populations, Filipinos displayed a peculiar urge to mix socially with whites. As one observer noted, "The Japs and Chinese have never mixed with 'white women' to any extent, . . . not to the extent that the Filipino does anyway."[20] This behavior was diagnosed as a distinctive racial pathology among the Filipino population, characterized by a reckless attraction to white women and a defiant attitude toward social conventions. Filipinos were also described as socially adventurous, with a love for public spectacle and indulgence. Claims makers argued that Filipinos possessed an insatiable sexual passion that gave rise to a host of deviant practices, including criminality and moral turpitude. For "experts" testifying at the Commonwealth Club's forum the race-mixing issue was a primary concern, and on Filipino immigration, participants felt that they had a duty to speak "frankly" and "fairly" about the sensitive topic, even though the task was not a pleasant one. Speakers repeatedly alluded to troubling "moral conditions" observed in western communities with large Filipino populations. Investigators dispatched by the organization discovered instances in which "members of the white races [we]re living illicitly with Filipinos," a phenomenon that in some instances had led to intermarriage.[21] Investigators noted that Filipinos did not seem content to limit their social circles to other residents of segregated Chinatowns or Asian enclaves, remarking that Filipinos were unusual in that they did "not desire the company of the Japanese or Chinese" but instead "desire[d] the society of whites."[22]

This unwillingness of Filipinos to abide by the color line was repeatedly portrayed as a source of conflict that stirred up the passions of white men unaccustomed to competing with other groups for the affections of white women. Judge D. W. Rohrback of Watsonville highlighted this issue, arguing that "the American people will find in [the Filipinos] a problem they did not find with the negro, who usually understood how to act, but these Filipinos feel they have the perfect right to mingle with white people and even to intermarry and feel resentful if they are denied that right."[23] Popular media accounts of the issue repeated unsubstantiated claims made by nativist leaders that Filipinos had "declared preference" for blond women. This was taken as evidence of Filipinos' covetous attraction to their racial "betters" since blond hair served as a powerful symbol of white racial purity. Some of these problems were blamed on their inability to adapt to the fast-paced modern life they encountered in American society. The Reverend John F. Wilson remarked that Filipinos were "attracted by vice" but were also in some ways unwitting victims of American consumer culture: "The glitter and glare of this great Western life have simply overwhelmed him. He has found it is possible to align himself with white girls here and there for small sums of money."[24] The *Los Angeles Times* offered a similar observation a few months later, noting that Filipinos were "bewildered by the broad freedom" they experienced in the United States. Unable to handle their newfound autonomy, they drifted into a state of cultural "intoxication" that led them into ill-advised associations with white women in a desperate attempt to gain social footing.[25] White women who reciprocated Filipinos' affections were also subject to public scrutiny. Some of these women were dismissed as youthful victims of their own adolescent whims—too immature and naive to understand the consequences of their actions. Others, such as the so-called taxi-dance girls, were seen as morally suspect, crossing the racial Rubicon for personal profit or to satisfy their deviant sexual desires.

In 1930, the U.S. National Committee on Law Observance published a national report on crime trends, focusing on the delinquent tendencies of America's foreign-born population. The report asserted that Filipinos' sexual deviancy often led them into a life of crime as they relentlessly pursued the affections of white women. According to this argument, Filipino men needed to put on airs (e.g., fancy clothes, a nice car) and shower white women with expensive gifts to gain their attention. Paying for these things required money that working-class Filipinos did not have, so they eventually turned to crime to pay for their profligate lifestyle. Filipinos, moreover, often competed with one another for the affections of white women, leading to fights and moral-order crimes. The Committee on Law Observance's report featured anonymous quotes from law-enforcement officials in Seattle to demonstrate the problem of Filipino criminality in western cities. One Seattle police officer declared that "the Filipino is bad; by nature he is a criminal. Their crimes are violent in nature. . . . In addition they intermingle with white girls more especially with prostitutes." A second officer added that Filipinos are "our great menace" and are "all criminally minded," a problem amplified by the fact that they are "great chasers of white women." A criminal court judge from Seattle provided an even more disturbing account of Filipino criminality, remarking that the newcomers were overrepresented in the city's crime blotter because of their deviant sociality. Their crimes were characterized as unusually vicious: "they slash, cut or stab at the least provocation," because, according to the judge, they arrived from the Philippines "untamed." The problem was again linked to crossings of the color line; Filipinos dressed themselves in the latest fashionable attire, projecting a "natty appearance" that attracted women of "various low types" including uneducated white women. The judge added that there was not a single Filipino in the United States who was not a "potential criminal."[26]

Defining Deviance

Sensational news stories about Filipino men socializing with white women were used by exclusionists to mobilize support for their campaign, believing that the issue of race mixing would touch a nerve with the white community. Nativist leaders such as D. W Rohrback, Paul Scharrenberg, and V. S. McClatchy were regularly featured in newspaper stories about Filipinos, and they used these media to transmit alarmist messages about interracial sex and marriage. These claims makers were recognized as legitimate spokesmen for the public interest and were afforded privileged access to the media and to government officials. They used their cultural authority to define Filipinos as a problem population and to bolster their own position as guardians of the social order. Two high-profile incidents in 1929 and early 1930 dramatize how public narratives of Filipinos as a sexual threat were constructed and disseminated.

The criminal case of a young immigrant named Perfecto Bandalan received sensational media coverage in Northern California in the late 1920s and was held up by claims makers as a representative example of the Filipino "boy crisis." In December 1929, police in the town of Watsonville conducted a late-night raid at a local Filipino boardinghouse. They discovered two partially clad white girls, Esther and Bertha Schmick, ages sixteen and eleven, asleep in a room with the twenty-five-year-old Filipino Perfecto Bandalan, who was quickly taken into custody. Front-page coverage of the case in the local media reverberated throughout the community, with many people assuming that the two young girls were being held against their will by a Filipino predator. News accounts of the case were marked by innuendo and rumor, claiming that the police had uncovered "shocking" conditions at the scene of the alleged crime. Police officers testified that when they conducted their raid at one-thirty in the morning, "the two young girls and their Filipino companion were only partially dressed, the room lights were not burning and 'lots of noise' was required to arouse them."[27] News accounts of the incident hinted that some nefarious activity had taken place in the darkness of the bedroom, though an equally plausible explanation was that the three were sound asleep in their night clothes at that late hour. Bandalan was immediately charged with "contributing to the delinquency of a minor," and police officials promised that other "serious girl charges" were being investigated.

Coverage of the trial emphasized the lurid nature of the alleged crime, even though the details of the actual events were left purposely vague. The *Salinas Index Journal* reported that the criminal complaint against Bandalan contained shocking revelations "which only few people would even dare visualize," adding suggestively that the immoral acts committed by the defendant were "of an unprintable nature."[28] The *Watsonville Evening Pajaronian* offered a similar analysis, reporting, "some of the things brought out in the trial were not only unprintable but revolting."[29] Such characterizations allowed the reader to let his or her imagination run wild as to what sexual transgressions had occurred between the "oriental" and the white girl. The judge in the Bandalan case set an unusually high bail of seventy-five hundred dollars for the defendant, to reassure the community that this dangerous villain would not be allowed to roam the streets while he awaited trial. The Schmick sisters were also taken into custody by the juvenile court, so medical authorities could conduct a thorough physical examination to see if "the Filipino" had "harmed" them. District attorney Albert Warth assured outraged citizens that his office would prosecute Bandalan to the fullest extent of the law. He acknowledged that there were "a lot of bad rumors about the affair, and if they are true, the consequences will be severe. We won't stop at half measures."[30]

The case, however, soon took some strange twists and turns, especially when it emerged that Bandalan was actually engaged to Esther, the older of the two girls, with her mother's blessing. It was also revealed that the younger girl was staying with Bandalan and Esther at the mother's request because the family was destitute and could not care for her. A prominent front-page photograph of the interracial couple smiling and embracing one another was published in two local newspapers. The provocative snapshot was accompanied by a caption describing the affair as the "strange case of a white girl in love with a Filipino . . . [and] a mother who sanctions her desire to wed the oriental."[31] Esther confirmed to a local paper that her relationship with Bandalan was indeed consensual: "Yes, I love him and I'll marry him." And a reporter visiting the Schmick family residence observed that the home's walls were "lined with photos of the 16-year-old girl and her dark-skinned sweetheart," corroborating that the girl's mother embraced the relationship.[32] Mrs. Schmick pleaded for Perfecto's release from jail, claiming that "he was a good boy" who loved her daughter and treated the whole family well. This unconventional attitude about her daughter's interracial relationship seemed to contrast with that of the girls' father, Alex Schmick, who it was soon revealed had filed the initial police complaint against Bandalan that led to his arrest. Mr. Schmick claimed that he filed the police report after becoming outraged by his daughter's interracial associations. Yet his seemingly righteous motives in the affair soon came under scrutiny when his wife dropped a bombshell at a court hearing, declaring that her husband had in fact offered to "sell the girl to the oriental" for five hundred dollars and had only called the police when he did not receive his payoff.

Authorities had their hands full with the various charges and counter-charges that were leveled during the court hearings. Alex Schmick offered an implausible defense of his role in the affair. He admitted that he had broached the idea of a monetary payment from Bandalan when he had asked for Esther's hand in marriage, requesting "$1,000 to take care of the consequences" (five hundred for him and five hundred for his wife). He told police, however, that his demand for compensation had been misunderstood, suggesting that he made the monetary request in jest. His wife disputed this statement, noting that Perfecto and Esther had actually been dating for some time and that her husband "squealed" to the police only after becoming frustrated because "the Filipino would not buy the girl for $500."[33] Mr. Schmick later turned this charge around on his wife, claiming that it was she who wanted money so she could "live on easy street." Both parents apparently believed that Perfecto had wealthy parents in the Philippines who would provide money to the family and help the couple "build a fine house" after the wedding.[34]

The prosecution of the case was made even more difficult by Bandalan's unwillingness to cooperate with authorities. Police repeatedly questioned him about whether he had agreed to "buy" the girl from Mr. Schmick. His response that "he didn't know" was interpreted by authorities as evidence of his evasiveness. Bandalan's response was not surprising, though, since he was interrogated without legal counsel and likely believed the payment demanded by the family to be some sort of connubial custom. Police investigators were also stunned by disclosures that Esther Schmick confessed to past involvement with other Filipino boyfriends. She admitted under questioning to "having had several Filipino sweethearts in the past—her first one at the age of 15."[35]

News that Esther had been "keeping company" with "Orientals" for over a year, with her parents' knowledge, painted a troubling picture of a white family gone awry. The publicity surrounding the case served as a warning to respectable citizens about the dangers of Filipino settlement. After all, their daughters might face a similar fate, if they did not properly socialize their children about the inviolability of the color line in American life. Some of the harshest criticism was aimed at Esther's parents, whose permissive attitudes about interracial associations were deemed contemptible. Mrs. Schmick admitted to having regularly accompanied the couple on automobile rides to attend social events. Her public approval of the relationship was even more disquieting, and she was condemned in the media for unashamedly "championing the dusky suitor for the hand of her daughter." Alex Schmick did not escape scrutiny either, although he took credit for filing the initial criminal complaint against Bandalan. He ended up facing criminal charges himself a month later, when he was arrested at the county courthouse while attending a hearing for the Bandalan case. He was charged with spousal dereliction for failing to provide "food, clothing and shelter" for his family, including his wife, two daughters, and two young sons who were not involved in the criminal case.[36] Although the criminal charges against both Bandalan and Schmick were relatively minor, their symbolic importance was not. The Bandalan affair was held up as a cautionary tale of a family who had fallen so low that they allowed their daughter to engage in intimate associations with Filipinos. It also served as a reminder about the collective responsibility of all white citizens to remain vigilant in their observation of the color line. Those who did not would suffer the same fate as the Schmick family: public humiliation and ostracism for their moral laxity.

Just a month after the Bandalan case, another incident made headlines in the Watsonville area. A sixteen-year-old girl named Carrie Victorini "disappeared" during the last week of January 1930. She was the daughter of a local rancher, Manuel Victorini, and she had a contentious relationship with her family. Carrie Victorini was reported missing the evening of January 26 after being remonstrated by her parents for "consorting with Filipinos." Initial media reports of the case claimed that the missing girl had been "kidnapped by Filipino laborers." News accounts raised the possibility that she may have subsequently committed suicide after recognizing the shameful nature of her actions.[37] These reports turned out to be false, when it was discovered that Victorini had run away from home to be with her Filipino boyfriend, Carmilo Chavi. Chavi, however, refused to take in the runaway, likely fearing reprisals from her parents or from vigilantes who had been patrolling the area and attacking Filipinos caught with white women.

Though Carrie's whereabouts were unknown, law enforcement officials declared that she was being "held by Filipinos" somewhere in the region.[38] Police launched a "statewide search" for the girl but were stymied by the lack of cooperation from Filipinos and by Carrie's apparent unwillingness to be found. In the absence of concrete leads, investigators theorized that the girl had been secreted away through a clandestine underground network of "oriental" dwellings and boardinghouses in Northern California. Rumors that she was being passed around "from one Filipino bunkhouse to another to prevent her parents from rescuing her" ignited outrage among locals. Carrie was spotted by local rancher Elmer Struve, who found her hanging around in the Filipino quarters at his ranch. He ordered her back home to her parents, but she again slipped back into the company of Filipinos, further frustrating investigators. The idea that the girl was "missing" of her own volition was viewed with skepticism by many in the white community, who preferred to view her as a prisoner of the local "Filipino colony."[39] Police finally discovered her on January 31, 1930, at a hotel in San Jose where she had been staying for a couple days. Police interrogated Carrie, looking for evidence of a kidnapping and demanding the names of those who abetted her escape. Investigators believed that Filipinos had transported her by automobile from Watsonville to San Jose, and they hoped this evidence might be used to criminally charge someone with her disappearance. Carrie repeatedly asserted that she had left of her own will to escape a troubled relationship with her parents. She gave police conflicting stories about how she got to San Jose, initially claiming that she walked the fifty-mile trek and later claiming she got a ride from an unknown individual. Although no one was ever charged in her disappearance, suspicions remained about the complicity of local Filipinos in the incident. Carrie Victorini was returned back to her parents, and her case quickly faded away from the headlines. But the incident added to the public narrative depicting Filipino men as sexual predators who preyed on young white girls.

These two episodes were frequently cited by nativists as evidence of the need for stricter enforcement of lax racial checkpoints. Alarmist messages about Filipino men preying on young white girls struck a powerful chord in white communities in the West that were experiencing rapid cultural transformation and economic uncertainty. Moral panics about sexual predators had long been used in the South as a political bludgeon against African Americans, whose civil rights claims were dismissed as a front for their real desire—unfettered access to white women. The public discourse surrounding the Bandalan and Victorini episodes played on these same anxieties, allowing nativist leaders to put their own spin on the well-worn southern defense of the color line by asking white Californians, "Do you want your daughter to marry a Filipino?"

Gateways to Miscegenation

The proliferation of taxi-dance halls on the West Coast during the 1920s was another issue that drew critical attention from nativist leaders, since many of these establishments permitted interracial dancing. These venues were denounced by claims makers as sites of moral turpitude and sexual deviancy that facilitated Filipino infiltration into white society. The dance halls were characterized as analogous to brothels, places where Filipino men paid money for intimate contact with white women at private clubs hidden from public scrutiny. The popularity of these establishments reinforced the common perception of Filipino men as morally suspect, driven by an unquenchable sexual desire for white women. David Barrows declared that their "vices are almost entirely based on sexual passion." This pathology was "inordinately strong" among the Filipinos and could not be restrained by individual willpower. For Barrows, Filipinos remained undercivilized despite decades of corrective colonialism in the islands. This lack of self-control led the Filipino male to the "lowest and least fortunate associations, . . . frequent[ing] the poorest quarters of our towns, . . . spend[ing] the residue of his savings in brothels and dance halls, which in spite of our laws, exist to minister to his lower nature."[40] The women who worked at the venues were also suspect, portrayed as disreputable individuals or as prostitutes who rented their bodies to the highest bidder, regardless of race. Moral guardians publicly rebuked taxi dancers and dance-club owners, who endangered white hegemony by facilitating miscegenous encounters in spite of community antipathy toward such interactions. White dancers and proprietors were held up as the public face of racial infidelity, and subjected to voluble public scorn. As breeding grounds for interracial contact and deviant sexuality, dance halls represented a dangerous breach—one that required remedial intervention from concerned community leaders on behalf of the common good.[41]

The generalized aversion to interracial intimacy in American society was bolstered during this period by the rise of the eugenics movement, which grafted the language of science onto popular prejudice. Since Filipinos were widely considered to be of inferior racial stock, their liaisons with white women evoked fears of social degeneration.[42] Amalgamation between Filipinos and whites was said to be particularly troubling since such couplings invariably combined the worst elements of both populations. According to Commonwealth Club associate Vaughn McCaughey, the "eugenic" problem on the West Coast was exacerbated by the "heavy influx of the very lowest grade of Filipino labor." This low-grade population inevitably found its way to the vice worlds of American cities, where they mixed with low-class white women at taxi-dance halls. These commercial venues fostered a "type of race mingling which [was] highly undesirable," between "promiscuous hordes . . . who are at the social bottom." Since the taxi dances purportedly encouraged illicit sexual relations outside marriage, they undermined antimiscegenation laws aimed at preventing amalgamation. The prospect of interracial children produced by Filipino-white relationships raised another set of concerns, since they involved "hybridizing at the bottom, often under the most wretched of circumstances," between "lower racial stocks."[43] The main problem, according to Commonwealth Club officer Frederick Duhring, was blood contamination. He warned that Filipino-white relationships tended to lower "the blood strain" and therefore depressed the general "character" and "health" of the white population. Filipinos had to be segregated, he argued, because "we already have enough people in this country who are pulling us down."[44]

C. M. Goethe, an influential West Coast nativist who led and financed the California Joint Immigration Commission, repeatedly spoke out in public forums on the dangers of amalgamation. Goethe argued that miscegenation was the key rationale for restricting Filipino immigration:

> Filipinos are vain, unreliable and of a rather low mentality, since labor agents in the [Philippine] islands tend to select those of a lower mentality as being more docile. . . . These men are primitive jungle folk and their primitive moral code accentuates the race problem. . . . The Filipino tends to interbreed with near moron white girls. The resulting hybrid is almost invariably undesirable. The ever increasing brood of children of Filipino Coolie fathers and low grade white mothers may in time constitute a serious social burden. . . . Primitive island folk such as Filipinos do not hesitate to have nine children, while parents of white stock find educating three a problem of finance. Filipinos, at the theoretical rate of nine children to the family, will have 729 great-grandchildren as against the white parent's twenty-seven.

He concluded, "Immediate exclusion is tragically necessary to protect our American seed stocks."[45]

The proliferation of commercial leisure establishments during the 1920s offered a unique challenge for nativist leaders, who had focused much of their previous energy on ratcheting up enforcement of antimiscegenation laws in western states. Prohibitions on interracial marriage, however, did not stop the informal race mixing that occurred at private venues such as taxi-dance halls that catered to Filipino men, and as a result, these types of clubs came under increasing scrutiny from nativists and social reformers.

The War on Dance Halls

Taxi-dance halls emerged on the West Coast in the early decades of the twentieth century and reached their peak popularity during the 1920s and 1930s. They were classified as "closed" clubs, which meant that entry was restricted to female employees and men who were screened for admission at the door. This type of organization allowed for greater regulation of the female entertainers, who interacted with club patrons and offered a more respectable alternative to brothels and other vice-world establishments. It also allowed proprietors of interracial clubs to restrict the entry of white men who might initiate violence. Social reformers and civic leaders denounced dance halls as sites of moral degeneracy because they promoted "illicit" intimacy between young unmarried partners. Though only a small percentage of the clubs allowed mixed-race dancing, these establishments received an inordinate amount of attention. A number of western cities passed ordinances outlawing taxi clubs, and other communities increased levels of police surveillance of dance-hall activities to keep an eye out for potential racial contraventions.

The popular appeal of taxi-dance halls was problematic for moral entrepreneurs since these establishments brought together unmarried men and women in close intimate contact behind closed doors. Social reformers and civic leaders looked at the clubs as gateway institutions that led to more unwholesome sexual behaviors. The assertive social and courting practices of Filipinos made the taxi-dance establishments even more of a concern, since the venues provided a private space for interracial socializing outside the watchful eye of authorities. Not surprisingly, the nightclubs fostered resentment among white men who considered white women to be their exclusive sexual property. Social reformers spent significant resources investigating the proliferation of taxi-dance halls, and their findings were often troubling. The scholarly community also took an interest in these leisure establishments, focusing on the clubs as incubators of deviant behavior and modern youth culture. A sociologist studying taxi-dance halls in one West Coast city offered a typical illustration of this social-problems approach to the phenomenon. During his fieldwork, he observed "hoodlums and women . . . of a lower type" dancing as "vulgarly and obscenely as they wished." Young attendees were "stimulated by primitive music, the dim lights, [and] the hot dance air," and young women were encouraged to "seek sex expressions in vulgar forms" with any man who was willing to pay.[46]

Another study, conducted by the Delinquency Unit of the U.S. Children's Bureau in 1932, focused on the "social hygiene" problems raised by Filipino interactions with white women. The report stated that the "excess of males" among the Filipino population led them to seek companionship across the color line, which produced a backlash from the white community. The report acknowledged that "race prejudice makes it quite impossible for the young Filipino to mingle socially on equal footing with young white boys and girls of his own class." Moreover, most "respectable places of amusement" frequented by whites were off-limits to nonwhites. This led Filipinos to seek out female companionship in less savory places such as dance halls, which in turn fostered "unwholesome" encounters with white women of low social standing at mixed-race clubs. The Delinquency Unit's report noted that it was only the "less respectable, hardened type of taxi dancer that signs up for work in a hall catering to men of another race," which again raised the prospect of amalgamation among the lowest elements of the population. Mixed-race dance halls were characterized as havens for prostitution, and the young women who were lured to work in these establishments were invariably drawn to the criminal underworld. The dance halls, at their worst, led to full-fledged relationships between Filipinos and whites, with "children springing from the matings." The fallen women who entered into miscegenous unions inevitably brought the woman's whole family into disrepute, since "public disapproval [fell] so heavily on any white girl who dares accept a Filipino as a social equal." The bureau's report ended with an entreaty to law-enforcement officials and social-reform agencies to redouble their efforts to regulate or reform taxi-dance halls across the country.[47]

Campaigns to close down the dance halls that catered to Filipinos emerged in a number of West Coast cities. One of the earliest took place in 1925 in San Diego, where law-enforcement officials and civic leaders targeted a dance hall frequented by Filipinos. One newspaper headline exclaimed that city officials had finally declared "war" on the city's dance halls.[48] Police Judge J. Chambers used a public hearing held at San Diego City Hall to condemn mixed-race venues. He used "harsh terms" to describe a cluster of clubs in the lower end of town frequented by Asian immigrants. The judge accused dance-hall promoters of "trying to re-create a segregated district like the ancient 'Stingaree,'" a reference to the nickname of the former Chinatown district in San Diego. Judge Chambers denounced the venues as "illicit resorts," adding that "a virtuous girl who accepts employment in such places becomes a social outcast in within thirty days." A taxi-dance establishment run by a Filipino named David Gilito was singled out by the judge for surreptitiously evading a city ordinance prohibiting mixed-race dance clubs. Gilito's venue, like many others catering to Filipinos, reclassified the female employees as "teachers" rather than taxi dancers, a change in status that exempted them from the discriminatory law. Judge Chambers dismissed this legal sleight of hand and instructed San Diego's chief of police to "start making arrests and bringing the girls into [his] courtroom," where he could evaluate whether the girls were really dance "teachers" or "merely forbidden hired girls."[49]

A similar campaign followed a few years later in Oakland, California. Complaints about a proliferation of Filipino dance halls led Oakland officials to adopt a citywide ban on interracial dancing. A number of clubs skirted the rules and reopened as dance training schools, with white instructors again serving as partners for Filipino men. Local officials launched an investigation of the dance establishments, looking for evidence of moral-order violations. An undercover sting carried out by the police department and public health commissioner found numerous cases in which clubs seemed to be violating the spirit of the law. In one instance, investigators "found an American girl dancing with Filipinos in a hall at Forty-Seventh Street and Shattuck Avenue." Police padlocked the club, and a young woman found working there was taken into custody. Arresting officers informed the malefactor that she was in violation of a local ordinance banning "mixed color dancing." The woman, however, claimed exemption from the law because she was "half Filipino," an identity she adopted based on the fact that "she was married to a man of that race." Police investigators rejected her unusual identity claims, and the club's permit was revoked.[50] Efforts to clamp down on mixed-race clubs in Oakland proved more difficult than expected, as proprietors cleverly reclassified their businesses as dance academies to circumvent the city's prohibition on taxi-dance establishments.

Pressure from civic and reform groups led Oakland city prosecutor Earl Warren to "open war" on the mixed-race dance halls. It was during these years as the Alameda district attorney that Warren earned the law-and-order reputation that bolstered his ascendancy to the governorship of California and then later to the position of chief justice of the U.S. Supreme Court. Warren seized on the dance-hall controversy to curry favor with political powerbrokers from the Oakland Civic Center executive board. He bragged that his office had "closed places in Albany and Alameda which catered to Filipinos and had white girls for dancing partners" and emphasized that his eradication campaign was just getting started.[51] According to Warren, his officers discovered two white girls, Jeanette and Roma Paris, working at a club called Maryland Dance Academy on San Pablo Avenue. This finding prompted Warren to initiate a grand-jury investigation of dance-hall conditions throughout Alameda County. Efforts to enact a blanket closure of all the city's dance halls failed, since many of the clubs were law abiding and did not allow mixed-race dancing. In lieu of a citywide ban on dance halls, Warren promised vigilant enforcement of ordinances barring the operation of mixed-race establishments. This mandate would be aided by "rigid supervision" of all club proprietors as well as interviews with the female employees about their "moral character," before the clubs would be allowed to operate legally within the city limits.[52]

The crusade against taxi-dance halls also picked up steam in Southern California in the late 1920s. Police closed down a dance hall in the agricultural town of Ontario after a police sting discovered that white girls were being "rented out to Filipinos" for ten cents per dance. Police officials declared the club a "menace to the youth of the community" and placed proprietor A. C. Ballard in jail.[53] A few months later, a dance hall was closed down in Santa Barbara County after authorities declared its mixed-race entertainment "immoral and improper and not in the best interests of the community."[54] Publicity surrounding the proliferation of taxi-dance establishments in Los Angeles during the summer of 1929 led civic leaders to call for a mass closure of all such places of business as part of an effort to clamp down on the city's vice trade. The Los Angeles Police Commission launched an investigation into conditions at the dance halls and issued a report stating that its officers had "found Caucasians and Asians intermingling and creating conditions against the moral welfare of the city."[55] The Police Commission recommended closing all the city's taxi-dance establishments, but it faced opposition from club operators, who argued that it was unfair to shut down all dance halls based on the activities of the few disreputable venues. A compromise was reached allowing for stricter regulation of the taxi clubs from city officials. Under the new rules, all girls employed at the dance halls had to be fingerprinted by police and were subject to regular checkups by authorities. The city attorney's office ruled that Los Angeles's ban on "the mingling of races" at dance halls was legally binding and enforceable by police, so concerns about the issue were allayed for the time being.[56]

The issue flared up again a few months later, when city investigators looked into a Filipino dance hall known as the Lyceum Club, at 231 South Spring Street. When undercover police agents tried to gain entrance to the venue, they were assaulted by Filipino patrons and thrown out of the club. The case was delayed for a few months when charges of corruption and payoffs to investigators by club owners came to light, throwing the whole case into question. Los Angeles mayor John Porter and chief of police Roy Steckel took up the issue in earnest, lobbying the city council to adopt a new ordinance shutting down all the city's dance halls. Chief Steckel testified before the council that his office had received scores of complaints about the "vice conditions in which these halls are implicated, . . . particularly in reference to Filipinos," adding that he believed it "advisable to close the taxi halls entirely."[57] Mayor Porter also testified before the council, decrying the problem of "girls dancing with Filipinos" at the proceedings. Objection to mixed-race dancing by the arch-conservative Porter was not surprising considering his checkered political pedigree. He had been a Ku Klux Klan leader in San Diego before moving to Los Angeles and had accepted the KKK's endorsement when he ran for mayor in 1928.[58] The efforts of Porter and Steckel again ran into opposition from the city's dance-hall proprietors, most of whom did not allow mixed-race dancing. These business operators claimed that it was unfair to shut down all the clubs because of the actions of a few bad apples and argued furthermore that closing their establishments would throw a thousand women in the city out of work. Filipino organizations in Los Angeles also raised their voices in protest, condemning the racially charged tone of the anti-dance-hall campaign.[59] City officials eventually decided not to enact a total ban on dance halls but did authorize tighter surveillance of the clubs. The council passed an ordinance mandating that female dancers register with the city's crime prevention unit and fill out identification cards to keep track of their activities. City officials also declared that any taxi dancers "found living with men without being married . . . shall be discharged as dancers and not permitted to work in any other halls in the city."[60]

Nativists and social reformers had placed the "problem" of the taxi-dance halls on the public agenda, fueling moral panics about vice and interracial sexuality. Efforts by officials to close down or regulate mixed-race clubs were often stymied by the ingenuity of owners, employees, and customers. While the anti-taxi-dance campaign caused headaches for taxi-hall operators, they repeatedly found ways to circumvent regulation from social-control agencies. Whether by reclassifying their establishments as dance academies or by locating their clubs just outside the city limits, beyond the reach of municipal authorities, enterprising proprietors and their eager patrons found ways to subvert the color line. Frustration with the ineffectiveness of state officials in solving the dance-hall issue led to a series of violent confrontations, as private citizens turned to popular direct action to enforce racial boundaries.

White Riots

By the late 1920s, the debate over Filipino immigration reached a fever pitch on the West Coast. Newspapers across the region featured stories depicting increasing levels of hostility directed toward the Filipino community. Lurid media accounts detailing Filipino interactions with white women struck a discordant note with white workers already experiencing anxiety about competition with the newcomers in the labor market. Filipino associations with white women continued to attract public attention despite efforts to clamp down on interracial marriage and gateway institutions such as taxi-dance halls. The failure of the federal government to impede the flood of cheap labor across the nation's borders or to prevent Filipinos from mixing socially with white women led local citizens to take the law into their own hands, often turning to vigilante justice to punish perceived malefactors.

The earliest recorded anti-Filipino race riot occurred in Yakima, Washington, in 1927. Tensions had been building for some time over the employment of Filipinos in the harvest of hops, apples, cherries, and potatoes in the rich agricultural region of central Washington State. These tensions came to a boiling point in November 1927, when white mobs initiated a campaign to "deport" local Filipinos from the Yakima Valley. Headlines in the local newspaper described the troubling situation: "Gang Action Climaxes Weeks of Growing Ire against Imported Laborers in Competition with White Men: Improper Relations with Girls and Women Aggravates Anger of Townsmen."[61] Large armed mobs of men "swarmed" into the town of Toppenish and attacked Filipino laborers for two successive days. On the first night of rioting, armed gangs of men raided the homes of Filipinos, smashing up furniture and beating the residents with clubs. Filipinos were rounded up by the mob and "told to leave the valley as soon as possible under threat of violent death." They were then "forcibly deported" by the vigilantes, who placed them onto trains leaving for the west side of the state. Those Filipinos that remained in town after the first day of mob action were instructed that "they would be hung if found in the valley after dark."[62]

The riot was sparked by news that the police in the nearby town of Toppenish "had uncovered instances where Filipino men have had improper relations with white women and girls. The Filipinos are also said to have repeatedly bothered white women and girls on the streets of Toppenish despite efforts of the police department."[63] One Toppenish resident expressed the sentiment of the mob: "The Filipino has become a nuisance, with their parading up and down the streets and standing on the corners speaking to white girls. . . . We do not want the [Yakima Indian] Reservation Orientalized."[64] The rioters were eventually subdued by a sheriff's patrol which located a large mob forming outside the neighboring town of Wapato. The members of the agitated gang "were heavily armed and apparently determined to kill every Filipino they found." Sheriff L. D. Luce played down the racial volatility underlying the confrontations, stating that organized vigilantes were simply "young men desirous of excitement." The few Filipinos who remained in town were placed in police custody and put in jails in nearby Sunnyside to protect them from the roaming mobs.[65] A labor official sent to investigate the causes of the riots interviewed the Toppenish police chief and other local residents, who cited the insolent behavior of Filipinos as the primary source of trouble in the region. Police chief William Mann condemned young Filipino immigrants for acquiring "familiarity with white girls and women" through flashy clothing and their talent as musicians. According to Mann, the Filipinos seduced naive young girls with their showmanship, inflaming the girls' sexual passions with their sentimental songs and charismatic swagger. He compared the behavior of Filipinos to that of blacks in the South, suggesting that both groups employed the same cunning techniques to seduce white women. Encroachment across the color line aroused strong race feeling among the local white population, a sentiment captured by one "prominent" Toppenish citizen, who declared, "if I had my way I would declare open season on Filipinos, and there would be no bag limit."[66] Racial animosity in the region gathered momentum in succeeding years, which witnessed regular dynamite attacks on migrant labor camps carried out by nightriders against Yakima Valley farms that hired Filipino labor.

Vigilante violence quickly spread to other parts of the state. In September 1928, in the town of Cashmere, Washington, a gang "150 citizens" surrounded two busloads of Filipino workers who had been contracted by growers to harvest crops at area farms. Mob leaders informed the newcomers that the Cashmere Valley was "not a healthy place" for them to be and instructed them to return to Seattle. The group of "terror stricken" Filipinos were forcibly detained and escorted back over Blewett Pass accompanied by a convoy of the vigilantes. A similar deportation campaign unfolded in the neighboring town of Wenatchee later that same week. The Wenatchee Packing Corporation had hired a small group of Filipinos to work the graveyard shift at its fruit-packing plant. As news of this arrangement spread, Dan Small, the plant's manager, was warned by local residents that he would be subject to reprisals for his "objectionable" and "un-American" actions. A throng of two hundred "irritated white people" stormed the basement of the local Woolworth's store, where the Filipinos were being quartered, and ordered all of them to leave town before the end of the day. Expulsion campaigns carried out by local citizens groups became commonplace in the region for the next few years.[67]

Vigilante initiatives took off in California during this same period. One early incident took place in 1928 in the town of Dinuba, California. Local residents "threatened race war" against Filipinos after a series of brawls outside a number of summer dances sponsored by the town's American Legion affiliate. Filipinos were accused of "forcing unwelcome attentions" on white girls in public places, leading to run-ins with local thugs and police officers. A large group of Filipinos showed up for one of the dances, despite warnings not to attend any more events. They were met by an angry crowd of white youths and fifty armed Legionnaires, who had been deputized by local authorities. Police deputies "herded the Filipinos to the foreign quarter across the tracks" to avoid a confrontation with the mob, but the whites chased them and "challenged Filipinos to cross tracks to fight." Authorities were able to prevent the confrontation from getting out of hand but condemned the local Filipinos, who they maintained were responsible for provoking local whites with their defiant behavior. The root of the problem, according to one local journalist, was that Filipinos insisted on "their rights to attend dances and escort white girls about the city."[68]

Antagonism toward Filipinos took a more volatile turn in the nearby town of Exeter in 1929 when a group of laborers was contracted to work the local grape and fig harvest. Concern about Filipino interactions with local women had been festering for over a year and had resulted in intermittent confrontations between the Filipinos and local whites. Harassment of Filipinos on the streets of Exeter became commonplace during the summer months and got more intense during the fall harvest. They were routinely assaulted and shoved off sidewalks and taunted with racial slurs by white residents. At a local carnival, roving bands of white hoodlums threw projectiles at Filipinos who were seen talking to white women. The situation grew worse when a local white man, Adolph Borgman, and two friends attacked a Filipino who they claimed had insulted a white woman in their company. The Filipino slashed his assailants in self-defense, and Borgman was sent to the local hospital. News of the episode spread quickly, and three separate mobs, made up of one hundred to three hundred men "bent on revenge," were organized in town. They proceeded to five local ranches that hired Filipinos, and attacked any they found with clubs and rocks, forcing two hundred farmworkers to flee the district. The mobs set fire to barns and bunkhouses at two local farms, causing serious property damage. One local newspaper stated that the "chief friction between the races" was the "insistence by Filipinos that they be treated as equals by white girls."[69] This behavior exacerbated hostility that already existed in the community over competition in the agricultural labor market, especially in the region's burgeoning lettuce industry.

The spread of racial violence in the region led the *Watsonville Evening Pajaronian* editorial page to call on the federal government to grant the Philippines its independence, believing that such a move would prevent further

Filipino immigration to the United States. The editorial also implored Congress to take up the issue of "what can be done about sending back to Manila a large proportion of the natives that are now on this coast." Claiming that Filipino immigration had become a bigger problem than the Chinese and Japanese had been, the paper declared that the Exeter incident was "merely a scab coming off a slight festering boil, that ere long, is likely to break forth in a nasty eruption entailing grave consequences."[70] A *New York Times* editorial also characterized the Exeter clash as a harbinger of a "new race problem" in the United States. While condemning the lawlessness of the attacks, the *Times* asserted that a "Filipino was responsible" for the violence, suggesting that the vigilantes were justified in attacking the individual accused of stabbing Borgman but had gotten carried away in their drive to carry out retributive justice against all Filipinos.[71]

Assaultive behavior targeting Filipinos took an even more ferocious turn a couple of months later in the city of Watsonville, California, in January 1930. A confluence of events contributed to the volatile situation. Sensationalist reportage of the Perfecto Bandalan and Esther Schmick affair had dominated headlines in the local newspapers for much of December and January. The opening of new Filipino taxi-dance hall in the area put the issue of interracial intimacy back in the spotlight. The dance hall was located in the town of Palm Beach, just outside the city limits, to avoid scrutiny from Watsonville authorities. A few days later, a local newspaper published a copy of a resolution passed by the Northern Monterrey Chamber of Commerce condemning Filipino immigration as a threat to the community from a "moral and sanitary standpoint." The statement also denounced Filipinos as "a menace to white labor." The resolution was drafted by nativist crusader Judge D. W. Rohrback, who subsequently embarked on a media campaign to raise public awareness about the Filipino problem. He told one local newspaper that Filipino exclusion was the only way to prevent "the deterioration of the white race in the State of California." He warned his fellow citizens that "American men and women [were] thrown out of labor markets into crime, indolence and poverty" because Filipinos worked for lower wages. Judge Rohrback also spoke out forcefully on the putative perils posed by Filipino-white miscegenation: "if the present state of affairs continues there will be 40,000 half-breeds in the State of California before ten years have passed." The judge was careful to note, however, that he did not "advocate violence" against Filipinos but rather wanted the United States to "send those unwelcome inhabitants from our shores [so] that the white people who inherited this country for themselves and their offspring might live."[72]

A local Filipino organization published a pamphlet called *The Torch* as a response to Judge Rohrback's inflammatory charges. The pamphlet's author, David De Tagle, accused Rohrback of suffering from "Filipinophobia," a condition evidenced by his hysterical and incoherent public statements on the issues of race relations and immigration. The pamphlet mocked Rohrback's alarmist screeds on the Filipino issue, pointing out the overtly racist underpinnings of his claims. The part of the pamphlet that attracted the most attention was its defense of Filipinos' freedom to interact socially with whomever they pleased, regardless of race. *The Torch* boldly asserted that Filipinos would not be "treated as slaves" nor be relegated to segregated labor camps and Chinatowns on the margins of society. De Tagle reminded his American neighbors that Filipinos were taught the egalitarian values of Abraham Lincoln in their U.S.-run primary schools in the Philippines, adding that they were raised on "the Christian principle that God created all men equal, . . . so we do not believe in racial superiority." De Tagle added that Filipinos were only asking for the same rights and protections that white Americans were accorded in the Philippines, where they freely dated and married Filipinos without fear of reprisal. Ten thousand copies of *The Torch* were distributed in Watsonville and the surrounding towns, and it immediately set off a furious reaction from local whites, who saw the pamphlet as a provocation—a public challenge both to the color line and to asymmetrical gender norms that treated Euro-American women as the exclusive property of white men. Within days of the pamphlet's appearance, tensions reached a boiling point, as word spread about Filipinos' demands to be treated as social equals.[73]

On January 19, 1930, a mob of local whites attempted to raid the Monterrey Bay Filipino Club in Palm Beach, because of rumors that white girls were working at the "Filipino pleasure club." They were initially turned away by armed guards, but later that evening carloads of vigilantes roamed the streets looking for Filipinos, and police broke up a number of large brawls.[74] Over the next five days, the situation deteriorated, as terror and violence reigned throughout the region. News accounts of riots blamed the Filipinos for the bloodshed because of their defiance of local racial conventions. For example, the *Salinas Index Journal* stated that the conflict was "precipitated by resentment of the white populace of Watsonville to the maintaining of the Monterrey Bay Filipino club." It described the white women who worked at the establishment as rogue outsiders who showed up in Watsonville after angry white citizens had run them out of a taxi-dance club in Santa Barbara County several months earlier.[75] The next night, an even larger and more organized group "formed Filipino hunting parties, running in groups from

35 to over a hundred persons." The crowd was heavily armed and drove out to a bunkhouse at the McGowan Ranch, firing a volley of gunfire into the residences. The vigilantes had unwittingly attacked a residence that housed only Japanese workers. A mob leader shouted, "Are there any Filipinos in the joint?" Though the Japanese occupants answered no, the attackers "emptied their guns" into the home anyway, before speeding off.[76]

Revanchist sentiment gathered momentum over the next few days as the throngs of vigilantes increased in size and volatility. A group of about five hundred whites "on an open warpath against all Filipinos" surrounded that Palm Beach dance hall on the evening of January 21. The mob had secured gasoline bombs to burn down the premises with the Filipinos inside, but the police arrived in time to prevent the arson. The white entertainers were "ordered from the club" and told to return back to Southern California. Members of the mob voiced their displeasure by shouting down the police officers as "Goo-goo lovers." The raiders split up into smaller groups and set upon various ranches and homes known to house Filipinos. One gang threw a brick through a Filipino home, with the message, "You black so-and-so's let our white girls alone."[77] Another group of fleeing Filipinos was captured by a hunting party and thrown off the Pajaro Bridge. The "infuriated whites" stormed various Filipino residences, including one on San Juan Road, where thirty Filipinos were attacked with pistols and clubs. The mob discovered another set of Filipinos hiding under a house in fear for their lives, and they were "dragged out and mauled unmercifully" by the vigilantes. A Filipino boardinghouse on Van Ness Avenue was also set upon by a mass of three hundred white men, who fired on the residents; this time, however, the Filipinos fought back, returning gunfire and foiling the attackers.

At the Murphy Ranch three miles south of Watsonville, vigilantes fired a volley of gunshots into a Filipino bunkhouse, killing one worker, Fermin Tobera, and wounding another. Those captured while fleeing were beaten with clubs and other heavy weapons as a crowd of hundreds of onlookers, who had driven out to the ranch to revel in the onslaught, cheered on the rioters. The murder of Tobera attracted nationwide media attention, briefly painting white Californians in a critical light for engaging in the kind of racial brutality that was more common in the South. A number of arrests were made in connection with the anti-Filipino rioting, but widespread community support for the vigilantes made prosecution difficult. Eight Watsonville men, most of them in their late teens and early twenties and members of prominent local families, were eventually charged in connection with the rioting. Some of the defendants admitted that they had taken part in the vigilante campaign but claimed their actions were justified. One of the men, R. A. Smith, said he was walking with a female acquaintance on a Watson-ville street when she was "insulted" by an unknown Filipino. A fight ensued as Smith tried to protect her honor from the dark-skinned suitor. Later that night, Smith organized some of his friends to carry out a raid on a laborers' camp to "round up the insulting Filipino and turn him over to police." The raiding party kicked in the door of the residence, but not finding their tar-get they simply robbed some of the victim's possessions and left.[78] Another defendant, Edsel Frey, was described as the likely shooter who killed Fer-min Tobera at the Murphy Ranch. Witnesses claimed that they had seen Frey with a rifle at the camp, and one of his shoes was found at the crime scene during the investigation.

Court hearings for the defendants featured a circuslike atmosphere, and the judge in the case was none other than notorious anti-Filipino crusader D. W. Rohrback. In an ironic twist, Rohrback received an anonymous threat-ening letter during the trial promising "more trouble" if he did not show favoritism toward the white rioters. A preliminary hearing degenerated into chaos as fanatical supporters of the vigilantes swarmed the courtroom and knocked court officers off their feet as the crowd surged forward, cheering on the defendants and offering them hugs of encouragement. The crowd was so disruptive with cries of support and interruptions that Judge Rohrback had to halt the proceedings and continue the case for a later date.[79] The trial was eventually moved to the nearby town of Salinas, since a fair trial in Wat-sonville was unlikely. Eight defendants pled guilty to directly participating in the events that led to Fermin Tobera's death. Trial judge H. S. Jorgensen expressed sympathy for the young white men who had taken part in the anti-Filipino rioting and did not feel that their actions warranted a significant criminal penalty. He imposed a punishment of a two-year term in the state penitentiary for the murder of Tobera, but he suspended the sentences, so the defendants did not actually serve any prison time for their crimes.[80]

The violence spread to other areas in the region in the weeks and months after the Watsonville riots. A series of vigilante attacks targeting Filipinos occurred in San Francisco. On January 27, two Filipinos, Jose Francisco and Reseguno Peralta, were "set upon and severely beaten" by a gang of men who saw them escorting two white women at the corner of Turk and Larkin streets. The assailants fled before police arrived, leaving the two men badly injured. The San Francisco police's response to the attack was to arrest the two Filipino victims for "disturbing the peace," because of their role in pro-voking the assault by parading around in public with white women. Francisco protested the charges, telling police that the woman he was escorting at the time of the assault was actually his wife, explaining that they had recently been married in Tijuana. Both men were convicted anyway and given thirty-day sentences by police judge George Steiger, who was a vocal opponent of Filipino immigration.[81] Later that same day, three Filipinos were assaulted by white taxicab drivers at the intersection of Jones and Sutter streets. The cabdrivers asked the victims, "Are you Mexicans or Filipinos?" When the men responded, "Filipinos," they were beaten by the assailants.[82] A couple days later, a Filipino busboy, Augustin Vallego, was attacked by a group of "intoxicated whites," who hit him in the head with a heavy weapon after he left work at midnight. Judge Steiger, who presided over a number of these cases, blamed the victims for the upsurge of vigilante violence in the city, telling an audience at the American Citizenship Council of San Francisco that Filipinos had provoked the attacks because of their aggressive pursuit of white girls and their sexual deviance.[83]

The city of San Jose also saw a number of street clashes between whites and Filipinos. A confrontation on January 28, 1930, resulted in one white man, Alfred Johnson, being stabbed and four Filipinos being severely beaten during a melee. News of the knifing infuriated the city's white residents, who saw Johnson as a martyr for a community that felt like it was being overrun by the local Filipino "colony." Area citizens organized a series of mass meetings to discuss plans to expel the Filipinos from the community by any means necessary. Police, however, intervened before the planned pogrom was launched, arresting local white resident Leonard Brestle for "advocating a campaign of terrorism" aimed at driving Filipinos out of the region. Brestle and his associates had devised an elaborate plan to dynamite Filipino homes and gathering places in San Jose.[84]

Searching for Scapegoats

As the national media spotlight on the riotous events of 1929 and 1930 brought unwelcome exposure to Northern California's explosive racial fault lines, public figures and community representatives sought to deflect charges of rampant racism and lawlessness in the region. They repeatedly downplayed the catalytic role of nativist leaders and local elites in triggering the violence. Instead they blamed the Filipinos themselves, along with a host of outside agitators, for fomenting the unrest and stirring up an "outbreak of race feeling." They painted white citizens as the real victims of the recent events, characterizing the pogroms as legitimate acts of racial self-defense against a Filipino population hellbent on shattering the region's precarious social order. Local media accounts frequently cited the publication of *The Torch* as a primary cause of the violence, referring to its "defiant utterances directed towards Americans," most notably the "assertion that Filipinos have as much right to American girls" as white men do.[85] This combined with the continued employment of white women at taxi-dance halls had ignited "race feeling" among local residents already feeling bitter about labor competition. The public deportment of Filipinos was characterized as brazen and subversive—a threat to a social structure predicated on voluntary adherence by nonwhites to the rules of racial caste. Media narratives empha-sized the belligerent attitude of Filipinos, who abetted "ill feeling" with a "swag-ger and dressy contempt . . . for their white competitors." One visiting journal-ist described the newcomers' penchant for exhibitionism and public spectacle, noting that Filipinos could often be seen "dressed in their very best, parading down the main streets of the towns" in which they lived and worked. In addition, they made "fairly good lounge lizards, . . . neat, sociable, and often exceedingly accomplished. . . . This aspect of the Filipino invasion has particularly aroused the Californians."[86] The *San Francisco Chronicle* editorial page also weighed in on the issue, asserting that the anti-Filipino riots had "occurred under provoca-tion." The *Chronicle* declared that the recent outbreaks of violence:

> illustrated why there should be no Oriental immigration to America. Our people are race-conscious to an abnormal degree. A violation of the race taboo arouses us more than a serious crime. And the first of race taboos is women. Racial aliens may undercut us, take away our jobs, surpass us in business competition or commit crimes against our laws, and we will be only a little harder on them than we would be on aliens from Europe of our own race. But let them start to associate with our women and we see red.

The editorial added that Filipinos' frequent violations of the color line did not make for "good will" among peoples who should be kept "socially apart."[87] Interpretations such as these were the dominant frame used to explain the upsurge in racialized collective action on the West Coast. The upsurge in revanchist sentiment that swept across the West Coast during this period was portrayed as a forceful expression of popular sovereignty carried out by besieged white citizens angry that the federal government was not doing enough to protect them from the Filipino menace.[88]

Public accounts of the bombing of the Filipino Federation of America (FFA) clubhouse in Stockton, California, offers another textbook case of how the media and local elites placed the onus for outbreaks of racial violence on the actions of the Filipino population. The Filipino Federation site served as a combination headquarters, rooming house, and dance hall and had been the site of a number of political and labor organizing meetings in Stockton. On the evening of January 29, 1930, just a week after the Watsonville riots, a bomb was thrown into the FFA clubhouse from a passing automobile. The drive-by attack demolished the front section of the building and seriously injured some of the occupants, who were asleep at the time of the raid. The incident brought more unwelcome media scrutiny about the hostility faced by Filipinos in the region. Stockton officials, however, offered a bizarre theory of the bombing, suggesting that it was local whites, rather than Filipinos, who were the intended victims of the assault. Authorities characterized the bombing as part of an elaborate "Anti-White Plot" carried out by Filipinos to advance their self-serving political agenda. Police investigators claimed that the bombing had been carried out by the immigrants themselves "to arouse sympathy for Filipinos in the race riots and the fight for Philippine independence." The main evidence offered by authorities of Filipino involvement was the fact that none of the occupants sleeping in the building had been killed by the bomb. According to Stockton police captain Frank Fredericks, the residents "could not have escaped death unless they had been forewarned." This flimsy evidence led police to assert that the attack was a clever scheme hatched by local Filipinos, who sought political gain by "casting blame on whites." No actual evidence of a Filipino plot was ever uncovered, but a few days after the attack, five white youths were arrested, after it was learned that one of the boys had bragged to his mother the day before the explosion that the Filipino headquarters was going to be bombed.[89]

The *Los Angeles Times* also weighed in on the upsurge of anti-Filipino violence sweeping the region, amplifying the role of "Mercenary Women" and outside agitators in "fan[ning] the flames of racial discord" to advance their nefarious agendas. White taxi dancers were said to be at the root of the recent troubles, compelling young Filipinos to spend all their money on fashionable clothes and gifts to impress their potential paramours. These taxi dancers preyed on the lonely Filipino's quest for female companionship until he became an "impudent, indolent stupid dolt insupportable in the social and economic plans, and ripe for the reign of reprisal." The Filipinos were easily exploited by the hardened women of the dance-hall circuit, who reveled in the attention and gifts showered on them. Filipinos' ever-increasing need for money to feed their lavish lifestyles made them easy prey for radical labor organizers, who manipulated their desires to be treated as racial equals. This reckless quest for social equality made the Filipino laborer "a dupe to communism," which offered false promises of political and social betterment.[90]

The assertion that communist agitators had played a role in the California rioting was a frequent claim made by political elites. This accusation was based in part on the arrival of renowned labor leader Pablo Manlapit in Watsonville.[91] Manlapit, now based in Los Angeles, visited the area to investigate the riots and to press authorities to bring the assailants to justice. His presence in Watsonville was immediately derided as incendiary, aimed at "stir[ring] race hatred" against whites. Manlapit published a special issue of the Filipino American newspaper *Ang-Bantay* that described the anti-Filipino riots as "Wholesale Murder." The article was immediately denounced as "inflammatory propaganda" that wrongly fixed responsibility for the violence on white vigilantes and local authorities. Manlapit was condemned by the media as the organizer of violent labor strikes in Hawaii and as "an active communist in Los Angeles."[92] Efforts by public figures to assign blame to outside agitators was aided by the appearance of the Young Communist League (YCL) in the aftermath of the riots. The YCL distributed circulars condemning the role of local elites in fomenting anti-Filipino violence. The circulars were denounced as an attempt to challenge local agribusiness interests through radical labor agitation. Business and political leaders were particularly troubled by the flyer's call for interracial unionism. The YCL appealed for class solidarity in the face of repression: "Stand Together! . . . An Injury to Filipino Workers is an Injury to the American Workers! . . . Defend the Working Class Against American Legion and Fascist Attack. Join the Young Communist League! Join the Communist Party USA!" The leaflet was criticized in the local media as "lurid and dangerous propaganda" for its advocacy in interracial political activism and for implicating local elites in facilitating anti-Filipino violence.[93] The efforts of Pablo Manlapit and the YCL did little to help the situation of the aggrieved Filipino community. In some ways the presence of these political actors actually hindered their cause, inasmuch as it allowed local elites to deflect attention away from the racist origins of the riots and shift focus to the imaginary role of outside agitators in stirring up discord. That both Manlapit and the YCL arrived in the region after the main outbreaks of violence had ended and that no acts of aggression were ever directly linked to these groups was lost in the larger narrative of a white community under siege by dangerous outsiders determined to upset the social order.

The arrival of representatives from the Philippine government in Watsonville in the weeks after the violence added to the sense that outside forces were trying to unfairly lay blame on beleaguered white citizens. Philippine officials demanded a full-scale investigation of the mayhem by the U.S.

government, and federal officials did make some cursory inquiries into the events in Northern California, including queries from Francis Parker, head of the Bureau of Insular Affairs, and Patrick Hurley, secretary of war. This did not sit well with state leaders, who resented the involvement of the federal government in local affairs. The motivations of Philippine officials were called into question, as a calculated bid for sympathy to advance their demands for national independence. When the Philippine government held a national day of mourning to honor Fermin Tobera as a martyr, it was portrayed in the California media as a cheap political stunt that unfairly held whites accountable for the proliferation of racial violence on the West Coast. Local observers took narratives of white racial victimhood even further, claiming that Filipino "gang chiefs" were exploiting the situation to plot reprisals both against whites in Los Angeles and against American servicemen in the Philippines.[94]

In the wake of the rioting, state and local authorities enacted a number of measures aimed at heading off further race trouble. Filipinos were prohibited from attending public dances and taxi halls in many localities across the state, including Stockton, Turlock, Modesto, Santa Barbara County, and Stanislaus County. Meanwhile, clubs in Los Angeles that admitted Filipinos were closed down indefinitely, as police attempted to avoid potential violence.[95] More controversial was a decision by the California State Athletic Commission to ban all Filipino boxers from fight cards with white boxers in the state. William Hanlon, chairman of the state boxing commission, explained that the ban was issued to prevent possible race riots at sports arenas where large crowds gathered. The commission's decision had a strange twist of irony, as it sought to "eliminate any possibility of violence occurring at a boxing program."[96] Hanlon was "particularly fearful of the consequences" of bouts in which Filipinos beat white boxers, an occurrence that happened with great frequency. The State Athletic Commission's anxiety was fueled by the Filipinos' "disagreeable habit of winning their fights," a fact that "enrages the noble white man, who considers successful prize-fighting a proof of superiority."[97] Hanlon's decision did not sit well with local boxing promoters, who made good money off interracial bouts and resented meddling from state officials in their business. Filipinos, many of whom avidly followed their fellow countrymen's legendary exploits in the ring, also took exception to the state's injunction, feeling that they were being punished for the criminal acts of white rioters.[98]

As news of the anti-Filipino riots spread across the country, the violent outbreaks on the West Coast attracted attention from Congress. The notoriety surrounding events in California offered exclusionists an opportunity to revisit the issue of immigration restriction and Philippine independence. Congressional representatives from that state defended the malicious actions of their white constituents and held up the riots as evidence of the unassimilability of Filipinos. Arthur Free, U.S. congressman from the San Jose/Santa Clara area, represented a district where much of the anti-Filipino violence took place. Representative Free declared that the rioting in his district was caused by the deviant behavior of Filipinos themselves and argued that the bloodshed was morally justified:

> The alleged slaughter of a Filipino in a riot between white laborers and members of the Filipino colony was in reality the forceful expression of a community craving to rid itself of vice dens run by Filipino colonists. . . . The Filipinos of Watsonville are of the very lowest type. . . . I am going to show that the so-called rioters were sorely tried by the vicious practices of the Filipinos in luring young white girls into degradation.[99]

Influential U.S. senator from California Hiram Johnson offered a similar explanation of events, arguing that the Filipinos "had brought the antagonism upon themselves." The main problem as he saw it was the inability of Filipinos to "harmonize socially" with Americans, a deficiency evinced by their "forwardness with white women." Filipinos' "peculiar propensity" to cross the color line, according to Senator Johnson, set them apart from "any other race that has come to us."[100]

The "Cheap Labor" Problem

In the wake of the rioting, California governor C. C. Young appointed a fact-finding commission to investigate Filipino immigration to the state. This followed on the heels of a similar investigation commissioned by Young just a year before on the problem of Mexican labor in California.[101] The inquiry was headed up by Will J. French, director of the state's Department of Industrial Relations, in cooperation with statistician Louis Bloch. French's report was entitled *Facts about Filipino Immigration* and purported to present an objective study of the "problems" associated with Filipino migration to the United States. Whether Filipino immigration was in fact a "problem" was not in question, since that assumption was already accepted as fact by the authors of the report. The study's ideological frame made it clear that the investigators already knew what they would discover. They simply needed "data" collected by objective state functionaries to lend their political assumptions intellectual authority. The report documented the history of Filipino migration to California, attempting to offer a reliable population survey that could shed light on their numbers in the state. This was a potentially important exercise, since nativists frequently exaggerated the number of Filipinos in the United States to inflate the seriousness of the putative problem. Yet the search for "facts" about the phenomenon in question was compromised by the explicit biases of the report's authors, who repeatedly used the term "invasion" to describe the arrival of Filipino immigrants.[102]

The state's report addressed two main problems associated with Filipino immigration. The first was the willingness of Filipinos to work for low wages, which allegedly priced native whites out of the labor market. The second problem emphasized by the report was the "preponderance" of single young males among the early immigrant cohorts, which in turn led to unhealthy levels of race mixing with women of other groups. Investigators identified a number of occupations in which Filipinos were "displacing native white workers," especially in hotel, restaurant, and domestic jobs. The report, however, offered no actual data on job displacement but simply inferred that if a Filipino was employed and a white person was unemployed, then de facto job theft had taken place. State investigators identified the alleged displacement of white workers along with resentment over race mixing as the root causes of the recent rioting in California. By employing the rhetoric of immigrant invasion, investigators could effectively place the issue within a social-problems discourse that emphasized the threatening nature of Filipino settlement. The California Department of Industrial Relations study, like the "investigation" carried out by the Commonwealth Club, was an exercise in political framing designed to reinforce claims that the Filipino problem had reached a crisis point with potentially dire consequences for the larger society.

Nativists amplified the threat posed by cheap Filipino labor, arguing that continued immigration imperiled the economic survival of American citizens. According to D.W. Ruhrback, "whole armies of white people come to canneries and driers, hoping to get employment, but the Filipino is there before them, ready and willing to do the work for a small wage. . . . The lettuce fields and orchards are dotted with Filipinos, while white labor, both men, women, and children suffer."[103] That there was little evidence to support claims that Filipinos were displacing white workers did not really matter. American trade-union leaders also played a primary role in inciting anxieties about Filipino labor displacing whites, seeing the newcomers as a convenient scapegoat during a time of acute economic uncertainty. Earlier campaigns launched by West Coast nativist and labor leaders had helped pressure the U.S. Congress to enact restrictive legislation against the Chinese and Japanese laborers, and these same forces believed that they would play a vanguard role in closing the nation's borders to the latest group of Asian invaders. Exclusionists realized quickly, however, that the Filipino issue could not be "solved so easily," since federal officials were reluctant to bar America's colonial wards from entering the United States.[104]

Trade-union opposition to Filipino immigration actually predated the violent events of 1929 and 1930. In fact, labor leaders on the West Coast had been agitating against the influx of Filipino labor as far back as 1926. Paul Scharrenberg, the leader and spokesman for the California State Federation of Labor, made opposition to Filipino immigration a personal crusade and lobbied the American Federation of Labor to adopt a series of resolutions opposing the entry of Filipino immigrants. He had long been active in campaigns against Asian and Mexican workers and viewed nonwhite workers as undesirable and unorganizable. Scharrenberg used his leadership position in the California State Federation of Labor to push his brand of conservative business unionism among skilled white workers. His probusiness ideology put him at odds with some of the state's other labor leaders, most notably his arch-nemesis Harry Bridges, whose radical organizing vision championed union membership for minority workers. Scharrenberg, like many nativist leaders, saw Filipinos' exemption from the 1924 Immigration Act as a slap in the face. He claimed that cheap Filipino labor invariably undermined the "American standard of living," putting white workingmen and their families at risk. Scharrenberg argued that workers on the West Coast had become "apprehensive of this new uncontrolled flood of cheap Asiatic labor." He added that "Filipinos have taken the place of white workers in the culinary trades; they have replaced white bell boys and elevator operators and made it more difficult for white hotel maids to find jobs. Steamships . . . have been manned by Filipinos while American seamen are vainly walking the docks looking for jobs."[105] The race riots that had taken place in Northern California were in Scharrenberg's eyes a direct consequence of labor displacement: "The race riots . . . and their bloody issue are inevitable as the result of the third invasion of California by Oriental labor. I predicted them and I predict that they will increase if this new swarming of 'cheap labor' from across the Pacific is not stopped."[106]

Alarmist messages about Filipinos displacing whites and endangering the American standard of living spurred a number of municipalities and organizations to enact resolutions aimed at driving them out of their communities. The economic and social turmoil of the Great Depression gave these campaigns extra traction as local communities attempted to monopolize scare resources and ward off potential competitors. The influential fraternal organization the Native Sons of the Golden West passed a series of resolutions asking Congress to bar immigration from the islands. The Native Sons denounced Filipinos as "politically, economically, and socially undesirable," imploring the federal government to take ownership of the problem. The Native Sons condemned Filipinos as a "vicious and criminal" population whose settlement in the United States represented a "permanent menace to the maintenance of American standards."[107] The California Joint Immigration Committee and the Commonwealth Club also lobbied for exclusion, with the latter group even hiring attorneys (with the assistance of California attorney general U. S. Webb) to develop a legal strategy to circumvent the exemption for Filipinos contained in the 1924 Immigration Act.[108] Other communities passed resolutions banning the employment of Filipino labor. The chamber of commerce of the city of Greenfield, California, passed a resolution demanding that "Filipinos be eliminated from this community as a labor factor and a social entity," proclaiming that the region's agricultural industry would effortlessly proceed without "the presence of little brown brother."[109] Cannery owners in the coastal city of Monterrey signed an agreement to "eliminate" the employment of Filipino labor in their industry. Cannery officials were responding to public pressure from the local American Legion post, which claimed that hundreds of white laborers were out of work because of the newcomers. The Legionnaires explained that Monterrey was "in danger of becoming a Filipino colony" unless social closure was enacted properly.[110] Further south, the West Hollywood Chamber of Commerce approved a similar resolution, mandating the hiring of "American citizens" over alien labor. The Hollywood resolution even went so far as to quote a passage from the Bible to justify the exclusionary policy.[111]

Resolutions and boycotts were not the only type of response to the problem of Filipino employment. Labor expulsions aimed at driving Filipinos out of the West Coast labor market were commonplace. Resentment about the employment of Filipino labor in Oregon led to a number of attacks in the early 1930s. In February 1930, Filipino laborer Vincent Catoda was assaulted and severely beaten by a gang of eight white men in Portland. Catoda was found lying bloodied and unconscious on a city sidewalk. He told the police that his attackers demanded to know the "whereabouts of other Filipinos," and when he refused to answer, he was assaulted.[112] A few months later, Filipino workers were driven out of a Seattle community by "white raiders" who opposed the employment of the Filipinos on lettuce and pea farms in the region, claiming that they worked for "half of the wages that white men demand." A group of armed residents conducted a late-night raid of the labor camp and kidnapped all of the Filipino workers. They were subsequently "taken on a ride" by vigilantes, dropped off miles outside town, and warned that they would be shot if they returned to work in the fields. Seattle police captain Owen McGill claimed that his officers found scores of Filipino laborers "running down roads toward their ranches, most dressed only in their underwear . . . frightened to death."[113] A nearby Filipino bunkhouse was burned to the ground two days later by angry citizens who had earlier issued threats to farm owners in the region who hired outsiders. Later that month a group of five Filipinos was attacked outside a movie theater in Shelley, Idaho, by a mob of white men, who beat them savagely and stripped them of their clothing.[114]

The final months of 1930 were particularly bloody for Filipinos. Anonymous letters featuring skull-and-crossbones symbols were sent to employers throughout the Santa Clara/Sunnyvale area, warning, "Work no Filipinos or we'll destroy your crop and you too." Another letter was sent to the Sunnyvale chief of police, threatening, "Get Rid of All Filipino or We'll Burn this Town Down." That week, a local bunkhouse was torched by vigilantes, killing Joaquin Somera, a Filipino laborer who was trapped inside.[115] A mob of three hundred white men and Indians raided a local hop ranch in Ukiah, California, and "forcibly deported eighty-five Filipinos," dropping them at a nearby railroad station with orders not to return to the county.[116] A few days later in Visalia, vigilantes threw a bundle of dynamite into a bunkhouse where one hundred Filipino workers were sleeping. Another bombing in El Centro, California, left a Filipino farmworker dead and another maimed, after a series of clashes between "disgruntled white laborers" and Filipino lettuce pickers in the Imperial Valley.[117] And in a gruesome scene, the bodies of two Filipinos were found hanged, while another "apparently burnt to death was propped up against the trunk of the tree" outside the town of Lodi.[118]

"Little Brown Brother" Becomes Big Red Menace

By 1931, a new variation on the problem narrative of Filipino labor began to emerge, adding more ammunition to nativists' rhetorical arsenal. Previous discourse emphasizing Filipinos' docility and tractability gave way to more ominous images of them as militant labor organizers with communist leanings. Acclaimed labor journalist Carey McWilliams described Filipinos' newly acquired reputation in the following way:

> The Filipino, militantly race-conscious, began to protest against his exploitation in California at an early date, and has grown increasingly rebellious. The Filipino Labor Union, restricted to agricultural workers, has seven locals with a membership of about 2,000. . . . The Filipino is a real fighter and his strikes have been dangerous.[119]

Initially excluded from the American Federation of Labor unions because of racial discrimination, Filipinos looked outside the structure of mainstream unions to find sympathetic organizational bases for their political grievances. They found willing allies in the communist trade-union movement, which during the 1930s adopted an aggressive program of class insurgency and interracial solidarity. Communist cadres on the West Coast were singular in their public condemnation of the unbridled racial violence faced by Filipinos, citing vigilantism and police harassment as instruments of racial and class repression. In addition, three unions affiliated with the American Communist Party—the Trade Union Unity League (TUUL), the Cannery and Agricultural Workers' Industrial Union (CAIWU), and the Agricultural Workers Industrial League (AWIL)—actively sought out Filipino members to strengthen their campaign against the dominance of the agribusiness oligarchy on the West Coast. By the early 1930s, communist organizers came to the conclusion that Filipinos were the most militant of California's workers and attempted to recruit them into the party ranks. An AWIL flyer was typical of their ideological position on ethnic labor solidarity:

> Hundreds of Americans, Mexicans and Filipinos are being discriminated against because of their activities . . . to improve our standards of living. The employers at all times are trying to divide the workers into races, groups, and nationalities. They divide us in order to wage a more successful struggle against us. The employers are united against us. We must be united in our struggle. No Race Discrimination! No division on lines of races and nationalities! Unity of all workers. Mexicans, Filipinos, Americans, Negroes and Orientals. This is the necessity of the moment.[120]

Though the efforts of these organizations were sometimes opportunistic, they did make genuine attempts to organize racially marginalized workers and often faced vigilante violence themselves as a result. The early 1930s has been described as a period of "Great Upheaval" by labor historian Cletus Daniel, because of the increasingly violent conflicts between labor and capital. The presence of Filipinos and Mexicans in these conflicts was particularly notable, since they had long been characterized as docile workers averse to labor militancy. Filipinos also formed independent ethnic unions such as the militant Filipino Labor Union (FLU), led by labor contractors D. L. Marcuelo and Rufo Canete, as well as smaller unions such as the Filipino Protective Union and the Filipino Labor Association. Though they borrowed some tactics from AWIL and CAIWU organizers, the FLU sought autonomy from the strategic and ideological strictures of the Communist Party. By 1933, Filipino labor activists in California had staged a number of meetings aimed at creating a broadscale statewide labor union that would advocate on behalf of all Filipino workers in the state, in the hope of creating a unified bloc of thirty-thousand-plus workers who could act in unison against intransigent employers.[121]

As labor relations in agriculture became more adversarial, the specter of radicalism came to dominate discussions about Filipino workers. By the early 1930s, Filipinos had been involved in a number of crippling strikes that had resulted in significant financial losses for agribusiness. At the same time, American officials expressed concerns about growing labor militancy in the Philippines, accusing communists of infiltrating the islands' labor movement. The increasing militancy earned the ire of both growers and civic leaders, who saw labor radicalism by nonwhite workers as a threat to the normal relations of power. AWIL was active in organizing a number of strikes in the fields of California, including a large multiracial strike carried out by field laborers in the Imperial Valley in 1930. Early attempts to unionize farmworkers by Communist labor organizers were met with stiff resistance from growers and police. In April 1930, AWIL called a mass meeting of agricultural workers to develop a new campaign to eliminate the labor contractor system and job speedups, in addition to calling for an increase in wages. Before the mass meeting was held, "the local sheriff led a group of deputies, policemen, and privately hired thugs into an AWIL meeting and removed all 108 persons found there to the El Centro County Jail."[122] Eight of the union leaders were prosecuted under the Criminal Syndicalism Law, including one Filipino leader who was convicted with the others during a show trial and sent to prison. Describing the authoritarian strategy employed against the militant labor activists, the commander of the local American Legion office stated, "The way to kill the red plague is to dynamite it out. That's what we did in Imperial County. The judge who tried the Communists was a Legionnaire,

50 percent of the jurors were veterans. What chance did the Communists have?"[123] By the early 1930s, AWIL was effectively destroyed by the authorities, who had placed most of the leadership in jail. CAIWU soon filled the vacuum left by AWIL, looking to learn from strategic mistakes made in previous campaigns. In November 1932, a CAIWU-led strike of Filipino and Mexican orchard workers took place in Vacaville, California. Growers and police organized specially deputized gangs of vigilantes to break up labor meetings. In a show of power by growers and authorities, "six strike leaders were taken out of the Vacaville jail and driven twenty miles out of town," where forty masked men "flogged them with tug straps, clipped their heads with shear clippers, and poured red enamel over them."[124] The labor action was eventually called off.

A strike by two hundred Filipino vegetable pickers in San Mateo, California threatened to spoil crop shipments when workers walked out, and demanded a wage increase from five cents an hour to twenty-five cents. Local ranchers were incensed that state labor officials had forced them to negotiate with Filipino strikers, whom they described as "Red agitators." Unwilling to cede to the demands of the workers, growers took the law into their own hands. When Filipinos refused to return to work, an armed group of citizens instructed them to "clear out or be driven out" of the community under threat of violence.[125] Repeated accusations of Communist influence among Filipino unionists reinforced public perceptions of Filipinos as disruptive troublemakers whose continued presence in the United States represented a serious social problem. The violent events of the late 1920s and early 1930s gave nativist leaders a springboard from which they would take their anti-Filipino crusade to the U.S. Congress. National notoriety surrounding the riots animated new calls for immigration exclusion and revived languishing legislative interest on the issue of Philippine independence.

5

"To Guard the Doors of My People"

Exclusion, Independence, and Repatriation

The volatile political events of the late 1920s and early 1930s placed a national spotlight on Filipino immigration and settlement, which up until that point, had been primarily a regional issue. Nativist leaders character- ized the race riots on the West Coast as the inevitable outgrowth of permis- sive government policies that allowed for the unrestricted immigration of another unwanted and unassimilable population. Restrictionists made effec- tive use of the newfound public attention paid to the issue and hoped this notoriety would galvanize public support for exclusion. Spokespersons for the anti-Filipino movement warned of even more violence and political strife unless the federal government interceded quickly to curtail the influx of newcomers from the Philippines. In the wake of the western race riots sev- eral legislative proposals were introduced in Congress aimed at restricting immigration from the Philippines to the United States.

Not surprisingly, congressional leaders from California played a central role in this debate with two members from that state's delegation, Represen- tative Richard Welch and Senator Samuel Shortridge, proposing Filipino- exclusion bills in 1930. Both lawmakers extolled the vanguard historical role played by their state in pushing for federal exclusion laws against Chinese and Japanese immigrants and called on citizens to raise once again the soiled banner of yellow perilism to shore up the nation's borders. At the same time, legislative efforts to grant the Philippines its independence gathered momen- tum in Congress. The push for independence was aligned with the aims of exclusionists insofar as a change in the political status of the Philippines would likely strip Filipinos of their right to migrate to the United States as American "nationals."

An eclectic mix of political actors took an interest in the Philippine ques- tion, including the American Federation of Labor (AFL), nativist groups, agri- business concerns, and "patriotic" organizations. Filipinos, both in the United

States and in the Philippines were also central players in this debate, seeing it as an opportunity to advance their aspirations for national sovereignty. These different constituencies had parallel but intersecting agendas that sometimes worked at cross-purposes, with exclusionists refusing to support indepen-- dence legislation unless it included an immigration quota and advocates of independence unwilling to vote for an immigration bill targeting Filipinos that did not also grant the Philippines its autonomy. The two camps eventually became entangled as proponents of both exclusion and independence realized that their political aims could not be realized unless they worked together.

The campaign for Filipino exclusion evolved along two interrelated tracks. The first focused on pressuring Congress to amend the 1924 Immigration Act to restrict Filipinos.[1] Advocates of this strategy, such as California attorney general U. S. Webb and organizations such as the Native Sons of the Golden West and the American Coalition of Patriotic Societies, believed that Congress should bar the entry of Filipinos regardless of their status as colonial wards. Lawmakers, however, expressed reservations about the potential negative diplomatic fallout from such a policy since it broke from international norms regarding the treatment of imperial subjects. The second approach was focused on pressing Congress to follow through on its longstanding pledge to grant the Philippines its independence. Advocates of this strategy included lawmakers from midwestern states and regional agribusiness concerns who saw independence as a way to restrict the import of Philippine commodities such as sugar, coconut oil, tobacco, and cordage that competed with American products in the domestic marketplace. Relinquishing U.S. sovereignty over the islands would bring an end to the so-called privileged status of Philippine imports, subjecting them to the same tariff restrictions placed on other foreign goods. Sponsors of independence bills did not initially consider Filipino immigration to be a high-priority concern and worried that adding an explicit exclusion provision to their legislative proposals might hinder their efforts to get a bill passed. Some groups, including labor unions and patriotic organizations such as the American Legion, threw their weight behind both exclusion and independence legislation, as they simply wanted the nation's borders closed to Filipino laborers and products by whatever means necessary.

Congressional leaders scheduled hearings on the issue of Filipino immigration in 1930, in the wake of the riots that had swept the West Coast. The hearings provided a valuable opportunity for nativists, inasmuch as it gave them a national platform to raise public awareness about the Filipino problem and to demand that the federal government intercede. The issue of Filipino immigration was hardly a new topic for political leaders in Washington, DC, who had considered bills aimed at curbing the entry of laborers and imports from the Philippines in previous years. The AFL began lobbying its allies in Congress in the mid-1920s to act on the Philippine question, but these initiatives failed to gain much traction. Trade-union leaders and their allies in the nativist movement saw their efforts as an extension of previous exclusionary crusades targeting the Chinese and Japanese and suggested that Filipinos posed an even greater menace to American society. Proponents of exclusion also claimed that the importation of duty-free products from the Philippines imperiled the U.S. economy since American businesses were forced to lower wages and lay off workers to compete with cheap Filipino goods.

The concerns raised by labor and nativist groups did not get a serious hearing from Congress until the outbreaks of violence on the West Coast put a spotlight on the Filipino issue, resulting in hearings conducted by the House Immigration and Naturalization Committee. Although the hearings gave exclusionists a high-profile platform to push their campaign, a legislative solution to the Filipino issue proved elusive. It was not until nativists aligned themselves with forces advocating for Philippine independence that they were able to move their agenda forward. Exclusionists eventually realized their goal with the passage of the Tydings-McDuffie Act in 1934, which granted the Philippines its independence and placed Filipinos under the most stringent immigration quota allotted to any country in the world. Anti-Filipino partisans took some satisfaction in this legislative achievement, but they also recognized that this was only a partial victory since it did nothing to remedy the problem of Filipinos already living in the United States. Consequently, nativist forces shifted tactics and began pressuring Congress to enact legislation aimed at sending the immigrant undesirables back to their homeland, hoping that such a move would finally solve the Filipino problem once and for all.

This chapter examines the strategic and ideological program of the manti-Filipino movement, tracing its evolution from a campaign to forestall immigration from the Islands to a pressure group advocating the repatriation of resident Filipinos back to the Philippines. Although West Coast nativists had a track record of success with previous crusades targeting Asian immigrants, they confronted a different set of political considerations in their drive to head off the "third Asiatic invasion." The unique political status of the Philippines was the chief obstacle facing exclusionists, but they encountered other roadblocks as well. Nativists had to contend with powerful countervailing forces opposed to restriction. These forces included western agribusiness interests which favored liberal immigration policies that preserved their access to foreign labor. Influential sectors of the federal government also opposed Filipino exclusion, especially officials from the Department of War who believed that restrictive legislation would offend Filipino allies and undermine American geopolitical interests in Asia. Filipino political leaders were also vocal in their opposition to the nativist agenda, arguing that exclusion without independence would set an ugly diplomatic precedent and hurt the international standing of the United States. The final obstacle facing exclusionists was their relatively low position on the congressional priority list. During the late 1920s and early 1930s, restrictionists in Congress were focused on legislation that would enact quota walls against immigration from Latin America, and political powerbrokers such as Albert Johnson believed that bills dealing with Mexican immigration took precedence over the Filipino matter.

Another Indispensable Enemy

Trade-union leaders played an early and important role in the movement for Filipino exclusion, reiterating their longstanding opposition to the presence of Asian immigrants in the United States. The passage of the Chinese Exclusion Act in 1882 was hailed by West Coast labor leaders as a major legislative victory that demonstrated their growing influence on the national political scene. Organized labor's crusade against Asian immigrants continued through the early decades of the twentieth century as it threw its support behind passage of the 1917 and 1924 Immigration Acts, which further curtailed immigration from Asia. Trade-union opposition to Asian immigration was motivated by the unshakable myth that the immigrants represented an unorganizable mass of "coolie" labor that imperiled the so-called American standard of living.[2] Yellow perilism proved a powerful ideological trope for western labor leaders, insofar as it provided a convenient scapegoat for white workers to project their discontents.

Trade-union interest in the Philippine question actually preceded the arrival of significant numbers of Filipinos to the United States. This concern was evident as early as 1923, when resolutions were introduced at the AFL's national convention urging Congress to grant the Philippines its independence. The AFL viewed the unfettered flow of both goods and labor from the islands as looming threats. Labor leaders railed against the tariff-free import into the United States of "cheap" Philippine products, which, they argued, undersold goods made by white workers. They also implored national leaders to prevent the entry of "cheap" Filipino labor, seeing them as the latest in a long line of peon labor exploited by employers to undercut gains made by union workers.

The AFL adopted a two-pronged strategy, endorsing narrowly crafted exclusion legislation during certain years and supporting the passage of legislation aimed at granting the Philippines its independence at other times. In 1924, the AFL's Executive Council petitioned lawmakers to enact one of the two independence bills before Congress and thereby answer the "earnest prayer and petitions" of Filipinos seeking national self-determination. The Executive Council believed that Philippine goods would be subject to tariff restrictions in the United States once independence was conferred. By the late 1920s, the AFL's policy on the Philippine question was heavily influenced by activists representing its West Coast chapters. The California (CSFL) and Washington State (WSFL) branches of the trade-union federation had taken up Filipino exclusion in earnest, passing resolutions at their state conventions during the late 1920s championing Filipino exclusion. Paul Scharrenberg, who had served as both president and secretary-treasurer of the CSFL was a central figure in the anti-Filipino movement. He praised the vanguard role played by West Coast trade unionists in protecting white workingmen from the scourge of coolie infiltration. Scharrenberg explained his union's stance in an article published in San Jose labor organ the *Union Gazette*:

> It has been the historic mission of the California labor movement to take the lead in every movement to preserve our state as a heritage to the white race. That grave responsibility is still with us. If it had not been for Dennis Kearney and his followers in labor's ranks, California, in its early days, would have been swamped by Chinese immigrants. If it had not been for the vigilance of the organized labor movement during the present century, California would be populated by several times the Japanese population, which is estimated at least 100,000. . . . California trade unionists owe a duty to themselves, their families, and their descendants to prevent the dumping of these undesirable Asiatics in our fair state. We must again take the lead in stemming the third Asiatic invasion of California.[3]

The immigration issue (as opposed to the independence issue) received national attention at the AFL's 1927 annual convention in Los Angeles when Daniel Murphy of the CSFL introduced a resolution supporting the exclusion of Filipino labor from the United States. The resolution stated that the influx of Filipinos had exacerbated the "racial and economic problems" on the West Coast. Objections raised in previous years about Chinese and Japanese immigrants, according to Murphy, applied "with equal force to" Filipinos. As a result, the AFL "strongly urge[d] Congress to enact legislation prohibiting Asiatic laborers from the Philippine Islands from migrating to the United States."[4] A similar resolution, introduced by Paul Scharrenberg along with Andrew Furuseth and Victor Olander of the International Seamen's Union was passed at the 1928 AFL convention. The 1928 motion endorsed a legislative proposal (HR 13900) sponsored by California congressman Richard Welch which sought to amend the 1924 Immigration Act to include Filipinos as a restricted class of entrants. The debate at the 1928 convention also revealed the increasingly racialized tone of the AFL's approach to the issue. Scharrenberg's resolution claimed that the presence of Filipino laborers in the United States "destroy[ed] American ideals" and "prevent[ed] the development of a nation based on racial unity." The resolution's authors argued that "nothing short of exclusion" could protect white workers from being overrun by cheap Filipino labor.[5]

The 1930 AFL convention in Boston saw an even broader coalition of trade unionists backing calls for immigration restriction and Philippine independence. New supporters included machinists, railway laborers, oil and refinery workers, and the International Brotherhood of Teamsters. The AFL's 1930 resolutions cited the West Coast race riots as evidence that the threat posed by Filipinos went beyond simple labor competition. Filipinos' brazen defiance of the color line was now front and center, with AFL officials blaming the violence on the islanders' tendency to "transgress upon the sanctity of our women in their forced efforts to assimilate." These misguided associations produced a "mongrel race" that undermined the social standing of white families.[6] The brand of racial protectionism advocated by the American Federation of Labor helped to reactivate anti-Asian sentiment on the West Coast and provided labor leaders with moral authority to act as defenders of the American standard of living.

"The Filipino Must Go!"

Congressional hearings on the subject of Filipino immigration in 1930 elevated the visibility of an issue that up to that point was primarily a regional concern. Support for restrictive legislation had been mounting on the West Coast for some time, as evidenced by a flurry of state and local measures seeking to prevent the entry of Filipinos during the 1920s. Officials in the western states passed a series of public decrees beseeching the federal government to enact stricter immigration controls. In April 1929, the Seattle City Council adopted a resolution petitioning Congress to limit or "terminate" the rights of Filipinos to enter the United States.[7] A month later, the California state legislature drafted a joint resolution petitioning the Congress to enact legislation placing restrictions on Filipino immigration. The edict read:

> WHEREAS the policy of unrestricted immigration as an aid to cheap labor has had a tendency toward the destruction of American ideals and American racial unity; and . . .
>
> WHEREAS, Filipinos have not been among those excluded under the immigration laws of the United States in accordance with our national policy of restrictive immigration, and
>
> WHEREAS the present absence of restriction on immigration from the Philippine islands opens the door annually to thousands of Filipinos, causing unjust and unfair competition to American labor . . . therefore, be it
>
> RESOLVED by the Assembly and the Senate of the State of California, jointly, That the Legislature of the State of California earnestly petitions Congress to enact legislation which will restrict immigration from the Philippine Islands; and which will prevent all Filipinos entering the United States who are afflicted with communicable diseases.[8]

This resolution passed overwhelmingly, by a vote of fifty-one to eight in the State Assembly and of twenty-two to two in the Senate, and was quickly sent to lawmakers in Washington, DC, for consideration. Along the same lines, California attorney general U. S. Webb asked Congress to bar the entry of Filipinos, arguing that exclusion was necessary to "preserve the racial integrity of the United States."[9] Civic organizations also pressed the federal government to take action. The Native Sons of the Golden West passed a resolution endorsing Filipino exclusion at their annual convention in San Francisco in May 1929. The Native Sons condemned Filipinos as a "vicious and criminal" population that had become a "permanent menace to the . . . peace and life of the communities in which they settle."[10] Similar resolutions were passed by the Commonwealth Club and the California Joint Immigration Committee (CJIC).[11] These public proclamations had no legal effect, but they provide a good barometer of nativist sentiment on the West Coast and growing frustration with the federal government for failing to contain the Filipino population. The symbolic political maneuvers along with the upsurge in revanchist violence during the late 1920s and early 1930s left little doubt that by the time Congress held hearings on the issue most California citizens readily endorsed the exclusionists' toxic refrain, "The Filipino Must Go!"[12]

The National Stage

Congressional attention to the Filipino issue was swift in the aftermath of the West Coast riots. Senator Millard Tydings of Maryland raised the issue of Filipino restriction on the Senate floor on January 29, 1930, just days after the Watsonville riots ended. Tydings implored his colleagues to act quickly on one of the various Philippine independence bills under consideration before Congress to head off further outbreaks of violence on the West Coast.[13] Bills aimed at outright immigration exclusion were also introduced, but the Filipino question took a back seat to legislation addressing the issue of restricting immigration from the Western Hemisphere (e.g., Mexico). Representative Albert Johnson, who chaired the House Committee on Immigration and Naturalization, was eager to amend the 1924 Immigration Act to place quota limits on immigration from Latin American nations. The issue had preoccupied legislators for a number of years and many legislators saw Mexican immigration as a more pressing matter than the Filipino issue.

The House Committee on Immigration and Naturalization held a series of hearings on Western Hemisphere immigration from 1926 to 1930, during which it debated a set of bills aimed primarily at bringing Mexicans under the restrictive quota system established by 1924 Immigration Act. In the early months of 1930, committee members considered restrictive legislation sponsored by Representatives John Box of Texas and Albert Johnson of Washington in the House and by Senator William Harris of Georgia in the Senate. The focus on "Western Hemisphere Immigration" was somewhat misleading, since the proposals in question clearly targeted the southern border of the United States. All the bills under consideration, in fact, accorded immigrants from Canada a favorable entry status, either exempting immigrants coming over the northern border from restriction altogether or granting Canadians a high "paper quota" of at least sixty-seven thousand persons per year.

The sudden addition of the Filipino question to the legislative docket in 1930 added another possible snag to the committee's efforts to advance a bill imposing quotas against Latin American countries. The spate of violent outbreaks in the western states gave the Filipino question some urgency that could not be ignored by lawmakers. House Immigration Committee member Arthur Free from San Jose, a vocal opponent of Filipino immigration, attempted to expand the exclusionary scope of bills already before the committee. Free threatened to stall the Box and Johnson bill unless a provision was attached adding Filipinos to the list of excluded groups. Free argued that legislation focused solely on the southwestern border would put the nation "no nearer to the solution of the immigration problems," since Filipinos would still be allowed unfettered entry to the United States.[14] He cited the recent race riots as evidence of the need to prioritize the Filipino issue and suggested that Mexicans were a far more tolerable population than other groups that had been imported for agricultural work in the region. Free singled out Filipinos and Puerto Ricans as the least desirable of all immigrant groups, noting that they were less desirable than even the "Chinaman or the Jap." He warned his colleagues that the "Filipinos . . . that are in California to-day . . . are the scum of the earth," who posed "a menace to our women."[15] Representative Free's attempt to hijack the Western Hemisphere immigration legislation by attaching an amendment barring entrants from the Philippines was rebuffed by Chairman Johnson and other legislators who feared that the issue would derail their efforts to enact Mexican restriction. Representative Richard Welch, another Californian, also tried to jump into the fray, introducing a last-minute Filipino exclusion bill during the same session in late February, but was told his measure would have to wait until March, when the committee could give the issue a separate hearing.

Holding concurrent hearings on Filipino and Mexican restriction created some dilemmas for legislators, who were split over which group posed a greater threat to American society. Advocates of Mexican restriction for the most part hailed from the West and the South. Support for tighter immigration controls was strong in the western states especially during the Depression years, when white workers were competing directly with Mexicans for agricultural and railroad jobs. Support for restriction was also robust in the South, where the Ku Klux Klan was exercising its political muscle during a tumultuous period of social and economic change. Sponsors of exclusionary legislation such as Harris (Georgia) and Box (east Texas) seized on these anxieties, arguing that immigration and racial competition had harmed the living standards of white working families.[16]

Welch reintroduced his Filipino exclusion bill, HR 8708, on the House floor on March 25, 1930. This was not the first time he had proposed such legislation, having sponsored a similar bill in 1928. The 1928 bill, HR 13900, had been jointly drafted with members of the California Joint Immigration Committee and sought to amend subdivision (b) of section 28 of the 1924 Immigration Act, which exempted citizens of America's imperial possessions from quota restrictions.[17] The bill, however, was tabled without a hearing and disappeared from the legislative docket. Welch reintroduced his bill as HR 8708 in March 1930 to much greater attention. The key provision of the Welch bill aimed to amend the term "alien" as defined in the 1924 Immigration Act to include citizens of the Philippine islands. This change in definition would subject Filipinos to the restrictive quotas established under the 1924 act. Senator Samuel Shortridge, yet another Californian, also introduced a Filipino exclusion bill to the Senate Immigration Committee. Shortridge told constituents in Long Beach that his bill was motivated by a desire "to guard the doors of my people" from the latest wave of Asiatic invaders flooding across California's borders.[18] Both legislative proposals cited the recent race riots on the West Coast as a key rationale for terminating the right of Filipinos to enter the United States. Congressional restrictionists frequently recycled nativist talking points, warning of continued racial strife if the federal government did not act quickly to remedy the matter. Congressional debates on the subject of exclusion repeated many of the same inflammatory charges that had been leveled against Filipinos on the West Coast and nativists leaders were frequently called as expert witnesses during the congressional hearings on the Filipino question. Nativist ideologues were recognized as legitimate spokespersons for the public interest, and their claims were accorded a disproportionate degree of attention and authority by lawmakers.

These claims makers did not go unchallenged, however, as a number of political representatives from the Philippines also testified before the congressional committee. Filipino leaders refuted the racist characterizations of their community made by exclusionists and questioned the propriety of the United States' barring its own imperial subjects from entering the borders of the "mother country." Philippine spokespersons had their own political agenda at the hearings as well, seeing the forum as an opportunity to advance the cause of national self-determination. Exclusion without independence, they argued, violated American principles of liberality and fair play, and they called on federal authorities to live up to their lofty political rhetoric touting the United States as a beneficent imperial power. Restrictionists also faced opposition from the White House and federal agencies such as the Department of War and the State Department, which believed that the Philippines (and Filipinos) played a valuable political and military role for the United States in the Asia-Pacific region. Immigration exclusion would likely be perceived as a slap in the face to Filipinos and might undermine American interests in that part of the world. Agribusiness groups, especially those from Hawaii, also exposed immigration restriction on purely instrumental grounds, inasmuch as they depended on the steady flow of tractable labor from the Philippines to replenish the plantation workforce. Filipino leaders and their allies played an important role in derailing the passage of exclusion bills and ultimately helped shift legislative focus to the issue of Philippine independence. Their political maneuvering, however, came at a steep cost, as Filipinos were forced to accept immigration quotas as a trade-off to secure ratification of an independence bill.

Competing Interests

By the time Congress held hearings on immigration from the Philippines, the desirability of Filipino exclusion was not really a matter of debate, with most senators and representatives accepting the premise that immigration from the islands constituted a serious social problem. There were, however, significant differences of opinion on how to resolve the matter. On one side were advocates of outright immigration restriction, who believed Congress should bar Filipinos from the United States irrespective of their status as American nationals. Hardcore exclusionists worried that the issue of Philippine independence was a political hot potato that was best dealt with as a separate legislative matter. On the other side were those who believed that exclusion could be implemented in a more diplomatic and honorable way, favoring independence as a means to curtail immigration. The granting of Philippine independence, they argued, would allow the United States to avoid a rather ugly diplomatic precedent—being the first imperial state to ban its own political subjects from entering their sovereign state. The passage of an independence bill, moreover, would yield the added bonus of placing Philippine imports under tariff quotas. This was a major concern of midwestern congressional representatives from states with large sugar-beet and/ or dairy industries, who had long railed against the import of cheap Philippine goods such as cane sugar and copra (coconut oil) that competed with their products.[19]

The Shortridge bill was first introduced on the Senate floor as a standalone exclusion bill (S. 4183) on April 16, 1930, but Shortridge quickly shifted tactics and reoffered his proposal a week later as an amendment (S. 51) to Senator William Harris's Mexican-exclusion bill, which already had significant support in Congress. The Shortridge amendment was modeled on the Chinese Exclusion Act of 1882. The senator explained that the "main and vital purpose" of his provision was to "prevent the coming of what may be called the laborer class,"[20] exempting students, merchants, and government officials from quota limits. The bill targeted only immigration to the "Continental United States," a proviso added to appease Hawaiian sugar planters, who opposed any legislation that would hinder the unfettered flow of Filipino labor to the islands. The Shortridge amendment was designed to act as a stopgap measure, with the exclusion provision remaining in force for five years from the date of ratification. The temporary fix advocated by Shortridge proceeded on the assumption that a Philippine-independence bill would be passed during that five-year interval, rendering the need for a separate exclusion bill moot. Shortridge introduced into the Senate record dozens of letters and telegrams from concerned citizens to illustrate popular support for exclusion. These letters were mostly from West Coast labor and patriotic organizations that endorsed Filipino exclusion. Speaking on behalf of his own bill, the California senator explained that temporary restriction was an urgent issue that could not be delayed while Congress dragged its heels on the question of Philippine independence. Exclusion, he argued, was vitally necessary because the "Oriental" and "Caucasian" branches of the human family were not culturally compatible, a truism evidenced by the outbreaks of racial violence on the West Coast. The problems associated with Filipino immigrants, moreover, demonstrated once again that Asians were antagonistic toward the nation's social and political institutions. The American form of government, Shortridge declared, could not survive unless the "dominant and controlling race" reclaimed control of the nation's borders and sealed them off against alien trespassers.[21] Filipino immigration posed an unusually potent threat in this regard, because of Filipinos' unique political status and because of their peculiar propensity for race mixing. That the inhabitants of the Philippines had unfettered access to the United States created a potentially ruinous problem, since "hundreds of thousands" or "perhaps millions" of Filipinos would immigrate, intermarry with whites, and produce a large class of mixed-race children with full citizenship rights. Shortridge took pains to emphasize that his opposition to Filipino immigration was not born of racial animus—he simply wanted the Philippine people "to remain where god placed them and where history found them." The alarmist rhetoric about miscegenation and political disorder struck a chord with South Carolina senator Coleman Blease, a fervent white supremacist who in 1928 had proposed an amendment to the U.S. Constitution seeking a nationwide ban on interracial marriage. Blease advised his colleagues to "to shut the gates now" to Filipino immigration to help the nation ward off the rising threat of racial mongrelization.[22]

Although many members of the Senate supported Filipino exclusion in principle, Shortridge had a difficult time securing votes for a stand-alone immigration bill that did not address the independence issue. Opposition to the Shortridge amendment came from two separate camps. One group was made up of senators from midwestern states, who would not get behind a bill that ignored their demands for a tariff wall against Philippine imports. They argued that Philippine-independence legislation was a more comprehensive solution to the problem, since it would restrict the entry of both commodities *and* labor from the islands. Politicians such as Arthur Vandenberg of Michigan and William King of Utah were key figures in this group. Both were labeled "sugar-beet senators" because of their desire to block the entry of imported Philippine cane sugar in favor of the domestic beet variety grown in their states. Others, such as Harry Hawes of Missouri and George Norris of Nebraska, represented dairy-producing states concerned about the importation of Philippine coconut oil (an ingredient in margarine and other products) that competed with staples such as shortening and butter. Another smaller group of congressmen, mostly from the northeastern states, opposed Filipino exclusion on political grounds. The most vocal proponent of this faction was Hiram Bingham of Connecticut, who believed that the barring Filipinos while they were still colonial subjects violated American principles of international amity and fair play. Bingham served as the chairman of the Senate Committee on Territories and Insular Affairs and was more attuned than others to the potential diplomatic fallout likely to result from the implementation of a callous restriction policy barring American dependents. Bingham had allies in the U.S. State Department, which also considered exclusionary legislation harmful to U.S. political interests in the Asia-Pacific region and sought to stall Congress from passing any bill that undermined America's stature in the global community.[23]

The Shortridge amendment to the Harris exclusion bill finally came up for a vote on the Senate floor on April 23, 1930, where it was defeated by a margin of forty-one to twenty-three, with thirty-two abstentions. While the majority of senators present during the debate supported the immigration exclusion in principle, the issue of independence remained a major sticking point. The rather large number of abstaining votes on the Shortridge amendment partly reflected lingering uncertainties about the wisdom of enacting an exclusion policy targeting people under U.S. sovereignty and the likely diplomatic fallout that might ensue from such an action. The fact that no political representatives from the Philippines had been allowed to formally weigh in on the Shortridge legislation also struck some senators as a potential public-relations problem.

The Filipino-exclusion question received a more protracted deliberation in the House of Representatives, where Immigration Committee chairman Albert Johnson scheduled formal hearings on Representative Richard Welch's exclusion bill. This piece of legislation was even more malicious than the Shortridge amendment, seeking to reclassify Filipinos as "aliens ineligible to citizenship." This change was designed to strip them of their status as U.S. nationals, thereby subjecting them to the exclusionary quota system established by the 1924 Immigration Act. In Welch's speech introducing HR 8708, he warned his colleagues that Filipino migration and settlement in the United States constituted one of the "gravest problems that has ever faced the people of the Pacific Coast." He referenced the recent outbreaks of violence on the West Coast, which in Welch's view "reveal[ed] the intense jealousy and racial hatred which the Asiatic immigrants have aroused." His characterization of the race riots again shifted blame from the white perpetrators of the attacks to the Filipino victims, whose actions had "aroused" a violent reaction from besieged communities. He cautioned his fellow congressmen that the Filipino "problem is bound to become so acute that it will test every power of our State governments on the West Coast." Welch employed a novel argument to support what he called the "ethics" of immigration exclusion, citing the benefits of restrictive controls instituted by American officials in the islands in the period immediately following annexation. The implementation of Chinese exclusion laws in the Philippines had, according to Welch, kept other "races of invading Asiatics" from overrunning the islands, saving the Filipinos themselves from racial extinction. This led Welch to ask, "Do we not . . . in all fairness, have a moral right to protect the racial integrity of our own people by excluding a race which scientists, as well as our own instinct, tell us should not mix their blood with ours?"[24] Welch's suggestion that a double standard was at work, one that permitted Filipinos to protect themselves from undesirable racial groups, but did not allow Americans the same right of racial protection was bizarre. The Chinese exclusion laws he spoke of had been instituted by the American colonial officials in consonance with U.S. immigration policy and were not provisions that Filipinos had demanded out of racial antipathy against the Chinese.[25] This argument was part of a larger strategy employed by nativists to deflect charges of racism and imperial malevolence. Restrictionists repeatedly portrayed their actions as defensive and perhaps even altruistic, aimed at protecting both whites and Filipinos from the conflicts that emerged when two incompatible racial groups were forced to live side by side.

The hearings on the Welch bill began on April 10, 1930. Among the witnesses invited to the proceedings were "distinguished Californians" U. S. Webb and V. S. McClatchy, as well as a number of other restrictionists such as John Trevor of the American Coalition of Patriotic Societies and William Hushing of the American Federation of Labor. Welch kicked off the hearings by stressing the unique burden that the citizens of California and the American West had borne when it came to dealing with immigration problems. Unlike other parts of the country, this region faced an unceasing onslaught of aliens from both the southern and Pacific borders. He argued that California had become a "dumping ground for Filipinos . . . and Mexicans" but promised that citizens of the western states were ready to play a vanguard role in shoring up the nation's borders as they had done in previous decades against the Chinese and Japanese. Welch's address drew heavily on nativist talking points and his opening remarks presaged the exclusionists' political playbook. This strategy relied heavily on alarmist rhetoric about job displacement, sexual impropriety, and public health hazards, employing the language of crisis to galvanize public support and demand government interdiction.

Welch asked his colleagues to visualize the menace posed by forty-six thousand young, unmarried Filipino "troops" marching across the country "in mass formation," swarming across the border like an invading army. This "invasion," according to Welch, had already produced tragic consequences, as American citizens were displaced by cheap Filipino labor, driving white workingmen to desperation and criminality.[26] John Trevor of the American Coalition of Patriotic Societies testified that white families were suffering downward mobility because of Filipino labor and called on Congress to bar further entrants from the Philippines in the "interest of the public welfare."[27] Nativist testimony repeatedly returned to the theme of racial victimhood to underscore the injurious effects of Filipino immigration. J. Edward Cassidy, another representative from the American Coalition, testified in support of HR 8708, asserting that ancient Egypt and Rome had collapsed because they failed to restrict the entry of undesirable immigrants, a mistake that led to their territories being overrun by the "tide of colored races." He added that exclusion was desirable on patriotic grounds, since the influx of unassimilable immigrants such as Filipinos made the country vulnerable to foreign infiltration and subversion. Cassidy maintained that Americans "who ha[d] any spark of patriotism" supported Filipino exclusion as a means to preserve racial and national unity.[28] A key challenge for West Coast nativists was to convince people in other parts of the country that the issue would soon affect their communities. They cautioned their colleagues in Congress that though

Filipino immigrants were "our problem to-day," they "will be yours tomorrow." In other words, it was imperative for Congress to resolve the Filipino crisis now before it spread to the rest of the nation.

The American Federation of Labor, not surprisingly, sent representatives to testify before the committee in support of the Welch bill. W. C. Hushing, the legislative representative of the AFL, and Andrew Furuseth of the International Seamen's Union recycled the usual charges of job displacement and downward economic mobility for white families. Most of the evidence they provided was anecdotal, offering little in the way of concrete data about white workers losing their jobs to Filipinos. The simple fact that a Filipino held any job in the United States while white workers were unemployed was proof of displacement. The only possible explanation for the employment of Filipinos, according to Hushing and Furuseth, was that they were cheaper and more tractable than white workers. It followed from this logic that "cheap" Filipino labor depressed the "American standard of living" by pushing down wages and eroding the gains won by trade unionists during previous decades.

The Southern Strategy

Western nativists knew that they could not win passage of an exclusion bill without another large bloc of votes in Congress. Movement spokesmen saw southern Democrats as their natural allies on issues of racial exclusion, regularly invoking the specter of miscegenation in a bid to win support from the representatives from that region. Restrictionists portrayed Filipinos' demands for social equality and minority rights in the United States as a thinly veiled smokescreen for their real agenda: interracial marriage with white women. This same accusation had long been levied by white leaders in the South to disparage the civil rights demands of African Americans, who, according to segregationists, possessed an irrepressible desire for conjugal access to white women. Nativist point men warned that Filipinos would soon be intermarrying with white women in the eastern and southern states if congressional leaders did not throw their support behind exclusion.[29]

Restrictionists claimed that Filipino men had a peculiar talent for winning the affections of white women and had proven themselves adept at evading proscriptions on interracial marriage. J. Edward Cassidy reminded the committee that even though the number of Filipinos intermarrying with whites was small, the "mongrel stream" resulting from such unions multiplied rapidly, producing hybrid children "of the worst type."[30] This point was underscored by V. S. McClatchy, who painted a grim picture of white racial decline in the face of unrelenting waves of Asian migration over previous decades. Admixture with Filipinos, he argued, violated the laws of nature and degraded the blood of the white race. The arrival of increasing numbers of Filipinos had pushed the situation to a crisis point, forcing western leaders such as McClatchy to demand from Congress "protection against the colored races of the Orient." He dismissed charges that recent campaigns to expel Filipinos from the West Coast were motivated by hate or malice, claiming instead that white citizens had acted in self-defense to reclaim their communities and their nation from an alien onslaught. The struggle to defend America's Pacific border was described as a high-stakes conflict that was already playing itself out in the Hawaiian Islands. McClatchy pointed to Hawaii as a "terrible example of the penetration of colored races" into an American domain. The demographic majority of Asians in Hawaii offered a cautionary tale that illustrated the dangers of laissez-faire immigration policy. Hawaii, according to McClatchy, was "hopelessly lost to the white race" due to the lax attitude of federal lawmakers. The nightmare scenario that had unfolded in Hawaii was likely to be repeated in "white man's country" if lawmakers did not fortify the nation's western border. This scenario, he warned, was a matter of great urgency for American citizens, since if California went "colored," it would quickly "spread all over the United States."[31]

Nativist ideologues believed that the specter of miscegenation, more than any other issue, might win support from congressional leaders in the South. McClatchy testified to the committee that most of the rioting that had occurred on the West Coast was because Filipinos did not "mingle well with other racial elements." This was largely due to the "extreme unassimilability" of the Filipino people, as evidenced by their reckless and arrogant defiance of the color line. McClatchy and other exclusionists defended the recent outbreaks of violence against Filipinos as a natural and instinctual response to violations of racial taboos regarding interracial intimacy. He described Filipinos as a "proud and aggressive" race that presented trouble "we never had with the Japanese, Mexicans or Chinese." The operation of taxi-dance halls, in particular, was held up by nativists as a "provocative cause" of racial resentment among local whites. McClatchy cited an editorial from the *Gilroy Dispatch* justifying violence against Filipinos, drawing a direct parallel between whites' opposition to race mixing in the West and in the South. According to the piece, Filipinos operated outside the bounds of societal conventions, "openly and brazenly" pursuing white women "to satisfy their lust." This practice was "enough to make the blood of any white man, or decent man boil" and thus explained the ferocity with which local citizens attacked the Filipino problem. McClatchy was careful to highlight the editorial's conclusion, asking committee members rhetorically, "What would our southern fellow Americans say if the southern negroes were to open dance halls with white entertainers saying they preferred white women to negresses? There would be a riot in the South, there would be a massacre."[32]

Many of these same themes were taken up by California attorney general U. S. Webb, who saw the preservation of national and racial boundaries as inseparable. Webb testified that racial incompatibility between whites and Asians was a "chemical fact," arguing that Filipino-white admixture led to the dissipation of white racial hegemony. He told the committee that America's position as a global power could not be sustained without the "complete predominance of white blood" and asked the federal government to do its part to preserve the integrity of the national community.[33] Webb drew a direct comparison between the "race feeling" aroused by Filipinos in the West and that associated with African Americans in the South. He condemned Filipinos' "boastful arrogance" on matters of interracial intimacy and expressed frustration that so many white women reciprocated romantic interest. Webb declared "great sympathy with the South" on the necessity of racial segregation and reproved political leaders from the North and East who lacked an understanding of the terrible burdens borne by whites in the West and South. He warned that the race riots that had recently occurred on the West Coast were simply a preview of even greater conflicts to come if Congress did not act to bar the nation's doors to Filipinos.[34]

While many in Congress were concerned about the defiant attitude of the Filipino community, the prospect of barring immigration from the Philippines while it was still under the sovereignty of the United States proved to be a major stumbling block for exclusionists. Many lawmakers recognized that America's international standing required them to abide by certain international norms and conventions, even if these rules caused some friction on the domestic front. Filipino leaders also played an important adversarial role in the exclusion debate, demanding that American leaders adhere to established precedent regarding the treatment of imperial subjects and insisting that the Philippines be granted its independence as a precondition for any change in Filipinos' immigration status.

The Opposition Speaks

Filipinos testifying on the Welch bill had their own agenda for the hearings. They saw the forum as an opportunity to make the case for independence and to challenge racist claims made by their adversaries. The Philippine delegation included Manuel Roxas, speaker of the Philippine House of Representatives; Camilo Osias, Philippine resident commissioner; Manuel Briones, House majority leader; and Pedro Gil, House minority leader. Joining them in opposition to the bill was a representative from the U.S. War Department and lobbyists from the Hawaiian Sugar Planters Association. Filipino leaders had two main objectives at the hearings: The first was to challenge the political and legal propriety of the United States' excluding its own colonial wards. Their second goal was to steer the debate away from immigration restriction and back to the question of Philippine independence, a legislative solution that would allow both sides to claim a measure of victory. Philippine officials had pressed the case for national self-determination for decades without making much headway, so the immigration hearings offered a timely, though somewhat awkward, opportunity to move their political aims forward. Filipino representatives expressed some embarrassment about appearing before the committee in light of the racist and insulting charges leveled at the Filipino community during the hearings, but the hostile climate did not prevent them from confronting their adversaries' head on and taking them to task for their racism and hypocrisy. Their status as American subjects, they argued, entitled them to special treatment, especially since they had proven themselves to be loyal allies of the United States during World War I.

Manuel Roxas laid out the key themes of the opposition strategy, engaging in a protracted back and forth with committee members, who at times seemed confused about the precise legal status of Filipinos in the United States. Roxas challenged a key premise of the Welch bill—that the U.S. Congress could legally reclassify Filipinos as aliens, as defined in the 1924 Immigration Act. Recalling earlier debates surrounding Filipinos' naturalization status in the United States, he pointed out that U.S. courts had definitively recognized that Filipinos were American "nationals" and not "aliens." To change their status now would give the term "alien" a "wholly arbitrary meaning" inconsistent with established legal precedent. Roxas reminded the committee members that American officials had always framed their role in the Philippines as a benevolent one, rooted in "principles of fair-play, righteousness, and justice." To enact restrictive legislation would call into question the "guiding norm[s] of American conduct" and would likely create resentment against the United States in the islands, upsetting cordial relations between the two governments.[35] Roxas also drew on the rhetoric of American exceptionalism to defend the special status of Filipinos, noting that U.S. policymakers had always touted their brand of imperialism as a more munificent and progressive type of sovereignty, a tradition that could not be reconciled with the belligerent aims of the Welch bill.

Roxas spent significant time responding to nativists such as McClatchy and Webb, whose testimony was riddled with misinformation and specious claims. He ridiculed Webb for suggesting that the United States might solve the problem of Filipino immigration simply by selling the Philippines to another imperial power. The notion that Filipinos were "owned as mere chattels, as a herd of oxen, and [might] be disposed of as such" was, according to Roxas, wholly inconsistent with political and moral norms undergirding American dominion in the islands. This was a compelling point, insofar as Filipinos had U.S. sovereignty imposed on them by force and were powerless to "disentangle themselves" from this imperial attachment. Other members of the Philippine delegation reminded the members of the Immigration and Naturalization Committee that Filipinos "owed allegiance" to the United States and lived under the American flag. Passage of the Welch bill, they argued, would set a troubling precedent, singling out the United States as the world's only imperial power to ban its own political subjects from entering the "mother country." Roxas drove this point home by highlighting the fact that Filipinos had never been excluded from Spain during its three centuries of colonial rule in the islands, even though Spain, unlike the United States, "was a selfish, imperialistic power!" This clever contrast between Spanish colonial policies and the ostensibly more humane character of American empire effectively communicated the odious nature of the Welch exclusion bill.[36]

Filipino leaders also argued that the Welch bill was inconsistent with the "innate sense of justice and fair play of the American people." It would be unfair, they testified, to exclude immigrants from the Philippines because Filipinos did not have the reciprocal right to exclude Americans from immigrating to the Philippines. Pedro Gil testified that a prohibition on Filipino immigration while the Philippines were still under the U.S. flag would be "unjust" and "un-American." If Congress wanted to restrict Filipino immigration, it first needed to grant the islands their independence, which would give Philippine leaders the reciprocal authority to exclude Americans from their country. Furthermore, the change in status proposed in the Welch bill would place Filipinos in the rather strange position of being able to travel freely under an American passport to any country in the world—except the United States.[37]

The Filipino delegation also questioned the motivations of congressional restrictionists, portraying the Welch bill as a clear case of racial discrimination, a charge that nativists repeatedly denied. Roxas acknowledged that Congress had the right to regulate immigration but asked the committee why it was singling out Filipino nationals for exclusion while allowing "aliens" from countries such as England, Germany, Canada, and Poland to enter the United States in relatively high numbers. If the restrictionists were really interested in protecting "American laborers," why were lawmakers permitting "250,000 quota immigrants" per annum to enter the country and compete with American workers, as allowed under the 1924 Immigration Act? Filipino leaders asserted that U.S. nationals, who lived under the American flag, should receive priority in matters of immigration over "aliens" of foreign allegiance.[38]

This imperial-allegiance argument was bolstered by the testimony of General Francis Lejeune Parker, who represented the War Department. General Parker was the chief of the Bureau of Insular Affairs, the agency within the federal government that held jurisdiction over America's insular possessions. He maintained that the unique relationship between the United States and its insular subjects entitled Filipinos to special consideration in matters of immigration policy. He testified that approximately twenty-five thousand Filipinos had volunteered to serve in the U.S. military during World War I, a fact that demonstrated their "whole-hearted loyalty and patriotism to the United States." Having demonstrated their allegiance through faithful wartime service, Filipinos deserved to be treated with more respect and dignity by American lawmakers. Parker suggested that the exclusion of loyal Filipino subjects would represent a heavy-handed exercise of state power, especially while tens of thousands of unloyal "aliens" from nations such as Mexico entered the country every year without restriction. The State Department opposed the legislation for similar reasons, believing that Filipino exclusion could hurt America's reputation in Asia. The positions taken by the War and State departments reflected the political imperatives of the Hoover administration, which believed that the islands provided military and commercial value to the United States, and President Hoover threatened to veto legislation, including the Welch bill, that might destabilize U.S. interests in the region.

The testimony provided by the Philippine delegation and General Parker clearly gave the Immigration Committee pause. It became clear over the course of the hearings that barring Filipinos while they were still under the American flag would create a major public-relations headache for the United States as it vied for power and prestige in the global arena. By the end of the 1930 hearings on Filipino immigration, it became clear that restrictionists did not have the votes for passage of the Welch bill. It became increasingly clear to nativists that they would have to shift gears and look more seriously at the issue of Philippine independence. The fact that some members of the Philippines delegation agreed that it would be "fair" for the United States to exclude Filipinos if they were first given their autonomy would provide the necessary political cover for those skeptics worried about the diplomatic consequences of exclusion. Filipinos, of course, resented the indignity of accepting exclusion as a trade-off for national sovereignty, but they saw little choice but to accept this Faustian bargain as the high price to be paid for their dreams of self-determination.

Independence from the Philippines

In 1931, Arthur Free offered a bill, HJ Resolution 478, seeking to place a quota of five hundred per year on Filipino immigrants, but this proposal was stalled by House Immigration Committee chairman Albert Johnson, who tried again to prevent the Filipino issue from derailing higher-priority legislation aimed at curtailing Mexican immigration. This setback finally convinced nativist leaders to abandon efforts to secure passage of a stand-alone exclusion bill. This new strategy was reflected in the actions of the AFL, which switched tactics in 1931 and made the passage of a Philippine independence bill the sole focus of its agitation on the Filipino issue. Though the AFL had passed resolutions endorsing independence during previous years, it had spent an equal amount of effort lobbying on behalf of Filipino exclusion. Labor leaders made it clear that they would not support any independence measure that did not contain a clear and unequivocal provision mandating the immediate exclusion of Filipino labor. Organized labor's political campaigning on behalf of independence put it in strange company, finding itself working toward the same legislative goal as midwestern agribusiness interests. Among the various agricultural organizations pressuring Congress to divorce the United States from the Philippines were the National Grange, the American Farm Bureau, the National Dairy Union, and the National Beet Growers Association.[39] These were some of the same organizations that had opposed the Shortridge and Welch bills because they did not contain provisions restricting the entry of Philippine products. Trade-union leaders and agribusiness concerns, which just a year before had been on opposite sides of the Philippine question, were now allies working toward the common goal of Philippine independence as a means to stem the flow of Filipino laborers and imports into the United States. That fact that Philippine leaders were also lobbying for the cession of U.S. sovereignty in the islands made the issue even more compelling.

Over the next two years (1932–1933), Congress considered a variety of bills aimed at conferring Philippine independence. Senator William King, who hailed from the sugar-beet-producing state of Utah, proposed a bill granting immediate independence to the islands, a change in status that would subject Philippine cane sugar to tariff restriction. A proposal from Senator Hiram Bingham called for the creation of a joint commission to study the practicability of independence and then issue a report on its findings before the Congress acted on legislation. This was likely a stall tactic by Bingham, a respected internationalist who preferred an amiable and gradual termination of Philippine-American ties. Senator Arthur Vandenberg of Michigan, a Republican loyalist acting on behalf of the Hoover administration, offered a legislative proposal aimed at delaying formal independence. His plan proposed a commonwealth-type status for the Philippines that would allow the United States to maintain remote control over the islands indefinitely. None of the bills gained much traction, as the various factions pressing for independence—agribusiness, labor unions, and nativists—differed over the features of the various proposals. The King bill, granting immediate independence, did not get much support, since the general consensus in the Senate was that some sort of probationary period was needed to prevent the Philippines from descending into anarchy after the exit of American overseers. The exact length of the probationary period was a serious source of conflict, with proposals ranging from a relatively brief eight-year transition period to the much longer twenty-five-year interval favored by the War Department. While there was a general agreement among congressional leaders about the necessity of a probationary period for Philippine independence, questions remained about how immigration and tariff barriers would be implemented under the various proposals. Would restrictive quotas on Philippine immigrants and products begin with the passage of an independence bill, or would the free entry of Filipino laborers and commodities continue during the probationary period? Would the Filipino people accept immigration and trade restrictions as part of an independence bill, or would they continue to demand "special privileges" even after formal ties were severed?

Support for Philippine independence picked up new momentum in 1932 with the introduction of concurrent bills by Harry Hawes of Missouri and Bronson Cutting of New Mexico in the Senate and by Butler Hare of South Carolina in the House. The Senate and House bills shared the same basic outlines and eventually merged into a single legislative proposal after some back and forth between the two legislative bodies. The American Federation of Labor, powerful agribusiness interests, and Philippine delegates Sergio

Osmena and Manuel Roxas all testified at hearings on the new bill. The initial versions of the Hare and Hawes-Cutting bills did not directly deal with the issue of immigration exclusion, due to concern that such a provision would offend the Filipino people and derail support for the legislation in the Philippines. California congressmen Hiram Johnson (Senate) and Richard Welch (House) considered this issue to be a deal breaker and quickly inserted an exclusion clause into the Hare-Hawes-Cutting bill.[40] That the motivations of American lawmakers in pushing this legislation forward were less than noble was not lost on Filipino leaders, who remarked that congressional support for national autonomy was as much about "independence of America *from* the Philippines" (emphasis added) as it was about independence for the Philippines.[41]

The Hoover administration was strongly opposed to independence and tried through various channels to delay the passage of the Hare-Hawes-Cutting bill. These methods included adding unfriendly amendments, offering alternative legislation, and recruiting Hoover allies to filibuster the bill. None of these tactics worked, however, and the Hare-Hawes-Cutting bill passed in December 1932. The legislation, however, still had two significant obstacles to overcome before it would be passed into law. First, it had to prevail over the likely veto of President Hoover. In addition, the bill required ratification by the Philippine legislature before it could take effect, though the bill's sponsors assumed that Filipino leaders would rubber-stamp the proposal. Congressional leaders were prepared for Hoover's veto and had the necessary votes to override it.

The bill's supporters were caught by surprise when the Philippine legislature, which had long demanded independence, vetoed the bill in early 1933 after Manuel Quezon, president of the Philippine Senate, raised strong objections. Not surprisingly, Filipino leaders wanted to begin their sovereign status on the most advantageous terms possible and were not happy with key provisions of the Hare-Hawes-Cutting bill. The issue was also complicated by the fact that Quezon was locked in a power struggle with Sergio Osmena and Manuel Roxas, as both camps jockeyed for control of the postindependence regime. Most Philippine leaders had reservations about the tariff and immigration provisions in the bill but figured that this was the price to be paid for independence. Some opponents of the Hare-Hawes-Cutting bill also expressed concerns about the continued presence of U.S. military bases in the islands, which for many Filipinos symbolized a threat to national sovereignty. Quezon believed that he could negotiate a better deal with the incoming Roosevelt administration, one that would adjust the restrictive immigration and trade quotas laid out in the Hare-Hawes-Cutting bill. Roosevelt's representatives informed Quezon, however, that these issues were not negotiable and that restrictionists might demand even harsher terms if Filipinos continued to press the issue. This seemingly endless political maneuvering did not sit well with nativist leaders, who believed that Filipinos were getting cold feet about the exclusionary provisions contained in the bill. They criticized Filipino leaders for reneging on the deal and called on federal officials to settle the matter once and for all. California labor boss Paul Scharrenberg wrote an article entitled "What Do Filipinos Want?" which voiced the concerns of exclusionists. Scharrenberg stated that it was "hard to figure out just what our little brown brothers are after. . . . Evidently they themselves have not the slightest idea that a free and independent nation must stand upon its own two feet and accept the same treatment with respect to tariff and immigration as is accorded to other nations." He called for the "prompt enactment of a Filipino exclusion bill—with or without independence. The evils of Filipino immigration are altogether too serious. The solution to of that evil must not be delayed or tied to an academic debate over independence."[42]

The only area in which Philippine leaders were able to win any concessions was on the issue of military bases, with Quezon negotiating the withdrawal of U.S. Army bases and gaining a promise to revisit the issue of Navy bases during the Commonwealth period. The revised Hare-Hawes-Cutting bill was reintroduced in 1934 by its new sponsors, Senator Millard Tydings of Maryland and Representative John McDuffie of Alabama, and it was passed by Congress in March 1934. The Tydings-McDuffie Act mandated a ten-year probationary period under which a Commonwealth government supervised by the United States would assist in the transition to self-rule. The Philippine legislature was instructed to draft a national constitution patterned on the U.S. republican system. The Philippine Constitution was approved by President Roosevelt in March 1935.[43]

The ten-year probationary period mandated by the Tydings-McDuffie Act revealed the separation anxiety of American officials, who believed that the Philippines would descend into chaos without another decade of paternal supervision. And though formal independence would not be enacted for ten years, two important exclusionary provisions prescribed by the act would be put into force immediately. Section 6 of the act established quotas for Philippine products such as sugar, coconut oil, and cordage, and graduated tariff duties were placed on other goods, slowly limiting the access of Filipino products to the American market. Not surprisingly, the act contained no provision allowing the Philippine government to reciprocally levy any duties or quota restrictions on the entry of U.S. products, allowing American goods unfettered access throughout the Commonwealth period. More important, Section 8 of the Tydings-McDuffie Act reclassified the Philippines as a "foreign country" vis-à-vis U.S. immigration law. American immigration authorities were now obliged to treat Filipinos "as if they were aliens" in all matters pertaining to their right to enter the United States. This change in status made them subject to the limitative restrictions established in the 1917 and 1924 Immigration Acts.

Federal officials granted the Philippines a quota of a mere fifty immigrants per year during the Commonwealth period. This meager quota reflected the lingering hostility to Filipino immigrants on the West Coast and was only half the number of entries allocated to other Asian nations such as China and Japan, which received one hundred slots per annum under the 1924 Immigration Act. The ration of fifty entrants per year for Filipinos was characterized as a compromise figure, since American lawmakers had actually considered the unprecedented step of completely cutting off all immigration from the islands. Adding insult to injury, Filipinos would be barred altogether from immigrating to the United States at the end of the ten-year probationary period because they had not been allocated a quota under the terms of the 1924 Immigration Act.[44]

West Coast exclusionists celebrated the passage of the Tydings-McDuffie Act as a reaffirmation of the principle of Asian exclusion, which in their minds had been undermined by the free entry of Filipinos. Representative Richard Welch sent a letter to Paul Scharrenberg lauding the victory of Filipino exclusion after a long, hard-fought political battle. Scharrenberg included a copy of Welch's communiqué in an article he wrote called "Filipino Exclusion as Accomplished Fact," which was published in various labor publications across the state of California. Welch declared that Filipino exclusion was "an accomplishment of which we can both be proud," noting that it had spurred a new effort in Congress to reduce the quota allocated to Chinese and Japanese immigrants from one hundred to fifty per year to put them on equal par with Filipinos. He added, "The very fact that the Filipinos, who were practically wards of ours, have been placed on a quota of fifty annually is assuring that the bars will not be let down for other Asiatics."[45]

A Problem Not Solved

U.S. officials lauded the Tydings-McDuffie Act as a political victory for both Americans and Filipinos. For most Americans, the new bar on immigration from the Philippines was the most obvious benefit of act. The *Washington Post* declared the exclusion of Filipinos to be "Benefit No. 1

resulting from independence" and reported that American officials were acting swiftly to implement provisions enforcing immigration restriction. The State Department appointed Henry Day as chief consular official in Manila to supervise the new quota system and to collect a newly instituted head tax from those departing the islands. Day's appointment set an unusual precedent, as he was the first foreign service officer ever to serve in such a capacity on what was technically "American soil." The Philippines' change in status had other consequences as well, since Filipino representatives serving in the U.S Congress in Washington, DC, were reclassified as aliens, a thorny problem considering the United States' prohibition on "aliens" serving in that body.[46]

While nativist leaders celebrated the new restrictions on immigration from the Philippines, they still expressed concern about the problems posed by the tens of thousands of Filipinos already in the United States. Racial antagonism toward Filipinos remained strong on the West Coast and had spread to other parts of the country by the mid-1930s. The Filipino "boy crisis," for instance, still attracted sensational attention on the West Coast. Newspaper headlines in Southern California in November 1933 warned readers of a so-called white slavery ring operating between Los Angeles, San Luis Obispo, Pismo Beach, and Bakersfield. The outfit was accused of luring young girls into a prostitution racket that catered to Filipinos in the region. Art Maron, a Filipino chauffeur from Los Angeles, was charged with being a principal player in the ring, driving young white women to and from various hotels in the Southland region, where they were "forced to submit to the advances of Filipinos." Sensational reporting about the case reinforced the public perception of Filipinos as possessing a pathological attraction to white women, a compulsion that gave rise to a secretive criminal enterprise aimed at enslaving young white girls in California. In March 1934, Maron and his three codefendants were convicted of pandering and conspiracy and were sentenced to serve one- to ten-year sentences in state prison.[47]

Hostility toward Filipinos also remained strong in Northern California during the mid-1930s. Police in Sacramento broke up the attempted lynching of a thirty-two-year-old Filipino who allegedly attacked a local white woman. A mob of twenty-five men captured Jose Banez and "looped a rope around his neck and were running frenziedly thorough the alley looking for a pole from which to hang their victim." He was rescued when police spotted Banez being dragged down the street by the bloodthirsty mob.[48] A high-profile incident made headlines in San Francisco when law-enforcement officials uncovered an underground network of "Mixed Race Parties" at which

Filipino men and white women socialized in private homes across the city. Police raided a residence at 1139 Turk Street, described as a Filipino "community house" where many these parties were held, and arrested six Filipinos and three white women who were identified as ringleaders of the social network. The Filipinos—Robert Gabriel, Peter Suguitan, Joseph Mariana, Steven Datoe, James Asperas, and Florence Martinez—were charged with vagrancy and held on one thousand dollars bail each, after freely admitting to having frequented the gatherings. The three white women—June Furness, Gloria Lane, and Kay Deane—ranged in age from twenty-two to twenty-three but were all described as "looking much younger" than their ages. During the hearings, municipal judge Sylvain Lazarus expressed outrage at the "shocking conditions resulting from intermingling of Filipinos and white girls." Lazarus was particularly disgusted by the casual attitude of the three white female defendants, who expressed no shame or guilt about their actions. The *San Francisco Chronicle* noted that all three women wore fur coats to the trial, likely purchased by high-spending Filipinos who enjoyed their company. One of the women, June Furness, was accused along with Peter Suguitan of assaulting another white woman who had attended one of the parties. Judge Lazarus "blew up" in the courtroom after hearing revelations of social liaisons between hundreds of San Francisco girls with "flashily dressed 'little brown men.'" He condemned the "strange influence" the men had on "tender" young girls, whose morals were being corrupted through their unwholesome associations with Filipinos. Lazarus directed the three female defendants to be held in quarantine to undergo medical examination by health officials. The judge ordered San Francisco chief of police William J. Quinn to "clean up" conditions in the city and instructed the San Francisco Police Department to "take into custody all white girls seen in company with Filipinos, together with their escorts."[49]

Widespread unemployment during the early years of the Great Depression added to resentment in the region about the continued presence of Filipinos in the United States. In April 1932, eighty-seven Filipino laborers were "driven out" of Banks, Oregon, by white laborers and farmers. Filipinos had been hired to harvest the area's strawberry crop but were ordered to evacuate the district after a "mass meeting of whites" declared them a menace to the local economy. The next year, a bombing campaign was orchestrated by residents of the Yakima Valley to drive Filipino agricultural workers out of the region. A local white Citizen's Committee "requested" that Japanese truck farmers on the Yakima reservation stop employing and/or subleasing agricultural land to Filipinos. The committee cited "unfair competition with white labor and mingling with white women" as its principal objections to Filipinos. The Japanese initially refused to cooperate with this order, and during March and April 1934, nightriders tossed dynamite and planted bombs on farms that employed Filipinos.[50]

The growing labor militancy of Filipino workers also remained in the spotlight. A series of large-scale strikes and labor actions disrupted the agricultural industry in California and reinforced perceptions of Filipinos as a disruptive force in American political life. A major strike in 1933 saw workers across the state engaged in simultaneous labor actions. The walkout affected the state's peach and lettuce crops, as well as pear orchards, grape vineyards, and cotton and sugar-beet fields. The industry faced millions of dollars of losses due to the loss of perishable crops. In addition, the walkout by Filipino and Mexican fieldworkers threatened the jobs of innocent white cannery workers who were idled by the strike. Seven hundred Filipino lettuce pickers in Salinas were singled out for their intransigence, selfishly striking right before the harvest to leverage a pay increase from employers during this brief window of vulnerability. Soon, over three thousand lettuce pickers and sugar-beet toppers across the region had joined the strike, which was led by the Filipino Protective Union and CAIWU. Local authorities denounced attempts by these radicals to "paralyze the entire fruit industry of the state." Community sentiment turned against the Filipino workers, who were driven out of the town of Escalon by "fifty white men" who told the islanders that it "was the community's wish" that they leave the city.[51] Portrayals of Filipinos as "congenital insurgent[s]" became commonplace in popular accounts of their labor activities. Filipino labor activist Ricardo Ramos was arrested and convicted in Los Angeles for distributing literature to strikers and picketers at Terminal Island inviting them to join the Communist Party. A week later, two thousand Filipino agricultural workers in Salinas declared that they would engage in a sympathy walkout during the San Francisco general strike of 1934, raising fears about their alliance with radical labor leader Harry Bridges.[52]

The FLU was involved in a series of lettuce strikes in 1933 and 1934. The 1934 lettuce strike was initially a joint effort between the Filipino fieldworkers and white shed workers. The white workers were represented by the AFL, however, and bargained separately, agreeing to a settlement that ignored the demands of the FLU. The lettuce growers had verbally approved arbitration with the FLU but backed out of that agreement once the AFL union negotiated an accord with the white workers. The FLU called for a strike, causing problems for white shed workers, who could not profit from their new contract without a lettuce crop to pack. The militancy of the FLU worried growers and authorities, who had seen Filipino workers walk out in support of the San Francisco general strike just two months earlier. Local media coverage repeatedly mentioned that both Filipino strike leaders, Marcuelo and Canete, were married to white women, adding another layer of antagonism to the volatile situation. Growers, police goon squads, and deputized white citizens launched a "determined drive to clear the Salinas Valley lettuce field of all Filipinos." They expelled eight hundred workers from the community and justified their campaign as necessary to rid the community of Filipino labor organizers, who were "under the domination of communist agitators."[53] A street sign in Salinas warned Filipino workers, "This is White Man's Country. Get Out of Here if You Don't Like What We Pay."[54] A group of vigilantes showered the camp of FLU president Rufo Canete with gunfire and burned it to the ground, resulting in the death of a Filipina woman, Marguerite Vitacion.[55] Relying on the usual playbook, Salinas authorities initially blamed the attack on Filipinos, even though all the witnesses to the incident insisted that the raiders were white men.[56] The police expressed little interest in finding the vigilantes and instead arrested Canete for "inciting a riot" in connection with his labor activism.

Despite the combined efforts of growers, vigilante groups, and sympathetic law-enforcement officials to suppress the FLU, the strike was successful. The walkout was called off on September 24, 1934, and the strikers went back to work, with significant pay raises and recognition of their union.[57] The FLU victory, however, created bad blood with growers and local authorities, who no longer viewed Filipinos as a long-term solution to their labor problems. Crippling strikes led by Filipino and Mexican workers in Santa Barbara County and the Imperial Valley the same year added to the backlash against Filipinos on the West Coast.[58] The escalating militancy of Filipino labor led George P. Clements, head of the Los Angeles Chamber of Commerce's Agricultural Division, to condemn Filipinos as "the most worthless, unscrupulous, shiftless, diseased, semi-barbarian[s] that ha[ve] ever come to our shores."[59] Farm operators on the West Coast who during previous years had tolerated Filipinos and opposed restriction began to rethink their stance as the social and political costs of hiring Filipino workers grew. Nativist leaders took advantage of the growing frustration with the intransigence of the Filipino population to press for new federal legislation aimed at ridding the country of the problem once and for all.

"A Disguised Form of Deportation"

Some of the key figures behind the campaign for Filipino exclusion launched a new campaign aimed at repatriating those immigrants still residing in the United States back to the Philippines. A mass deportation of Filipinos similar to campaigns carried out against Mexicans during the early 1930s was not practicable because of the unique political attachment between the United States and the Philippines. Congressional restrictionists and nativist leaders, however, got creative in their efforts to facilitate a mass exodus of Filipinos. Lawmakers came up with a novel legislative solution that might achieve the result of a large-scale deportation without the political fallout. U.S. officials set about crafting a federal policy aimed at convincing Filipinos to leave the country voluntarily, with Uncle Sam providing financial and logistical assistance to facilitate their departure.

Representative Samuel Dickstein, who chaired the House Immigration and Naturalization Committee, proposed an early version of this legislation in 1933. The bill, House Joint Resolution 549, was specifically aimed at repatriating "unemployed" Filipinos back to the Philippines, with government assistance. The federal government would provide logistical support for transportation to the islands and a financial appropriation from Congress would pay for their one-way passage back to the islands. Dickstein's proposal was couched in humanitarian terms as an effort to help indigent Filipinos return home during a time of economic distress. Lawmakers also believed that the departure of large numbers of Filipinos would help to quell the racial antagonism on the West Coast, which continued to flare up on a regular basis through the mid-1930s. Among the notable witnesses appearing at the hearings in favor of the resolution were U.S. Secretary of Labor William Doak, Major General John L. Dewitt of the War Department, and William Hushing of the American Federation of Labor, who never missed an opportunity to discuss the menace posed by Filipino immigration. Officials from Los Angeles County were also called to testify before the committee since they claimed to be overburdened by Filipinos seeking public assistance from the local relief agencies. The assertion that Filipinos put a serious strain on state welfare rolls was accepted as an article of faith, even though data compiled by the Federal Emergency Relief Administration (FERA) cast doubt on these claims. According to FERA, Filipinos made up only 135 of 64,403 people on the Los Angeles County welfare rolls, hardly a significant portion of those requesting public assistance.[60]

The appearance of municipal officials was particularly significant since Los Angeles County had served as ground zero for a federal campaign to expel tens of thousands of Mexicans during the late 1920s and early 1930s, an operation held up as a successful model for repatriating Filipinos. William Doak had been a central figure in the Mexican-repatriation drive, serving as President Hoover's point man in marshaling the Department of Labor's personnel and resources to round up undesirable aliens and deport them. Persons of Mexican ancestry, both immigrants and citizens, were expelled en masse during raids throughout most of the Great Depression.[61] The mass repatriations carried out during this period were supposed to free up jobs for American citizens by eliminating cheap alien labor from the job market. Public officials also hoped that the repatriation campaign would lessen the burden on public-relief agencies, which had their hands full with citizens and noncitizens alike. The Dickstein measure was designed to achieve the same goals, though it was framed in humanitarian terms, inasmuch as the federal government was trying to "help" indigent Filipinos relocate to friendlier environs. The real motives of the legislation were betrayed by the testimony of many witnesses at hearings on the bill, such as Representative Richard Welch and the AFL's William Hushing, who hailed the bill as a much-needed government intervention that would reduce the supply of cheap Filipino labor. Though labor representatives lauded the aims of the Dickstein bill, some members of the Immigration and Naturalization Committee wondered if their enthusiasm was misplaced. Representative Thomas Jenkins of Ohio reminded those at the hearings that the proposed legislation only applied to "unemployed" Filipinos and was not a mass repatriation act. This distinction was of little importance to Hushing, who admitted that the AFL's position on Filipinos was simply to "get them out of the country as soon as possible."[62]

William Doak heartily endorsed HJ 549 and sent a special assistant, Murray Garsson, to Southern California to do some "heavy investigation" of the Filipino situation and then report his findings at the hearings. Garsson's testimony asserted that the number of Filipinos had reached epidemic proportions in California, a situation that reinforced the need for aggressive government action on the matter. He introduced wildly inflated estimates of the Filipino population in the United States and of the total number of those who were unemployed to inflate the scale of the problem. Garsson suggested that there were as many as 150,000 Filipinos living on the U.S. mainland and 60,000 residing in Los Angeles County alone, figures at odds with the Census Bureau's count of 45,000 total living in the continental United States. He estimated that 80 percent of the Filipinos in the United States were unemployed, a situation that caused severe hardships for the communities in which they resided. Garsson drove this point home by telling the committee about the dire conditions he discovered while investigating a "Filipino colony" in Los Angeles. He described visiting a Filipino home where fifteen or sixteen men lived together in a single room, "sharing beds in shifts of three" and rotating sleepers twenty-four hours a day. These practices, according to Garsson, were typical among Filipinos and posed a possible public-health risk to the communities around them. Other witnesses at the hearings on the Dickstein bill assured committee members that there was widespread support for repatriation among Filipino leaders, who recognized that economic and social competition in the United States had reached a crisis point. Committee members discussed the logistics and costs of a repatriation operation, even though Filipino leaders criticized the bill as a thinly veiled deportation act. Advocates of the Dickstein measure suggested that as many as thirty thousand Filipinos would voluntarily repatriate if their travel was subsidized by the federal government.[63]

Lawmakers were eager to put this process into motion, with the initial plan focused on using military transports to send the repatriates back to the Philippines en masse. The logistics of such an endeavor, however, were not as simple as originally thought, since army and navy ships were already running at maximum capacity with service personnel. Representative Charles Millard of New York expressed frustration with the lack of space on the military transports, asking General John Dewitt if there was any way to make more room on their vessels to move Filipinos out of the country at a quicker pace. Dewitt informed the congressman that he opposed exceeding the vessels' carrying capacity, noting that the ships had a finite number of beds and were not designed to function as cattle cars. Millard responded that the military transports could actually take three times as many repatriates as Dewitt claimed, since Filipinos "were accustomed to sleeping in three shifts," a reference to Murray Garsson's earlier testimony. The general balked at the idea, arguing that such a practice would create hardships for military personnel and would likely be viewed as a callous approach to the matter.[64] The lack of space on army and navy vessels compelled lawmakers to look into commercial liners as a more expeditious way to ship out Filipinos, even though the cost of such an undertaking concerned some committee members. Frustration with the growing cost estimates of the repatriation campaign led some lawmakers to question the whole "free trip" idea and to suggest that Filipino officials be asked to reimburse the U.S. government for the costs of repatriation.

Although support for repatriation on the committee was unanimous, HJ 549 was eventually tabled, unable to secure a spot on the legislative calendar. The bill was reintroduced again a few months later, with some minor revisions, as HJ 118. The proposal, however, did not contain a clear provision barring Filipino repatriates from returning to the United States, which became a sticking point for restrictionists, who wanted assurances that there would be no right of return. Dickstein argued that a ban on return was implicit in the measure because of the so-called pauper's provision already enforced through Section 23 of the 1917 Immigration Act. Under the pauper's provision, aliens were exempted from returning to the United States upon acceptance of federally funded deportation. This did not convince skeptical lawmakers such as Representative Thomas Blanton, who argued that the pauper's provision only applied to aliens, which might allow Filipino nationals to skirt the rule.[65] Restrictionists also argued that it was unfair for Congress to use public funds to repatriate Filipinos without concrete assurances to taxpayers that repatriates would not return to the United States a short time later. Dickstein's failure to adequately address the right-of-return issue led to the bill's defeat in February 1934. Restrictionists in Congress did not wait long to reintroduce an amended measure, with the necessary proviso barring Filipino reentry. On March 6, 1935, the indefatigable Richard Welch sponsored HR 6464, which contained clear-cut language prohibiting the return of Filipinos who had been "deported." Immigration and Naturalization Committee members Martin Dies of Texas and Thomas Jenkins of Ohio applauded Welch for putting together a bill that would "make it impossible for Filipinos to return to the United States." The only weakness of the legislation, according to Dies, was that it made repatriation "voluntary," a problem that allowed Filipinos to stay in the country even though they were no longer welcome.[66] A final amended version of the bill, cosponsored by Hiram Johnson in the Senate, was signed into law on July 10, 1935.[67]

Media observers extolled the virtues of the new policy, suggesting that the mass departure of the islanders was in the best interest of both Americans and Filipinos. The *San Francisco Chronicle* encouraged Filipinos to take advantage of the Repatriation Act, declaring that they would be "happier in their own land and California would be better off." Leading African American newspaper the *Chicago Defender* concurred, noting that Filipinos had worn out their welcome in the United States and suggesting that their "love [of] American Life and Blonds" had turned public opinion against them. The paper criticized the ever-increasing "criminal class" of Filipinos, who wore "exaggerated clothes" and "infest[ed] the taxi-dance halls night after night," wasting all their money on ill-advised leisure activities.[68]

Projections about the number of potential repatriates were implausibly high, based on the inflated estimates proffered by exclusionists. Colonel Daniel W. MacCormack, commissioner of the Immigration and Naturalization Service (INS), headed up the federal campaign to organize the Filipino exodus. The first order of business was to conduct a nationwide survey to determine the number of denizens willing to leave. Lawmakers originally earmarked $450,000 to finance the repatriation program, with the expectation that as many as forty thousand Filipinos would leave the country. Upon completion of the survey in February 1936, however, MacCormack discovered that the number of potential applicants was much smaller than anticipated, with only around one thousand Filipinos showing interest. The Congressional Appropriations Committee trimmed the budget for the program to $100,000, which included both transportation funds and money to pay for a series of nationwide newspaper advertisements to promote repatriation. The lack of interest from Filipinos surprised many people, especially in light of the exaggerated claims touted by exclusionists. This setback offered an early sign that the dream of a mass repatriation of Filipinos was going to fall well short of early estimates. The fatal flaw of the legislation, according to the *Los Angeles Times*, was that the bill was "voluntary," allowing the resident nationals to stay in the United States and underbid whites in a tight depression labor market.[69] MacCormack explained that the discrepancy between preliminary projections and the actual number of applications was due to a propaganda campaign waged by labor contractors who profited from the exploitation of Filipino immigrants. He expressed disappointment in the low numbers, alluding to the fact that only seventy-seven applications for repatriation had been formally filed during the first six months of the program and adding that the "prospect of persuading the approximately 40,000 Filipinos to go home is not nearly so bright now as it was when the bill was enacted."[70]

MacCormack ordered immigration officials on the West Coast to launch a promotional blitz to "counteract" skepticism about the program in the Filipino community. Edward Cahill, commissioner of immigration in San Francisco, and Walter E. Carr, district director of the U.S. Immigration Service in Los Angeles, took the lead in the day-to-day logistics of repatriation on the West Coast.[71] Federal officials also targeted Filipinos living in other parts of the country and provided logistical support to get these individuals to California, where they could be shipped out. The Department of Labor chartered a special train that departed from New York City in April 1936 to pick up Filipinos at designated stops across the country and to transport them to San

Francisco, where they would board the *President Coolidge* ocean liner bound for the Philippines. The train passed through Cleveland, Chicago, St. Louis, and Denver on a month-long voyage across the country.

Time magazine documented the journey, noting that the Filipinos were enjoying the "free ride" that took them "halfway across the world entirely at the expense of the U.S. Government." The magazine remarked that the "subsidized exodus" of Filipinos was welcome news in the western states, where they had become "problem children" for Pacific coast authorities. The *Time* article featured commentary from San Francisco judge Sylvain Lazarus, highlighting a fiery exchange he had with Quintin Paredes, the Philippine resident commissioner in Washington, DC, over the judge's description of Filipinos as savages. Lazarus told *Time* that no racial group in San Francisco had supplied the criminal courts with more business than the Filipinos, noting that almost all of their crimes had "as background intimate relations with white girls." The desirability of an effective repatriation campaign was magnified by the sexual sophistication of Filipinos, who, according to Lazarus, "practice[d] the art of love with more perfection than white boys."[72] The pervasive threat of amalgamation gave the repatriation issue added urgency, insofar as the continuing presence of Filipinos in the United States increased the likelihood of continuing violence and disorder.

As the December 31, 1936, deadline for repatriation approached, exclusionists had little to show for their efforts. Officials tasked with carrying out the program were forced to request an extension from lawmakers in Washington, DC, to continue the campaign. Congress extended funding for an extra year to allow immigration officials on the West Coast to drum up support for a program they characterized as "the most considerate piece of legislation of the type ever conceived by a government." Walter E. Carr promoted the virtues of repatriation in the Southern California media and disputed the perception promoted by Filipino leaders that the program was little more than a "disguised form of deportation." He told the *Los Angeles Times* that immigration authorities were engaged in a humanitarian effort and that Filipinos were beneficiaries of American munificence. Advocates of repatriation emphasized the "special privilege" that Filipinos held, noting that "Uncle Sam" was generously funding their passage back to their country of origin.

Filipinos living in the United States, however, questioned the liberal intentions of American authorities, especially since "alien" immigrants also received the same "special treatment" of free federally funded transportation when they were deported for criminal convictions or political subversion. U.S. officials continued their public-relations blitz, telling potential repatriates they would be traveling to the Philippines on "luxuriant ocean liners with Uncle Sam paying their passage and all expenses and wishing them bon voyage, . . . [to be] greeted in Manila by brass bands and songs of welcome." Officials noted that Filipinos could even take their "automobile" or "blond wife" with them if they could afford the extra passage.[73] The issue of wives and children of Filipino immigrants became an unexpected quandary for West Coast officials, who discovered that a number of their potential targets were unwilling to leave the United States without their families. In Los Angeles, which was said to have the largest concentration of Filipinos on the West Coast, only "117 men, eight women, twenty-seven children and six white wives" had been repatriated through October 1936. A measly 157 Filipinos left the country through the repatriation program by the end of 1936, a figure far short of the tens of thousands promised by exclusionists. Carr explained that the lack of provision for the passage of Filipinos' families had created a serious obstacle for immigration officials. He revealed that his office had entered into an arrangement with the Los Angeles County Welfare Department to pay for the passage of children of interracial unions to avoid the burden of leaving them in the United States. Carr added, however, that "no provisions ha[d] been made for white wives of Filipinos," noting that the families had to come up with the pricey steamship fares, which were more than one hundred dollars, out of their own savings.[74] Coming up with this kind of money was no small burden for potential repatriates, most of whom were poor and/or unemployed.

In the meantime, exclusionists shifted some of their focus to tightening up loopholes in federal law that they believed allowed Filipinos to circumvent racially restrictive immigration laws. West Coast labor leaders singled out the illicit entry of Filipino seamen into the United States. Filipino and Chinese sailors were regularly hired by shipping companies in Asian ports and became a popular source of labor for the global merchant fleets.[75] Labor spokespersons such as Andrew Furuseth and Paul Scharrenberg claimed that there were thousands of Filipino seamen working on American ships, taking jobs away from white seafarers. They also alleged that Asian crewmen jumped ship at unsupervised West Coast ports and thus evaded surveillance of U.S. authorities. Western trade unionists won a victory with the passage of the 1936 Merchant Marine Act, which restricted the employment of alien seamen. Section 302 of the act mandated that all crew members on American cargo ships be U.S. citizens, a provision aimed at restricting the surreptitious entry of Asian seafarers through West Coast ports.[76] In addition, federal authorities moved to deport six hundred Filipinos who had arrived in the United States after the passage of the Tydings-McDuffie Act. These individuals had actually left the Philippines before the act had been formally signed into law but landed in the United States after the law went into effect. The Philippine resident commissioner's office expressed concerns about the increasingly aggressive tactics of federal authorities in scrutinizing the status of Filipinos in the United States. Philippine officials were inundated with letters from Filipinos who were being threatened with deportation on specious grounds. Still others who were legal residents of the United States complained that they were being denied reentry to the country after traveling abroad. The Philippine government eventually took up the plight of Esteban Conti as a test case of the Filipinos' new immigration status, demanding that he be released from detention on Ellis Island as a legal resident of the United States.[77]

The Filipino Repatriation Act was extended two more times through December 31, 1940, in a last-ditch effort to convince Filipinos to leave the country.[78] A mass exodus of Filipinos, however, never materialized. By the end of 1938, *Time* magazine called the repatriation program the "Philippine Flop," characterizing the $237,000 spent on the operation as a disappointment. The magazine speculated that the campaign had failed because the "boys [were] loathe to leave a country, where as a California judge remarked, they boast of enjoying the favors of white girls because they are a very superior grade of lovers." This did not surprise renowned labor journalist Carey McWilliams, who predicted that very few Filipinos would apply for the act since they viewed the Welch bill as a "trick, and not a very clever trick, to get them out of the country" because of their labor militancy and political activism. The program officially ended during the fiscal year 1941, having repatriated 157 Filipinos in 1936, 580 in 1937, 502 in 1938, 392 in 1939, 425 in 1940, and 134 in 1941, for a total of 2,190. These numbers fell far short of the thirty to forty thousand predicted by exclusionists.[79]

As the 1930s came to a close, the standing of Filipinos in the United States was more precarious than ever. Though clearly not welcome in the United States, many Filipinos were wary of returning to the Philippines with little money and few opportunities for employment. The Tydings-McDuffie Act occasioned some important changes in the character of Philippine-American relations, most notably a modification in the immigration status of Filipinos. Those still living in the United States remained an outcast population living on the margins of American society. The outbreak of World War II soon provided an unexpected opportunity for Filipinos to stake their claim to civic recognition and belonging in American society.

6

"Another Mirage of Democracy"

War, Nationality, and Asymmetrical Allegiance

The years leading up to World War II witnessed a series of domestic and international political shifts that profoundly altered the contours of U.S.-Philippines relations. The Tydings-McDuffie Act of 1934, as discussed in the previous chapter, established a framework for Philippine independence, but full autonomy was not scheduled to go into effect until the completion of a ten-year probationary phase, set to end in 1946.[1] During this period, a Commonwealth government was established in the islands and tasked with implementing a national constitution and managing the transfer of sovereignty. For most residents of the Philippines, life under the Commonwealth system did not differ markedly from the previous period. Excepting for changes to their immigration status and new restrictions on Philippine goods entering the American market, asymmetrical power relations between the two societies remained firmly in place. All decisions made by Commonwealth officials were subject to approval by the United States, thus safeguarding American commercial and geopolitical interests in the islands from any potential nationalist initiatives aimed at appropriating land or resources held by the U.S. government or U.S. corporations. Two provisions of the Tydings-McDuffie Act reinforced these asymmetrical ties: The first decreed that Filipinos still "retained allegiance" to the United States during the ten-year trial separation phase. Another section of the act authorized the president of the United States to conscript "all military forces organized by the Philippine Government" to fight under the American flag at any time during this period. These provisions served as powerful reminders of Filipinos' continuing political obedience to the imperial center, and both obligations took on unexpected importance as the two countries were drawn into World War II.[2]

The Japanese invasion of the Philippines in December 1941 brought the planned transfer of sovereignty to a standstill, leaving the political status of Filipinos in limbo once again. The Commonwealth's defense system, at the time of the attack, was under the control of the U.S. military command. American forces in the islands were poorly organized and underresourced, even though the Japanese government made no secret of its desire to establish an imperial bulwark in the region. That the Roosevelt administration showed so little interest in shoring up the islands' defenses in the lead-up to the war struck a discordant note with many Filipinos, since the United States had long justified its imperial presence in the Philippines as a protective enterprise aimed at forestalling military intervention by hostile foreign powers. Within months of the initial attack, American commanders left for Australia, and the archipelago fell under the control of the Japanese imperial army. Japan's wartime occupation of the Philippines raised the specter of Filipinos having to answer to their third colonial sovereign in less than fifty years. The political future of the islands, however, was far from settled, since the United States maintained its claims of sovereignty over the Philippines even after American officials withdrew in early 1942. Though disappointed by the retreat of American military forces, most Filipino leaders still saw their political fortunes as inextricably linked to the United States. An active guerrilla movement quickly emerged in the islands, waging a protracted insurgency campaign against the occupation government. Many guerrilla units worked in tandem with U.S. commanders in the Pacific, viewing an Allied victory in the war as the best way to realize their aspirations for national self-determination.

The wartime crisis gave rise to a new set of political dilemmas for Filipinos, especially those living in the United States, who viewed the war as a chance to defend their native soil from Japanese aggression, as well as an opportunity to prove their fidelity to their adopted homeland and its democratic institutions. Filipino Americans expressed their eagerness to join the fight against the Axis powers, but their transient political status complicated initial efforts to volunteer for military service in the United States, since recruitment guidelines contained no protocol for the domestic enlistment of U.S. nationals. Bureaucratic uncertainty regarding their eligibility for American military service was eventually resolved, and they would soon play a significant role in both the domestic and international war effort. The wartime sacrifices of Filipinos, like those of other racial minorities, took on a complex set of meanings as they pledged their undivided loyalty to a nation that had long treated them as an unwanted and unwelcome presence. Their zealous allegiance is all the more remarkable considering Filipinos, just a few years before, had been subject to a vitriolic campaign aimed at barring their entry into the United States and a federally orchestrated drive to repatriate all those who still remained in the country back to the Philippines.

In the year leading up to the war, Filipino American leaders had begun to ratchet up their demands for full political enfranchisement in the United States. In 1940, labor organizer (and part-time sociologist) Trinidad Rojo published an open letter to U.S. leaders that augured many of the grievances that were taken up by community activists during the war. Rojo declared, "We, Filipinos, owe allegiance to the United States. In case of war we are duty bound to lay down our lives for the STARS AND STRIPES. If the American flag imposes upon us the duty to die for it, if necessary; in all fairness, it must also give us the right to live as American citizens if we choose to do so. If the American flag does not do this it crucifies the ideals of justice and democracy." He added, "we are victims of a Philippine-American relationship which started before most of us were born. Certainly we are not responsible for that relationship. . . . we are here because America is in the Philippines. We are asking you no special privilege. We simply ask you to grant us the naturalization rights which the Americans enjoy in our government. . . . Your naturalization law is consistently inconsistent toward us. It is a record against you rather than us."[3]

Frustrations like those expressed by Rojo did not prevent Filipinos from ardently throwing their support behind the Allied war mobilization. Community spokespersons and activists expressed the belief that their participation in the war effort would demonstrate their identification with, and allegiance to, the United States and its democratic covenant. By defending the cause of American freedom abroad, they reasoned, they could stake a greater claim to civil rights at home. This faith in the inclusionary potential of U.S. democracy was, in part, a response to wartime public-relations campaigns launched by the federal government. U.S. officials actively promoted ethnic pluralism as a touchstone of Americanism and counterposed these patriotic principles to the racialist ideology of the Axis powers. Domestic civil rights leaders took advantage of the shifting wartime political culture, and their agitation led to an expansion of political rights and economic opportunities for minorities. Yet the war also produced bitter disappointment for many loyalists, alienated by the rapid resurgence of prewar patterns of racial and class subordination and by their exclusion from many of the generous postwar entitlement programs available to white GIs. Filipinos, in particular, expressed a strong sense of resentment about the asymmetrical character of wartime obligations, especially in the immediate aftermath of the conflict, when U.S. officials moved quickly to limit America's political and economic liabilities in its war-devastated former colony. This sense of frustration continued after the war and was made even more acute by the failure of the United States to deliver on its wartime pledges of commensurate veterans benefits and civic recognition as a reward for Filipinos' wartime service.

The United States and the Global Crisis

Though the United States did not officially enter World War II until December 1941, it had been operating behind the scenes of the conflict for a few years. Tensions between Japan and the United States had been building for some time, and American war intelligence had been preparing for a confrontation in the Pacific theater for months. It was no secret that Japan harbored designs on the Philippines, seeing the archipelago as part of its larger imperial vision in the Pacific. The surprise attack on the Pearl Harbor naval base in Hawaii by Japanese forces on December 7 was followed a few hours later by full-scale assault on the Philippines. The islands' defense system was quickly overwhelmed, due in no small part to strategic blunders by U.S. commanders, who failed to launch American aircrafts as the offensive began. As a result, Japanese planes flew into the archipelago unopposed and quickly destroyed most of the U.S. air fleet, which remained parked on the ground. General Douglas MacArthur, head of the U.S. Pacific command in the Philippines, pleaded for reinforcements, but none were forthcoming, and the ragtag collection of Filipino and American fighters were left to wage a hopeless campaign against the tactically disciplined and better-equipped Japanese army.[4]

Filipinos living in the United States, like most of their fellow residents, were caught up in the patriotic fervor that swept the country following the Japanese offensive. This zeal was amplified as reports of high civilian causalities in the Philippines spread. Filipinos appeared in droves at recruiting offices to volunteer for service in the U.S. armed forces. To their surprise, the volunteers learned that they were ineligible for military service because of their status as noncitizen nationals. Filipinos had served in the American military before World War II (with the majority serving in the U.S. Navy), but they had joined in the Philippines under the auspices of the colonial government.[5] Though Filipinos were eventually made eligible for military service, the enlistment fiasco served as another reminder of their liminal political condition and the impairments they still faced under U.S. law. Their outlier political status came under new scrutiny in a wartime political climate in which issues of loyalty, patriotism, and civic duty took on new urgency.

The fact that Filipinos "owed permanent allegiance" to the United States was more of an abstract principle than a clear set of political obligations. The contours of this relationship began to take clearer shape in the late 1930s and early 1940s as global military conflicts intensified. Filipinos were swept up in the international turmoil, and their political status in the United States was in a constant state of flux. Over the course of the war, they were subject to a series of arbitrary edicts from the federal government regarding their standing vis-à-vis the national state. At certain times and for particular wartime measures, Filipinos were classed as "aliens," but in other circumstances and for different directives, they were deemed to be "citizens" or "nationals." The fact that an individual could be both alien and citizen at the same time was a striking departure from established legal norms and offers a window into the political anxieties of U.S. policymakers, who sought to exercise greater administrative control over all persons residing within the nation's jurisdictional borders. The wartime schizophrenia about the legal standing of Filipinos recalled previous disputes over their eligibility for citizenship, landholding, and intermarriage. And to the extent that these determinations were arbitrary and enacted from the imperial center, they also served as a reminder that Filipinos remained enchained to American empire even as the United States and the Philippines moved inexorably toward political divorcement.

The United States began preparations for its possible entry into World War II well before the attack on Pearl Harbor. Among the notable steps it took was the enactment of a series of laws, known as the Neutrality Acts, from the mid- to late 1930s, which proclaimed the ostensibly neutral stance of the United States with regard to conflicts raging between belligerent states in Europe and Asia. Another important piece of war-era legislation was the Alien Registration Act of 1940, which required all "aliens" living within U.S. borders to be registered and fingerprinted by the federal government as part of a campaign to prevent foreign subversion and political radicalism. In a similar vein, the Nationality Act, also passed in 1940, revised the statutory definition of American nationality to recodify laws pertaining to citizenship, denationalization, and expatriation. And finally, the Selective Service Acts of 1940 and 1941 were adopted to facilitate the mobilization of the nation's fighting forces during the war. This legislation was particularly important since military service was generally viewed as the highest expression of civic patriotism during wartime.

Navigating this new political terrain proved vexing for Filipinos, who found their standing in American society even more precarious than it was before the war. The U.S. government classified them as "aliens" when it came to their liability under the Alien Registration Act. Yet federal officials classed them as "citizens" or "nationals" with reference to the enforcement of the Neutrality Act and the Selective Service Act. Despite the apparent contradictions of these decisions, there was an underlying logic at work. When it came to exacting maximal loyalty and martial sacrifice from Filipinos, U.S. authorities considered them to be citizens, with the requisite obligation to defend the nation and provide military service to the state during the war. When it came to the state's reciprocal obligation to extend the full spectrum of rights and protections accorded to citizens, then Filipinos were classed as aliens or nationals, with a limited claim to civic benefits and privileges.

Not surprisingly, the U.S. government placed a high premium on national loyalty and patriotic conformity during the war. To this end, authorities went to great efforts to identify and isolate possible threats to national security, particularly alien subversives whose loyalties were questionable. The fact that, legally speaking, Filipinos owed imperial allegiance to the United States did not eliminate questions about their individual fidelity to the American government, since they were, in the minds of most whites, of a suspect racial strain. The war provided a unique opportunity for Filipinos and other persons of Asian descent to demonstrate their commitment to the nation's democratic institutions and, in doing so, to challenge longstanding claims about their cultural unassimilability.

The Shifting Boundaries of the Wartime State

The Neutrality Acts of the 1930s were intended to keep the United States out of the various military clashes erupting around the globe. A majority of Americans were reluctant to get involved in these conflicts, and isolationists in the U.S. Congress effectively blocked efforts by interventionists to directly confront Axis aggression. The Neutrality Acts reflected the isolationist mood of the country and forced the Roosevelt administration to maintain an official posture of nonalignment with reference to conflicts in Europe, Asia, and Africa, even though its sympathies with the Allied nations were clear. The first of these laws, passed in 1935, instituted an arms embargo that prohibited the export of war materials to belligerent nations. The law was amended in 1936 and 1937 to expand the embargo to include other types of commerce, including an injunction against certain types of financial transactions with warring states in Europe.[6]

The final Neutrality Act, passed in 1939, refined the earlier trade prohibition and added a ban on the travel of American citizens to designated combat zones. Filipinos did not believe that this law affected them, since they were not U.S. citizens. The neutrality legislation, however, yielded unexpected consequences for Filipinos, who were suddenly (and provisionally) classified as American citizens. Section 16(f) of the 1939 Neutrality Act contained an unusually broad definition of the term "citizen" as "any individual owing allegiance to the United States." The boundaries of national citizenship, at least for the purposes of this statute, were defined in a broad "geographical sense," covering residents of the "States," "Territories," and "insular possessions" of the United States (including the Philippines and the Panama Canal Zone).[7] The 1939 act's ban on travel to combat zones, which included many global commercial hubs (including the United Kingdom, France, Canada, Australia, and South Africa), had some significant consequences for Filipinos, since such a large number of them made their living as merchant seamen in the international shipping trade. The travel limitations imposed by this new legislation were particularly galling, insofar as the U.S. government had placed restrictions on the employment of Filipino seafarers just three years before, on the basis of their status as "aliens." Recall the Merchant Marine Act of 1936, a piece of legislation championed by West Coast nativist leaders that was enacted to protect the monopoly position of American seamen by severely restricting the number of aliens that could be employed on U.S.-registered vessels. The Merchant Marine Act's statutory definition of the term "alien" explicitly included Filipinos to discourage American shipping companies from hiring them.[8]

In 1940, a group of Filipino sailors challenged the Neutrality Act's travel ban in U.S. federal court in New York, arguing that the law unfairly threatened their livelihood and restricted their freedom of association on dubious legal grounds. The case involved fifty-three seamen who were hired to work on the SS *Panamanian* in Newport News, Virginia. The cargo ship was scheduled to depart for Great Britain, which by this time had been declared a designated combat zone. When it tried to clear port in Baltimore, it was held up by the U.S. Customs Service, which ordered all Filipino crewmembers to quit the vessel before the *Panamanian* would be permitted to leave the country. The owner of the ship (registered to a Panamanian corporation) quickly fired the Filipinos and replaced them with a foreign crew. The fifty-three Filipino crewmen filed a lawsuit against the shipping company, Compania Transatlantica Centroamericana, claiming damages of $35,895 in lost wages and living expenses. The owners of the SS *Panamanian* responded that the plaintiffs were disqualified (as U.S. citizens) from employment on their vessel under the provisions of the 1939 Neutrality Act. The fact that Filipinos were U.S. citizens, the company argued, rendered the employment contract between the two parties null and void.[9]

The case hinged on the appellants' contention that the Neutrality Act's definition of the term "citizen" was arbitrary and inconsistent with previous precedent regarding Filipinos' political status in the United States. The appellants argued that they had previously been classed as aliens for the purpose of other legislative enactments, such as the 1924 Immigration Act (after Tydings-McDuffie) and the 1936 Merchant Marine Act. The Neutrality Act's reclassification of Filipinos as citizens, according to the petitioners, imposed an artificial definition of the term that rendered it meaningless. District court judge G. Murray Hulbert accepted many of the factual claims asserted by the Filipino petitioners regarding their anomalous political status and acknowledged that they had generally been classified as aliens when it came to recent legislative enactments. Yet he ultimately dismissed the relevance of the plaintiffs' arguments, ruling that the U.S. government was empowered to conduct foreign affairs in whatever manner it saw fit, even if it resulted in inconsistent or arbitrary legal definitions. The court ruled in favor of Compania Transatlantica, declaring that Filipinos were American citizens for the purposes of the Neutrality Act. The judgment was also a victory for the federal officials who had issued the original order demanding that the Filipino crewmembers quit the vessel before it could clear port.[10]

Belonging to a State

A very different verdict on the status of Filipinos was rendered with reference to another piece of wartime legislation, the Alien Registration Act of 1940, also known as the Smith Act.[11] The purpose of this law was to bolster the regulatory powers of the federal government with regard to the detention and expulsion of aliens whose political affinities were deemed "subversive." The legislation was a response to prewar anxieties about foreign infiltration and internal subversion that took root during the late 1930s.[12] The Smith Act targeted "traitorous fifth columnists" who "urge[d] disloyalty" among American armed-forces personnel. The statute, however, was broadly written and was also used to root out "seditious" activities not directly related to military security, such as left-wing political activism, narcotics trafficking, and offering aid to undocumented immigrants.[13] New aliens attempting to gain entry into the country after passage of the law were subject to a systematic vetting process, and all aliens over the age of fourteen already residing in the United States were required to register, be fingerprinted, and to fill out a "probing" questionnaire about their political activities at a local post office, under threat of imprisonment and likely deportation.[14]

The Alien Registration Act, like the 1939 Neutrality Act, employed a geographic definition of the United States to determine who would be subject to the law, but U.S. lawmakers used a different set of criteria to delineate the boundaries of the national polity. The territories of Alaska, Hawaii, Puerto Rico, and the Virgin Islands were, under this legislation, included within the rubric of the United States, thereby exempting residents of these territories from the provisions of the act. The Philippines, however, was excluded from the statutory definition of the United States, and Filipinos were thus required to register with the federal government as aliens.[15] This aroused significant resentment within the Filipino community, insofar as Filipinos believed that their compulsory allegiance to the United States distinguished them from "alien" immigrants whose political attachments were less certain.

The legality of the Alien Registration Act was challenged by Filipino lawyer and activist Braulio Gancy.[16] The forty-four-year-old Gancy had criticized the act since its inception, in public speeches and writings, and refused to register as required by law in 1940. Federal immigration officials in Minnesota arrested him on February 19, 1944, after his public activism on behalf of Filipino citizenship rights attracted the attention of local authorities.[17] Gancy acted as his own counsel at trial and argued that he possessed "dual citizenship" in both the Philippines and the United States. He stressed that the U.S. government had long differentiated the political condition of Filipinos from that of aliens and that their unique position in the American polity was a matter of settled law. Filipinos' status as U.S. nationals, he argued, placed them in an intermediate legal classification outside the statutory purview of the Alien Registration Act. Trial judge Gunnar Nordbye rejected all of Gancy's factual claims and told the defendant that the "anomalous" political standing of Filipinos gave them no special immunity with reference to the law in question. Nordbye acknowledged that the 1940 Registration Act did not actually define the term "alien" anywhere in the statute but cited opinions from the commissioner of immigration and naturalization as well as the attorney general that had construed the law to include "any person not a citizen of the United States." The unique status of Filipinos was not lost on the judge, who praised them for their loyalty and courage on behalf of the American war effort. Nordbye opined, however, that if Filipinos were truly loyal, they would happily comply with the Alien Registration Act as a display of wartime patriotism. Gancy's motion to quash the indictment was rejected by the court, and he was convicted and held for sentencing. Facing incarceration, he issued a public plea to Manuel Quezon, exiled Philippine Commonwealth president (who happened to be in Florida at the time of the trial), to aid him in an appeal of his case to the U.S. Supreme Court. But no intervention was forthcoming, and Gancy was sentenced to prison.[18]

Anxiety about alien disloyalty and fifth-column espionage was a chief preoccupation of American policymakers throughout this period. In a speech before a national conference of law-enforcement officials in August 1940, President Roosevelt and his attorney general, Robert Jackson, called on local, state, and national lawmakers to work in tandem to root out "internal enemies" who threatened American security. Roosevelt implored state and federal authorities to enact additional legislation aimed at combating "subversive acts, seditious acts and those things which might slow up or break down our common defense program." This entreaty was reinforced by Jackson, who warned that fifth columnists had already infiltrated the country and were actively "proselyting [sic] for alien beliefs" in an effort to soften up the nation's defenses.[19] Heightened anxieties about foreign subversion reflected an increasing recognition from American political leaders that the United States would soon be drawn into the war and that the nation faced a clear and present threat from domestic radicals.

The Selective Service Act of 1940 was a response to these concerns, and the enactment of this military draft bill sent an unambiguous message to the Axis powers about the war footing of the United States. The act was the first peacetime military conscription in the history of the country and generated significant opposition from isolationists in Congress. The Selective Service law decreed it the "duty of every male citizen . . . and every male alien residing in the United States" between the ages of twenty-one and thirty-six to register for the military draft. Only aliens who had declared their intention to become citizens were subject to the draft, and nondeclarant aliens were unconditionally exempt from service because of their indeterminate loyalties.[20] Interestingly, Filipino nationals residing in the United States were initially left outside the statutory scope of the 1940 Selective Service Act and, in fact, were not technically eligible to enlist in the U.S. armed forces at the time of the law's passage. Filipinos' outlier classification again raised questions about where they fit into the American polity and what obligations they held to the United States during wartime. The Filipino question received some much-needed clarification a month later, in October 1940, with the ratification of another piece of war-era legislation, the Nationality Act of 1940.

The new nationality code revised the rules pertaining to the exclusion and deportation of immigrants, giving American officials greater authority to expel individuals whose political loyalties were deemed suspect. The law barred from naturalization persons with "subversive" political affiliations and established procedures for the expatriation (loss of nationality) of military deserters and persons with suspected ties to the political affairs of a foreign state.[21] The act's emphasis on undivided allegiance to the national state reflected wartime anxieties about the country's large foreign-born population and paranoia about domestic subversion. The Nationality Act also provided incentives for foreign-born residents to establish their loyalty to the United States, with a provision that expedited the conferral of citizenship to alien residents who enlisted in the U.S. armed forces.

A key section of the 1940 Nationality Act provided some clarity with regard to the administrative status of Filipinos in the United States. The term "nationality," as used in the new legislation, lacked a precise definition but, broadly speaking, referred to the status of "belonging to a state."[22] The act, however, established a two-tiered definition of nationality to differentiate discrete classes of U.S. nationals. Citizens were, by definition, nationals as fully vested members of the American nation-state. Noncitizen inhabitants of "outlying possessions" such as the Philippines, Guam, and Samoa were also nationals but occupied a different tier of the U.S. polity as fractional, nonvested members.[23] What both groups had in common was the shared condition of "owing permanent allegiance to a state," a political designation that carried with it certain civic obligations. Foremost among these responsibilities was the duty to faithfully support and defend the United States "against all enemies, foreign or domestic."[24] Yet there was a clear distinction between the two classes of nationals. Citizen nationals possessed the highest category of political rights granted by a state and were entitled to the full array of privileges and protections guaranteed by the U.S. government. In this sense, the state also "belonged" to its citizens, since obligations between the two parties were reciprocal and mutually reinforcing. Filipinos and other noncitizen nationals, on the other hand, occupied a second-tier status within the U.S. polity, and their claims on state resources and protections were bounded. So while the noncitizen national held the same duties as the citizen to support and defend the American nation during wartime, the state's obligations to them were tentative and conditional. The 1940 Nationality Act provided an important affirmation that Filipinos still "belonged" to the United States, regardless of their impending independence. This determination had important consequences for Filipinos during the war, as they were called on to fulfill their obligations to the United States through patriotic service.

The Dilemmas of Loyalty

Wars, by their very nature, foreground questions of loyalty and civic duty. Efforts to marshal patriotic conformity took on a new urgency with the formal entry of the United States into World War II in December 1941. Citizens and noncitizen nationals alike were called on to demonstrate their undivided fidelity to the United States and to work for the common defense. In the days following the Japanese attacks on Pearl Harbor and Manila, Filipinos across the country showed up in droves at local recruiting centers to enlist in the U.S. armed forces, only to be turned them away by military officials. Noncitizens were allowed to join the armed forces but were required to file a declaration of intention to become a citizen when they enlisted. Filipinos could not meet this requirement, since they, like other Asian immigrants, were racially ineligible for naturalization.[25]

Filipino community organizations in the United States quickly organized a letter-writing campaign, imploring the federal government to allow them to participate directly in the war effort. Letters and telegrams poured into Washington, DC from all corners of the nation. Frank Reyes, a community spokesperson from New Orleans, sent a wire declaring that the city's Filipino residents were ready to serve the U.S. government in whatever capacity it deemed necessary. Filipino cannery workers in Alaska held a mass meeting during which they pledged their support for the U.S. government and announced a boycott of Japanese businesses. Community leaders in Los Angeles sent a telegram declaring "100 percent loyalty" to the American war effort.[26] Philippine Resident Commissioner J. M. Elizalde aggressively pursued the issue in Washington, DC, lobbying Congress and the Roosevelt administration to amend the law to allow Filipinos to serve in the American armed forces. Secretary of War Henry Stimson acknowledged Filipinos' willingness to "join us in common cause" but stated that a change in the law would be required before they could be admitted into the U.S. armed forces. The federal government acted quickly on the issue, and on December 20, 1941 (less than two weeks after Pearl Harbor), Congress passed Public Law 360, modifying the Selective Service Act.[27]

The amended Selective Service Act of 1941 made it the legal duty of every male citizen and "every other male person residing in the United States" between the ages of eighteen and sixty-five to register with the Selective Service. The revised act, like previous versions, contained a provision allowing noncitizens from neutral countries (Filipinos were initially placed in this class) to apply for relief from military service, but not without punitive sanction, since any individual in this category who applied for a deferment was permanently debarred from becoming a citizen of the United States.[28] Filipinos, though, expressed little interest in deferment, celebrating their newly acquired service status as a welcome opportunity to join in the global fight against fascism.

Upon the passage of Public Law 360, President Roosevelt sent a letter to Resident Commissioner Elizalde, commending Filipinos for their "willingness to join with us in common cause," contributing as junior partners in the international struggle for freedom and democracy. Joining in the war effort, according to Roosevelt, would allow Filipino immigrants living in the United States to show the same kind of courage that their coethnics had shown fighting the Japanese in their homeland during the early weeks of the war.[29] The national headquarters of the Selective Service System announced that "all registrants who are citizens of the Philippine Commonwealth are deemed nationals of the United States and shall be reclassified in the same manner as citizens of this country." Filipino leaders in the United States hailed the ruling as a victory and pressured community members to quickly register with the Selective Service to demonstrate their willingness to join the war effort. Interestingly, the law did not modify the rules barring Filipinos from voluntary enlistment in the armed forces; it simply made them eligible for the military draft, and most were inducted into the U.S. Army. Lack of choice aside, most Filipinos were simply happy to join the fight against the Axis powers in whatever capacity, especially since the new draft law was passed on the same day (January 2, 1942) that Manila fell to invading Japanese forces.[30]

The Filipino community's public zeal for the Allied war effort was publicly hailed by U.S. officials, who were eager to highlight stories that trumpeted the pluralistic character of American society. These expressions of wartime loyalty were far more complex than they appeared at first glance, and media coverage of minority participation in the war often confused contingent patriotism with blind support for the United States and its ruling system. Public endorsements of the U.S. war campaign were often accompanied by sharp public criticism that appropriated the symbols and vocabulary of patriotism to call the United States to task for failing to live up to its democratic covenant.

Carlos Bulosan, the Filipino writer and labor activist, eloquently articulated this double-edged patriotism in his heralded essay "Freedom from Want," published in the *Saturday Evening Post*. The wartime loyalty of Filipinos and other racial minorities, according to Bulosan, was aspirational, founded on a reasoned faith in the yet-unrealized promise of American democracy. His essay celebrated the virtues of the nation's democratic institutions and the righteousness of the Allied campaign against fascism. Yet he was careful to point out that the faith of minority groups in the United States as a beacon of liberty had "been shaken many times and . . . crippled" by entrenched practices of racial exclusion and economic subordination. Bulosan condemned Axis aggression and accented the threat that fascist ideology posed to democratic ideals, but he also identified lynch mobs, union-busting employers, and racial segregation on the home front as equally insidious threats to the viability of U.S. democracy. He concluded his essay by proclaiming that America's "march to freedom [was] not complete" and would not be realized until the United States extended full social and political citizenship to all those who resided within the nation's borders. Bulosan's essay was part of a larger effort launched by the Filipino American community aimed at projecting a new meaning onto the term *patriotism*, replacing its uncritical embrace of national chauvinism and the American ruling system with an aspirational allegiance to the principles of multiracial democracy and class solidarity.[31]

The double consciousness expressed by Bulosan was echoed by other Filipinos, who understandably had mixed feelings about being asked to fight for a country that still treated them as social inferiors. War service, they argued, entitled them to participate as equal partners in the nation's democratic covenant. Activists were quick to point out lingering barriers to equality in the United States, highlighting the fact that Filipinos as a class of persons remained racially ineligible for citizenship in the United States even though they were now subject to military conscription. Moreover, they continued to face discriminatory restrictions in employment, landholding, and family rights. The last issue was particularly contentious, since antimiscegenation laws deterred Filipino enlistees from marrying their white partners in states such as California before they went off to war.

Reconciling the American government's rhetoric of national unity and democratic pluralism with the everyday experiences of racism and exclusion presented a maddening challenge for Filipinos in the United States. Rosario Macabebo, who was among the first group of Filipino draftees inducted into the army, explained this dilemma well in a letter to the editor published in the *San Francisco Chronicle*: "I am now called upon to fight for the Stars and Stripes to risk my life and to sacrifice it if necessary, to pour out my blood in order to help, in my little way, to preserve the democratic way of life. I consider it a privilege to make this sacrifice. I have no intention of avoiding this highest of duties, but I do protest against the glaring denials directed against me!" The denials that he was referring to included racial restrictions on citizenship, proscriptions on family rights, and occupational segregation. Macabebo declared it "undeniably unfair" that he and other Filipinos "should be made to defend the democratic way of life" overseas but "at the same time be denied the enjoyment of that same democratic way of life" at home in the United States. He reassured his fellow Americans that Filipinos would indeed fight to preserve the nation's democracy but asked that his "protest be heard, for it is the voice of thousands," including other minority servicepersons who found themselves in the same situation.[32] Macabebo and his fellow Filipino conscripts did not shy away from demanding a greater stake in America's democratic institutions as a condition of their service. This civil rights strategy paralleled the celebrated "double-V" campaign launched by African American activists, who had similarly linked the victory over the fascism and authoritarianism abroad with victory over racism and subordination back in the United States.[33] The nation's wartime emergency provided a provisional opening for these kinds of claims, as minority groups insisted on greater political recognition in exchange for their patriotic efforts.

American officials worked closely with Filipino American leaders to develop a national strategy to make the best use of the population. The mobilization of the Filipino American community included not only those who served in the armed forces but also the many thousands who assisted the war effort on the home front in a variety of capacities. This included volunteering with the civilian defense corps, organizing a nationwide series of successful Red Cross blood drives, and coordinating local campaigns to buy war bonds. Filipino labor was also mobilized to fill shortages in the West Coast defense industry and played a prominent role in the nation's "Food for Victory" campaign. Filipino leaders in the United States waged an aggressive public-relations campaign to marshal support for the Allied war campaign and placed pressure on rank-and-file community members to do their share to help the war effort. By publicly touting the war sacrifices of their community, Filipino leaders hoped that their highly visible patriotism would help to chip away at lingering racial stereotypes about their community and serve as the basis for a new public narrative that highlighted their commitment to democratic institutions. The patriotic milieu of the country allowed Filipinos to exploit what historian Lucy Salyer has called "the warrior ideal of citizenship" to contest racialist definitions of American national belonging and bolster their civil rights claims.[34]

The War at Home

After Public Law 360 made Filipinos eligible for the military draft, federal officials debated the best way to utilize them. Plans were quickly made to establish a special Filipino unit of the U.S. Army that would be based in California. Many Filipinos, however, were exempt from military service, since a large percentage of the population was already in their mid-thirties, beyond the customary draft age. Selective Service administrators channeled many of the older volunteers into civilian support roles in vital war industries that were facing labor shortages. Jose Imperial, who ran the Philippine resident commissioner's Pacific Coast Office, coordinated campaigns in Seattle, Sacramento, Los Angeles, and the San Francisco Bay Area to organize blood drives and to solicit community pledges for defense bonds. Local initiatives were also commonplace. Two companies of Filipino World War I veterans in Los Angeles were recruited to serve in the state's Civilian Defense Corps, providing logistical support for emergency-preparedness operations on the West Coast. Community organizations across the nation worked with local Red Cross offices to carry out blood drives and benefit dances. In New York City, community leaders organized a "Bomber a Day for MacArthur" fund. Similarly, seven hundred Filipino shipyard workers in Honolulu coordinated a "Bomber for Bataan" campaign drive that established a special defense-bond account to raised funds equal in value to the cost of a plane that would be used against Japanese occupation forces in the Philippines. Moreover, Filipinos in the state of Hawaii oversubscribed by nearly 100 percent above their one-million-dollar quota of war-bond purchases, and similarly high rates of contribution were matched by community organizations in California.[35]

Filipino Americans also played a key role in wartime production industries. Though the Selective Service System is generally associated with administering the military draft, officials at the agency also helped to manage workforce needs for the defense industry and other vital sectors of the national economy. Wartime labor shortages in the West Coast defense industry worried federal officials, who needed munitions plants running at full speed to meet critical production schedules. As a result, Filipino, African American, and Mexican American men and women, along with large numbers of white women, were recruited to fill jobs in the region's sprawling manufacturing apparatus, which produced the nation's aircraft, warships, and armaments. Filipinos and other minorities initially had difficulty finding employment in the defense industry, where racial discrimination was rampant. Civil rights leaders, led by A. Phillip Randolph, pressed the Roosevelt administration to clamp down on discriminatory hiring practices and to open up these jobs to minority workers. These demands won support from the American Legion, whose political ideology of unalloyed patriotism was consistent enough to embrace minorities who demonstrated their willingness to sacrifice for the national defense. The Legion issued a public resolution in early 1942 demanding that "Filipino and Negro citizens be given work in defense plants and that prejudices against them because of their race be dropped."[36] Significant numbers of Filipino men and women did eventually find employment in the defense plants and shipyards on the West Coast, filling slots at airplane manufacturers such as Lockheed, Douglas, Vultee, and Boeing. Others took positions at naval shipyards including the Kaiser, Wilmington, and San Pedro installations in California and the Bremerton and Todd Pacific facilities in the Seattle area, contributing directly to the production of America's "arsenal of democracy."[37]

Although the move into wartime industrial employment was partly fueled by patriotism, Filipino workers were also motivated by new opportunities for social mobility. The wages and labor conditions in defense plants were much better than in the agricultural labor market, where most Filipinos still toiled. Federal authorities, however, worried about a mass exodus of the Filipinos from the fields to the factories. Agricultural production was deemed essential to the war effort, since someone needed to harvest the crops that fed the nation's armed forces as well as the civilian population. Filipino farmworkers were called "soldiers of the soil" to highlight their critical contributions to food production. Low wages and a tight labor market, however, made it difficult to keep laborers on the farms when higher-paying defense jobs in the cities were readily available. Filipinos and Mexicans who, during the 1930s, had been subjected to repatriation campaigns by the U.S. government now found themselves in high demand by federal authorities, who needed them to rescue the nation's agricultural system.[38]

American officials worked with Filipino leaders in California to increase participation in the federal government's "Food for Victory" campaign. Filipinos, however, rejected the federal government's proposition that they simply toil away in the fields for below-market wages out of patriotic duty. Community leaders stressed their commitment to the nation's war effort but demanded fairer compensation for their labor and asked the federal government to subsidize their wages to make up the pay differentials between the agricultural sector and higher-status jobs in the cities. Early antagonism between Filipinos and Japanese on western farms made the situation difficult. Before the war, many Filipinos worked on Japanese-run farms, but tension between the two groups after the invasion of the Philippines led them to "boycott" Japanese farms in the early months of the war, before internment. The walkout worried public officials, since Filipinos made up such an important segment of California's agricultural labor force. The problem was particularly acute in regions such as the Salinas Valley, which produced nearly 60 percent of the nation's lettuce and more than 30 percent of the carrots for the national market and which relied heavily on Filipino labor. Japanese-run farms accounted for a significant percentage of the productive acreage in the region up through the early 1940s, in spite of the state's alien land laws.[39] By the spring of 1942, the Japanese had been stripped of their property and relocated to internment camps, leaving a significant void in agricultural production.[40]

Filipinos were recruited to help fill this labor vacuum but demanded a wage increase of fifteen cents an hour and deferment from the military draft. They also insisted that their participation in the "Food for Victory" campaign be publicly recognized as an alternative form of patriotic war service, so that they were not viewed as slackers for avoiding military duty. Large numbers of Filipinos eventually participated in the nation's wartime agriculture program alongside Mexican nationals recruited by the American government under the newly implemented bracero contract-labor program.[41] Filipino leaders trumpeted their work on the home front as evidence of their patriotism and commitment to American values and institutions. While their domestic efforts garnered praise from their compatriots, their efforts on the battlefield attracted even more attention and provided an opportunity to gain political legitimacy and prove their "Americanness."

From the Home Front to the Battle Front

In January 1942, the War Department revealed the formation of the First Filipino Infantry Battalion, a special unit of the U.S. Army. Military authorities planned to have the Filipino corps play a front-line role in the Allied campaign in Asia. Secretary of War Henry Stimson explained that the battalion was formed in recognition of the "intense loyalty and patriotism of those Filipinos who are now residing in the United States." Their conscription into the American army, according to Stimson, would provide them with the "eventual opportunity of fighting on the soil of their homeland," which by the spring of 1942 was fully under Japanese control.[42]

Appeals to ethnic solidarity were a key part of this mobilization, as both American officials and Filipino leaders emphasized the brutality of the Japanese occupation and the threat it posed to plans for Philippine independence. Public demonstrations of martial nationalism were often accompanied by expressions of enmity toward Japanese, both at home and abroad. The Filipino Federation of America pledged the undivided loyalty of its members to the U.S. government and promised to "crush the enemies of democracy." The federation added that it was the "duty of every Filipino" to do his or her part in the fight to preserve the "high ideals and principles of

American democracy." Philippine Resident Commissioner Elizalde played a central role in marshaling Filipino patriotism. His office worked closely with the War Department and with Filipino World War I veterans living in the United States to rally support for the war program. Elizalde bragged that the Filipinos' fighting spirit was high, noting that men such as Andy Flores, Mariano Sulit, and Stanley Astorga—all veterans of World War I—had personally expressed the willingness to pay the ultimate sacrifice to defend the cause of democracy and freedom against the threat of global fascism. Flores left little doubt about his commitment, telling the *Washington Post*, "I am ready to die. . . . I only ask to kill two Japs for my one life." Sulit, who had served under General Douglas MacArthur, offered a similar declaration, telling the *New York Times* that "Filipinos everywhere . . . are clamoring to get a crack at the Japanese" and were anxiously awaiting the American government's sanction to take on the Axis armies.[43] Jose Imperial of Philippine resident commissioner's Pacific Coast Office was tasked with getting Filipino communities in the western states organized behind the nation's war mobilization. The War Department's decision to create an all-Filipino regiment was partly a result his endeavors. Imperial's efforts paid off, with sixteen thousand men registering for the draft in California alone.[44]

The First Filipino Battalion received its regimental colors in February 22, 1942, and was officially activated into service at Camp San Luis Obispo on April 1. The unit was made up primarily of draftees but also included members of the Philippine Commonwealth Army who were stranded in the United States during the war. Filipinos were technically allowed to serve in "white" units of the U.S. armed forces but were strongly encouraged to join up with the racially organized outfit. The number of enlistees swelled quickly and reached regiment strength by the summer of 1942 (the formation of a second regiment followed a few months later). The two Filipino units eventually included around seven thousand men and were organized under the auspices of the California National Guard, training at bases in Northern and Southern California. A third regiment, made up of Filipino national guard members from Hawaii, was also supposed to merge with the other two units but was prevented from joining the war effort by the Hawaiian Sugar Planters Association, which invoked martial-law emergency provisions to keep them on island plantations in support of wartime food production.[45]

The commander of the First Filipino Regiment was Lieutenant Colonel Robert Offley, who was chosen to lead the unit because he had lived for a few years in the Philippines as a child, when his father was an American military governor in the islands. Offley was assisted by Captain Abdon Llorente, a

World War I veteran who was brought into the unit to assuage grumblings from rank-and-file soldiers about the lack of a Filipino officer in the command.[46] The regiment received the majority of its training at Camp Beale in Marysville, California. The activation of this unit was widely praised by national leaders and military officials as evidence of Filipino patriotism and was held up as a stirring example of the shared commitment of the United States and the Philippines to the values of freedom and democracy. This rhetoric of shared sacrifice and pluralistic solidarity, however, was often offset by conditions on the ground, where the color line remained a powerful barrier to social inclusion.

One of the immediate dividends of military service was an expansion of political rights for Filipino GIs. In early 1942, Congress passed the Second War Powers Act, which, among other things, amended the 1940 Nationality Act (discussed earlier) to provide expedited naturalization for aliens or nationals serving in the U.S. military. Like similar legislation enacted during World War I, the statute offered the reward of American citizenship in exchange for military service. The wartime enactment waived the declaration-of-intention, five-year residency, and English-language requirements for servicepersons. It also established procedures for the naturalization of soldiers serving overseas by roving examiners from the Immigration and Naturalization Service (INS). The Second War Powers Act also contained some important restrictive provisions. Any soldier dishonorably discharged from the military was disqualified from receiving the benefits of the law. And like similar legislation passed to bolster military recruitment during World War I, the statute limited eligibility to those whose service was rendered during the "present war." In addition, only veterans who filed their petitions before the statute's deadline on December 31, 1946, were entitled to receive the benefits of the legislation. The act was a partial victory for the political recognition of one segment of the Filipino population, who through their military attachment were now entitled to citizenship.[47] The majority of Filipinos in the United States, however, remained disqualified from national membership, since the act did not abolish the racial prerequisites to citizenship mandated by American naturalization law but only temporarily modified the rules to meet the political imperatives of the wartime state.

Barriers to Belonging

Filipino GIs embraced positive public narratives about their contributions to the war effort, believing that their patriotic sacrifices would translate into greater social and cultural acceptance. U.S. officials regularly portrayed the

Filipino enlistees as courageous partners in the nation's fight for freedom. The stubborn hold of racism, though, proved difficult to dislodge, resulting in disappointment and alienation for many Filipinos. Members of the First Filipino Regiment transferred to Camp Beale, outside Marysville, in early 1943, after a long stretch of combat training at Fort Ord in Monterrey Bay. They mistakenly assumed that their patriotic service had earned them some goodwill from local residents. A group of five hundred soldiers from the camp decided to go into the Marysville on a weekend pass soon after their arrival for some well-earned leisure time. When they tried to sit down for a meal at a restaurant in town, they discovered that they were not welcome. The proprietor of the restaurant told the soldiers, "We don't serve Filipinos here," even though they were wearing their army dress uniforms. The servicemen soon discovered that the same policy was in force at all the other restaurants in town, leaving them to go hungry on what was supposed to be a day of fun and indulgence.

Other forms of recreation in town were off limits as well. Filipino GIs were denied admittance to local movie theaters (or forced to sit in the colored section). Married Filipino soldiers who had arranged to have their wives meet them in town for the weekend discovered that no hotel would rent them a room, forcing the couples to spend the night at the local bus station. Discriminatory treatment was not limited to the small town of Marysville. Men from the First Filipino Regiment discovered "even worse" discrimination in Sacramento and described similar tales of racist treatment in San Francisco.[48] Moreover, as persons of Asian ancestry, they were often mistaken for Japanese, so like the Chinese, they were compelled to wear large buttons on their clothing identifying themselves as Filipinos when they went out in public, to prevent potential reprisals from white vigilantes. These types of experiences produced a profound alienation among those who still found themselves racially excluded from the American mainstream. Filipino writer and infantryman Manuel Buaken reflected bitterly on this contradiction, noting the wide gap between the rhetoric of ethnic tolerance and egalitarianism promoted by American leaders and the pervasive and often violent racism encountered by minorities on a daily basis. Buaken described wartime platitudes about freedom and inclusion as "another mirage of democracy," a public artifice that camouflaged a more "gruesome" reality of racial discrimination and second-class treatment for minorities in the United States.[49]

Filipinos faced other hardships, as they were still denied many basic rights available to their compatriots. Though many Filipinos worked in West Coast agriculture as part of the government's "Food for Victory" program, they remained subject to alien land laws in California. Family rights remained a contentious issue for Filipinos in the United States, especially for those serving in the armed forces. In addition, a number of Filipino soldiers who were married to Japanese American women faced the prospect of having their families placed in internment camps while they were sent off to war.

Legal barriers to intermarriage hit Filipino soldiers particularly hard, since almost all of them were based in California, where antimiscegenation statutes remained in force. Those wishing to wed their white girlfriends (including Mexican women, who were technically classified as "white") before being sent off to overseas combat were bitterly disappointed that their status as American soldiers did nothing to modify the state's racially restrictive marriage laws. Antimiscegenation statutes produced some practical dilemmas beyond the obvious injustice of not being able to marry the partner of one's choosing. A Red Cross representative assigned to the First Filipino Regiment at Camp Beale was inundated with emergency aid requests in the spring of 1942 from servicemen denied family allowances from the military because they were not legally married. Many of the men, moreover, could not name their partners or children as beneficiaries for military life insurance policies for the same reason, since children of these relationships were classified as "illicit" and therefore ineligible to receive insurance disbursements. Filipino soldiers and their families at Camp Beale appealed to their commander, Colonel Robert Offley, and to regiment chaplain Eugene Noury, asking them to petition state officials for relief from racial prohibitions on intermarriage in California. Offley expressed public support for Filipino families: "My men are spirited, loyal soldiers of the United States Army. They are eager to do their part [in the war]. They deserve peace of mind about the financial and social welfare of their loved ones, before they go overseas."[50]

With Offley's blessing, Chaplain Noury lobbied state and federal officials on the issue, seeking a legal remedy. Noury drafted an "Open Letter" to the governor of California, seeking a repeal of antimiscegenation laws that prohibited Filipino-white intermarriage. The chaplain's letter to the governor asserted, "I'm sure you will agree with us that in this time of war there should be no place for racial discrimination anywhere in the country." The letter criticized discriminatory laws against intermarriage as inconsistent with the nation's wartime commitment to pluralism and tolerance. Noury highlighted the inconsistency between asking Filipinos to sacrifice their lives for freedom and democracy abroad when they were denied basic civil rights at home. That policies of racial chauvinism were so closely associated with the ideology of the enemy made these discriminatory practices even more odious.

Despite repeated lobbying efforts by military officials, the governor and the state legislature refused to amend California's statutory prohibition on interracial marriage. With no remedy forthcoming, Colonel Offley and Filipino leaders devised an alternative plan to circumvent the state's antimiscegenation laws. They granted emergency furloughs to Filipino soldiers to caravan in groups with their fiancées to New Mexico, where they could be legally married. The trip was partly subsidized by Camp Beale's Red Cross branch and took place a month before the regiment was scheduled to ship out for combat. Now legally married, the wives of Filipino soldiers and their children were finally eligible for military family allowances and life insurance, providing some measure of solace for those heading off to war.[51]

A smaller group of servicemen also faced challenges on the family front. Approximately a dozen Filipino soldiers were married to Japanese American women on the West Coast. When President Roosevelt issued Executive Order 9066 in February 1942, these men faced the prospect of having their wives and children rounded up and relocated to internment camps. These multiethnic couples objected to the evacuation order, citing their patriotism and "Americanness" to challenge unfounded claims of Japanese disloyalty. Filipino leaders in Seattle and San Francisco worked with renowned ACLU attorney Ernest Besig to issue one of the first constitutional challenges to Roosevelt's internment order. The ACLU strategized that the patriotic service of Filipino soldiers might offer a way to legally intercede on behalf of Japanese Americans, since the internment order was framed around racially tinged claims of political disloyalty. The test case involved a Seattle couple, Filipino labor activist Mamerto Ventura and his wife, Mary Asaba Ventura. The couple filed for a writ of habeas corpus in federal district court in Washington State to prevent the internment of Mrs. Ventura, an American-born citizen of Japanese ancestry. The Venturas' petition asserted that the federal government's curfew and internment order "unlawfully and unfairly restrained [Mrs. Ventura] of her liberty." They argued, moreover, that the government had failed to show that Mrs. Ventura, an American citizen, had ever held allegiance to any nation other than the United States, rendering the legal basis for the evacuation order illegitimate.[52]

Federal district judge Lloyd Black rejected the petitioners' claims out of hand, asserting that the blood loyalty of Japanese in the United States was inherently suspect, making detention a necessary evil. His ruling provided a preview of the legal reasoning adopted by federal officials in later, more well-known internment cases such as those of Mitsuye Endo, Fred Korematsu, and Gordon Hirabiyashi. Judge Black invoked an early version of the infamous "military necessity" argument, suggesting that the wartime emergency on the West Coast justified the revocation of Mrs. Ventura's Fifth and Fourteenth Amendment rights. He dismissed the Venturas' pleas for constitutional protection as nothing more than a "technical right" that was being used by the petitioners to undermine the military security of the nation. Black scoffed at Mary Ventura's claim that she was a "loyal and devoted" American citizen, suggesting that Japanese (and perhaps Filipinos) on the West Coast were prospective "fifth columnists" who "were pretending loyalty" to the United States while secretly abetting plans for a potential attack on Seattle by enemy parachutists.[53]

This stubborn disconnect between the wartime rhetoric of ethnic pluralism and the lived realities of racial subordination produced resentment among Filipino soldiers. The hardships they faced on the West Coast reminded them that they remained on the periphery of American society. Their continued exclusion from the mainstream of American life tarnished the meaning of citizenship for many Filipinos, who believed that their sacrifices deserved greater recognition. The struggles of Filipinos in the United States paralleled those of their compatriots back home in the Philippines, who faced even greater adversity under Japanese rule.

Fight for the Philippines

The occupation of the Philippines by Japanese forces in the early months of the war created political dilemmas for both Americans and Filipinos. American officials had long justified their continued colonial presence in the Philippines as a protective enterprise necessary to safeguard the islands from foreign invasion, and the islands' military apparatus was under the command of the U.S. military at the time of the Japanese invasion. Despite this sanctimonious rhetoric, U.S. policymakers made little effort to buttress the islands' military defenses in the lead-up to the war, even though it was well known that Japan harbored imperial designs on the Philippines. The looming threat of a Japanese invasion in the summer of 1941 did, however, prompt President Roosevelt and Secretary of War Henry Stimson to authorize two interrelated initiatives aimed at shoring up the U.S. military position in the islands in preparation for a possible attack. The first action reorganized the structure of the Pacific command. On July 26, 1941, the Roosevelt administration established the United States Army Forces Far East (USAFFE) as the nation's new military command post in Asia. Retired Major General Douglas MacArthur, who at the time of the command change was serving as field marshal of the Philippine Commonwealth Army, was selected to head USAFFE.[54] On that same day, Roosevelt issued Executive Order 81, which placed the military forces of the Philippine government under the command of the general officer of United States Army and the secretary of war. Incorporating the Philippine Commonwealth Army into the U.S. military command provided a major boost to the U.S. forces in the Asia-Pacific region, placing more than one hundred thousand Filipino troops (an estimated 200,000– 250,000 eventually served) at MacArthur's disposal.[55] This was on top of the twelve thousand members of the Philippine Scouts, an official branch of the U.S. Army made up of local recruits.[56] The induction of Philippine soldiers into USAFFE had some potentially significant consequences. As nationals serving in the U.S. military, they would theoretically qualify for American citizenship, as stipulated by Section 701 of the Second War Powers Act of 1942, discussed earlier.[57] They were also potentially eligible for the generous federal entitlements and veterans-assistance programs that were available to the American soldiers whom they served alongside.

The fierce resistance of the Philippine defense forces to the Imperial Japanese Army was front-page news in U.S. media, which featured daily headlines about the courageous exploits of Filipino and American fighters facing an unrelenting onslaught. Filipino leaders, in concert with MacArthur, had requested military reinforcements from the secretary of war in the months before the invasion, but no help were forthcoming, leaving the islands vulnerable. Japanese troops quickly overran the country with superior numbers and armaments, and MacArthur along with the rest of the U.S. commanders fled the Philippines in March 1942. The United States' obligation to protect the Philippines from foreign military aggression, which had long served as a major justification for continued American presence in the islands, came under renewed scrutiny from Filipinos facing an uncertain political future. The compulsory induction of the Philippine Commonwealth Army members into the U.S. military command added to this sense of betrayal, since it laid bare the asymmetrical obligations between the two societies. Filipinos in the Philippines, like those living in the United States, were subject to military conscription because they "owed permanent allegiance" to the United States. What the United States owed to its Philippine subjects in return was much less clear, leaving many Filipinos to believe that wartime political obligations were one-sided. The failure of the U.S. government to live up to its pledge to protect the islands created significant resentment among the Philippine populace and renewed doubts about America's political integrity during a time of international crisis. This bitterness, though, was tempered by an even greater sense of enmity toward the Japanese occupiers, who angered the local population with their heavy-handed tactics and the routine abuse of civilians.

After the retreat of American forces, General MacArthur was forced to rethink his strategy in the islands. He maintained remote control of the Philippine Commonwealth forces from his Asia-Pacific command center in Australia, directing both conventional army units and guerrilla outfits that were resisting Japanese occupation. Political and military officials in the United States emphasized their solidarity with the Philippine people and took pains to highlight the shared burden of both peoples during the wartime crisis, characterizing the two groups as coequal partners in the global fight against fascism. During the early months of the war, Filipino and American troops fought side by side in defending the islands against overwhelming odds. Widely publicized accounts of battles such as the notorious "Bataan Death March" (in which an estimated eleven thousand prisoners of war died) stressed the shared suffering of Filipinos and Americans. U.S. newspapers also highlighted the courage of Filipino fighters, extolling their fortitude in carrying out strikes against the Japanese occupation government. Military officials were quick to point out that the first Congressional Medal of Honor (the U.S. military's highest decoration) awarded to an enlisted man during the war went to a Filipino, Jose Calugas, who had served as a mess sergeant with the Philippine Scouts. He received the award for "conspicuous gallantry and intrepidity above and beyond the call of duty" for his actions during the battle of Bataan. According to official reports, he had run one thousand yards across a battlefield under heavy Japanese artillery fire to commandeer a field-gun position after all the other members of his squad had been killed. Calugas then organized a volunteer unit to man the artillery battery and hold off advancing Japanese forces.[58] Public narratives drawing attention to the shared sacrifice of Filipinos and Americans, however, masked some rather dramatic disparities in how the burdens of war were borne.

By April 1942, Filipino forces were, for the most part, operating on their own and saw little in the way of direct logistical support from the American command in Australia. They lacked modern weapons, regular access to food, and sometimes even shoes. This did not mean that Filipino fighters were not actively engaging their adversaries. Small guerrilla units remained active in the countryside, carrying out frequent strikes against occupation forces. The consequences of joining the Filipino resistance, were severe, as anyone identified as a Philippine guerrilla or accused of collaborating with local insurgents faced certain torture and/or execution. Yet the opposition persisted, with MacArthur issuing orders to loosely organized guerrilla units that regularly hit Japanese targets and carried out valuable surveillance on troop movements. The courage and resolve of Filipino fighters under these arduous conditions earned plaudits from U.S. officials.

Yet when it came time to reciprocate the loyalty shown by Filipino allies, American officials consistently fell short. This was particularly true when it came to issues of remuneration and benefits. Military commanders such as General MacArthur and Secretary of War Stimson maintained that Filipino inductees were entitled to the same health and compensation benefits as American soldiers.[59] Moreover, they pledged to do something about the vast inequality in pay received by American and Filipino soldiers, an issue that had created significant resentment in the Philippines. Delivering on these promises, however, proved difficult and became a source of contention as the war dragged on. The issue became even more controversial when Filipino veterans tried to claim benefits they were entitled to after the war. This issue of pay disparity was a grievance that predated the war, having been raised before by the members of the Philippine Scouts, who for decades had complained about receiving lower compensation than their American colleagues.[60] The pay that Philippine conscripts received was less than half of what American GIs earned, even though they held the same obligations and served at the will of the general officer of the United States Army.

Early in the war, MacArthur had publicly announced that Filipino soldiers would receive "equal pay and allowances" to those earned by Americans, "regardless of nationality." The War Department supported the pay-equalization initiative but could not implement such a policy without approval from Congress. Legislation instituting this policy ran into opposition from congressional leaders despite lobbying from the military officials.[61] MacArthur went as far as to issue an executive order mandating a sixfold pay increase for Commonwealth soldiers, submitting the directive to Philippine vice president Sergio Osmeña for his signature. Word of the new policy spread quickly and was widely hailed as an act of good faith by the U.S. government. Unfortunately, Congress had not authorized the equal-pay policy, creating confusion among Filipino leaders, who mistakenly assumed that MacArthur had received the necessary approvals before issuing the equalization order. American lawmakers, though, balked at the idea of boosting the pay of Filipino soldiers to the same level as U.S. soldiers, claiming that such a policy would be too expensive. A compromise bill that increased the pay of Commonwealth inductees from seven dollars a month to eleven dollars a month (the rate paid to the Philippine Scouts) passed the U.S. Senate in June 1942.[62]

Testimony from War Department officials on behalf of the bill explained that the importance of the matter went beyond a simple matter of fairness for Filipinos serving under the U.S. command. The pay-disparity issue was regularly cited in Japanese propaganda in the islands as yet another example of callous racial "discrimination" practiced by the white imperial powers in Asia. Members of the House Rules Committee nonetheless blocked the equal-pay legislation, claiming that raising the compensation of Filipino soldiers would not silence Japanese propaganda or make their charges of discrimination by the United States against its nonwhite soldiers "any closer to the truth."[63] Philippine leaders, along with War Department officials, continued to lobby Congress for a legislative remedy as unrest spread among the ranks of Commonwealth soldiers tired of empty promises regarding their value to the American war effort. Congress, however, disregarded the issue, and pledges of equal pay for equal sacrifice promised by MacArthur and the War Department quickly faded after the war ended.

Filipinos' courage and sacrifice in the armed forces, alongside their wartime contributions on the home front, did increase their standing among lawmakers in Washington, DC. Filipino leaders used this newfound political capital to challenge racial bars to naturalization. Although rules for admission to American citizenship had been temporarily modified to include those who served honorably in the armed forces, Filipino civilians (including those who worked in the American defense industry or civilian corps) remained racially disqualified. The exclusionary bases of American naturalization law came under increasing scrutiny as the war dragged on, especially as U.S. leaders ratcheted up criticism of the loathsome racial policies of the Nazi regime. Japanese propaganda promoting a "Greater East Asia Co-Prosperity Sphere" in Asia as an alternative to centuries of white colonial rule in the region compelled American leaders to rethink certain racist policies targeting Asians. Filipinos, like other minority groups, pressed the federal government to live up to its professed creed of inclusionary democracy or face criticism for assenting to the enemy's ideology of racial supremacy.

The continuing racial exclusion of Filipinos from naturalization exemplified the pervasive disconnect between rhetoric and reality. The Philippine resident commissioner's office launched a nationwide campaign to pressure Congress to amend the country's naturalization laws. The passage of the Magnuson Act in 1943, which granted citizenship rights to Chinese in the United States, bolstered the Filipino movement for civic recognition. Key actors in this drive included Diosdado Yap, the community activist and publisher of *Bataan* magazine, and Manuel Adeva of the Philippine resident commissioner's office. They coordinated a letter and telegram drive involving various community groups from across the United States.[64] Filipino activists cited their substantial contribution to the Allied war effort to leverage political concessions from the federal government. The campaign for Filipino citizenship rights picked up steam in 1944 as a series of bills aimed at granting naturalization privileges to the islanders were introduced in Congress. In November 1944, the House Immigration and Naturalization Committee held hearings on six different bills that proposed naturalization rights for Filipinos. Bill sponsors included Vito Marcantonio (NY), Harry Sheppard (CA), C. Norris Poulson (CA), Dan McGehee (MS), Jennings Randolph (WV), and Joseph Farrington (HI).[65] Filipino representatives highlighted their community's wartime service as evidence of their fitness for citizenship and emphasized the ways in which racist policies undermined America's international standing. They also pointed out that persons of Chinese descent in the United States had been granted naturalization rights the year before, which set a new political and legal precedent regarding Asian eligibility. The admission of Chinese to citizenship in 1943 struck a raw nerve with some Filipinos, who believed that they should have been given priority on the naturalization issue because of their status as American nationals who held compulsory allegiance to the United States. Moreover, the racial exclusion of Filipinos had become a difficult proposition to defend over the course of the war, since it placed them in the same disadvantaged category as Japanese immigrants.

The congressional hearings were chaired by New York Congressman Samuel Dickstein, who had played an important role in legislative campaigns to exclude and repatriate Filipinos during the mid-1930s. The introduction of six different naturalization bills in 1944 was evidence of just how dramatically the mood of Congress had changed regarding the civic fitness of Filipinos over a relatively short period of time. The irony of this attitude adjustment was not lost on soldier and writer Manuel Buaken, who asked, "How many Americans are truly sincere in granting us this [citizenship] privilege? We know . . . that the military expediency is a large factor" behind Congress's newfound inclusionary impulses.[66] Congress's motivations aside, Filipino activists seized the opportunity to advance their longstanding campaign for civic recognition in the United States.

The hearings provided a platform for both Filipino and American leaders to contrast the legacy of exclusion with the larger geopolitical transformations sweeping the globe. The case for repealing racial prerequisites to citizenship was bolstered by testimony from a variety of American backers including representatives from patriotic organizations and trade unions, support that was ironic since these same groups had led the movement to exclude Filipinos just a decade before. The Roosevelt administration also threw its weight behind the legislation, seeking to blunt international criticism of America's hypocrisy on racial issues. The six bills under consideration differed in method and scope. The legislation offered by Representative Poulson (HR 3633), for instance, extended naturalization rights only to Filipino veterans of World War I who had missed the previous deadline set by Congress that required applicants to apply within six months after honorable discharge from military service.[67] The Farrington bill (HR 2776) was a product of economic anxiety about labor shortages on Hawaii's plantations and in the defense sector, where Filipinos made up a significant percentage of the workforce at Pearl Harbor and other military facilities.[68] Hawaii officials believed that the reward of citizenship might induce Filipinos to stay in the islands after the war instead of returning to the Philippines to take part in the rehabilitation of their homeland. The other four bills offered fairly straightforward modifications to U.S. naturalization law aimed at extending to Filipinos the same citizenship privileges available to persons of the white, African, and Chinese "races."

There was strong support among members of the House Immigration and Naturalization Committee for extending American citizenship rights to Filipinos, but there were some important differences of opinion about how far the law should go. Filipino activists and their supporters stressed two key arguments in making their case for a broad revision of American naturalization rules: First, they contended that their longstanding imperial attachment to the United States merited special consideration when it came to expanding the boundaries of national membership. Second, they cited their patriotic service to the Allied war effort as evidence of their fitness for citizenship.

Concerns about America's image in Asia compelled lawmakers to act quickly. Anxiety among U.S. officials and military commanders about the effectiveness of Japanese propaganda in the Pacific theater highlighting the exclusionary policies of the white colonial powers pushed Congress to take action. Filipino leaders also pressed the issue of mutual reciprocity between the two nations, noting that Americans had long had held naturalization rights in the Philippines, making the disqualification of Filipinos from U.S. citizenship all the more inequitable. This point was driven home by the testimony of Diosdado Yap, who advised the committee that it was "obviously contradictory" for Congress to "claim that America accepts the Philippines as an equal in the family of nations," while at the same time treating Filipinos on "unequal terms . . . prevent[ing] them from becoming U.S. citizens."[69] In the same vein, Filipino leaders such as A. L. Luartes, an officer of the Veterans of Foreign Wars from Camden, New Jersey, and Ramon Pobre of the Filipino National Council of Chicago called on lawmakers to live up to their lofty rhetoric of equality and freedom or run the risk of losing credibility in the international community. Pobre implored Congress to start treating his compatriots "on equal terms with our other allies in this war" in order to "bolster their morale and their determination to resist and . . . fight our common enemy." He reminded the House committee that Japanese military propaganda in the islands cited "anti-Filipino exclusion law[s]" as proof that Americans considered Asians to be despised racial inferiors who would never be accepted as social equals in the United States.[70]

Most of the testimony focused on the bills submitted by McGehee (HR 4826) and Sheppard (HR 4229). Both bills sought to amend Section 303 of the 1940 Nationality Act to add Filipinos to the list of races (whites, persons of African descent, and Chinese) eligible for citizenship. They differed in one important aspect: Sheppard's bill sought to waive the certificate-of-arrival and declaration-of-intention requirement ("first papers") for Filipinos, but the McGehee bill did not. The certificate-of-arrival requirement (proof that an immigrant entered the country legally) was a particularly thorny issue for Filipinos, since up until the 1934 Tydings-McDuffie Act, they were classified as American nationals and not as immigrants. As a result, immigration authorities did not register their admission when they entered the country before 1934, making it impossible for petitioners to provide an official certificate or record of arrival.[71] The declaration-of-intention requirement (discussed in chapter 3) was similarly problematic in that it added another complication to the application process. According to U.S. nationality law, petitioners were subject to a two-year waiting period after filing their declaration of intent before they could become citizens. Advocates of Filipino naturalization rights desired a waiver of this requirement to avoid having them wait another two years after passage of legislation to actually take advantage of the statute.

The hearings featured testimony from a diverse range of political actors, with most speaking on behalf of either the Sheppard or McGehee bill. Representatives from the Roosevelt administration played a significant role in pushing the naturalization bills, primarily in recognition of the solidarity demonstrated by Filipinos over the course of the war. Richard Ely of the Department of Interior and Edward Shaughnessy of the Immigration and Naturalization Service both appeared as expert witnesses, explaining the Roosevelt administration's position in favor of the Sheppard bill, which waived the first-papers requirement for Filipinos. In addition, Secretary of State Edward Stettinius Jr., Secretary of Interior Harold Ickes, and Attorney General Francis Biddle gave written testimonies expressing their support for the enactment of the proposed legislation. Ely and Shaughnessy both emphasized the importance of waiving the first-papers provision for Filipinos in recognition of their anomalous political status as American nationals and because of their compulsory allegiance to the United States.[72] Similar motives undergirded the testimony of S. E. Wilkins, representing the Veterans of Foreign Wars of the United States (VFW), and James Moore of the American Legion's National Legislative Committee. The ideological commitment of the VFW and American Legion to martial citizenship, a principle which equated military service with national citizenship, undergirded their involvement in the issue.

By the early 1940s, Filipino veterans from World War I had established a number of local VFW and Legion posts across the country, and leaders from these branches pressured the national organization to take up the issue in recognition of their patriotic sacrifices. The success of these efforts was illustrated in a resolution passed by the American Legion during its 1944 national convention endorsing enactment of naturalization legislation, since the "Filipino people have proven their loyalty to the United States in time of our national emergency, as well as in peace," and because "they have supported the American ideals of democracy and proven themselves worthy of the trust placed in them."[73] VFW and American Legion spokespersons, like those representing the Roosevelt administration, made it clear that that their support of Filipino naturalization was a quid pro quo reward for their wartime service and was not to be interpreted as abrogating in any way the power of Congress to regulate citizenship rights on the basis of racially selective criteria. The potential consequences of extending naturalization privileges to Filipinos was a point of contention among certain committee members, who debated whether the law should apply only to those who arrived before the passage of the 1934 Tydings-McDuffie Act (who entered as "nationals") or whether it should also include those who came after 1934 as "aliens."

The specter of large numbers of Filipinos entering the United States with full citizenship rights did generate some anxiety among Immigration and Naturalization Committee members. Chairman Samuel Dickstein, along with Ely and Shaughnessy, were careful to remind their colleagues, however, that Filipinos had since 1934 been subject to a tiny quota of fifty persons per annum, which limited the potential pool of applicants. The most voluble resistance to modifying rules for naturalization came from Representative A. Leonard Allen, who raised concerns about the racial consequences of rushing to incorporate Filipinos into the American body politic. This was not surprising, since the Louisiana congressman had been a vocal opponent of granting citizenship rights to Chinese during the committee's deliberations the year before, accusing pro-Chinese witnesses of recklessly advocating "social equality" between the races. During the hearings on Filipino naturalization, Representative Allen repeatedly interrogated witnesses about the racial makeup of the Philippine population. He asked Representative John Phillips, who testified on behalf of his colleague Harry Sheppard's bill, if it was true that Filipinos had a high propensity toward criminal behavior, expressing surprise at the California congressman's assertion that their crime rates were no higher than those of whites. He also quizzed Phillips about the frequency with which Filipinos "fraternized" with Japanese on the West Coast, raising the possibility that the two groups had joined together in some sort of Asiatic blood alliance. Allen took up a similar line of inquiry with Diosdado Yap, asking him what "racial stock" the Filipinos traced their lineage to. Yap responded that leading ethnologists of the period had classified them as belonging to the brown or Malay race. That answer did not satisfy Allen, who demanded to know whether Filipinos were members of the "Negro race," in addition to voicing concerns about their "racial connection" to the Japanese. The Louisiana congressman was particularly surprised when Yap told the committee that he was married to a white woman. Allen was incredulous when Yap suggested that "thousands" of Filipinos had wed American citizens in recent years. He then asked Yap, "Have they married Caucasians?" After being told that many had indeed tied the knot with white women, Allen demanded to know if there had "ever been an instance" when Filipinos had done the unthinkable and intermarried with members of the "Ethiopian race."[74]

Attempts to inject questions about the racial desirability of Filipinos into the hearings did not make much headway, primarily because the "Asiatic" bar had already been lifted for the Chinese. Moreover, as Diosdado Yap reminded the committee, state-sanctioned racial discrimination was both "un-Christian" and "un-American," particularly in light of the nation's proclaimed wartime commitment to ethnic toleration. Though there was strong support from the House committee for enacting one of the bills, the legislation had failed to come up for a vote when the 78th Congress went into recess in December 1944. McGehee and Sheppard reintroduced their bills again in early 1945, hoping for a different result. Filipino leaders maintained pressure on Congress to recognize their sacrifices with the reward of citizenship.[75] The notoriety of the First and Second Filipino Regiments and their important contributions to the West Coast defense industry bolstered their campaign.[76] The San Francisco veterans' organization the Filipino Fighters for Freedom used its newly acquired political capital to pressure the state's elected officials to back its cause. Winning the support of California lawmakers marked a remarkable sea change in attitude in the state that just a decade earlier had served as the launching point of a nationwide Filipino exclusion crusade.[77]

House members passed a version of the McGehee naturalization bill in 1945 (now known as HR 776), but the legislation got stalled in the Senate over disagreements regarding the bill's language. At the same time as the fight for Filipino citizenship rights was taking place in Congress, a similar campaign was being orchestrated to extend naturalization privileges to immigrants from India. The political standing of Indians as British imperial subjects paralleled the situation of Filipinos in some important ways. Both populations were called into military service by colonial authorities during the war, and both Indians and Filipinos earned praise from Allied leaders for their valor on the battlefield. There was considerable support in Congress for relaxing racial bars to immigration and naturalization for Indians. Representatives Emanuel Celler (NY) and Clare Boothe Luce (CT) both submitted bills extending citizenship privileges to Indians in 1944, with language that was very similar to legislation aimed at Filipinos.[78] The two naturalization bills were eventually merged into a single piece of legislation popularly known as the Luce-Celler Act, which was passed by Congress on July 2, 1946.[79] The new law amended the Nationality Act of 1940, making "persons of races indigenous to India, and . . . the Philippine Islands" racially eligible for citizenship in the United States.

While the legislation enlarged the boundaries of the national community to include Filipinos and Indians (along with Chinese), the Asiatic bar remained in place. Eligibility for naturalization under the Luce-Celler Act was limited to those persons who had a "preponderance of blood" of the prescribed races, a requirement aimed at disqualifying mixed-race persons with more than 50 percent "ineligible" blood. This blood-quantum provision was designed to prevent persons of more than 50 percent Japanese ancestry from gaining admission to American citizenship through the quotas allotted to the Philippines or China.[80] The law established an austere quota cap of one hundred immigrants per year for Indians but did not address the situation of Filipinos, whose previous quota of fifty per annum had expired as stipulated in the Tydings-McDuffie Act.[81] The limitative quotas stipulated in the Luce-Celler Act, however, were partially blunted by other legislative actions during this period, most notably, the War Brides Acts of 1945 and 1947 and the Veterans' Alien Fiancées Act of 1946, which allowed foreign wives, fiancées, and children of soldiers to enter the country as nonquota immigrants.[82] This set of family-reunification statutes allowed veterans, including those of Filipino descent, to skirt restrictive quotas by sponsoring their alien wives and children. In the years following the war, approximately sixteen thousand Filipino women entered the country as war brides, a phenomenon that reflected the changing gender dynamics of postwar Asian migration to the United States.[83]

The passage of the Luce-Celler Act marked an important triumph for Filipino leaders and activists. Antonio Gonzalez, president of the Filipino Inter-Community Organizations of the Western States, declared that the naturalization bill removed "for all time the stigma of inferiority attached to Filipino nationality and race" and afforded Filipinos living in the United States a greater opportunity to pursue the full benefits of American democracy.[84] This newly acquired civic recognition came just days before another monumental change in political status was set into motion with the formal relinquishment of U.S. sovereignty in the Philippines. The cession of American rule in the islands was framed as a well-earned reward granted to Filipinos, who had finally shown themselves to be ready for democratic self-rule. American officials had maintained a vocal public commitment to Philippine independence throughout war, a position stressed during the occupation to counterbalance wartime propaganda issued by the Japanese government promising its own version of autonomy for the islands. As the war drew to an end in the summer of 1945, the Truman administration assured Filipino leaders that the United States planned to honor the terms of the Tydings-McDuffie Act as soon as a civilian government could be reestablished. American officials had long planned to relinquish sovereignty in the islands on the Fourth of July, a symbolic gesture aimed at highlighting the paternal role of the United States in readying Filipinos for independence during its five decades of colonial supervision. President Truman issued a presidential proclamation of independence on July 4, 1946, declaring that the people of the Philippines had at long last "demonstrated their capacity for self-government," thus earning them the right to direct their own affairs. That same day, Truman also established a new immigration quota of one hundred per year for the Philippines.[85]

Although Philippine leaders justifiably celebrated the twin achievements of national independence and the dismantling of the racial bar to citizenship for Filipinos in the United States, these accomplishments turned out to be in many ways partial victories. American officials voiced concerns about the potential political and financial obligations associated with postwar reconstruction in the Philippines and sought to limit U.S. liability to the former colony, which had been ravaged under its watch. At the same time, lawmakers moved aggressively to secure a privileged position for American business interests in the postwar Philippine economy. One issue that loomed large was the status of the more than two hundred thousand Filipinos who had been inducted into USAFFE during the war. Congressional leaders expressed concern about the fiscal obligations associated with providing generous veterans benefits to this large cohort, especially since the United States was already obliged to provide large financial outlays for postwar reconstruction of the war-devastated islands. There were also potential political costs, as many, if not all, of these men were technically eligible for U.S. citizenship according to the provisions of the Second War Powers Act. Although President Truman had established an immigration allotment of one hundred persons per year for the Philippines in 1946, this large population of Filipino veterans would potentially be exempt from entry quotas if they first became American citizens. The resolution of these issues reveals how the hierarchical power dynamics between the two countries continued to shape Philippine-American relations even after the formal enactment of independence.

The Bell Trade Act was one important piece of postwar legislation that underscores the inequalities undergirding the postwar relationship between the two natioins. The law, enacted in April 1946 and to take effect after the transfer of sovereignty, secured an advantageous position for American capital in the Philippine economy. The act established absolute quotas on Philippine commodities such as sugar, tobacco, rice, and coconut oil entering the U.S. market, to shelter domestic agricultural producers from competition for the first eight years of the agreement. The legislation was pushed through Congress at the bidding of American agribusiness interests, which continued their longstanding crusade against "cheap" imports from the islands.[86] At the same time, the new trade agreement mandated unfettered access to the Philippine market for American export products and commercial interests. The bill contained a series of so-called "parity" clauses establishing preferential trade status for American businesspeople by granting them equal rights with Philippine citizens regarding the "disposition, exploitation and development" of the nation's natural resources and commercial opportunities. The act was designed to supersede a clause in the Philippine constitution that gave preference to Filipino citizens in the development of the nation's economic resources, and it included a provision allowing the president of the United States to terminate the trade agreement if he determined that the Philippine government was "discriminating against citizens of the

Unites States" or against American business enterprises. And lastly, Congress accorded a generous immigration allowance for American citizens in the islands, requiring the Philippine legislature to allow a quota of "not . . . less than a thousand" per year at a time when Filipinos were still limited to fifty per annum in the United States (expanded to one hundred per year a few months later). The aims of the Bell Act were clear: it established a neocolonial trade system that sustained unfettered and preferential access to the Philippine market for American citizens while a the same time maintaining quota walls aimed at restricting the entry into the United States of Filipino products.[87] The lopsided terms of the Bell Act ensured that unequal economic relations between the two nations would continue in the postwar period.

With the date of independence approaching (July 4, 1946), American policymakers were confronted with a daunting set of political obligations in the Philippines. The United States clearly bore responsibility to assist with the (soon to be former) colony's postwar reconstruction efforts, especially since the islands had been overrun and despoiled under America's watch. Political realities, however, quickly set in, as Congress looked anxiously at mounting commitments, both political and financial, which had accrued to the United States during the conflict. One of the most pressing issues facing congressional leaders was how to deal with the rising price tag of entitlements promised to Filipino veterans. The ranks of native fighters had swelled over the course of the war to between 200,000 and 250,000 soldiers, and so too did the potential fiscal outlays associated with back pay, health care, and GI benefits for those who had served under the U.S. military command. In addition, most, if not all, of these veterans were theoretically eligible for American citizenship as a consequence of their military service (as long as they applied by the December 31, 1946, deadline). Congress moved quickly to limit American liability in the islands, pushing through new legislation aimed at downgrading the status of Filipino GIs to exclude them from generous federal entitlements available to other veterans.

Wartime pledges of pay and benefit equity touted by U.S. officials to enlist the loyal service of Filipinos in the fight against the Axis powers came under increasing scrutiny in the months after the war. As the patriotic contributions of Filipinos in the United States and the Philippines slowly faded from the headlines, support in Congress for generous entitlements promised during the war diminished. With the conflict over, new political realities set in, especially the mounting costs of postwar reconstruction efforts across the globe. The international political commitments of the United States spawned new legislative initiatives aimed at disentangling the United States from its imperial obligations to the Philippines. Congress enacted a series of bills disqualifying Filipino soldiers from liberal social-welfare programs available to other GIs, creating a separate benefit class for these veterans that disqualified them from many entitlements. Lawmakers were greatly concerned with the long-term federal outlays associated with providing veterans benefits (medical care, life insurance, pensions, and GI Bill programs) to the large number of Filipinos who had served in various capacities under the command of the general officer of the United States Army. The murky status of many of these fighters, which included veterans of the Commonwealth Army as well as members of guerrilla units who operated in concordance with American commanders, added an extra layer of scrutiny to the issue. The looming independence of the islands, scheduled for July 4, 1946, provided political cover for U.S. lawmakers looking for ways to externalize the costs of veterans' care to the beleaguered Philippine government. Congressional leaders justified the retraction of previously pledged benefits by claiming that American obligations to Filipinos were dissolved with the impending handover of sovereignty.

On February 18, 1946, Congress passed the First Supplemental Appropriation Rescission Act, the first in a series of laws popularly known as the Rescission Acts. These laws downgraded the status of Filipino serviceperson, placing them in a separate administrative classification from that of other U.S. soldiers. As the statute's title implies, the legislation *rescinded* previously allocated appropriations related to war spending, including disbursements for veterans.[88] According to the Rescission Act, members of the Philippine Commonwealth Army who were inducted into the U.S. armed forces "pursuant to the military order of the President of the United States dated July 26, 1941, shall not be deemed to be or have been in service in the military or naval forces of the United States" for the purposes of "conferring rights, privileges, or benefits" accorded to other veterans, except as specified by Congress.[89] Philippine Commonwealth Army soldiers, according to the law, were only eligible for two programs: the National Life Insurance Act of 1940 and service-related disability or death pensions provided by the federal government. Their qualification for these two programs came with a catch: Filipinos veterans could only receive benefits at a ratio of one peso per dollar. This rate of compensation represented a sizeable disparity in payouts, since the U.S. government had artificially set the value of the peso at fifty American cents on the dollar, meaning that they were eligible for only half the allowances paid to other veterans. Adding insult to injury, the legislation excluded Filipinos from all other veterans programs, including the Servicemen's Readjustment Act (the "GI Bill"), the Mustering Out Payment Act of 1944, hospitalization and medical care for service-related disability, and burial and funeral allowances. In one small bright spot, however, the act clarified that Filipino veterans who had already received certain benefits (such as hospitalization expenses or disability allowances) would not be asked to reimburse the United States.[90]

The Rescission Act was understandably viewed as a betrayal by Filipino servicemen, who had been promised pay and benefit reparations. They had been eligible for the same veterans programs as American soldiers during the war and were never told that this was a temporary arrangement. As late as the fall of 1945, the Federal Bureau of Veterans Affairs ruled that Philippine soldiers were eligible for full benefits, so the retraction of previously held rights represented a sharp departure from established policy.[91] The retroactive nature of the law was especially troubling, since no mention of Filipinos' differential or provisional status had been made when American officials were mobilizing them into service. Philippine leaders vigorously protested the rescission of benefits and insisted that American policymakers make good on their wartime pledges to Filipino soldiers. Carlos Romulo, the Philippine resident commissioner, repeatedly called out his colleagues in the U.S. Congress, imploring them not to become "accessories to injustice" by backtracking on previous pledges of equal treatment. He reminded them that an indissoluble political bond linked the two nations, noting that Filipinos fought as "soldiers of the Army of the United States, as American nationals fighting in defense of the American flag on soil over which the United States had full sovereignty." Romulo urged Congress to restore full benefits eligibility to Filipino veterans in recognition of their valorous sacrifices on the battlefield. He condemned the payout rate of one peso per dollar for pensions and life insurance as a callously discriminatory policy since it provided Filipinos only half the allowance given to American GIs. According to Romulo, "The bullets they faced, and the shells and bombs, made no distinction between them. . . . The terror, the determination, the courage of battle drew no line of discrimination between Filipino and American." Why, he asked, was the United States now dishonoring the service of its imperial loyalists by retroactively denying them rights they had previously been entitled to?[92]

The two-tiered system of benefits recalled the "separate but equal" doctrine wielded against African Americans in the Jim Crow South, in that it stamped Filipino GIs with a "badge of inferiority" that disenfranchised them from the rights and rewards available to their fellow veterans. Romulo continued to press Congress to redress the inequities contained in the first Rescission Act, to no avail, and the Filipino disqualification proviso was reaffirmed in subsequent Supplemental Appropriation and Rescission bills in 1947, 1948, and 1949.[93] President Truman explained that dissolution of America's legal and political obligations to Filipino GIs did not nullify America's "moral obligation" to these veterans. These policies marked an important shift in posture, reframing the obligations of the United States to Filipino veterans as a matter of charity rather than of civil rights or the imperial responsibility. In other words, the United States was no longer *legally bound* to provide for the welfare of its colonial fighters who had been marshaled into service during the war, but it might assist with their care on a voluntary basis as an act of postcolonial beneficence.[94]

Controversy surrounding the issue of the eligibility of Philippine nationals for U.S. citizenship paralleled disputes over veterans benefits. The Second War Powers Act of 1942 established liberalized naturalization criteria for alien servicepersons in order to promote enlistment. The legislation stipulated that the commissioner of the Immigration and Naturalization Service send representatives to military bases overseas during the war to carry out naturalization proceedings for soldiers stationed abroad. Congress amended the Second War Powers Act on December 28, 1945, setting a deadline of December 31, 1946, for soldiers to file citizenship petitions under the statute.[95] Philippine servicemen, like other noncitizen soldiers, were technically eligible for naturalization under the liberalized wartime provisions, though few in the islands were aware of the policy. Not surprisingly, the prospect of tens of thousands of Filipino veterans becoming U.S. citizens by virtue of their military service alarmed some American officials. The Truman administration had explicitly set an immigration quota of one hundred per year for the Philippines after the war, but Filipino veterans who took advantage of the special naturalization program for U.S. servicepersons would be exempted from quota restriction, since they would be American citizens.

The ability of Filipino veterans to take advantage of the wartime naturalization program was hindered by logistical obstacles. The Philippines was under Japanese occupation until the summer of 1945, so no INS official was sent to the islands to carry out examinations until the war had ended. In August 1945, the U.S. vice consul in Manila, George Ennis, was granted authority to conduct naturalization proceedings in the islands. A month later, Attorney General Tom Clark issued a ruling that veterans of the Philippine Commonwealth Army were eligible for U.S. citizenship under the act.[96] This decision did not sit well with Ugo Carusi, the commissioner of the INS, who wrote a memo to Clark on September 13, expressing concerns about the political consequences of granting naturalization rights to the two hundred thousand or more Filipinos who had served in the war. The INS had originally ruled that Philippine army veterans were eligible for citizenship but reversed its position after the Rescission Act amended the status of Philippine GIs. After consultation with Commissioner Carusi on the matter, Attorney General Clark revoked Vice Consul Ennis's authority to naturalize Filipino servicepersons on September 26, 1945. Carusi claimed that the INS intervened on the issue in response to concerns raised by an anonymous Philippine government official about a mass emigration of Filipinos to the United States as a consequence of the naturalization policy. The revocation of Ennis's authority, however, raised questions about the legality of this intervention. The U.S. Congress has plenary power under the Constitution over immigration and naturalization law, so the unilateral intervention of the attorney general and the INS (both part of the executive branch) were of questionable constitutionality. An internal memorandum issued by INS deputy Edward J. Shaughnessy admitted that its actions were suspect, creating a "rather anomalous situation" in which the United States recognized "the legal right of these persons" to become citizens while at the same time making it "impossible for such persons to acquire these benefits." In other words, the INS acknowledged that Filipino servicemen were eligible for American citizenship under the Second War Powers Act while at the same time admitting that the revocation of Ennis's authority had made it impossible for these veterans to effectuate their right to naturalization.[97]

The attorney general and INS commissioner's efforts to undermine congressional intent regarding Filipino citizenship rights was eventually contested on grounds that the executive branch did not have the authority to contravene the plenary power of the legislative branch with regard to naturalization policy. The Philippines was still under U.S. sovereignty when Ennis's naturalization power was revoked, and INS officials provided no coherent legal justification for their intervention. Moreover, American authorities' claims that they were acting at the behest of an unidentified Philippine government official came under increasing scrutiny, as Filipino activists demanded remedy in U.S. courts. The public record did not support the claims made by INS officials about Philippine opposition to emigration. No Filipino officials publicly expressed any concern about a potential exodus of immigrants from the country during the postwar period, and the Commonwealth legislature proposed no analogous policy to discourage postwar emigration from the islands. The fictive claim that the Philippine government

wanted to restrict outmigration was also belied by the fact that Filipino officials worked in concert with the U.S. Congress on a policy to recruit fifty
thousand Filipinos to go to Japan to participate in that country's reconstruction efforts after the war.[98]

The INS was eventually compelled to send another naturalization officer, P. J. Phillips, to the Philippines to process petitions in August 1946,
after a nine-month dead period. His arrival, in August, however, left only
four months for Filipino veterans to file their citizenship papers before the
December 31, 1946, deadline. And while Phillips administered applications
for Philippine servicemen, the law was not widely advertised and the some
petitioners were rejected or ignored without clear explanation.[99] For instance,
Lorenzo Fortuno and Antonio Tirona filed citizenship papers before the
December 1946 deadline but had their applications denied because, according to the INS, "[no] purpose would be served . . . by the submission of
such an application to our office." Other petitioners, such as Felix Layug,
Godofreda Magalued, Canuto Mangila, and Alfredo Nerpiol, filed citizenship papers while they were still in the armed forces, but their applications
were simply ignored by INS officials.[100] By the end of 1946, approximately
eleven thousand Filipino veterans had taken advantage of the naturalization
provisions of the Second War Powers Act. The majority of these men were
drawn from two groups: members of the First or Second Battalions based in
California, who were naturalized en masse before they were sent overseas,
and members of the Philippine Scouts, who were an "official" branch of the
U.S. armed forces. At least one thousand of these petitioners were granted
citizenship outside the United States by INS officers traveling to U.S. military bases across the globe, so there was a clear precedent for extraterritorial
naturalization.[101] The figure of eleven thousand newly minted citizens was a
relatively small number, considering American officials' own internal estimates suggested that around 270,000 Filipinos were eligible for U.S. citizenship under the act. While the reinstatement of an INS officer to the Philippines affirmed the naturalization eligibility of Filipino veterans, American
authorities did little to facilitate this benefit and in a number of cases denied
petitioners their statutory rights by ignoring or rejecting their applications
without justification.[102]

The war-bred aspirations of Filipinos for more just and equitable treatment from the United States produced both triumphs and disappointments.
In the aftermath of the war, the Philippines was finally granted its independence, and racial bars to naturalized citizenship in the United States were
overturned. Filipino Americans were able to claim a greater stake in Amer-

ica's democratic institutions, and their war service improved their standing in communities that just a decade before had waged campaigns to expel Filipinos from the United States. For those who had been inducted into the American armed forces in the Philippines during the war, things were less rosy. Their fight for veteran's benefits and back pay remains a contentious political issue to this day. The issue of citizenship for Filipino veterans who served in the war received little attention in the decades immediately following the war, but it was revived in the early 1970s as part of the American civil rights movement. Former Filipino GIs, along with U.S.-based attorneys and civil rights activists, took up the issue, filing a series of legal challenges that sought the retroactive conferral of citizenship. This issue also remains unresolved and continues to serve as a rallying point in the Filipino community, where the specter of empire continues to haunt Philippine-American relations.

Epilogue

The advent of Philippine independence ushered in a new era in Filipino American politics, though the political trajectory of the two nations has remained closely intertwined throughout the postcolonial era. The status of Filipinos in the United States, to be sure, saw some marked improvement in the period after the war. Racial barriers to citizenship were dismantled as result of the wartime efforts of Asian Americans, and other discriminatory measures, such as proscriptions on intermarriage and property rights, became increasingly untenable, leading states to repeal many of these laws in the years immediately following the war. Filipinos in the United States, however, still faced significant obstacles as the community tried to rebuild itself in the postwar era. Limitative quota restrictions on Filipino immigration to the United States, instituted in the aftermath of the war period, constrained community growth and development, and the population did not see significant demographic replenishment until the mid-1960s. The gap between the rhetoric of egalitarianism and the lived experience of second-class citizenship and segregation proved difficult to dislodge, as the nation quickly reverted back to old patterns of social closure and boundary maintenance. Conditions in the Philippines were also slow to improve in the postwar period, as the newly independent nation set about rebuilding the war-ravaged homeland. Although formal colonial rule ended in 1946, relations of dependency and external control remained firmly in place. American meddling in the Philippines in some ways became more insidious in the postwar period, as U.S. policymakers and multinational corporations used "soft power" to impose their will and shape the political and economic trajectory of the islands. The continued presence of American military bases in the Philippines, moreover, provided a stark reminder about the enduring legacy of U.S. imperial power in the archipelago and the ease with which that power might be used against the local population if it threatened U.S. political-economic interests in the region.

The Philippine case reminds us that long-term patterns of stratification and subordination do not change overnight, especially when those in power have a vested interest in maintaining the status quo. Legislation extending citizenship rights to Filipinos in the United States or an administrative decree granting national independence to the Philippines did not occasion a clean break from the hierarchical practices that characterized the earlier era, any more than the passage of civil rights legislation in the 1960s quickly ended customs of social segregation and racial antipathy against African Americans. That Filipino World War II veterans are still locked in a political battle to obtain the rights and benefits promised to them during the war underscores the ways in which the politics of race and empire still resonate today. Only after decades of community activism has the U.S. government displayed a willingness to honor all the wartime promises made to Philippine veterans, though recent progress on the issue seems to be directly related to the fact that the cost of following through on these pledges has lessened considerably now that there are so few veterans still alive.

Other legacies of empire remain salient and help us to link the imperial past with the postcolonial present. The global migration regime initiated during the early decades of U.S. rule in the Philippines was reactivated in the 1960s. The influx of nurses from the Philippines is a very visible example of this phenomenon. Employers recruited Filipinas because of attributes linked to the imperial period: their English-language capacity and their training in an American-designed education system. The demand for Filipina nurses also recalls previous patterns of Filipino labor recruitment, reflected in the desire of employers to hire less-expensive and politically vulnerable immigrant labor in an industry that was becoming increasingly unionized. The demand for Filipina domestic workers in the global economy is also linked to demand for inexpensive labor with English-language skills. Filipinos, according to many employers, make good domestics because they are "naturally" subordinate and display an instinctive attraction to low-paid domestic labor. Narratives about Filipino nurses and domestics in many ways parallel older stereotypes about the naturally subordinate character of Filipino agricultural laborers, who were thought to enjoy backbreaking stoop labor. In recent years, the Philippine government has appropriated the stereotype of Filipino subservience to enhance the marketability of its overseas contract workers, carving out a special niche in the global service economy.

This book at its heart is about the entanglement of domestic and international boundary controls, a topic that remains relevant today. Nativist sentiment has been an enduring feature of the American political landscape. There is no shortage of nativist pundits and public officials railing against immigrants, criticizing the federal government for "failing to protect" the integrity of the nation's borders. Nativist spokespersons use racially coded language to warn of an impending "invasion" of immigrants from Latin America who want to "reconquer" the United States. The popular association of contemporary immigrants with deviancy, economic displacement, and unassimilability, moreover, offers a sober reminder that the discourse of social problems remains salient even today. Like the activists discussed in this book, claims makers have mobilized resources to define immigration as an urgent social problem or a "crisis," hoping that alarmist rhetoric will mobilize public support and force a change in federal policy. The recent upsurge in nativist sentiment has been accompanied by the mobilization of private citizens groups in the U.S. border region that have taken it upon themselves to arrest or "deport" immigrants in the name of the public welfare. This hostile climate has also given rise to new folk heroes such as Sheriff Joe Arpaio, an anti-immigrant crusader who brazenly uses racial profiling to round up suspicious-looking residents (i.e., Latinos) in Phoenix, Arizona. Though Arpaio is an agent of the state, he often uses extralegal methods to carry out his campaigns, regularly violating the Fourth, Fifth, and Fourteenth Amendment rights of arrestees. That he regularly deputizes a "posse" of between two and three thousand private citizens to assist with his crusade is eerily reminiscent of earlier expulsion campaigns described in this book. The notion that history is repeating itself provides us with an opportunity to identify patterns and lessons from past battles at the boundaries. The political debates associated with the age of globalization bear a striking resemblance to those that characterized the age of empire. None is more than obvious than the difficulty of addressing seemingly irreconcilable phenomena such as the unfettered mobility of global capital, labor-market demands in the industrialized states, and calls for stricter immigration and national controls in the global North. Whether we will witness a replay of the restrictionist era or whether we will see a new, more humane approach to these complex issues remains to be seen.

Notes

1. The three-day waiting period was popularly referred to as the "Gin Marriage Law." It was ostensibly aimed at preventing inebriated couples from entering into ill-advised marriages.

2. De Onate appeared in a handful of Spanish-language films under his stage name, Ralph Novarro. *San Francisco Examiner,* October 26, 1934, 1, 11; *New York Times,* October 26, 1934, 23; *Time,* November 5, 1934, 8.

3. *Los Angeles Times,* October 25, 1934, 1; *New York Times,* October 26, 1934, 23; *Berkeley Daily Gazette,* October 26, 1934, 13; *San Francisco Call Bulletin,* October 25, 1934, 1.

4. Rumors of an elopement to a neighboring state or to Mexico against the family's wishes briefly spread in the newspapers, but these reports turned out to be false. *Oakland Tribune,* October 25, 1934, 2.

5. *Washington Post,* October 24, 1934, 1; *San Francisco Chronicle,* October 26, 1934, 1; *Sacramento Bee,* October 24, 1934, 1.

6. *New York Times,* October 25, 1934, 12. L. J. Difani, the state senator representing the Riverside district, also intervened in the case, claiming that he had been "retained" by a private party to investigate the bridegroom's lineage. He showed up at the county clerk's office to scrutinize the marriage application materials.

7. Colonel Neblett also warned De Onate that he would be subject to "legal action" if the couple traveled to Mexico to get married. It is unclear what sort of legal sanction would have applied since Filipino-white couples regularly went to Mexico to circumvent California's miscegenation statutes. *San Francisco News,* October 24, 1934, 1; *San Francisco Call Bulletin,* October 25, 1934, 1.

8. McAdoo was one of the frontrunners for the Democratic Party's presidential nomination in 1924. The 1924 Democratic convention was marred by conflict over the role of Ku Klux Klan in the party. The Klan wielded significant power in the national party and sought to shape the 1924 platform and influence the selection of a presidential candidate. McAdoo sought support from Klan delegates at the convention, calculating that their support might get him enough votes to win the Democratic nomination. Though he was not a Klan member, it is worth noting that he was willing to solicit their support to advance his political ambitions. McAdoo was a son of the South, born in Georgia (in 1863) and raised in Tennessee. His father and uncle both served as officers in the Confederate army during the Civil War. D. Chalmers, *Hooded Americanism: The History of the Ku Klux Klan* (Durham, NC: Duke University Press, 1987), 203–212; W. Wade, *The Fiery Cross: The Ku*

Klux Klan in America (New York: Oxford University Press, 1998), 197–199; Z. Armstrong, *Notable Southern Families* (Chattanooga, TN: Lookout, 1918), 142.

9. De Onate cited among other things his tall, six-foot-two frame as evidence that he was not Filipino. *Oakland Tribune*, October 24, 1934, 1; *New York Times*, October 26, 1934, 23; *San Francisco Examiner*, October 25, 1934, 3; *Los Angeles Times*, October 24, 1934, 1.

10. Some news reports listed the sister's name as "Nena West," who was married to an American man in Seattle. Their father, Pablo Lopez De Onate, was a Spanish colonial official (a judge in the Zambales Province). Their mother, Isabel Novarro Rafael, was born in the Philippines. The insistence of Rafael and Mercedes that their Manila-born mother was of pure Spanish blood is not surprising considering their family's elite social status. The fact that the siblings gave conflicting accounts of where their parents were from suggests some selective memory about the family history. Rafael's account is particularly dubious, since Philippine records showed that he had been born in 1902, not in 1896 as he claimed on his marriage application. *San Francisco Examiner*, October 25, 1934, 3; *San Francisco Call Bulletin*, October 25, 1934, 1.

11. Pablo Lopez De Onate died in 1901. Isabel Novarro later married Phillip Whitaker of Manila, who became Rafael and Mercedes's stepfather. Isabel died in 1917. Although it is impossible to verify Whitaker's claims about his former wife's being of Filipino extraction, it is not clear what motive he had to lie about it. Rafael and Mercedes, on the other hand, might have had a reason (racial passing) to fudge their mother's background and to play up their whiteness. *San Francisco News*, October 25, 1934, 3; *Oakland Tribune*, October 25, 1934, 2.

12. *Los Angeles Times*, November 11, 1934, 1.

13. *Los Angeles Times*, November 9, 1934, 1, 3; *San Francisco News*, October 26, 1934, 3.

14. *Los Angeles Times*, November 9, 1934, 1, 3; *Los Angeles Times*, November 11, 1934, 1–2; *Los Angeles Times*, November 12, 1934, 3; *New York Times*, November 8, 1934, 25.

15. *Los Angeles Times*, February 20, 1937, 1; *Los Angeles Times*, February 27, 1937, A1; *Los Angeles Times*, March 24, 1937, A1; *Los Angeles Times*, April 3, 1937, A1.

16. *Los Angeles Times*, May 25, 1940, 8; *New York Times*, May 26, 1934, 21.

17. De Onate did appear in a few uncredited roles in films after his divorce, under his stage name, Ralph Novarro.

18. H. Blumer, "The Future of the Color Line," in *The Selected Works of Herbert Blumer: A Public Philosophy for Mass Society*, edited by S. Lyman and A. Viditch (Urbana: University of Illinois Press, 2000), 208–209.

19. It is worth noting that the De Onate scandal occurred just a few months after the passage of the Tydings-McDuffie Act in 1934, which granted the islands "independence" (to be awarded after a ten-year probationary period). A provision of the act placed the Philippines under a restrictive immigration quota of fifty persons per year. Filipinos who entered the United States before 1934 were not affected by the quota restrictions and could still travel freely in and out of the country. I discuss this issue in greater detail in chapter 5.

20. Hawaii was formally annexed in 1898 as an "incorporated territory," setting it apart from "unincorporated territories" such as the Philippines, Puerto Rico, and Guam. American sugar barons had previously tried to take over the Hawaiian islands in 1893 but were stymied by President Cleveland, who vetoed the annexation resolution. The Organic Act of 1900 granted collective naturalization to native Hawaiians as U.S. citizens, a decision that stood in sharp contrast to the treatment of Filipinos, Puerto Ricans, and

Chamorros (the indigenous people of Guam), whose racial fitness was subject to a different level of scrutiny. 31 Stat. 141; 23 Op. Atty. Gen. 345 (1901).

21. Regarding the political status of Puerto Ricans and Filipinos, the Supreme Court declared that "there is an implied denial of the right to American citizenship until Congress should signify its assent thereto." *Downes v. Bidwell*, 182 U.S. 244. See also *Balzac v. United States*, 258 U.S. 298.

22. M. Ngai, *Impossible Subjects: Illegal Aliens and the Making of Modern America* (Princeton, NJ: Princeton University Press, 2004), 22–55; E. Nakano Glenn, *Unequal Freedom: How Race and Citizenship Shaped American Citizenship and Labor* (Cambridge, MA: Harvard University Press, 2002), 18–37; E. Lee, *At America's Gates: Chinese Immigration during the Exclusion Era* (Chapel Hill: University of North Carolina Press, 2003), 19–46; R. Waldinger, "Foreigners Transformed: International Migration and the Making of a Divided People," *Diaspora* 12(2) (2003): 247–272.

23. The Bureau of Immigration and Naturalization was the institutional forerunner to the Immigration and Naturalization Service (INS). The 1906 act set standardized forms and fees for all courts of record in an effort to clamp down on fraud and competition among courts, which charged different fees to attract naturalization business. The new forms mandated by Congress required petitioners to list their "color" and "complexion" as part of their declaration of intention. 34 Stat. 596.

24. B. Anderson, *Imagined Communities: Reflections on the Origin and Spread of Nationalism* (New York: Verso, 1991).

25. J. Gusfield, *Contested Meanings: The Construction of Alcohol Problems* (Madison: University of Wisconsin Press, 1996), 17. See also J. Gusfield, *The Symbolic Crusade: Status Politics and the American Temperance Movement* (Urbana: University of Illinois Press, 1986). On the construction of race as a social problem, see S. Hall et al., *Policing the Crisis: Mugging, the State and Law and Order* (New York: Holmes and Meier, 1978).

26. Though the Tydings-McDuffie Act was passed in 1934, the probationary period did not officially begin until after Philippine officials drafted a constitution establishing the structure of the new Commonwealth Government. The Philippine constitution then had to be approved by the Roosevelt administration and later ratified by the Filipino electorate, which happened in 1935. The act stipulated that the United States would surrender sovereignty over the islands on July 4, 1946, ten years after the inauguration of the Commonwealth Government under the new constitution. 48 Stat. 456.

NOTES TO CHAPTER 1

1. M. F. Jacobson, *Barbarian Virtues: The United States Encounters Foreign Peoples at Home and Abroad, 1876–1917* (New York: Hill and Wang 2001), 221–260; S. Miller, *Benevolent Assimilation: The Conquest of the Philippines, 1899–1903* (New Haven, CT: Yale University Press, 1984), 13–30. For a more general overview of the U.S. imperial vision, see W. Lafeber, *The New Empire: An Interpretation of American Expansion, 1860–1898* (Ithaca, NY: Cornell University Press, 1998).

2. L. Thompson, "The Imperial Republic: A Comparison of Insular Territories under U.S. Domination after 1898," *Pacific Historical Review* 71 (4) (2002): 535–574; R. Smith, *Civic Ideals: Conflicting Visions of Citizenship in U.S. History* (New Haven, CT: Yale University Press, 1999), 436–438; P. Kramer, *The Blood of Government: Race, Empire, the*

United States, and the Philippines (Chapel Hill: University of North Carolina Press, 2006), 162–165.

3. Jacobson, *Barbarian Virtues*, 26–37, 222–229; L. S. Stavrianos, *Global Rift: The Third World Comes of Age* (New York: William Morrow, 1981), 380–382; T. Bender, *A Nation among Nations: America's Place in World History* (New York: Hill and Wang 2006), 182–245.

4. The paternalistic outlooks and accompanying benevolent impulses were key themes of Progressive Era ideology. Racial issues were increasingly looked at from a "social problems" perspective that cataloged the putative deficiencies of nonwhites and the challenges of assimilation. See Jacobson, *Barbarian Virtues*, 179–220; J. Go, "Racism and Colonialism: Meanings of Difference and Ruling Practices in America's Pacific Empire," *Qualitative Sociology* 27 (1) (2004): 35–58.

5. H. Gannett, "The Philippine Islands and Their People," *National Geographic Magazine* 15 (3) (1904): 91–112; V. Rafael, *White Love and Other Events in Filipino History* (Durham, NC: Duke University Press, 2000), 19–50.

6. B. Anderson, *Imagined Communities: Reflections on the Origin and Spread of Nationalism* (New York: Verso, 1991), 164–169, 184–185.

7. The treaty needed the approval of a two-thirds majority of the Senate to be ratified, and it ultimately passed by single vote above that threshold.

8. W. Williams, "United States Indian Policy and the Debate over Philippine Annexation: Implications for the Origins of American Imperialism," *Journal of American History* 66 (4) (1980): 810–831; Bender, *Nation among Nations*, 219–226; Thompson, "Imperial Republic," 545–560.

9. The population of the Philippines was estimated to be 8 to 10 million. This stood in contrast with the territorial populations in Puerto Rico (953,000), Cuba (1.5 million), and Guam (8,661). The Hawaiian Islands, which were annexed separately, had a population of just over 100,000. *The World Almanac and Encyclopedia 1901* (New York: Press Publishing, 1901), 96–113.

10. *Historical Statistics of the United States, 1789–1945* (Washington, DC: GPO, 1949), 250.

11. Jacobson, *Barbarian Virtues*, 225–227; Lafeber, *New Empire*, 353–365; E. Hobsbawm, *The Age of Empire, 1875–1914* (New York: Vintage, 1987), 66–67.

12. A. Beveridge, *The Meaning of the Times* (1908; repr., Freeport, NY: Books for Libraries Press, 1968), 43–45; Kramer, *The Blood of Government*, 116–120.

13. Henry Cabot Lodge (R-Massachusetts), *Congressional Record* (1900), 2632; see also O. P. Austin, "Problems of the Pacific: The Commerce of the Great Ocean," *National Geographic Magazine* 13 (8) (1902): 303–318.

14. Quoted in H. Beale, *Theodore Roosevelt and the Rise of America to World Power* (Baltimore: Johns Hopkins University Press, 1956), 72.

15. Williams, "United States Indian Policy," 827.

16. Secretary Hay informed the commission, "the President wishes to know the opinion of the Commission as inserting in treaty provisions on the subject of citizenship of inhabitants of Philippines which will prevent extension of that right to Mongolians . . . and also whether you consider it advisable to provide, if possible, for recognition of existence of uncivilized native tribes in the same manner as in Alaska treaty." *Foreign Relations* (1898), 961.

17. Samuel McEnery (D-Louisiana), *Congressional Record* (1900), 1862.

18. Beveridge, *Meaning of the Times*, 72.

19. Senator John Daniel of Virginia, for example, questioned why the United States was determined to consecrate Filipinos "with the oil of American citizenship" when the population of the islands was nothing more than a "mess of Asiatic pottage." John Daniel (D-Virginia), *Congressional Record* (1900), 1430.

20. James Berry (D-Arkansas), *Congressional Record* (1899), 1298.

21. Benjamin Tillman (D-South Carolina), *Congressional Record* (1900), 1261.

22. John Daniel (D-Virginia), *Congressional Record* (1899), 1431.

23. George Gilbert (D-Kentucky), *Congressional Record* (1900), 2172.

24. John Dalzell (R-Pennsylvania), *Congressional Record* (1900), 1959.

25. Francis Newlands (D-Nevada), *Congressional Record* (1900), 2001.

26. Inasmuch as the prospect of Filipino civic equality threatened the racial foundations of American society, the choice facing Congress was either to "immediately withdraw from the Philippines" or, "if we are determined to retain them, we must immediately proceed to exterminate their inhabitants." George Turner (Silver Republican/ Democrat-Washington), *Congressional Record* (1900), 1055.

27. George Gilbert (D-Kentucky), *Congressional Record* (1900), 2172.

28. For a discussion of U.S. officials' concerns about the relationship between Philippine annexation and Chinese immigration, see *Foreign Relations* (1899), 207–217, which details Secretary of State John Hay's views on exclusion as well as the response from Chinese officials. 32 Stat. 176–177. The extension of Chinese exclusion to U.S. territories was formalized in 1902. 33 Stat. 428.

29. The provisions of the Teller Amendment put Cuba in a separate category from the Philippines and Puerto Rico. The Teller Amendment precluded formal annexation of Cuba, but Congress imposed a "protectorate" status over the island, which allowed the United States to maintain remote control over Cuba's political affairs.

30. Jacob Bromwell (R-Ohio), *Congressional Record* (1900), 2043.

31. Sereno Payne (R-New York), *Congressional Record* (1900), 1941.

32. Jacob Bromwell (R-Ohio), *Congressional Record* (1900), 2043.

33. Thomas Spight (D-Mississippi), *Congressional Record* (1900), 2105.

34. Francis Newlands (D-Nevada), *Congressional Record* (1900), 1994; William Williams (D-Illinois), *Congressional Record* (1900), 2162; William Lindsay (D-Kentucky), *Congressional Record* (1900), 2696.

35. Albert Beveridge cited the long history of nonconsensual rule over Native Americans to dismiss anti-imperialists' claims that Filipinos would be entitled to constitutional rights by virtue of the United States' imposing sovereignty over Filipinos. He mocked his colleagues who argued that the "Declaration [of Independence] applies to all men, how dare you deny its application to the American Indian? And if you deny it to the Indian at home, how dare you grant it to the Malay abroad? . . . There are people in the world who do not understand any form of government [and] must be governed. . . . And so the authors of the Declaration themselves governed the Indian without his consent." Albert Beveridge (R-Indiana), *Congressional Record* (1900), 710.

36. Most of the Insular Cases dealt with litigation questions involving Puerto Rico, but the decisions rendered by the Court also applied to the Philippines. *De Lima v. Bidwell*, 182 U.S. 1; *Downes v. Bidwell*, 182 U.S. 244; *Fourteen Diamond Rings v. United States*, 183 U.S. 176;

Dorr v. U.S., 195 U.S. 138. The *Fourteen Diamond Rings* and *Dorr* cases specifically dealt with the Philippines. The *Rings* case involved an American soldier who had smuggled some rings back to the United States without paying customs duties. Among other things, the justices affirmed that the United States held title to the Philippines even though Filipinos had taken up arms against the imposition of American rule. The Court rejected the claim that the United States had sought to "subjugate the people of a foreign country," declaring instead that it was "preserving order and suppressing insurrection in the territory of the United States." 183 U.S. at 178. The *Dorr* case took up the issue of whether residents of the Philippines were entitled to the constitutional right to a trial by jury. 195 U.S. at 138.

37. *Downes v. Bidwell*, 182 U.S. at 244; *Dorr v. U.S.*, 195 U.S. at 148. See also Smith, *Civic Ideals*, 434–438; C. Burnett and B. Marshall, *Foreign in a Domestic Sense: Puerto Rico, American Expansion and the Constitution* (Durham, NC: Duke University Press, 2001).

38. The first Philippine Commission conducted its work during the height of the annexation debate. U.S. Philippine Commission, *Report of the Philippine Commission to the President*, 4 vols. (Washington, DC: GPO, 1900). The Department of War study, which came out soon after, went into even greater detail about the population characteristics of the Philippines.

39. U.S. Bureau of Insular Affairs, *The People of the Philippines—A Letter from the Secretary of War* (Washington, DC: GPO, 1901), 1.

40. U.S. Philippine Commission, *Report of the Philippine Commission*, 1:137–141. On colonial surveys as instruments to measure the "traffic habits" of subject populations, see B. Anderson, *Imagined Communities*, 169.

41. U.S. Philippine Commission, *Report of the Philippine Commission*, 1:11.

42. The commission asserted that should the Negrito "as he exists to-day be compared to the African, a sufficient number of characteristics will be found to indicate a relationship with the latter race." Ibid., 3:334.

43. Ibid., 1:11.

44. Ibid., 1:12.

45. Ibid., 3:343. Racial admixture between Anglo-Saxons and Filipinos raised different anxieties about the deleterious effects of such amalgamations on the white population. The European mestizos were rejected by both Filipinos and Anglos, giving rise to a complicated "mental condition" in which members of this group continually strove to "attain the respect and consideration accorded to the superior class" even though their native blood linked them to "the other side." In vain, they attempted to "disown their affinity to the inferior races . . . while on the other hand jealous of their true born European acquaintances." U.S. Bureau of Insular Affairs, *The People of the Philippines*, 51–52.

46. Ibid., 52–54; U.S. Philippine Commission, *Report of the Philippine Commission*, 2:19.

47. This theme was evidenced in the secretary of war's claim that, "true to their Malay instincts, all tribes of the Philippine people can not resist the desire to mutilate the bodies of their fallen enemies." U.S. Bureau of Insular Affairs, *The People of the Philippines*, 36.

48. U.S. Bureau of the Census, *Census of the Philippine Islands*, 4 vols. (Washington, DC: GPO, 1905), 1:44; see also Gannett, "Philippine Islands and Their People."

49. U.S. Philippine Commission, *Report of the Philippine Commission*, 2:228–229.

50. Ibid., 2:33.

51. U.S. Bureau of Insular Affairs, *The People of the Philippines*, 18; Gannett, "Philippine Islands and Their People," 92–99.

52. U.S. Philippine Commission, *Report of the Philippine Commission,* 3:384.

53. U.S. Bureau of the Census, *Philippine Census,* 1:504.

54. Quoted in U.S. Bureau of Insular Affairs, *The People of the Philippines,* 18.

55. The most comprehensive discussion of the relationship between America's world's fairs and empire building is R. Rydell, *All the World's a Fair: Visions of Empire at America's International Expositions, 1876–1916* (Chicago: University of Chicago Press, 1984).

56. *Los Angeles Times,* June 26, 1904, C9; Rydell, *All the World's a Fair,* 160–173.

57. *Los Angeles Times,* July 1, 1904, A4.

58. *Los Angeles Times,* April, 24, 1904, E10.

59. Rydell, *All the World's a Fair,* 171–172.

60. *Washington Post,* May 7, 1904, 5.

61. *Portland Oregonian,* December 19, 1904, 5; *Los Angeles Times,* April 24, 1904, E10.

62. *Los Angeles Times,* November 18, 1904, 4.

63. *Washington Post,* August 9, 1904.

64. *New York Times,* August 9, 1904, 7; *New York Times,* August 10, 1904, 7.

65. Rydell, *All the World's a Fair,* 194–196; *Chicago Tribune,* October 3, 1904, 6.

66. *Washington Post,* September 17, 1905, A10.

67. *Portland Oregonian,* September 6, 1905, 10.

68. *Portland Oregonian,* September 5, 1905, 14; *Portland Oregonian,* September 6, 1905, 10.

69. *Portland Oregonian,* September 13, 1905, 12. Exhibition manager Richard Schneidewind objected to the Humane Society's characterization of native customs. He claimed that Igorottes were "barbarians," rather than "savages," though the distinction he was making between the two terms is not clear. *Portland Oregonian,* September 14, 1905, 14.

70. *Portland Oregonian,* September 15, 1905, 14.

71. *Los Angeles Times,* January 14, 1906, 10.

72. *New York Times,* August 10, 1905, 7.

73. *Seattle Post-Intelligencer,* June 22, 1909, 3. For a good overview of the Alaska-Yukon-Pacific Exposition, see S. Lee, *Claiming the Oriental Gateway: Pre-war Seattle and Japanese America* (Philadelphia: Temple University Press, 2011).

74. *Seattle Post-Intelligencer,* June 20, 1909, 10.

75. *Seattle Daily Times,* June 7, 1909, 1, 6.

76. *Seattle Post-Intelligencer,* July 5, 1909, 2.

NOTES TO CHAPTER 2

1. U.S. Philippine Commission, *Report of the Philippine Commission to the Secretary of War 1911* (Washington, DC: GPO, 1912), 167. The Pensionado Act was approved by the Philippine Commission in August 26, 1903 (Act No. 854), and the first group of 102 students arrived in November of that year, with a total of 289 Filipinos eventually taking part in the program. Filipino students continued to come to the United States in the following decades but not generally under government sponsorship like the first group of pensionados. The largest concentration of these students was on the West Coast. B. Lasker, *Filipino Immigration to the Continental United States and Hawaii* (Chicago: University of Chicago Press, 1931), 369–375; D. Fujita-Rony, *American Workers, Colonial Power: Philippine Seattle and the Transpacific West, 1919–1941* (Berkeley: University of California Press, 2003), 51–65;

Y. L. Espiritu, *Home Bound: Filipino American Lives across Cultures, Communities, and Countries* (Berkeley: University of California Press, 2003), 23–45.

2. Executive Order, April 5, 1901 (Pres. McKinley). The order called for the enlistment of up to five hundred Filipinos a year in the U.S. Navy. It was amended a few months later, on June 25, to include natives of Guam. The amended order also changed the language of the decree, striking out the term "Filipino" and replacing it with the "natives of the Islands of the Philippines," presumably to prevent Chinese residents of the Philippines from taking advantage of the program. On the settlement of former navy men in the United States, see Lasker, *Filipino Immigration*, 25, 59–63.

3. On the relationship between the global capitalist expansion and labor migration, see L. Cheng and E. Bonacich, eds., *Labor Immigration under Capitalism: Asian Workers in the United States before World War II* (Berkeley: University of California Press, 1984); S. Sassen, *The Mobility of Labor and Capital: A Study in International Investment and Labor Flows* (New York: Cambridge University Press, 1990).

4. H. Gannett, "The Philippine Islands and Their People," *National Geographic Magazine* 15 (3) (1904): 91–112.

5. G. May, *Social Engineering in the Philippines* (Westport, CT: Greenwood, 1980); A. Calata, "The Role of Education in Americanizing Filipinos," in *Mixed Blessing: The Impact of the American Colonial Experience on Politics and Society in the Philippines*, edited by H. McFerson (Westport, CT: Greenwood, 2002), 89–92; see also C. Ceniza Choy's work on the establishment in the Philippines of U.S.-style nursing schools staffed by American nurses and medical personnel. She shows a clear linkage between colonial policy, educational networks, and emigration. C. Ceniza Choy, *Empire of Care: Nursing and Migration in Filipino American History* (Durham, NC: Duke University Press, 2003), 17–40.

6. American officials outlawed the public display of the Philippine flag as a seditious act until 1919, when the newly empowered Philippine legislature repealed the ban (Act No. 2871). In 1920, Philippine lawmakers passed Act No. 2928 adopting the Philippine flag as the official flag of government. The statute, however, contained a provision that mandated that the U.S. flag be given a position of preeminence in all public displays, "whenever the Philippine flag is hoisted in public jointly with the American flag, . . . the American flag shall be placed above the Filipino flag when both are in vertical line." 15 Public Laws P.I. 271–272 (1920); W. Cameron Forbes, *The Philippine Islands*, 2 vols. (Boston: Houghton Mifflin, 1928), 2:341.

7. U.S. Secretary of Labor, *Labor Conditions in Hawaii* (Washington, DC: GPO, 1916), 39.

8. R. Takaki, *Pau Hana: Plantation Life and Labor in Hawaii* (Honolulu: University of Hawaii Press, 1983), 19; U.S. Secretary of Labor, *Labor Conditions in Hawaii*, 11.

9. On the centrality of sugar production to American imperial expansion, see C. Ayala, *American Sugar Kingdom: The Plantation Economy of the Spanish Caribbean, 1898–1934* (Chapel Hill: University of North Carolina Press, 1999). Ayala's book offers a particularly cogent analysis of the evolving relationship between new corporatized plantation regimes in Latin America and local systems of labor control. For a good overview of the central role of sugar in fueling modern capitalist development, see S. Mintz, *Sweetness and Power: The Place of Sugar in Modern History* (New York: Penguin, 1986).

10. American sugar interests carried out a coup against the Hawaiian monarchy in 1893 but were rebuked in their efforts to have the U.S. government support their action

by formally annexing the islands. The plantation oligarchs got their wish a few years later when the McKinley administration backed up their power play as part of its expansionist crusade in 1898.

11. Civil Governor Taft and members of Philippine Commission were initially hesitant about signing off on the export of Filipinos to Hawaii without certain guarantees about labor protections for plantation workers. M. Dorita Clifford, "The Hawaiian Sugar Planter Association and Filipino Exclusion," in *The Filipino Exclusion Movement, 1927–1935,* edited by J. M. Saniel (Quezon City, Philippines: Institute for Asian Studies, 1967), 14; R. Alcantara, *Sakada: Filipino Adaptation in Hawaii* (New York: University Press of America, 1981), 3–10.

12. This quotation comes from an investigator with the U.S. Bureau of Labor, who was summarizing the views of planters he interviewed during a survey of economic conditions in the islands. Planters had unsuccessfully tried to bring in Korean and Chinese immigrants to offset the growing demographic power of the Japanese, but restrictive immigration laws hindered these efforts. Planters had more success with playing Filipinos against the Japanese, since they could be brought into the United States in large numbers. U.S. Department of Commerce and Labor, *Bulletin of the Bureau of Labor* (Washington, DC: GPO, 1906), 402; *Los Angeles Times,* December 28, 1922, 17.

13. This quotation comes from the sugar-industry newsletter *Planters' Monthly,* quoted in E. Beechert, *Working in Hawaii: A Labor History* (Honolulu: University of Hawaii Press, 1985), 183; the superintendent of labor in Hawaii described the arrival of Filipino workers as "our only salvation." U.S. Commissioner General of Immigration, *Industrial Conditions in the Hawaiian Islands* (Washington, DC: GPO, 1913), 43.

14. Clifford, "Hawaiian Sugar Planter Association and Filipino Exclusion," 17; see also E. Wentworth, *Filipino Plantation Workers in Hawaii* (San Francisco: Institute of Pacific Relations, 1941); 23 Stat. 332.

15. U.S. Commissioner General of Immigration, *Industrial Conditions in Hawaiian Islands,* 40–41.

16. Keefe's report on economic conditions in Hawaii criticized the HSPA for low wages and exploitative living conditions that discouraged "white labor" from coming to work on the plantations. He asserted that the recruitment of Filipinos was a conscious strategy by the planters to depress wages in the industry through the use of "oriental" labor. He claimed that Filipinos undercut the process of "Americanization" in the islands because of their low standard of living and suggested that they were prone to criminality and laziness. His official report, published in 1913, included a supplement omitted from the original version of the document presented to Congress in 1911. The supplement, which pertained to the "undesirable character" of Filipinos, was left out of the original report at the request of Charles Nagel, secretary of commerce and labor, because of its provocative racial tone. According to Keefe, he withdrew the offending items when he received assurances from Nagel that President William Howard Taft and Secretary of War Jacob Dickinson would intervene to restrict emigration from the Philippines on a voluntary basis, in a manner similar to the Gentleman's Agreement, in order to avoid offending Filipinos. His addendum to the published report made it clear that he felt betrayed that no action was ever taken to restrict emigration from the Philippines. U.S. Commissioner General of Immigration, *Industrial Conditions in Hawaiian Islands,* 4–5, 40–41; Clifford, "Hawaiian Sugar Planter Association and Filipino Exclusion," 15–16.

17. Philippine officials, many of whom were closely tied to the U.S. colonial regime, made meager efforts to check on the well-being of their nationals working in Hawaii. On a few occasions, a Filipino representative was appointed to investigate complaints about labor abuses in the islands. The most notable of these was Cayetano Ligot, a probusiness official who took bribes from plantation owners and declared working conditions to be good. Ligot denounced unionization efforts among Filipino workers and actively worked to undermine union leaders. M. Sharma, "Labor Migration and Class Formation among Filipinos in Hawaii, 1906–1946," in Cheng and Bonacich, *Labor Immigration under Capitalism*, 597–598; Clifford, "Hawaiian Sugar Planter Association and Filipino Exclusion," 17–18.

18. This is the equivalent of about thirty-two million in 2010 U.S. dollars. It is not hard to imagine how this large flow of money into the Philippines spurred additional emigration.

19. Remittances rose to five million dollars a year by the 1930s. Sharma, "Labor Migration and Class Formation," 590–591.

20. Beechert, *Working in Hawaii*, 174, 200–213; Reinecke, *The Filipino Piecemeal Strike of 1924–1925* (Honolulu: University of Hawaii Press, 1996), 29–37.

21. Lunas usually carried whips to discipline workers in the fields, a method that evokes images of plantation slave masters in the American South. There were many reports of laborers receiving medical treatment after brutal whippings from lunas. Takaki, *Pau Hana*, 74–75.

22. Manlapit was an important figure in the early Filipino labor movement in Hawaii and the U.S. mainland. He hailed from Batangas province in southern Luzon and had briefly worked on a plantation when he arrived in Hawaii in 1910. He later worked at a law office in Honolulu, where he took up his career as a labor leader. Manlapit was a skilled orator but proved to be an unpredictable organizer who relied on charismatic authority rather than thorough planning in the labor campaigns he led. M. Kerkvliet, *Unbending Cane: Pablo Manlapit, a Filipino Labor Leader in Hawaii* (Honolulu: University of Hawaii Press, 2003), 23–28; R. Alcantara, "The 1920 Hawaii Plantation Strike," in *Festschrift in Honor of Dr. Marcelino Foronda, Jr.*, edited by Emerita S. Quito (Manila: De La Salle University Press, 1987), 190–199.

23. The role of Manlapit during the 1920 strike was controversial, though there is little doubt that he was genuinely devoted to improving the lives of Filipino workers, even when it came at a great personal cost. The strike was actually called without his authorization by rank-and-file workers who were frustrated with his erratic leadership. Kerkvliet, *Unbending Cane*, 26–28, 53–60; Alcantara, "1920 Plantation Strike," 200; Beechert, *Working in Hawaii*, 199–210.

24. In addition to historical evidence that suggests that the bribery charge against Manlapit was a complete fabrication orchestrated the HSPA, the HSPA ran a sophisticated smear campaign against him that included paying informants to try and undermine his credibility. Kerkvliet, *Unbending Cane*, 26–28; Alcantara, "1920 Plantation Strike," 200–201.

25. Clifford, "Hawaiian Sugar Planter Association and Filipino Exclusion," 20–21.

26. Quoted in Alcantara, "1920 Plantation Strike," 182.

27. Beechert, *Working in Hawaii*, 208–209, 214–215.

28. Ibid., 217–223.

29. The *Advertiser* was equally harsh in its denunciations of the strikers, who it blamed for all the violence. The newspaper editorialized about the strike leaders, "if happily they are dead, well and good." *Honolulu Advertiser,* September 11, 1924, 1, 4; *Honolulu Star-Bulletin,* September 11, 1924, 14; Reinecke, *Filipino Piecemeal Strike,* 82.

30. Reinecke, *Filipino Piecemeal Strike,* 80; According to the *Advertiser,* Filipino strike leaders had been given "too much sympathy" by the public, which encouraged their radical ambitions. *Honolulu Advertiser,* September 13, 1924, 14.

31. Reinecke, *Filipino Piecemeal Strike,* 85–86.

32. Beechert, *Working in Hawaii,* 223; Kerkvliet, *Unbending Cane,* 53–58; Reinecke, *Filipino Piecemeal Strike,* 45–70.

33. Beechert, *Working in Hawaii,* 183, 251.

34. R. De La Pedraja, *The Rise and Decline of U.S. Merchant Shipping in the Twentieth Century* (New York: Twayne, 1992), 22, 97–98; Lasker, *Filipino Immigration,* 211–216.

35. Clifford, "Hawaiian Sugar Planter Association and Filipino Exclusion," 21; Lasker, *Filipino Immigration,* 204–211.

36. Commercial fishing (including the canning of fish) is classified by the U.S. government as part of the agricultural sector—"farming" the ocean.

37. The output of canned salmon grew from 2.4 million cases in 1910 to 4.4 million in 1920 to 8.4 million cases in 1930. *Report to the Secretary of Interior by Alaska Governor* (Washington, DC: GPO, 1921), 37; J. Whitehead, *Completing the Union: Alaska, Hawaii, and the Battle for Statehood* (Albuquerque: University of New Mexico Press, 2004), 46.

38. In one case, mainland recruiters anchored their ship three miles outside Hawaii's territorial jurisdiction and secreted a group of more than one hundred Filipinos under cover of night to the waiting vessel, which then departed to the West Coast. Clifford, "Hawaiian Sugar Planter Association and Filipino Exclusion," 16.

39. C. Friday, *Organizing Asian American Labor: The Pacific Coast Canned-Salmon Industry* (Philadelphia: Temple University Press, 1994), 127; Fujita-Rony, *American Workers, Colonial Power,* 98–104.

40. Friday, *Organizing Asian American Labor,* 40–41, 127–133; J. Masson and D. Guimary, "Pilipinos and Unionization in the Alaska Canned Salmon Industry," *Amerasia* 8 (2) (1981): 5–9.

41. Masson and Guimary, "Pilipinos and Unionization," 4–7.

42. Ibid., 4–5; Friday, *Organizing Asian American Labor,* 129, 178.

43. The CWFLU was formed by Filipinos in Seattle in 1932 and received a charter from the AFL (Local 18257) in 1933. The AFL was generally hostile to the idea of organizing Filipino workers but made an exception in this case. Chris Friday suggests that the AFL changed its tune out of fear that the Communist-controlled Cannery and Agricultural Industrial Workers Union (CAIWU) was making successful inroads with ethnic workers on the West Coast. By the end of the decade, the union had more than two thousand Filipino members but also had black, Hawaiian, Japanese, and Native American members in its ranks. Friday, *Organizing Asian American Labor,* 137–140, 145; S. Jamieson, *Labor Unionism in American Agriculture* (New York: Arno, 1976), 218–219.

44. For a good overview of the history of California agriculture, see L. Jelinek, *Harvest Empire: A History of California Agriculture* (San Francisco: Boyd and Fraser, 1982); and A. Olmstead and P. Rhode, "The Evolution of California Agriculture, 1850–2000," in *California Agriculture: Dimensions and Issues,* edited by Jerry Siebert, 1–28 (Berkeley, CA:

Giannini Foundation of Agricultural Economics, 2003). The ascendancy of California agriculture was aided greatly by the creation of well-funded grower's cooperatives that engaged in national marketing campaigns that branded California agricultural products: Sunkist, Sun Maid, Calpak/Del Monte, and Di Giorgio Fruit Corp.

45. The southern agricultural regions of the state, especially Los Angeles County and the Imperial Valley, tended to be dominated by Mexican labor, although Filipinos worked certain crops in the Imperial Valley, where they were often brought in as a counterweight to Mexican workers, who participated in a number of crippling strikes during this period. C. Daniel, *Bitter Harvest: A History of California Farmworkers* (Ithaca, NY: Cornell University Press, 1981), 67–69; L. Fischer, *The Harvest Labor Market in California* (Cambridge, MA: Harvard University Press, 1953), 5–8, 38–40.

46. The ascendance of popular California products such as lettuce and asparagus (both fresh and canned) was also aided by advances in horticultural science that developed sturdier, less perishable varietals of these commodities, such as "iceberg lettuce" and "palmetto" asparagus, which could be shipped on refrigerated rail cars to East Coast markets without spoiling. K. Starr, *Endangered Dreams: The Great Depression in California* (New York: Oxford University Press, 1996), 180; C. McWilliams, *Factories in the Fields* (1939; repr., Berkeley: University of California Press, 2000), 254–255; C. McWilliams, *Brothers under the Skin*, rev. ed. (Boston: Little, Brown, 1951), 236–244; *Los Angeles Times*, December 17, 1930, A4.

47. Another consequence of heightened levels of border enforcement was an alarming increase in wage rates for farmworkers due to labor shortages. Growers in the Imperial Valley claimed that their wage bill doubled during 1926 because of restrictive immigration policies. Agribusiness interests in California convinced the Department of Labor to intervene and broker a "Gentlemen's Agreement" between immigration officials and growers that would legalize undocumented Mexican workers by deducting their visa fee and head tax from their wages. *Los Angeles Times*, February 3, 1926, 6; M. Ngai, *Impossible Subjects: Illegal Aliens and the Making of Modern America* (Princeton, NJ: Princeton University Press, 2004), 93–94; Z. Vargas, *Labor Rights Are Civil Rights: Mexican American Workers in Twentieth-Century America* (Princeton, NJ: Princeton University Press, 2004), 34–36.

48. The number of Filipinos coming directly to the U.S. mainland from Philippines by the end of the decade increased significantly. By 1929, the number of West Coast arrivals coming directly from the Philippines (45 percent) was roughly equal to the number of those arriving from Hawaii (45.3 percent). This shift reflects the aggressive advertising efforts of the Dollar Line and the Los Angeles Steamship Company in the Philippines. California Department of Industrial Relations, *Facts about Filipino Immigration* (San Francisco: R&E Research Associates, 1930), 19–27.

49. California Department of Industrial Relations, *Facts about Filipino Immigration*, 57; McWilliams, *Brothers under the Skin*, 232–240; *Los Angeles Times*, August 15, 1933, 1–2; *Los Angeles Times*, August 16, 1933, 1–2.

50. *Los Angeles Times*, June 10, 1923, VI16; *Los Angeles Times*, July 29, 1923, VI1.

51. According to the 1930 U.S. Census, California had the largest population of Filipinos (30,470) on the U.S. mainland. Washington State was second, with 3,480, followed by Illinois (2,011), New York (1,982), and Oregon (1,066).

52. Jamieson, *Labor Unionism in American Agriculture*, 203–204.

53. California Department of Industrial Relations, *Facts about Filipino Immigration*, 12–14; McWilliams, *Factories in the Fields*, 13–132.

54. Quoted in California Department of Industrial Relations, *Facts about Filipino Immigration*, 73. Growers regularly defended their hiring of Filipino and Mexican workers by claiming that native whites refused to do fieldwork (or did it poorly). It is hard to evaluate such claims, which were likely self-serving, but whites certainly had more employment opportunities than other groups did. Native whites tended to monopolize higher-paying jobs in the packinghouses or canneries, and in a sense their jobs were made possible by the availability of "cheap labor" in the fields. *Los Angeles Times*, May 11, 1930, 5, 13; *Los Angeles Times*, April 5, 1930, 2; Daniel, *Bitter Harvest*, 53–64; BANC MSS, C-R 4, box 2, James E. Wood Papers, Bancroft Library, University of California at Berkeley, n.p.

55. California Department of Industrial Relations, *Facts about Filipino Immigration*, 12; D. Anthony, "Filipino Labor in Central California," *Sociology and Social Research* 16 (2) (1931): 155.

56. Farm operators in the 1920s viewed Chinese workers as ideal field hands. Popular memory held that the plodding "Chinaman" possessed the perfect combination of efficiency and subservience. Moreover, they kept to themselves socially and were averse to labor strikes—traits that distinguished them from Filipino workers. Daniel, *Bitter Harvest*, 64–67.

NOTES TO CHAPTER 3

1. The Johnson-Reed Immigration Act of 1924 established the infamous "national origins quotas," which effectively merged national and racial classifications into mutually corresponding categories of exclusion. In practice, the 1924 act promoted and sanctioned large-scale immigration from western Europe as an instinctive and affirmative component of national development. At the same time, it unilaterally barred immigrants from Asia. M. Ngai, *Impossible Subjects: Illegal Aliens and the Making of Modern America* (Princeton, NJ: Princeton University Press, 2004), 21–55; B. O. Hing, *Making and Remaking Asian America through Immigration Policy* (Stanford, CA: Stanford University Press, 1993), 32–34; J. Higham, *Strangers in the Land: Patterns of American Nativism, 1860–1925* (New Brunswick, NJ: Rutgers University Press, 1963).

2. E. G. Adams, "The Filipino Question," *Three Stars*, July 15, 1929 (reprinted from *the Dinuba Sentinel*), 1–2, 8. Adams represented the district of Merced County in California's Central Valley.

3. I draw on recent scholarship emphasizing the role of the modern state in constructing and managing the American racial hierarchy. The administrative apparatus of the state is endowed with the politicolegal authority to assign different social collectivities into disadvantaged racial categories that shape their life chances. M. Omi and H. Winant, *Racial Formation in the United States: From the 1960s to the 1990* (New York: Routledge, 1994), 77–88; Ngai, *Impossible Subjects*, 1–20; I. Haney López, *White by Law: The Legal Construction of Race* (New York: NYU Press, 1996). The nation-state regulates the incorporation of foreign immigrant labor in three important ways. First, it institutes a formal standard of exclusion/inclusion, defining who is eligible for entry into the territorial boundaries of the nation. Second, the state adjudicates who will be included within the political community of the nation, through the regulation of access to citizenship rights.

Third, the state determines how migrant workers are allocated and incorporated into specific positions in the relations of production and the organization of the labor market. Contemporary studies of racial inequality in the United States have focused on the role of race in structuring hierarchical relations between different groups. Max Weber's concept of social closure is particularly useful for understanding the historical dynamics of racial stratification. According to closure theory, a dominant social group monopolizes valuable social resources and opportunities by excluding or "closing off" access of those resources to outsiders. Recent scholarship in the field of race relations has explored the transformation of racial categories and boundaries across time and space, examining how ideologies of empire, nationality, and class were inextricably fused with questions of racial identification. T. Almaguer, *Racial Fault Lines: The Historical Origins of White Supremacy in California* (Berkeley: University of California Press, 1994); M. F. Jacobson, *Barbarian Virtues: The United States Encounters Foreign Peoples at Home and Abroad, 1876–1917* (New York: Hill and Wang 2001), 4–9; T. Holt, *The Problem of Race in the 21st Century* (Cambridge, MA: Harvard University Press, 2001).

4. The Treaty of Paris signed in 1898 had provided that "the civil rights and political status of the native inhabitants of the territories hereby ceded to the United States shall be determined by the Congress" but did not clarify the status of Filipinos until four years later in 1902. 30 Stat. 1754 (1898).

5. For examples, see *In re Ah Yup*, 1 F. Cas. 223 (C.C.D. Cal. 1878); *United States v. Wong Kim Ark*, 169 U.S. 649 (1898); *In re Saito*, 62 F. 126 (C.C.D. Mass. 1894); *In re Buntaro Kumagai*, 163 F. 922 (W.D. Wash. 1908); *In re Balsara*, 171 F. 294 (C.C.S.D.N.Y 1909).

6. 1 Stat. 103–104 (1790); 16 Stat. 256 (1870).

7. E. Lee, *At America's Gates: Chinese Immigration during the Exclusion Era, 1882–1943* (Chapel Hill: University of North Carolina Press, 2003), 19–46; Ngai, *Impossible Subjects,* 21–55; A. Zolberg, *A Nation by Design: Immigration Policy in the Fashioning of America* (Cambridge, MA: Harvard University Press, 2006), 199–242.

8. Congress took action in response to a series of scandals involving the fraudulent issuance of naturalization certificates, especially by corrupt officials affiliated with big-city political machines. President Roosevelt appointed a special commission in 1905 to "investigate and report on the subject of naturalization," and the commission's report confirmed widespread corruption in the naturalization courts. The commission recommended greater federal control over the citizenship process, and many of the report's suggestions were written into the 1906 Naturalization Act. The new bureau was housed in the Department of Commerce and Labor. *Report of the President's Commission on Naturalization,* 59th Congress, 1st session, House Document 46; Act of June 29, 1906, 34 Stat. 596.

9. Under the Philippine Government Act, the inhabitants of the Philippines were explicitly excluded from the precedent established in the Revised Statutes of 1878 (section 1891), which provided that the "Constitution and all laws of the United States . . . shall have the same force and effect within all the organized Territories, and in every Territory hereafter organized as elsewhere within the United States." 32 Stat. at 692; See Rev. Stat. of 1878, ch. 1, § 1891, 18 Stat. 325, 333 (1874). The term *nationals* was popularized by legal theorist Frederic Coudert, who served as an attorney for the plaintiffs in some of the early Insular Cases. F. Coudert, "Our New Peoples: Citizens, Subjects, Nationals or Aliens," *Columbia Law Review* 3 (1903): 13–32.

10. The guarantee of "protection" granted to U.S. nationals was vaguely defined. It certainly entailed diplomatic safeguards for Filipinos traveling abroad who carried U.S. passports, and Filipinos could request assistance from American embassies in foreign nations. Whether the inhabitants of the Philippines or other American territories were entitled to military protection from the United States against invasion by a foreign power was less clear.

11. *In re Bautista*, 245 F. 765 (1917).

12. 39 Stat. 545–546; 48 U.S.C. § 1002. The farcical nature of "Philippine citizenship" is evidenced by the fact that the application did not even require one to pledge loyalty to the Philippine government. Yet anyone who wished to become a naturalized Philippine citizen *was required* to affirm an oath of allegiance recognizing the "supreme authority of the United States of America in the Philippine Islands" and to uphold "true faith and allegiance thereto." 15 Pub. Laws, Act No. 2927, 267 (1920).

13. The first case involved Garcia Quino, a seventeen-year-old immigrant living in Ohio who wanted to file his naturalization papers and enlist in the U.S. Navy. Quino's attempt to enlist raised suspicions with naval recruiters because he looked Japanese. The second case involved Benigno Bocco, who had his naturalization petition rejected by the district attorney's office in Santa Rosa, California. *Washington Post*, January 6, 1907, 1; *Washington Post*, October 7, 1907, 1.

14. The law also modified the previous requirement that applicants under this category "renounce allegiance" to "any foreign sovereignty," a requirement that was inapplicable to Filipinos, who already owed allegiance to the United States. Act of June 29, 1906, § 30, 34 Stat. 606.

15. Ibid., 606; 8 U.S.C. 360 (1926).

16. *Revised Statutes of the United States*, 2d ed., 380. Section 2169 was recodified by the Act of February 18, 1875, to clarify racial limitations (18 Stat. 318, chapter 80). The Chinese Exclusion Act, in addition to curtailing immigration, also explicitly barred Chinese from naturalization. 22 Stat. 58, 61 (1882).

17. *Buntaro Kumagai*, 163 F. 922; *In re Knight*, 171 F. 299 (E.D.N.Y 1909); *Bessho v. United States*, 178 F. 245 (4th Cir. 1910).

18. *In re Alverto*, 198 F. 688 (E.D. Pa. 1912).

19. Ibid., 688; see also *Knight*, 171 F. 299.

20. It is difficult to divine what "congressional intent" was on the issue the eligibility of Filipinos under the 1906 act. The legislation emerged out of the House of Representatives (HR 15422) and was primarily focused on establishing uniform rules for naturalization throughout the United States. Congress wanted to exercise greater authority over the naturalization courts after a series of high-profile fraud and corruption scandals tarnished the legitimacy of the application process. The debate on the bill had very little to say about the issues of U.S. nationals and citizenship. When the bill moved on to the Senate for consideration, members of that body did try to add an amendment to the legislation that would have made Puerto Ricans eligible for naturalization. When the House failed to agree on the Senate amendments, a conference committee was formed to iron out the differences between the two bodies. The House eventually agreed to a vaguely worded amendment that qualified "persons not citizens who owe permanent allegiance to the United States" who also resided in any of the states or territories of the United States. The bill also accepted residency in a territorial jurisdiction as meeting the U.S. naturalization

law's residency requirement. *Congressional Record* (1906), 7033–7057, 9505, 9359, 9407, 9576, 9691–9692.

21. District courts are the lowest level of courts in the federal judiciary system. District court opinions are subject to discretionary review by higher courts (a U.S. Appeals Court or the U.S. Supreme Court) and may be overturned by appellate court judges if they believe that the law has been misapplied. Precedent setting decisions pertaining to constitutional questions or federal statutes tend to be handed down by the higher courts, and district court judges are bound to follow precedent established by the appellate courts.

22. The rather paradoxical idea that Filipinos' "permanent allegiance" could be easily reassigned from one imperial power to another by simple diplomatic fiat did not receive much scrutiny from American officials. The notion that Filipinos held any tangible allegiance to Spain or to the United States is curious considering that they had launched armed campaigns for national self-determination against both nations.

23. See, for example, the letter from U.S. Solicitor General John W. Davis to the secretary of labor, January 4, 1916, cited in *In re Mallari*, 239 F. 416, at 417 (D. Mass. 1916); see also the case of Monico Lopez, Naturalization No. 1340, heard by the Supreme Court of the District of Columbia on December 13, 1915, cited in Naval Digest, *Digests of Selected Decisions of the Secretary of Navy* (Washington, DC: GPO, 1921).

24. The court ruled that Mallari had improperly based his petition on an 1894 naturalization provision aimed at facilitating naturalization for noncitizen veterans of the U.S. Navy. Judge Morton ruled that Mallari was not qualified under the 1894 law because it was passed before the 1906 Naturalization Act that made Filipinos eligible. *Mallari*, 239 F. 416.

25. *In re Lampitoe*, 232 F. at 382 (S.D.N.Y. 1916).

26. In the first case, Marcos Solis, a veteran of the U.S. Navy, filed a petition for naturalization in Honolulu. Horace Vaughn, U.S. district attorney for the territory, opposed the application. Vaughn argued that Filipinos were racially disqualified from naturalization because of Section 2169. Judge Charles Clemons examined the various statutory interpretations of the 1906 Naturalization Act, as well as federal opinions on the status of Filipinos. He also noted the historical elasticity of Section 2169, pointing out that native Hawaiians had been "collectively naturalized" by the U.S. government even though "the majority of them were neither white persons nor Africans." Clemons dismissed the district attorney's objections and granted Solis's petition for naturalization. *In the matter of Solis*, 4 U.S. District Ct. Hawaii 686 (1916). The opinion handed down in the *Solis* case didn't hold up for long, as the same court produced a contrary ruling in the matter of Alfred Ocampo later that same year. Just two months after the *Solis* case, Judge Clemons resigned from his post and was replaced on the bench by none other than Horace Vaughn. This turnover in political players did not bode well for Ocampo's petition. Vaughn's opinion noted with some "embarrassment" that the Hawaii court had ruled the same matter just months before. The decision handed down in that case court had, in Vaughn's opinion, been wrongly construed. Vaughn employed a narrower interpretation of the 1906 Naturalization Act in the *Ocampo* case, maintaining that the act extended citizenship rights to "white persons" residing in the Philippines but not to other racial groups. To interpret the law otherwise, he argued, would open up naturalization to those of "the Chinese, the Japanese, and the Malay races." This reading of the 1906 act struck Vaughn as implausible and contrary to established precedent on the issue of Asian exclu-

sion. Ocampo's petition for citizenship was denied. *In the matter of Ocampo*, 4 U.S. District Ct. Hawaii 770 (1916); *Los Angeles Times*, October 15, 1916, II2. Vaughn later changed his tune and granted a number of Asian veterans naturalization papers. *Los Angeles Times*, January 22, 1919, 12; L. Salyer, "Baptism by Fire: Race, Military Service and U.S. Citizenship Policy, 1918–1935," *Journal of American History* 91(3) (2004): 858–859. Salyer's article offers an insightful analysis of the political debates surrounding the eligibility of soldiers of Asian descent under the 1918 act, highlighting the relationship between war service and federal naturalization policy.

27. Cultural definitions of race became increasingly common in the early decades of the twentieth century, as biological classifications came under increasing scrutiny. *In re Rallos*, 241 F. 686 (E.D.N.Y. 1917); see also *In re Young*, 198 F. 715 (W.D. Wash. 1912).

28. *Rallos*, 241 F. at 687.

29. Under this law, veterans of the U.S. military who met certain prescribed criteria were exempted from some of the standard prerequisites for citizenship applicants, such as the "declaration of intention" and "proof of residency" requirements. Veterans who applied under this provision were also exempted from having to produce "proof of good moral character," since recommendation for reenlistment by a superior officer was prima facie evidence of "good character." 38 Stat. 392 (1914).

30. *Bautista*, 245 F. at 765–766.

31. Bonaparte had previously served as the U.S. secretary of the navy in 1905, so he likely had some knowledge of the contributions of Filipinos serving in the U.S. military. 27 Op. Atty. Gen. 12 (1908); *Bautista*, 245 F. at 765–766. The court noted that a similar interpretation had been reached regarding the eligibility of Puerto Ricans in a Maryland district court (in *In re Giralde*, 226 F. 826 [D. Md. 1915]).

32. *Bautista*, 245 F. at 768–769. Chinese exclusion policies were imposed at the behest of the United States (32 Stat. 176; 33 Stat. 692; U.S.C. title 48, sec. 1013). Colonial officials later barred Chinese from becoming naturalized "citizens" of the Philippines (39 Stat. 546; U.S.C. Title 48, 1002). The Philippine Commission passed the *Chinese Registration Act* in 1903, requiring all Chinese in the islands to carry a certificate of legal residence. Anyone caught without a certificate was assumed to be an undocumented laborer and was subject to deportation. See C. Bouve, *A Treatise on the Laws Governing the Exclusion and Expulsion of Aliens in the United States* (Washington, DC: John Byrne, 1912), 117.

33. Mestizo petitioners who cited their European ancestry to claim naturalization rights did not see their claims resolved until the *Morrison* case. Here the Supreme Court took up the question of just how "white" one had to be to qualify for U.S. nationality. The justices again reaffirmed that Asians, including Filipinos, were racially ineligible for naturalization and further refined the terms of their exclusion from the American polity. The *Morrison* ruling explained that the "range of exclusion" for Asians was not "limited to persons of the full blood" but also included people of mixed ancestry as well. Justice Cardozo explained that "men are not white if the strain of colored blood in them is a half or a quarter, or, not improbably, even less, the governing test always being that of common understanding." *Morrison v. the People of California*, 291 U.S. at 82 (1934). The *Morrison* ruling thus effectively thwarted the legal strategy employed by petitioners who cited their partial whiteness as a qualifying factor for naturalization. The Supreme Court's decision, like those handed down in the lower courts, seemed to affirm a two-pronged approach to racial identification that drew arbitrarily on scientific and/or popular definitions. This

flexible approach to racial assignment bolstered the self-preserving powers of gatekeepers such as judges and local officials who were charged with bringing epistemological closure to the legal category "white."

34. Roughly two hundred thousand alien soldiers were naturalized during this period, which illustrates the dramatic impact of these policies. N. Ford, *Americans All! Foreign-Born Soldiers in World War I* (College Station: Texas A&M Press, 2001), 64; *INS Reporter* 26 (3) (Winter 1977–1978): 41–46; D. McGovney, "Race Discrimination in Naturalization Law," *Iowa Law Bulletin* 8 (1923): 129–161.

35. Act of May 9, 1918, 40 Stat. 542 (8 U.S.C. title 8, sec. 388).

36. Ibid., 542; see also *American Journal of International Law* 46 (1952): 259–262.

37. Salyer, "Baptism by Fire," 857–863.

38. The Supreme Court's decision in the *Thind* case included a number of bizarre claims to support its interpretation that Congress had explicitly meant to bar Asians from U.S. citizenship under the 1870 Naturalization Act. Among other things, the Court cited the creation of the "Asiatic barred zone" provision in the 1917 Immigration Act to support its contention that Congress had "intended" to deny naturalization rights to Asians. It was counterintuitive, said the Court, that Congress would extend naturalization rights to a group that it had later barred from entry into the United States. That the Court could determine the "original intent" of Congress in 1870 through a piece of legislation passed nearly fifty years after the original legislation reveals the absurd logic of the *Thind* ruling. *United States v. Bhagat Singh Thind*, 261 U.S. 204 (1923).

39. Salyer, "Baptism by Fire," 862–866. There was a protracted debate among policymakers about whether the 1918 act abrogated the racial prerequisites established under Section 2169. In the years immediately following the war, a significant number of Asians were naturalized under the act, but by the early 1920s nativist forces revived anti-Asian sentiment and pressed the federal government to restrict the naturalization of Asian veterans. One early test case was *In re Mascarenas*, 271 F. 23 (S.D. Calif. 1921), which deemed a Filipino veteran of the U.S. Navy theoretically eligible under the 1918 act. The court however, denied Mascarenas's application on technical grounds that he had not filed his petition in the prescribed timeframe of two years. The case was heard in the Southern District Court in California, which simultaneously ruled on another petition filed by a U.S. Army veteran of Korean descent, named Song. The petitioner was ruled racially ineligible. Song, unlike Mascarenas, did not owe allegiance to the United States, so he was deemed ineligible. *Mascarenas*, 271 F. 23; *En Sk Song*, 271 F. 23.

40. Toyota claimed he was eligible for naturalization under the 1918 act, which provided that "any alien" who had served in the U.S. military during the war was eligible. He was initially granted a certificate of naturalization in 1921, but his certificate was later canceled by a district court as having been "illegally procured." His appeal eventually made it to the Supreme Court. The Court ruled that the 1918 act and the subsequent naturalization legislation in 1919 aimed at "any person of foreign birth" did not eliminate racial prohibitions and were restricted to white persons and persons of African descent. *Toyota v. United States*, 268 U.S. 402 (1925).

41. The Court also weighed in on whether Asians were eligible under the Act of July 19, 1919 (41 Stat. 222), which provided that "any person of foreign birth" who had served during the war was eligible for naturalization. Toyota's attorney, Laurence Lombard, pointed out that at least 300 Asian veterans (213 in Hawaii and 87 on the mainland) had

been naturalized under the 1918 and 1919 acts. Lombard suggested correctly that the government had promised Asian recruits citizenship when it needed soldiers to conduct the war but later rescinded that promise once their service was over. *Toyota*, 268 U.S. at 406.

42. The Court emphasized that Filipinos had been racially ineligible before the 1918 act in order to counter the appellant's claim that Filipinos were already eligible under the 1906 act. Lombard asserted this argument as evidence of the government's intent to include other Asians in the later legislation. If Filipinos were already eligible in 1906, he argued, then it would be "unnecessary and superfluous" for the 1918 act to make them eligible again. *Toyota*, 268 U.S. at 405.

43. *Toyota*, 268 U.S. at 412.

44. *United States v. Javier*, 22 F.2d 879 (D.C. Cir. 1927); *Los Angeles Times*, November 12, 1924, 8; *Washington Post*, November 8, 1927, 22. A similar case, involving an applicant named Roque De La Ysla, was heard by the Ninth Circuit Court of Appeals in California in 1935. De La Ysla's petition was denied since he was not a veteran of the U.S. military, nor was he of the white or African race. Filipinos remained racially debarred from citizenship (excepting for soldiers) until 1946 (see chapter 6). *De La Ysla v. United States*, 77 F.2d 988 (9th Cir. 1935).

45. The 1918 Naturalization Act had been amended in 1929 (45 Stat. 1514), but the basic statutory intent remained the same. The judges both cases criticized the poor grammatical construction of the law, referring to a poorly placed semicolon in the statute that unintentionally exempted Filipinos from the six-month requirement. *Cariaga*, 47 F.2d 609 (1931) ; *Rena*, 50 F.2d 606 (1931); 8 USCA § 388.

46. M. Konvitz, *The Alien and the Asiatic in American Law* (Ithaca, NY: Cornell University Press, 1946), 171–190.

47. The offspring produced by Asian-white unions in the West were of particular concern, both because these "mongrel" children were accorded U.S. citizenship by birth and because the making of families increased the likelihood that Asians would settle permanently in the United States. P. Pascoe, "Race, Gender, and the Privileges of Property: On the Significance of Miscegenation Law in the U.S. West," in *Over the Edge: Remapping the American West*, edited by V. Matsumoto and B. Allmendinger (Berkeley: University of California Press, 1999), 215–230. Peggy Pascoe's *What Comes Naturally: Miscegenation Law and the Making of Race in America* (New York: Oxford University Press, 2009), came out as this book was going into production, so unfortunately I was not able to include her newest work on this topic into my discussion.

48. C. Curry, *Alien Land Laws and Alien Rights*, 67th Congress, 1st session, Doc. 89 (Washington, DC: GPO, 1921), 4.

49. These concerns were aptly conveyed in an article appearing in the *California Law Review* in 1933. The *Review* examined the historical roots of that state's miscegenation legislation, tracing its origins in southern segregationist policy. The article cited the influential case *Scott v. State of Georgia*, 39 Ga. 321 (1869), as forming the ideological basis of California's statutory prohibition on interracial marriage. *California Law Review* 22 (1933): 117.

50. The intermarriage issue also raised important questions about potential material disabilities that might affect the Filipino community, especially regarding questions related to the inheritance of familial wealth or property and the uncertain legal status of children born out of wedlock.

51. According to the *New York Times,* there were approximately nineteen thousand mestizo children who had been abandoned in the Philippines by their American fathers, with many of these children living in a "pitiful condition." The precarious status of these mestizo children was seen as evidence that "American blood does not mix successfully with Malay." American social reformers mobilized a campaign to save the mestizos from "exploitation and vagabondage" at the hands of the native population. *New York Times,* May 26, 1926, XX14; *New York Times,* October 18, 1925, XX4; *New York Times,* November 15, 1925, E6.

52. Cal. Stat. (1905), 554; see also L. Volpp, "American Mestizo: Filipinos and Anti-Miscegenation Laws in California," *UC-Davis Law Review* 33 (2000): 795–836; M. Osumi, "Asians and California's Anti-Miscegenation Laws," in *Asian and Pacific American Experiences: Women's Perspectives,* edited by N. Tsuchida (Minneapolis: Asian/Pacific Learning Resource Center, 1982), 1–37; Y. L. Espiritu, *Home Bound: Filipino American Lives across Cultures, Communities, and Countries* (Berkeley: University of California Press, 2003).

53. The relative paucity of public relationships between Chinese and Japanese men and white women was partly due to miscegenation statutes. Men from these two immigrant groups also benefited from legal provisions that allowed settlers from these nations to sponsor the migration of wives from their respective homelands.

54. Washington State was the exception. Legislation aimed at implementing an antimiscegenation law in Washington was considered in the mid-1930s. Filipino activists, primarily trade-union leaders, traveled to the state capital in Olympia to lobby against the proposed legislation. C. Friday, *Organizing Asian American Labor: The Pacific Coast Canned-Salmon Industry* (Philadelphia: Temple University Press, 1994), 145.

55. Section 60 criminalized marriages between whites and Negroes and Mongolians. Section 69 prohibited state officials from issuing marriage licenses to couples who did not meet the racial criteria set forth in Section 60.

56. *Los Angeles Times,* December 16, 1920, II10.

57. Quoted in N. Foster, "Legal Status of Filipino Intermarriage in Los Angeles," *Sociology and Social Research* 16 (1932): 447–448. Bishop was careful to note that his ruling only applied to Malays and did not apply to Filipinos of the Negrito or Chinese races.

58. *Los Angeles Times,* May 11, 1925, A17. The "Filipino Sheik" characterization evoked the classic racial imagery of the rapacious "Oriental" man preying on white women. *Los Angeles Times,* February 27, 1925, A11.

59. *Los Angeles Times,* May 11, 1925, A10.

60. Quoted in Foster, "Legal Status of Filipino Intermarriage," 446. He made repeated references to personal experience with similar legal matters relating to "Negroes" in the South. He declared that Filipinos, like Negroes, could only become "highly civilized" if they observed, "lines marked out by nature" and kept their "blood pure."

61. Attorney General, Opinion No. 5641, State of California (1926). Attorney General Webb argued (without any supporting evidence) that contrary to scientific authority, there were only three races: white, black, and yellow. Those persons classed by ethnologists as members of the red and brown races were simply a subset of the yellow race.

62. *San Francisco Chronicle,* February 27, 1930, 6.

63. According to the *California Law Review,* "common understandings" had become the dominant definition of race in the courts by the late 1920s. *California Law Review* 22 (1933): 117; Volpp, "American Mestizo," 817–818.

64. *Gavino C. Visco v. Los Angeles County,* No. 319408 (Sup. Ct. 1931); *Los Angeles Times,* June 4, 1930, A8; *Los Angeles Times,* June 6, A6.

65. *Los Angeles Times,* February 25, 1930, A2; *Los Angeles Times,* February 26, 1930, A1.

66. Quoted in E. Reuter, *Race Mixture: Studies in Intermarriage and Miscegenation* (New York: McGraw-Hill, 1931), 102. Judge Smith was a temporary replacement in Los Angeles Superior Court. Smith was from Calaveras County, which may help to explain his decision to overturn the Los Angeles County custom of granting marriage licenses to Filipinos.

67. Rumors floated during the trial that Moreno and Robinson had eloped to Tijuana, Mexico, to get married. Court officials claimed that the couple's rumored Mexico marriage would not be recognized as legal in the state, even though California had no law barring interracial couples from traveling to other jurisdictions to solemnize their union. The rumor turned out to be false, but the reaction of state officials is worth noting. *Los Angeles Times,* February 27, 1930, 9; *Los Angeles Times,* February 25, 1930, A2.

68. *Stockton Record,* March 6, 1930, 24.

69. *Los Angeles Times,* September 6, 1931, C12.

70. *Los Angeles Times,* October 11, 1931, A5; Foster, "Legal Status of Intermarriage," 448–450.

71. *San Francisco Chronicle,* March 22, 1930, 10.

72. *Los Angeles Times,* June 4, 1931, A8.

73. *Los Angeles Times,* June 6, 1931, A6; *Los Angeles Times,* March 5, 1930, 14; *The Three Stars,* November 1931, 4–5. Attorney General Webb's office issued a legal memorandum arguing that persons of Mexican descent were racially ineligible for U.S. citizenship based on the fact that they were of the "Indian" or "red" race. *Los Angeles Times,* October 8, 1929, 10.

74. *Los Angeles Times,* February 10, 1930, 14.

75. Armstrong also ruled that Filipina women who married white American men would remain classed as aliens ineligible for citizenship. This decision was important since it departed from the legal norm in the United States that held that immigrant women inherited the citizenship status of their husbands. *Los Angeles Times,* August 12, 1930, 4.

76. California attorney general U. S. Webb filed an amicus curiae brief in support of the Los Angeles County counsels' effort to deny the couple a marriage license. *Los Angeles Times,* April 12, 1932, 10; *Salvador Roldan v. Los Angeles County et al.,* 129 Cal. App. 267 (1933)

77. *Roldan,* 129 Cal. App. at 268–269; *The Three Stars,* December 1931, 37–39.

78. *Roldan,* 129 Cal. App. at 269–271.

79. *San Francisco Chronicle,* January 30, 1933, 3. At least one couple was able to bypass San Francisco City Clerk Mulcrevy's cordon during the brief window of time between the California Supreme Court's denial of the of the *Roldan* appeal and the passage of the amended miscegenation statute. Magno Basilides Badar and Agnes Regina Peterson were granted the first marriage license to a Filipino-white couple ever recorded in San Francisco. Peterson was described in news coverage as "an attractive blonde" who had been engaged to Badar for more than four years. Though the state legislature had passed its new statute banning Filipino-white marriages on the previous day (April 5, 1933), the new prohibition did not actually go into effect for thirty days and was not retroactive. *San Francisco Chronicle,* April 6, 1933, 1, 5; *San Francisco Chronicle,* April 1, 1933.

80. The appeal to have the case heard by the state supreme court was denied on March 27, 1933 (129 Cal. App. 267; 18 P.2d 706); *Los Angeles Times*, April 4, 1933, A6, 14; *Los Angeles Times*, March 30, 1933, 1.

81. Governor Rolph was himself a prominent member of the Native Sons of the Golden West, a nativist organization that sought to make California a "White Man's Paradise." Osumi, "Asians and California's Anti-Miscegenation Laws," 20; *Los Angeles Times*, April 6, 1933, 2; *San Francisco Chronicle*, April 6, 1933, 1, 5. Filipino community organizations in California lobbied against the bill, to no avail. *The Philippines Mail*, March 27, 1933, 3.

82. California's antimiscegenation statute was invalidated in *Perez v. Lippold*. The case involved Andrea Perez, a Mexican American classified as white for the purposes of the intermarriage law, and Sylvester Davis, an African American, who were denied a marriage license in Los Angeles County. *Perez v. Lippold*, 32 Adv. Cal. 757, 198 P.2d. 17 (1948).

83. Some states even went so far as to criminalize consensual sexual relations between Filipinos and whites. For example, in Nevada "co-habitation and fornication" between a Filipino and a Caucasian was classified as a crime punishable by "a fine up $500 and up to one year in jail." Quoted in H. Empeno et al., "Anti-Miscegenation Laws and the Filipino," in *Letters in Exile: An Introductory Reader on the History of Pilipinos in America*, edited by J. Quinsaat and UCLA Asian American Studies Center (Los Angeles: University of California Press, 1976), 69–70.

84. Initial attempts to bring Filipinos under Utah's miscegenation statutes ran into the same problems as in California, centering on disputes about whether Filipinos were Malays or Mongolians. Utah Attorney General Joseph Chez eventually ruled that Filipino-white unions were not subject to the state's miscegenation law, after "weeks of delving into history books and ethnologists' findings, that Filipinos are Malayans—not Mongolians." *Los Angeles Times*, June 11, 1937, 5. The Utah legislature responded a year later by adding Malays to the list of groups barred from intermarrying with whites.

85. *The Philippines Mail*, February 14, 1941, 1–2; *The Philippines Mail*, March 29, 1941, 2.

86. Filipinos were not restricted from marrying other nonwhites and sometimes found partners among the other outcast communities they encountered in the West. Filipinos had notably high intermarriage rates with Mexicans and blacks in Los Angeles County, forging new families and alliances out of difficult circumstances. C. Panunzio, "Intermarriage in Los Angeles, 1924–1933," *American Journal of Sociology* 47 (5) (1942): 690–701; J. Burma, "Interethnic Marriage in Los Angeles, 1948–1959," *Social Forces* 42 (2) (1963): 156–165.

87. Roosevelt and Taft had repeatedly intervened to bottle up passage of anti-Japanese statutes in the California legislature. Governor Hiram Johnson and key Republican allies in the state legislature helped to quash various anti-Japanese measures. Roosevelt and Taft rightly believed that the enactment of nativist measures would create a diplomatic rift with the Japanese government. Taft was also concerned about setting a precedent that allowed states to enact legislation that superseded the treaty-making power of the federal government.

88. S. Olin, "European Immigrant and Oriental Alien: Acceptance and Rejection by the California Legislature of 1913," *Pacific Historical Review* 35 (3) (1966): 309–311.

89. Exclusionists in the U.S. Congress recognized the euphemistic genius of the legal term "aliens ineligible to citizenship" and appropriated the California law's language to

draw up the exclusionary provisions of the 1924 Immigration Act. Instead of denying Asians admission to the country on the basis of explicit racial criteria, the 1924 act barred "aliens ineligible to citizenship" from entering the United States. By doing so, Congress avoided messy constitutional challenges that might have resulted from using forbidden racial classifications in constructing the statute. *California Law Review* 12 (1923–1924): 259, 270; Immigration Act of May 26, 1924, 43 Stat. 153, Section 13(c).

90. *Cal. Gen. Laws*, Act 262, § 1 Deering (1944); Webb quotation from a speech before the Commonwealth Club of San Francisco on August 9, 1913, quoted in Y. Ichihashi, *Japanese in the United States: A Critical Study of the Problems of Japanese Immigrants* (Stanford, CA: Stanford University Press, 1932), 275 (emphasis added); E. Azuma, *Between Two Empires: Race, History, and Transnationalism in Japanese America* (New York: Oxford University Press, 2005), 63–74; Olin, "European Immigrant and Oriental Alien," 311–312.

91. Japanese owned, leased, or contracted more than 450,000 acres of land in the state in 1919, according to the California Board of Control, a significant increase over the 99,000 acres under their cultivation in 1910. State Board of Control of California, *California and the Oriental: Japanese, Chinese, and Hindus* (Sacramento: California State Printing Office, 1920), 47; "Present-Day Immigration: With Special Reference to the Japanese," *Annals of the American Academy of American Political and Social Science* 93 (182) (1921): 13–54. For a representative exemplar of the Asian colonization argument, see P. Macfarlane, "Japan in California," *Collier's*, June 17, 1913, 5–6, 20–21.

92. California tightened up its land law again in 1923 to outlaw all types of cropping agreements and made forfeiture of the land to the state retroactive based on the date of the wrongful acquisition. Cal. Stat. (1923), 1020.

93. Curry, *Alien Land Laws and Alien Rights*, 4–5.

94. The rulings in the first two test cases, *Terrace v. Thompson*, 263 U.S. 197, and *Porterfield v. Webb*, 263 U.S. 225, were handed down on November 12, 1923. The opinions in the next two cases, *Webb v. O'Brien*, 263 U.S. 313, and *Frick v. Webb*, 263 U.S. 364, were issued a week later, on November 19. All the rulings upheld the legality of alien land statutes.

95. The constitutional questions surrounding the alien land laws were most explicitly addressed in *Terrace v. Thompson*, which involved a legal challenge to Washington State's property prohibition. In upholding the constitutionality of Washington's statute, the Court's ruling emphasized the suspect national loyalties of Asian immigrants to paint the success of the Japanese in western agriculture as a serious threat to the public interest. According to Justice Butler, the "quality of allegiance of those who own, occupy and use farm lands within its borders are matters of highest importance." The Court contended that it was "within the realm of possibility that every foot of land within the state might pass to the ownership or possession" of disloyal Asian settlers, a scenario that posed a national-security risk. That Asians owned less than 1 percent of the agricultural land in Washington State did not receive much attention from the Court. *Terrace*, 263 U.S. at 220.

96. Butler pointed out that the "considerations upon which Congress made such classification" (excluding Asian immigrants from naturalization) were "substantial and reasonable" and therefore did not constitute "arbitrary discrimination." In other words, if Congress can discriminate against Asian immigrants, the courts could as well. *Terrace*, 263 U.S. at 220–221; *Webb*, 263 U.S. 323; see also *Cockrill v. California*, 268 U.S. 258 (1925).

97. The applicability of alien land laws to Filipinos was affirmed in *Morrison v. People of State of California*, 291 U.S. 82, 92 (1934).

98. Washington lawmakers used the term "non-declarant aliens" believing that this language bolstered their contention that the law treated "all aliens alike" and was therefore not discriminatory. In other words, it barred only those persons who "refused" to become citizens. The fact that Asians had not declared their intent to become citizens was "proof" of their suspect loyalty and buttressed the state's claim that it was simply trying to protect itself from aliens of questionable allegiance.

99. Yakima Reservation Superintendent Evan Estep, quoted in G. Nomura, "Within the Law: The Establishment of Filipino Leasing Rights on the Yakima Indian Reservation," *Amerasia* 13 (1986–1987): 101.

100. Yakima Reservation Superintendent C. R. Whitlock, who replaced Estep in 1931, quoted in ibid., 101–102.

101. John Collier, Commissioner of Indian Affairs, quoted in ibid., 112.

102. Quoted in ibid., 105.

103. Deputy District Attorney Lloyd Wiehl, quoted in ibid., 107. The district attorney argued that it did not matter whether Filipinos were considered "aliens" by the federal government but rather whether they were considered "aliens" with respect to the state's alien land laws. The 1937 amendment essentially reclassified Filipinos as aliens, in contempt of federal policy on the status of American "nationals."

104. Ibid., 103–107.

105. *De Cano et al. v. State of Washington*, 110 P.2d 627, 631 (Wash. 1941).

106. Ibid., 633–635.

107. Nomura, "Within the Law," 112. Filipinos won relief from California's alien land law in 1945, successfully arguing that they fell outside the purview of the statutory term "alien." The legal rights of Filipinos were expanded significantly during the World War II period as a consequence of their contributions to the war effort. *Alfafara v. Fross*, 26 Cal. 2d 358 [159 P.2d 14] (1945).

NOTES TO CHAPTER 4

1. J. Gusfield, *Contested Meanings: The Construction of Alcohol Problems* (Madison: University of Wisconsin Press, 1996), 21–29. For more explicit discussion of race as social problem, see S. Hall et al., *Policing the Crisis: Mugging, the State and Law and Order* (New York: Holmes and Meier, 1978). From the nativist perspective, see V. S. McClatchy, "Oriental Immigration in California," in *The Alien in Our Midst: Selling Out Birthright for a Mess of Pottage*, edited by M. Grant and C. S. Davison, 188–197 (New York: Galton, 1924).

2. On the relationship between discourses of racial victimhood and extralegal violence, see L. Gordon, *The Great Arizona Orphan Abduction* (Cambridge, MA: Harvard University Press, 2001), 254–274; R. Brown, *Strain of Violence: Historical Studies of American Violence and Vigilantism* (New York: Oxford University Press, 1975), 118–133; G. Myrdal, *An American Dilemma: The Negro Problem and Modern Democracy,* vol. 2 (New York: Harper and Row, 1944), 558–569.

3. W. Anderson, *Colonial Pathologies: American Tropical Medicine, Race, and Hygiene in the Philippines* (Durham, NC: Duke University Press, 2006), 13–45; C. Choy, *Empire of Care: Nursing and Migration in Filipino American History* (Durham, NC: Duke University Press, 2003).

4. N. Shah, *Contagious Divides: Epidemics and Race in San Francisco's Chinatown* (Berkeley: University of California Press, 2001); N. Molina, *Fit to Be Citizens? Public*

Health and Race in Los Angeles, 1879–1939 (Berkeley: University of California Press, 2006); A. Kraut, *Silent Travelers: Germs, Genes, and the Immigrant Menace* (New York: Basic Books, 1994).

5. D. Mitchell, *Lie of the Land: Migrant Workers in the California Landscape* (Minneapolis: University of Minnesota Press, 1996), 93–98, 131–138; Y. L. Espiritu, *Home Bound: Filipino American Lives across Cultures, Communities, and Countries* (Berkeley: University of California Press, 2003).

6. Commonwealth Club of California, "Filipino Immigration," *Transactions* 24 (7) (1929): 318.

7. Ibid., 324. Barrows also served as the superintendent of public education in the Philippines before taking a full-time career in academia at UC-Berkeley in 1910. He served as UC-Berkeley's president from 1919 to 1923, before going back to teaching in the Political Science Department.

8. Ibid., 355.

9. *American Federationist,* June 1928, 713.

10. There were a number of meningitis outbreaks across the country in 1929, and Filipinos made up only a tiny fraction of those afflicted with the disease. *New York Times,* June 16, 1929, E2; *New York Times,* April 27, 1929, 6; *Los Angeles Times,* April 1, 1929, 6; *Los Angeles Times,* March 21, 1929, 11.

11. P. Scharrenberg, "Exclude the Filipinos," *Organized Labor* 29 (1928): 57–58.

12. This quotation is from the *Thirty-Second Biennial Report of the Department of Public Health of California,* quoted in E. Abel, "Only the Best Class of Immigration: Public Health Policy toward Mexicans and Filipinos in Los Angeles, 1910–1940," *American Journal of Public Health* 94 (6) (2004): 936.

13. Quoted in ibid., 937.

14. Ibid., 937; see also Lasker, *Filipino Immigration,* 107–113.

15. *Watsonville Evening Pajaronian,* January 10, 1930, 1.

16. *Salinas Index Journal,* January 11, 1930, 8. Left out of this discussion was the fact that Filipinos had little choice as to the conditions and circumstances under which they lived. Racial segregation in western cities forced them into the poorest, crime-ridden sections of town, and low wages for seasonal work limited their housing options. Agricultural camps provided by employers offered meager living arrangements, often consigning Filipino and Mexican workers to refurbished barns designed for livestock.

17. For examples of such characterizations, see E. Bogardus, "The Filipino Immigrant Problem," *Sociology and Social Research* 13 (5) (1929): 472–479; B. Lasker, *Filipino Immigration to the Continental United States and Hawaii* (Chicago: University of Chicago Press, 1931); T. Rojo, "Social Maladjustment among Filipinos in the United States," *Sociology and Social Research* 21 (5) (1937): 447–457. Emory Bogardus was a protégé of influential sociologist Robert Park, who helped to found the Chicago School of sociology. Bogardus helped to administer Park's influential "*Survey of Race Relations*" project on the Pacific coast. From his position as director of the sociology department at the University of Southern California and his editorship of the journal *Sociology and Social Research,* he helped to inspire a virtual cottage industry of articles about the "Filipino problem" in the United States.

18. For good general overviews of anxieties about interracial sex in the United States, see R. Moran, *Interracial Intimacy: The Regulation of Race and Romance* (Chicago: Uni-

versity of Chicago Press, 2001); M. Hodes, *Sex, Love, Race: Crossing Boundaries in North American History* (New York: NYU Press, 1999); P. Pascoe, "Miscegenation Law, Court Cases, and the Ideology of Race in Twentieth Century America," *Journal of American History* 83 (1) (1996): 44–69.

19. G. Steiger, "The Filipinos as I Meet Them," *Organized Labor,* February 8, 1930, 6.

20. Claims that Filipinos were singular in their interactions with white women were overstated. Anxieties about interracial mixing between other Asian groups and whites has been well documented by M. Lui, *The Chinatown Trunk Mystery: Murder, Miscegenation, and Other Dangerous Encounters in Turn-of-the-Century New York* (Princeton, NJ: Princeton University Press, 2005); J. K. W. Tchen, *New York before Chinatown: Orientalism and the Shaping of American Culture* (Baltimore: Johns Hopkins University Press, 1999); and BANC MSS, C-R 4, box 2, James E. Wood Papers, Bancroft Library, University of California at Berkeley, n.p.

21. Commonwealth Club, "Filipino Immigration," 319.

22. Ibid., 318.

23. BANC MSS, C-R 4, box 3, James E. Wood Papers, Bancroft Library, University of California at Berkeley, n.p.; U.S. Congress, *Immigration from Countries of Western Hemisphere,* House Committee on Immigration and Naturalization Hearings, 71st Congress, 2d session (Washington, DC: GPO, 1930), 199.

24. Commonwealth Club, "Filipino Immigration," 328.

25. *Los Angeles Times,* February 2, 1930, 3.

26. U.S. National Committee on Law Observance (Wickersham Commission), *Report on Crime and the Foreign Born* (Washington, DC: GPO, 1931), 362.

27. *Salinas Index Journal,* December 2, 1929, 1.

28. *Salinas Index Journal,* December 11, 1929, 1.

29. *Watsonville Evening Pajaronian,* December 12, 1929, 7.

30. *Salinas Index Journal,* December 3, 1929, 4.

31. *Salinas Index Journal,* December 4, 1929, 1.

32. *Salinas Index Journal,* December 2, 1929, 1, 5.

33. *Salinas Index Journal,* December 11, 1929, 29.

34. *Salinas Index Journal,* December 6, 1929, 1; *Salinas Index Journal,* December 31, 1929, 1, 5.

35. *Salinas Index Journal,* December 11, 1929, 29.

36. *Salinas Index Journal,* January 15, 1930, 1.

37. *Berkeley Daily Gazette,* January 31, 1930, 17.

38. *Los Angeles Times,* January 30, 1930, 1. This narrative was reminiscent of the white-slavery panics of the early twentieth century. See Lui, *Chinatown Trunk Mystery,* 10–11; K. Mumford, *Interzones: Black/White Sex Districts in Chicago and New York in the Early Twentieth Century* (New York: Columbia University Press, 1997), 3–17.

39. *San Francisco Chronicle,* January 30, 1930, 1.

40. Commonwealth Club, "Filipino Immigration," 322.

41. Kevin Mumford calls the taxi-dance hall the "quintessential border institution" to describe the space these establishments occupied between family-centered residential areas and the commercialized vice districts. Mumford, *Interzones,* 54–60.

42. A. Stern, *Eugenic Nation: Faults and Frontiers of Better Breeding in Modern America* (Berkeley: University of California Press, 2005), 86–91; H. Bruinius, *Better for All the*

World: *The Secret History of Forced Sterilization and America's Quest for Racial Purity* (New York: Vintage, 2007), 219–222.

43. Commonwealth Club, "Filipino Immigration," 340–341. Mccaughey was a former director of the Northern California branch of the "Survey of Race Relations" organized by Robert Park. He was also an affiliate of the Eugenics Society of the United States of America. "Survey of Race Relations," Box 9.1 (correspondence), Hoover Institution Archives, Stanford Library, Stanford University.

44. Commonwealth Club, "Filipino Immigration," 377.

45. C. M Goethe, "Filipino Immigration Viewed as Peril," *Current History* 34 (1931): 353–354.

46. E. Moore, "Public Dance Halls in a Small City," *Sociology and Social Research* 14 (1930): 260–262. The classic work on this topic is P. Cressey, *The Taxi-Dance Hall: A Sociological Study in Commercialized Recreation and Life* (Chicago: University of Chicago Press, 1932). Cressey was a Chicago School sociologist who developed a "theory of retrogressive life cycle" to explain how white women fell into a pattern of downward status mobility as a result of their work at taxi-dance halls.

47. A. Bowler, "Social Hygiene in Racial Problems—The Filipino," *Journal of Social Hygiene* 18 (8) (1932): 453–454. This was a special issue of the journal that focused on the hygiene problems of Filipinos, Native Americans, and African Americans.

48. *Los Angeles Times*, August 14, 1925, 8

49. Ibid.

50. *San Francisco Chronicle*, January 4, 1930, 1; *Oakland Tribune*, January 3, 1930, 1. For a good account of the attraction of white women to taxi halls, see C. Heap, *Slumming: Sexual and Racial Encounters in American Nightlife* (Chicago: University of Chicago Press, 2009).

51. *San Francisco Chronicle*, January 1, 1930, 1.

52. *San Francisco Chronicle*, January 8, 1930, 3; *Oakland Tribune*, January 7, 1930, 1.

53. *Los Angeles Times*, June 14, 1930, 14.

54. These laws paralleled increasing enforcement of antiprostitution laws and were framed as defensive statutes that protected the moral sanctity of the community. *Los Angeles Times*, September 12, 1929, 12; *Los Angeles Times*, April 17, 1929, A3.

55. *Los Angeles Times*, April 24, 1929, A12. See also L. España-Maram, *Creating Masculinity in Los Angeles's Little Manila: Working-Class Filipinos and Popular Culture in the United States* (New York: Columbia University Press, 2006), 51–72.

56. *Los Angeles Times*, May 10, 1929, A3.

57. *Los Angeles Times*, June 25, 1930, A14.

58. *Los Angeles Times*, June 1, 1929, A1.

59. *Los Angeles Times*, July 31, 1930, A8.

60. *Los Angeles Times*, January 13, 1931, A7.

61. *Yakima Morning Herald*, November 11, 1927, 1.

62. Ibid.

63. Ibid., 1–2.

64. *Yakima Daily Republic*, November 12, 1927, 9; *Los Angeles Times*, November 17, 1927, 8.

65. *Yakima Morning Herald*, November 11, 1927, 1.

66. Quoted in U.S. Congress, *Exclusion of Immigration from Philippine Islands*, House Committee on Immigration and Naturalization Hearings on HR 8708, 71st Congress, 2d session (Washington, DC: GPO, 1930), 81.

67. *Yakima Morning Herald*, September 20, 1928, 1; *Seattle Post-Intelligencer*, September 20, 1928, 7; *Seattle Post-Intelligencer*, September 21, 1928, 10; *Three Stars*, October 1, 1929, 1; *Three Stars*, June 1, 1930, 1.

68. *San Francisco Chronicle*, August 18, 1928, 12.

69. *Salinas Index Journal*, October 25, 1929, 10; *Salinas Index Journal*, October 26, 1929, 8; *Three Stars*, November 1, 1929, 1.

70. *Watsonville Evening Pajaronian*, October 30, 1929, 6.

71. *New York Times*, October 28, 1929, 20.

72. *Watsonville Evening Pajaronian*, January 10, 1930, 1.

73. *The Torch*, January 1930, 1–4; *Three Stars*, February 5, 1930, 1, 4.

74. *Watsonville Evening Pajaronian*, January 20, 1930, 1. The dance hall in question was actually owned by white proprietors, who sought relief from law enforcement for the constant harassment and property damage to their venue inflicted by vigilantes.

75. *Salinas Index Journal*, January 20, 1930, 1.

76. *Watsonville Evening Pajaronian*, January 21, 1930, 1.

77. *Watsonville Evening Pajaronian*, January 22, 1930, 1.

78. *San Francisco Chronicle*, January 24, 1930, 3; *Los Angeles Times*, January 24, 1930, 1.

79. *Los Angeles Times*, February 6, 1930, 3.

80. *Three Stars*, March 1, 1930, 1; *Three Stars*, April 1, 1930, 2.

81. *San Francisco Examiner*, January 28, 1930, 4; G. Steiger, "The Filipinos as I Meet Them," *Organized Labor*, March 8, 1930, 6.

82. *Los Angeles Times*, January 29, 1930, 2.

83. G. Steiger, "The Filipinos as I Meet Them"; *San Francisco Chronicle*, February 10, 1930, 6.

84. *San Francisco Examiner*, January 28, 1930, 4; *Berkeley Daily Gazette*, January 28, 1930, 1.

85. *San Francisco Chronicle*, January 24, 1930, 1; *Washington Post*, January 25, 1930, 7.

86. *Watsonville Evening Pajaronian*, February 8, 1930, 1 (sec. 2); *China Weekly Review*, February 8, 1930, 353.

87. *San Francisco Chronicle*, February 10, 1930, 11.

88. Anti-Filipino violence spread to other parts of the country as well. A Filipino man, Fleomino Montigo, was shot to death and his roommate, Adrian Elanparo, was badly beaten by a gang of Italian immigrants on their way home from work in October 1931. The attack occurred after a series of run-ins between Filipinos and white ethnics who vandalized a local Filipino clubhouse on the west side of Chicago, forcing them to relocate to the north side of the city. Vigilante violence against Filipinos even spread to places such as West Palm Beach, Florida, after local whites became enraged over an "episode involving a white girl." This alleged violation of the local color line, along with the rumored arrival of two thousand more Filipinos into the region led "200 irate white residents" to order the local "Filipino colony" to leave the state immediately or face serious consequences. *New York Times*, July 24, 1932, 6; *Los Angeles Times*, July 25, 1932, 3.

89. *Los Angeles Times*, January 30, 1930, 1; *Los Angeles Times*, February 4, 1930, 3; *San Francisco Chronicle*, February 2, 1930, 6; *San Francisco Chronicle*, January 30, 1930, 4.

90. *Los Angeles Times*, February 2, 1930, 3.

91. Manlapit resumed labor organizing in California soon after he arrived in August 1927. He was detained by the special "police radical squad" of the Los Angeles Police

Department in February 1928. LAPD officials accused him of involvement in a "red strike plot" that involved a walkout of six thousand asparagus workers and seven thousand Filipino sailors enlisted in the U.S. Navy. Manlapit was taken into custody during a raid on a meeting of the All-American Anti-Imperialist League, an organization affiliated with the Communist Party. The LAPD claimed that it had discovered evidence that Manlapit had been on the payroll of the Communist Party, at the rate of forty-five dollars per week, since arriving in California and that he was assigned to go on a national speaking tour on behalf of the Anti-Imperialist League. *Los Angeles Times,* February 25, 1928, A1.

92. Manlapit chaired a meeting of one thousand Filipinos in Los Angeles that drafted a protest resolution that he forwarded to California governor C. C. Young, asking that authorities investigate the riots and bring the vigilantes to justice. The Watsonville riots also attracted significant attention in the Philippines, where officials organized a national day of humiliation in Manila protesting anti-Filipino violence on the West Coast. Ten thousand people attended the event at Luneta Park, where they hailed Fermin Tobera as a martyr. Contrary to some claims, I have found no evidence of a similar march or rally organized by Manlapit in Los Angeles. *Los Angeles Times,* January 31, 1930, 2; *Los Angeles Times,* February 3, 1930, 1; *San Francisco Chronicle,* January 31, 1930, 3.

93. *Watsonville Evening Pajaronian,* January 25, 1930, 1; *San Francisco Chronicle,* January 26, 1930, 1. The Watsonville paper also condemned the YCL flyer for accusing Judge Rohrback of advocating "white supremacy." The YCL accurately equated the tactics of Rohrback and his allies with those of white vigilantes in the South, an observation that did not sit well with western nativists, who saw themselves in a different light.

94. *San Francisco Chronicle,* January 27, 1930, 1; *Los Angeles Times,* January 30, 1930, 2 .

95. *San Francisco Chronicle,* February 2, 1930, 6; *San Francisco Chronicle,* January 30, 1930, 4; *Berkeley Daily Gazette,* January 31, 1930, 17.

96. *New York Times,* January 30, 1930, 4; *Los Angeles Times,* January 30, 1930, 2. For a good overview of the role of boxing in Filipino American culture, see España-Maram, *Creating Masculinity,* 73–104.

97. *San Francisco Examiner,* January 30, 1930, 1.

98. *San Francisco Chronicle,* January 30, 1930, 4; *San Francisco Chronicle,* February 2, 1930, 6.

99. *San Francisco Chronicle,* January 26, 1930, 1.

100. *Los Angeles Times,* January 30, 1930, 2.

101. *Report of Governor C. C. Young's Fact Finding Committee, Mexicans in California* (San Francisco: California State Printing Office,1930).

102. The report, for instance, cites 1923 as the year "when the Filipino invasion began." An accurate calculation of population numbers was also problematic because investigators used Hispanic surnames of new arrivals to West Coast ports to classify migrants as Filipinos. French admitted that it was likely that a number of Puerto Ricans, Spanish, and Portuguese were counted as Filipinos, thus skewing the immigration numbers. California Department of Industrial Relations, *Facts about Filipino Immigration* (San Francisco: R&E Research Associates, 1930), 11, 19, 33.

103. *Salinas Index Journal,* January 11, 1930, 1, 8.

104. *Los Angeles Times,* June 14, 1930, 2; this article is a summary of the French report.

105. P. Scharrenberg, "The Philippine Problem: Attitude of American Labor toward Filipino Immigration and Philippine Independence," *Pacific Affairs* 2 (1929): 50.

106. *Berkeley Daily Gazette*, January 25, 1930, 1.

107. *Los Angeles Times*, May 21, 1929, 11.

108. Commonwealth Club of California, "Filipino Immigration," 319.

109. *Salinas Index Journal*, January 16, 1930, 1–2.

110. *Los Angeles Times*, August 16, 1930, 1; *San Francisco Chronicle*, August 16, 1930, 4.

111. *Los Angeles Times*, October 9, 1930, A10; the Bible passage cited was from Timothy 5:8: "if any provide not for his own, and especially those in his own house . . . he is worse than an infidel."

112. *Morning Oregonian*, February 7, 1930, 20; *Los Angeles Times*, February 7, 1930, 29.

113. *Seattle Daily Times*, May 7, 1930, 1, 4; *Seattle Daily Times*, May 8, 1930, 7; *Chicago Daily Tribune*, May 8, 1930, 16.

114. *Three Stars*, June 1, 1930, 3.

115. *San Francisco Chronicle*, August 14, 1930, 3.

116. *San Francisco Chronicle*, August 17, 1930, 13.

117. *Los Angeles Times*, December 9, 1930, 1; *Los Angeles Times*, December 12, 1930, 1.

118. *Three Stars*, August 15, 1930, 3.

119. C. McWilliams, "Exit the Filipino," *Nation* 116 (1935): 265. For an overview of Filipino labor activity outside California, see D. Fujita-Rony, *American Workers, Colonial Power: Philippine Seattle and the Transpacific West, 1919–1941* (Berkeley: University of California Press, 2003); and C. Friday, *Organizing Asian American Labor: The Pacific Coast Canned-Salmon Industry* (Philadelphia: Temple University Press, 1994).

120. AWIL circular, in BANC MSS, C-R 4, box 2, James E. Wood Papers, Bancroft Library, University of California at Berkeley, n.p.

121. Cletus Daniel, *Bitter Harvest: A History of California Farmworkers* (Ithaca, NY: Cornell University Press, 1981). Earl Warren, the Alameda County district attorney, argued that the goal for growers and law enforcement during the "Great Upheaval" was to find a way to "break the continuity" of migrant workers by hiring locally unemployed workers (with the cooperation of local officials who cut off their social-welfare provisions) or by reinforcing the rights of the "native community" against the aspirations of those they termed "alien" agitators. *San Francisco Examiner*, April 8, 1934, 3; *The Philippines Mail*, November, 27, 1933, 1; *The Philippines Mail*, December 25, 1933, 5.

122. L. Majka and T. Majka, *Farmworkers, Agribusiness, and the State* (Philadelphia: Temple University Press, 1982), 69, 130; S. Jamieson, *Labor Unionism in American Agriculture* (New York: Arno, 1976), 84–86, 179–186; *The Philippines Mail*, March 27, 1933, 1; *The Philippines Mail*, September 11, 1933, 3; *The Philippines Mail*, November 27, 1933, 1. On accusations of communist agitation in the Philippines, see *New York Times*, June 1, 1931, 1; *New York Times*, August 22, 1931, 28.

123. L. Majka and T. Majka, *Farmworkers, Agribusiness, and the State*, 69, 76.

124. C. McWilliams, *Factories in the Fields* (1939; repr., Berkeley: University of California Press, 2000), 215.

125. *Los Angeles Times*, January 24, 1934, 1; *Los Angeles Times*, January 25, 1934, 1; *Los Angeles Times*, January 31, 1934, A2.

1. Senator David Reed of Pennsylvania, cosponsor of the restrictive 1924 Immigration Act, introduced a bill, S.J. Resolution 207, that aimed to suspend all immigration from the Philippines to the continental United States for a period of two years. Presumably the two-year suspension would have given Congress time to draft restrictive legislation that took into account the unique colonial status of the Philippines.

2. A. Saxton, *The Indispensable Enemy: Labor and the Anti-Chinese Movement in California* (Berkeley: University of California Press, 1971), 104–137; E. Lee, *At America's Gates: Chinese Immigration during the Exclusion Era* (Chapel Hill: University of North Carolina Press, 2003), 23–46; A. Zolberg, *A Nation by Design: Immigration Policy in the Fashioning of America* (Cambridge, MA: Harvard University Press, 2006), 187–197.

3. Paul Scharrenberg, "Vital Issues Confronting the California Labor Movement," *Union Gazette*, March 31, 1928, 7, reprinted in *Sacramento Valley Union Labor Bulletin*, August 30, 1928, 1.

4. American Federation of Labor, *Report of the Proceedings of Annual Convention of the American Federation of Labor*, 1927, 156, 362. The California State Federation of Labor also introduced a series of similar resolutions asking Congress to ban immigration from Mexico during this same period. See the *California State Federation of Labor Proceedings*, 1927–1930.

5. American Federation of Labor, *Report of the Proceedings of the Annual Convention of the American Federation of Labor*, 1928, 124.

6. American Federation of Labor, *Report of the Proceedings of the Annual Convention of the American Federation of Labor*, 1930, 153.

7. Cited in *Congressional Record* (1930), 71st Congress, 2d session, 7525.

8. The bill was sponsored by E. G. Adams of Merced County (discussed in chapter 4). State of California (1929), 48th Congress, 1st session, 2690; *Los Angeles Times*, May 9, 1930.

9. *Watsonville Evening Pajaronian*, January 1, 1930, 1.

10. *Los Angeles Times*, May 21, 1929, 11.

11. The CJIC was an influential umbrella organization that brought together members of the American Legion, the Native Sons, the California State Federation of Labor, and the Grange, as well as high-profile political luminaries such former U.S. senator James Phelan.

12. This slogan was a reference to the old "The Chinese Must Go" adopted by nativists in the nineteenth century. *Watsonville Evening Pajaronian*, February 8, 1930, 2.

13. *Congressional Record* (1930), 71st Congress, 2d session, 2593–2597; *Berkeley Daily Gazette*, January 29, 1930, 1.

14. *Los Angeles Times*, April 6, 1930, 7.

15. U.S. Congress, *Immigration from Countries of Western Hemisphere*, House Committee on Immigration and Naturalization Hearings, 71st Congress, 2d session (Washington, DC: GPO, 1930), 222–223; *San Francisco Chronicle*, January 31, 1930, 2.

16. *Los Angeles Times*, April 26, 1930, A4.

17. HR 13900, 70th Congress, 1st session (1928), 9275.

18. *Los Angeles Times*, August 2, 1932, 2.

19. F. Golay, *Face of Empire: United States–Philippines Relations* (Manila: Ateneo de Manila University Press, 1998), 288–289; H. W. Brands, *Bound to Empire: The United States and the Philippines* (New York: Oxford University Press, 1992), 150–152.

20. *Congressional Record* (1930), 71st Congress, 2d session, 7512.

21. Ibid., 7511–7512.

22. *Congressional Record* (1930), 71st Congress, 2d session, 7512–7513. Blease's bills calling for a constitutional amendment barring interracial marriage were S.J. Res. 65 and S. 784, 70th Congress, 1st session, 343 (1928), 1000.

23. *Congressional Record* (1930), 71st Congress, 2d session, 1304; ibid., 6843; ibid., 7521–7526.

24. *Congressional Record* (1930), 71st Congress, 2d session, 6107–6108.

25. Chinese-exclusion laws were applied to the Philippines by acts of Congress in 1902 and 1904. 32 Stat. 176–177; 33 Stat. 428. See also *Sui v. McCoy*, 239 U.S. 139 (1915); *Uy Kai Hu v. McCoy*, 24 Phil. 151 (1913).

26. U.S. Congress, *Exclusion of Immigration from the Philippines Islands*, House Committee on Immigration and Naturalization Hearings on HR 8708, 71st Congress, 2d session (Washington, DC: GPO, 1930), 4.

27. Ibid., 16; M. Ngai, *Impossible Subjects: Illegal Aliens and the Making of Modern America* (Princeton, NJ: Princeton University Press, 2004), 117–120.

28. U.S. Congress, *Exclusion of Immigration from the Philippines Islands*, 83–86.

29. Ibid., 7–8.

30. Ibid., 83–86.

31. Ibid., 8–16.

32. Ibid., 36–38.

33. Ibid., 66.

34. Ibid., 81.

35. Ibid., 102.

36. Ibid., 105, 111.

37. Ibid., 130.

38. Ibid., 107–108.

39. *Washington Post*, January 30, 1930, 3; T. Friend, *Between Two Empires: The Ordeal of the Philippines, 1929–1946* (New Haven, CT: Yale University Press, 1965), 90–92; Golay, *Face of Empire*, 288–291, 313–317; Brands, *Bound to Empire*, 150–156.

40. U.S. Congress, *Independence for the Philippine Islands*, House Committee on Territories and Insular Affairs Hearings on HR 7233, 72d Congress, 1st session (Washington, DC: GPO, ,1931), 378–383; *Washington Post*, December 10, 1932, 2; Golay, *Face of Empire*, 288–289.

41. "Independence for the Philippine Islands," 6. This statement was issued by the Philippine legislature on the occasion of a visit to the islands by U.S. Secretary of War Patrick Hurley.

42. P. Scharrenberg, "What Do Filipinos Want?" *Seamen's Journal* 48 (February 1933): 22–23; *East Bay Labor Journal* 9 (14) (February 10, 1933): 2. See also P. Scharrenberg, "Philippine Independence," *Seamen's Journal* 48 (April 1933): 54–55. For views explaining Filipino concerns about the terms of independence, see *The Philippines Mail*, April 30, 1934, 1–4; *The Philippines Mail*, February 12, 1934, 2.

43. The Tydings-McDuffie Act (Public Law 127) contained an exemption for Hawaii, in response to incessant lobbying from plantation interests in the islands. Filipino immigrants were allowed entry into Hawaii at the discretion of the U.S. secretary of interior, on the "basis of the needs of the industries in the Territory of Hawaii." Filipinos in Hawaii, however, were barred from immigrating to the continental United States. 48 Stat. 462 (section 8); U.S. Department of Labor, Immigration General Order 209, June 8, 1934.

44. Filipinos had not been allotted a quota under the 1924 act because as American nationals they held the same status as American citizens under U.S. immigration law. 48 Stat. 464 (section 14); U.S. Department of Labor, Immigration General Order 209, June 8, 1934.

45. *East Bay Labor Journal,* April 13, 1934, 1; *San Francisco Labor Clarion,* April 13, 1934, 3. The immigration quota established by the Tydings-McDuffie Act was quite effective— the Filipino population on the U.S. mainland was 45,208 in the 1930 and 45,563 in 1940. U.S Bureau of Census, *Population Characteristics of Non-White Population by Race, 1940* (Washington, DC: GPO, 1943).

46. *Washington Post,* May 3, 1934, 9.

47. *Los Angeles Times,* November 29, 1933, A6; *Los Angeles Times,* November 29, 1933, A5; *Los Angeles Times,* March 13, 1934, A3.

48. *San Francisco Chronicle,* March 11, 1935, 1; *New York Times,* March 11, 1935, 36.

49. *San Francisco Chronicle,* January 22, 1936, 13; *San Francisco Chronicle,* January 23, 1936, 2; *San Francisco Chronicle,* May 17, 1936, 2. Lazarus continued his crusade against Filipinos in the succeeding months, describing them as an uncivilized population—"one jump from the jungle"—who in his estimation were "scarcely more than savages."

50. *Wapato Independent,* March 2, 1933, 1; *Wapato Independent,* April 20, 1933, 1.

51. *Los Angeles Times,* August 16, 1933, 1; *Los Angeles Times,* August 8, 1933, A6; *Los Angeles Times,* August 10, 1933, 14.

52. *Los Angeles Times,* July 10, 1934, A2; *Los Angeles Times,* July 17, 1934, 2; *San Francisco Chronicle,* July 15, 1934, 1.

53. *Los Angeles Times,* September 6, 1934, 1; *The Philippines Mail,* August 20, 1934, 1.

54. Quoted in H. Dewitt, "The Filipino Labor Union: The Salinas Strike of 1934," *Amerasia* 5 (2) (1978): 15; *San Francisco Chronicle,* September 6, 1934, 1.

55. *New York Times,* September 23, 1934, 6; *The Philippines Mail,* September 3, 1934, 1, 3. The harsh tactics employed against Filipino and Mexican workers during this period were pointedly summarized in a report published by the National Labor Relations Board that investigated California labor conflicts during this period: "the impression of these events . . . is one of inexcusable police brutality, in many instances bordering on sadism." L. Majka and T. Majka, *Farmworkers, Agribusiness, and the State* (Philadelphia: Temple University Press, 1982), 93.

56. *Los Angeles Times,* September 6, 1934, 1; *Los Angeles Times,* September 24, 1934, 3; *New York Times,* September 23, 1934, 6.

57. Dewitt, "Filipino Labor Union," 14–15 .

58. *Los Angeles Times,* March 20, 1934, A6; *Los Angeles Times,* November 26, 1934, 7.

59. *Pacific Rural Press* 131 (19) (May 9, 1936): 602.

60. *Los Angeles Times,* December 11, 1933, A7.

61. Rex Thompson, deputy superintendent of the Los Angeles County Department of Charities, testified at the hearings that California authorities had shipped out thirty thousand Mexicans during the previous year and were willing to assist with the repatriation of Filipinos. U.S. Congress, *To Return Unemployed Filipinos to the Philippine Islands,* House Committee on Immigration and Naturalization, Hearings, 72d Congress, 2d session (Washington, DC: GPO, 1933), 45–46. On Mexican repatriation more generally, see Ngai, *Impossible Subjects,* 72–74; G. Sanchez, *Becoming Mexican American: Ethnicity, Culture, and Identity in Chicano Los Angeles, 1900–1945* (New York: Oxford University Press, 1993), 211–224.

62. *Los Angeles Times*, January 20, 1933, 4; U.S. Congress, *To Return Unemployed Filipinos to the Philippine Islands*, 32–33; C. Coloma, *A Study of the Filipino Repatriation Movement* (San Francisco: R&E Research Associates, 1939).

63. U.S. Congress, *To Return Unemployed Filipinos to the Philippine Islands*, 7–9, 36; Doak and Garsson offered no explanation why their population figures differed so markedly from the census tabulations but implied that Filipinos were somehow entering the country through surreptitious means. Representative Richard Welch testified that he knew that Filipinos had "purposely evaded the census" because they did not want American officials to know their true numbers in the United States. Ibid., 5. Filipino leaders began criticizing Dickstein's bill as a camouflaged deportation measure starting in 1933; *The Philippines Mail*, May 29, 1933, 2; *The Philippines Mail*, April 24, 1933, 1, 4.

64. Millard rejected this notion that sleeping in shifts of three during the twenty-two-day sea voyage would constitute a burden on the repatriates, since Filipinos did not live "in a normal and rational manner" anyway. Ibid., 26–27.

65. *Congressional Record* (1934), 73d Congress, 2d session, 2062–2064; Dickstein suggested that Filipinos might be convinced to voluntarily sign a pauper's oath, thus making them ineligible to return to the Untied States. See Immigration Act of 1917, 39 Stat. 892.

66. *Congressional Record* (1935), 74th Congress, 1st session, 7883–7885, 7887; 49 Stat. 478 (1935); 49 Stat. 1462 (1936).

67. *Congressional Record* (1935), 74th Congress, 1st session, 10046, 10339, 10585, 11801. The bill included a provision that "no Filipino who receives the benefits of this act shall be entitled to return to the continental United States." E. Bogardus, "The Filipino Repatriation Movement in the United States," *Sociology and Social Research* 21 (1) (1936): 68–70.

68. *San Francisco Chronicle*, February 9, 1935, 8; *Chicago Defender*, February 23, 1935, 4.

69. *Los Angeles Times*, July 26, 1935, A4.

70. *Los Angeles Times*, February 8, 1936, 4.

71. *Los Angeles Times*, February 15, 1936, 2; *Los Angeles Times*, February 8, 1936, 4.

72. *Time*, April 13, 1936, 17.

73. *Los Angeles Times*, July 1936, 19; *Los Angeles Times*, March 21, 1937, C6; .

74. *Los Angeles Times*, October 4, 1936, 1–2.

75. It is difficult to know exactly how many Filipinos worked as merchant mariners. According to the U.S. Bureau of Navigation, there were 7,890 working in the industry in 1929 (about 2 percent of the total number of workers in the trade). This number is deceptive, however, since many of the Filipinos were only signed on for short stints (including single transoceanic tours—Manila to Hong Kong, for instance), not as permanent employees. The majority of these men (71 percent) worked in the foreign trade, primarily in the Pacific, so the claim often made by exclusionists that they were displacing whites is not supported by the data. B. Lasker, *Filipino Immigration to the Continental United States and Hawaii* (Chicago: University of Chicago Press, 1931), 59–60.

76. Charles Sanders, the chief of the Bureau of Navigation's shipping service, estimated that there were roughly fifteen hundred Filipinos working on American ships, although other estimates ranged as high as nine thousand men, who worked primarily as stewards' helpers and engine-room firemen. Ship owners claimed that Filipinos were particularly well suited to working in the high temperature of the engine rooms, because of their tropical background. The Merchant Marine Act of 1936 also restricted the number of "aliens" that could work on passenger ships, requiring that 80 percent of the crews be

American citizens beginning in 1936 and graduating to 90 percent of the crew by 1938. A number of Filipino worked as musicians on passenger vessels. *Los Angeles Times,* September 8, 1936, 21; *Los Angeles Times,* November 13, 1937, 17.

77. *Los Angeles Times,* September 30, 1937, 6; *The Philippines Mail,* October 11, 1937, 1, 3. The Department of Labor issued an order in 1935 ruling that six hundred Filipinos who had departed the Philippines before the passage of the Tydings-McDuffie Act but arrived in the United States after its ratification were subject to deportation. These individuals were initially held at the Angel Island detention facility while they appealed to stay in country. After a few months they were "paroled" to San Francisco's International Institute, and many of them moved on and started a new life in the United States while waiting for nearly a year to learn their fate. Immigration officials sent out letters in April 1935 asking these individuals to voluntarily return to Angel Island to be repatriated. It is not clear how many of these six hundred people actually returned. *The Philippines Mail,* April 15, 1935, 1. See also U.S. Department of Justice, *Administrative Decisions under Immigration and Nationality Laws,* vol. 2 (Washington, DC: GPO, 1947), 340–345.

78. 50 Stat. 165 (1937); 53 Stat. 1133 (1939).

79. *Time,* October 3, 1938, 10; *Nation,* September 4, 1935, 265; U.S. Department of Justice, *Annual Report of Attorney General of the United States, 1941–1942* (Washington, DC: GPO, 1942), 232.

NOTES TO CHAPTER 6

1. Though the Tydings-McDuffie Act was passed in 1934, the ten-year probation clock did start until 1936 because the law required that a series of steps be met before the probationary period could begin. These steps included the drafting and ratification of a national constitution, the approval of this constitution by the president of the United States, and the election of a transition government, which was complete in November 1935. Independence was set to begin on July 4, 1946, immediately following the expiration of the ten-year probation period. 48 Stat. 456, 463–465; T. Friend, *Between Two Empires: The Ordeal of the Philippines, 1929–1946* (New Haven, CT: Yale University Press, 1965), 151–168.

2. The Tydings-McDuffie Act required all Philippine government officials to sign an oath before taking office declaring adherence to the "supreme authority of and . . . maintain[ing] true faith and allegiance to the United States." The United States also maintained direct supervision and control over Philippine foreign and trade policy. The act mandated English as the language of instruction in all public schools. The decisions of Philippine courts were also subject to review and veto by the U.S. Supreme Court. Section 2(12) contains the provision allowing the U.S. president to call all members of the Philippine armed forces into service in support of American military operations. 48 Stat. 456–457.

3. T. Rojo, "An Appeal for U.S. Citizenship," *The Philippines Mail,* February 26, 1940, 1.

4. R. Maddox, *The United States and Word War II* (Boulder, CO: Westview, 1992), 100–106.

5. Executive Order, April 5, 1901 (President McKinley). The order called for the enlistment of up to five hundred Filipinos a year in the U.S. Navy. It was amended a few months, on June 25, to include natives of Guam. The amended Executive Order also

changed the language of the decree, striking out the term "Filipino" and replacing it with the "natives of the Islands of the Philippines," presumably to prevent Chinese residents of the Philippines from taking advantage of the program. The number of Filipino enlistees was increased after 1908, averaging more than 1,100 recruits per year between 1909 and 1916. These numbers increased dramatically during the World War I era, when approximately 11,400 were enlisted from 1917 and 1919. Filipinos, like African Americans, could only serve at the rank of mess attendant or steward and were prohibited from admission to other ranks in the U.S. Navy until 1948. Some 25,000 Filipinos served in the navy during World War I.

6. The acts did, however, include exceptions designed to stealthily aid the Allied powers. 49 Stat. 1081; 49 Stat. 1152; 50 Stat. 121.

7. 54 Stat. 12 (1939); 22 U.S.C.S. § 245j et seq. As far back as 1937, U.S. Secretary of State Cordell Hull instructed the Department of War to stop issuing passports to Filipinos who wanted to go abroad, citing the 1937 Neutrality Act's restriction on freedom of movement to belligerent nations.

8. As discussed in the previous chapter, Section 302 of the Merchant Marine Act of 1936 was passed with support of West Coast nativists such as Andrew Furuseth and Paul Scharrenberg. The act restricted the number of "aliens" that could be employed on American-registered ships and by 1938 mandated that such vessels have a crew of no less than 90 percent American citizens. The law was designed to protect white labor in the shipping industry from competition from cheap Asian labor. 49 Stat. 1985.

9. To avoid restrictions on commerce imposed by the Neutrality Act, American shipping companies often registered their vessels under foreign flags to circumvent travel prohibitions.

10. *Suspine et al. v. Compania Transatlantica Centroamericana,* 37 F. Supp 268 (1940); *New York Times,* March 15, 1941, 18.

11. The Alien Registration Act imposed criminal penalty of up to ten years in prison and a ten-thousand-dollar fine for violating the law. *Los Angeles Times,* May 26, 1940, 1; *Washington Post,* May 26, 1940, 1–2; 54 Stat. 670; 8 U.S.C. § 452; 6 Fed. Reg. 3826 (1941).

12. Conservatives claimed that communists had infiltrated the U.S. armed forces and urged rank-and-file military personnel to agitate for better pay and benefits and lobbied for improved living conditions.

13. Representative Martin Dies (D-Texas), who chaired the House Committee on Un-American Activities, eagerly endorsed the fingerprinting of aliens and subversives. Dies declared that the Communist Party was "incontrovertibly subversive" and also singled out an unnamed seven-thousand-member trade union, likely the ILWU, as dominated by alien radicals. Representative Emmanuel Celler (D-New York) offered a related bill authorizing the FBI to increase its wiretapping surveillance to combat "fifth column activities." *Washington Post,* May 26, 1940, 1.

14. Alien registrants had to pay a one-dollar registration fee to process their paperwork and were required to reregister with the federal government on a yearly basis. *Washington Post,* July 31, 1940, 13; *New York Times,* July 31, 1940, 11.

15. 54 Stat. 670. According to the U.S. Department of Justice, 45,282 Filipinos on the U.S. mainland registered under the Alien Registration Act. *The Philippines Mail,* March 28, 1942, 3.

16. Gancy was born in Cavite province in 1900, immigrated to the United States in 1927, and had lived in Minneapolis for just a few months at the time of his arrest. He attended Harvard Law School and later worked for the U.S. Department of Labor. At the time of his arrest, he was planning to launch a monthly political magazine called "Pacific World," which would help promote citizenship rights for Filipinos in the United States. *Chicago Tribune*, April 6, 1944, 15; *Washington Post*, February 22, 1944, 11.

17. Minnesota had also been the site of the first federal prosecution of the Smith Act in 1941, when members of the Socialist Workers Party and the Minnesota Teamsters Union were put on trial for their antiwar positions and wartime strike activities. See G. Stone, *Perilous Times: Free Speech in Wartime; From the Sedition Act of 1798 to the War on Terrorism* (New York: Norton, 2004), 255; R. Goldstein, *Political Repression in Modern America: From 1870 to 1976* (Urbana: University of Illinois Press, 2001), 252–253.

18. *United States v. Gancy*, 54 F. Supp 755 (1944); *Chicago Tribune*, April 6, 1944, 15; *Chicago Tribune*, April 20, 1944, 6. See also the case of Mimo Guzman, a Filipino immigrant accused by the FBI of inciting the "dark skinned races" to rise up against the United States. Guzman was alleged to be working in alliance with African Americans and Japanese to launch an uprising in the United States against white authorities, in order to establish "colored supremacy." He was charged with failing to register with the Selective Service. *New York Times*, August 1, 1942, 3. The Philippine resident commissioner's office also protested the registration of Filipinos as aliens under the act, arguing that the law disregarded their oath of allegiance to the United States. *The Philippines Mail*, September 16, 1940, 1–2.

19. The conference featured dozens of governors and state attorney generals, as well as representatives of the Department of Justice. The Roosevelt administration sought to centralize the data about alien and subversive activities through J. Edgar Hoover at the FBI, believing that Hoover's agency was best equipped to analyze and act on information about foreign subversion. *New York Times*, August 6, 1940, 1.

20. The inclusion of aliens within the legislation was aimed more at surveillance of foreigners than at actually drafting them into service. Since they were already required to register under the Alien Registration Act, this was a way to track those who did not register with the Selective Service. The act also singled out domestic subversives as threats to the common defense, barring alleged communists and German Bund members from filling job vacancies that came about as a result of military induction. 54 Stat. 885–887, 892.

21. 54 Stat. 1168–1170; G. Knight, "Nationality Act of 1940," *American Bar Association Journal* 26 (1940): 938–940.

22. M. Koessler, "Subject, Citizen, National, and Permanent Allegiance," *Yale Law Review* 56 (1946): 60–67.

23. The 1940 Nationality Act clarified the statutory qualifications for birthright citizenship ("Nationality at Birth") by delimiting the geographical border lines of American territoriality to exclude certain "outlying possessions," such as the Philippines, Guam, and Samoa. It also devised new regulations for jus sangunis citizenship ("Nationality through Naturalization") for children born abroad to one or more American parents and modified length-of-residency requirements for naturalization petitioners. Moreover, the statute laid out provisions for expatriation ("Loss of Nationality"). 54 Stat. 1137.

24. The requisite allegiance of the national to the nation in a democratic polity presumed a reciprocal set of obligations and duties from the state to protect and provide for the welfare of its members. 54 Stat. 1137.

25. Filipinos living in the United States were classified as "non-declarants," so they could not voluntarily enlist. Congress had temporarily lifted this requirement during World War I, but it remained in force in the 1940s. 28 Stat. 216; 54 Stat. 1137 (sec. 504); *New York Times*, September 3, 1941, 14.

26. *Washington Post*, March 24, 1942, 11.

27. *Washington Post*, January 3, 1942, 3; *Los Angeles Times*, January 17, 1942, 11.

28. Only those between the ages of twenty and forty-five were liable for military service; others were subject to serving the war effort on the home front as part of the country's civilian support apparatus. 55 Stat. 844–845.

29. *Los Angeles Times*, January 3, 1942, A1.

30. The law was not without some kinks. The initial version of the bill classed the islanders as 4C (neutral aliens seeking relief from military service), but a few weeks later, on January 2, 1942, the War Department recodified the islanders' draft status. *Los Angeles Times*, January 17, 1942, 11; B. Santos, "Filipinos in War," *Far Eastern Survey* 11 (1942): 249. A later ruling by the Bureau of Navigation in spring 1942 allowed Filipinos to enlist in the U.S. Navy, but only at the rank of mess attendant. *The Philippines Mail*, March 28, 1942, 1.

31. C. Bulosan, "Freedom from Want," *Saturday Evening Post*, March 6, 1943, 12. See also A. Espiritu, *Five Faces of Exile: The Nation and Filipino American Intellectuals* (Stanford, CA: Stanford University Press, 2005), 48–63.

32. *San Francisco Chronicle*, April 10, 1942, 16.

33. E. Foner, *The Story of American Freedom* (New York: Norton, 1999), 243–244; G. Gilmore, *Defying Dixie: The Radical Roots of Civil Rights, 1919–1950* (New York: Norton, 2008), 364.

34. Though Salyer's study is focused on World War I, her analysis applies equally well to the racial dynamics of the World War II. L. Salyer, "Baptism by Fire: Race, Military Service, and U.S. Citizenship Policy, 1918–1935," *Journal of American History* 91 (3) (2004): 848.

35. *Washington Post*, March 24, 1942, 11; *New York Times*, March 15, 1942, 35; Santos, "Filipino in War," 250; *New York Times*, December 23, 1941, 26; *Washington Post*, March 7, 1942, 17.

36. The American Legion's action should not be taken as an expression of a serious commitment to racial equality. At the same meeting that produced this resolution, a resolution was also passed calling for the immediate internment of "American citizens of enemy alien extraction (Japanese) whose loyalty is questionable." *Los Angeles Times*, February 23, 1942, 7. Discrimination remained rampant in the defense industry, even though in the summer of 1941, the Roosevelt administration had issued Executive Order 8802, barring discrimination in defense jobs and establishing the Fair Employment Practices Commission (FEPC) to oversee compliance. The FEPC, however, had little enforcement power, and the color line remained pervasive in industrial plants and shipyards. See Gilmore, *Defying Dixie*, 360–382; P. Klinker and R. Smith, *The Unsteady March: The Rise and Decline of Racial Equality in America* (Chicago: University of Chicago Press, 1999), 161–202; D. Kryder, *Divided Arsenal: Race and the American State during World War II* (Cambridge: Cambridge University Press, 2000), 52–66.

37. R. T. Feria, "War and the Status of Filipino Immigrants," *Sociology and Social Research* 31(1) (1946): 51.

38. *New York Times*, January 6, 1942, 10; *Washington Post*, February 18, 1942, 28; *Wall Street Journal*, February 20, 1942, 1.

39. *The Philippines Mail*, June 23, 1942, 1; *The Philippines Mail*, March 10, 1942, 1; *The Philippines Mail*, April 26, 1943, 1; *The Philippines Mail*, March 10, 1942, 1.

40. Some agricultural and business leaders initially expressed hesitation about Japanese internment because of the disruptive effects it would have on farm production. This opposition, however, was likely motivated more out of personal financial concerns about having profitable Japanese lessees moved off white-owned land and the prospect of having these illegitimate leasing arrangements scrutinized by authorities. In the wake of the Filipino walkout, California attorney general Earl Warren promised to aggressively investigate widespread violations of California's alien land laws. *New York Times*, February 22, 1942, 22; *New York Times*, December 17, 1941, 32. Japanese farmers were said to account for as much as 33 percent of the West Coast's truck-farm production, with large stakes in crops such as lettuce, celery, asparagus, tomatoes, and spinach. The War Relocation Authority had interned Japanese participate in the "Food for Victory" campaign in the camps because of their agricultural skills, growing fruits and vegetables to support the American war effort. *Washington Post*, May 4, 1942, 11; *New York Times*, May 10, 1942, 2.

41. By the spring of 1943, West Coast growers were asking for a sharp increase in the number of the more tractable Mexican contract laborers to supplant Filipino workers, who were accused by agribusiness interests of demanding "excessive wages." *Los Angeles Times*, April 28, 1943, 1; *Los Angeles Times*, March 7, 1942, 7.

42. *Los Angeles Times*, February 20, 1942: A1; Santos, "Filipinos in War," 249; A. Fabros, "The Fight for Equality in the U.S. Armed Forces in World War II by Uncle Sam's Colored Soldiers," *Filipino American National Historical Society Journal* 4 (1996): 46; J. Wingo, "The First Filipino Regiment," *Asia and the Americas* 42 (6) (1942): 562.

43. Astorga added that a large group of Filipinos in his adopted state of New York had signed a pledge to revenge the attacks on the Philippines and Pearl Harbor and to drive the Japanese out of the islands. *Los Angeles Times*, January 2, 1942, 4; *Washington Post*, January 3, 1942, 3; *New York Times*, January 13, 1942, 10.

44. Wingo, "First Filipino Regiment," 562.

45. Fabros, "Fight for Equality," 46–48; L. Revilla, "Pineapples, Hawayanos, and Loyal Americans: Local Boys in the First Filipino Infantry Regiment, U.S. Army," *Social Process in Hawaii* 37 (1996): 61–63; Santos, "Filipinos in War," 249. The Second Filipino Regiment was commanded by Colonel Charles Clifford and trained at Camp Cooke in Lompoc, California. The Second Regiment was later reduced to battalion strength after many of its members transferred to the First Regiment.

46. Llorente had previously worked as a professor of economics at the University of the Philippines and at the time of his commission was serving in the Philippine resident commissioner's office in Washington, DC. *Washington Post*, March 14, 1942, 15; *Washington Post*, July 28, 1942, 9.

47. The Second War Powers Act made noncitizens serving in the U.S. military eligible for expedited citizenship and sent naturalization officers overseas to swear in alien soldiers serving in the American armed forces. 56 Stat. 182.

48. M. Buaken, "Life in the Armed Forces," *New Republic* 100 (1943): 279; M. Buaken, "Our Fighting Love of Freedom," *Asia and the Americas* 43 (6) (1943): 357–359.

49. The Philippine resident commissioner's office helped organize a national campaign to distribute the buttons to Filipinos across the United States. *New York Times,* December 21, 1941, 35; *Chicago Daily Tribune,* December 28, 1941, 2; *Los Angeles Times,* December 27, 1941, 1A; M. Buaken, "Life in the Armed Forces," 279.

50. I. Buaken, "You Can't Marry a Filipino, Not If You Live in California," *Commonweal,* March 16, 1945, 535–536.

51. Ibid., 536. In addition to antimiscegenation laws, Filipinos remained subject to California's alien land law until well into the war. In April 1943, California attorney general Robert Kenny issued a ruling exempting Filipinos from the restrictive statute because of their patriotic efforts during the war. Kenny's ruling was made in response to a request from the Santa Clara County district attorney seeking an arrest warrant for a Filipino accused of violating the state's alien land law. *The Philippines Mail,* April, 26, 1943, 4; *The Philippines Mail,* January 31, 1942, 1.

52. *New York Times,* April 20, 1942, 4; *New York Times,* April 23, 1942, 15.

53. Judge Black dismissed Mary Ventura's claims of American allegiance, ruling that her professed beliefs were irrelevant. In his estimation, the Japanese imperial government believed all persons of Japanese ancestry to be loyal to the emperor. Black believed that American-born Japanese would be motivated by blood loyalty to assist the Japanese imperial army. *Ex Parte Ventura et al.,* No. 498, 44. F. Supp. 520 (1942).

54. T. Friend, *Between Two Empires: The Ordeal of the Philippines, 1929–1946* (New Haven, CT: Yale University Press, 1965), 200–210; A. Millett and P. Maslowski, *For the Common Defense: A Military History of the United States* (New York: Free Press, 1994), 400–405.

55. In addition, all "naval components" of the Philippine armed forces were also placed under U.S. Navy command. 6 Fed. Reg. 3825 (1941).

56. The Scouts were established during the early days of American rule in the islands and were initially drawn from the Macabebe ethnic minority. The Macabebes had been loyalists to the Spanish colonial regime in the Philippines, and they provoked enmity from other Filipinos for their fierce defense of colonial rule. After the Spanish-American War, the Macabebes switched allegiance to the United States, much to the chagrin of Filipino revolutionaries. They were originally deployed by American military commanders to take on local rebels and were soon after organized into an official branch of the U.S. military. As adjuncts of the U.S. military, the Scouts had better training and equipment than members of the Philippine army, which was neglected by the Commonwealth government. Moreover, many of the Scouts had combat experience in World War I and were familiar with methods of modern warfare. J. Woolard, "The Philippine Scouts: The Development of America's Colonial Army" (Ph.D. diss., Ohio State University, 1975), 10–24, 58–60; B. Linn, *Guardians of Empire: The U.S. Army and the Pacific, 1902–1940* (Chapel Hill: University of North Carolina Press, 1999), 19–32.

57. The act contained provisions for naturalizing soldiers serving overseas, and rulings from federal officials declared Filipino nationals eligible for this benefit. 56 Stat. 182–183 (1942).

58. *Washington Post,* February 18, 1942, 1; *Chicago Daily Tribune,* February 18, 1942, 4.

59. *San Francisco Chronicle,* March 20, 1942, 5.

60. The issue of unequal pay had actually led to a mutiny among Philippine Scouts in 1924. Instead of acknowledging the injustice of unequal pay, American leaders blamed the revolt on "Red leaders" in the islands who promoted radical agitation within the Scout ranks for political gain.

61. *Los Angeles Times*, March 20, 1942, 9; F. Golay, *Face of Empire: United States–Philippine Relations, 1898–1946* (Manila: Ateneo de Manila University Press, 1998), 465–466.

62. The pay rates to American GIs started at around fifty dollars a month for infantrymen, so the proposed raise in pay for Filipino soldiers to eleven dollars a month was still quite low.

63. MacArthur was eventually forced to rescind his equal-pay order. *New York Times*, June 20, 1942, 6.

64. Diosdado Yap told the House Committee on Immigration and Naturalization that he represented thirty-seven different Filipino organizations from across the United States and Hawaii. He held a Ph.D. and regularly traveled across the country giving lectures on Philippine-American relations. In addition to publishing *Bataan* magazine, he also wrote for the *Manila Chronicle*. The letter-writing campaign was indeed a nationwide effort, including letters and telegrams from a broad range of organizations, ranging from Gene Manual of the Filipino National Council in New York to Roy Baldoz of the Filipino Community Council of Yakima, Washington. U.S. Congress, *Naturalization of Filipinos*, House Committee on Immigration and Naturalization Hearings, 78th Congress, 2d session (Washington, DC: GPO, 1944), 12, 32–37.

65. Ibid., 1–3. New York Representative Vito Marcantonio was an early supporter of granting citizenship rights to Filipinos. He first introduced a bill aimed at extending naturalization rights to Filipinos during the 76th Congress in 1939. He reintroduced the legislation again in 1941, 1943, and 1944 but found little support in the House. *Congressional Record* (1939) (HR 7239), 9207; *Congressional Record* (1941) (HR 1844), 122; *Congressional Record* (1943) (HR 2012), 1373. Marcantonio was a passionate advocate of immigrant and labor rights in Congress and was allied with a number of radical political figures such as W. E. B. Du Bois, Earl Browder, and William L. Patterson, African American leader of CPUSA.

66. Buaken, "Our Fighting Love of Freedom," 359.

67. 40 Stat. 542; *American Journal of International Law* 46 (1952): 259–262.

68. Farrington estimated that ten thousand Filipinos worked in the Hawaii defense industry. Political and industrial leaders argued that the potential labor shortage that would result from the loss of Filipino laborers after the war would be devastating to the islands' economy. In the words of Farrington, "We need every able-bodied man who is there and we need every able-bodied Filipino." Quoted in U.S. Congress, *Naturalization of Filipinos*, 19–23. The HSPA had also tried to prevent the enlistment of Filipinos into the U.S. military and the Hawaiian National Guard during World War I for the same reasons.

69. U.S. Congress, *Naturalization of Filipinos*, 18; One high-profile example of this contradiction was Francis Burton Harrison, who became a naturalized citizen of the Philippines in 1936. Harrison had previously served as American governor general of the Philippines. He took his oath at a special ceremony attended by Manuel Quezon, Sergio Osmena, and sixty members of the Philippine National Assembly. *Los Angeles Times*, November 15, 1936, B14.

70. U.S. Congress, *Naturalization of Filipinos*, 4.

71. Filipinos who came to the United States after 1934 were required to file a certificate of arrival. The number who arrived after 1934 was quite small, since they were subject to the quota of fifty per annum established by the Tydings-McDuffie Act.

72. U.S. Congress, *Naturalization of Filipinos*, 5–8.

73. The VFW endorsed the Sheppard bill, but Wilkins emphasized during the hearings that his organization was concerned principally with the naturalization of Filipino World War I veterans. Ibid., 8–10.

74. Yap misleadingly told the committee that Filipinos had not intermarried with African Americans, likely because he worried that close association with blacks might negatively affect their chances for citizenship. Representative Allen's response to Yap's assertion was that Filipinos had been "using good sense" not to intermarry with blacks. The intermarriage issue was brought up as part of a larger set of civil rights claims demanded by Filipinos. Yap and others testified about how their subordinate racial status affected their ability to find employment, own property, and legitimize their families. Yap reminded the committee that antimiscegenation laws doubly handicapped them, because white women who married Filipinos also lost their citizenship, hindering their ability to find work and making their children bastards. Ibid., 10–17.

75. A Filipino naturalization bill was also offered by Jennings Randolph of West Virginia (HR 542). *Congressional Record* (1945), 27, 58, A319, A3119, A3313.

76. *San Francisco Chronicle*, April 4, 1946, 4.

77. This dramatic change in outlook was evidenced by passage in the California State Assembly of House Resolution 230 endorsing the enactment of the McGehee bill. As discussed in the previous two chapters, the California legislature had taken a leading role in advocating legislation seeking Filipino exclusion because of their unassimilability. Remember also the decisive action in the state legislature enacting a statutory prohibition on Filipino-white intermarriage because of their racial undesirability. That just a decade later they were supporting legislation extending citizenship rights to Filipinos is quite remarkable. *Congressional Record* (1945), 4929.

78. Celler actually submitted two Indian-citizenship bills in the same year (HR 4415 and HR 4636). In support of his bill, Celler remarked, "We cannot, on one hand, revile the Nazi theories of racial supremacy, and on the other, ignore the sinister implication of our immigration legislation that bars one people and not another." *Congressional Record* (1944), A1347, A1427. Luce explained that her bill (HR 4479) was aimed at boosting the morale of Indian troops in Asia and Northern Africa who had faced a steady stream of Japanese propaganda in the Pacific battlefront about the racial discrimination of the United States and England in Asia. Luce reassured constituents that the costs of enacting her legislation would be small, since only three thousand Indians already residing in the United States would be eligible for naturalization under her bill and India would be subject to an immigration quota of one hundred persons per year. *Congressional Record* (1944), A2195–2196.

79. Curiously it took two years for legislators to realize the utility of merging the two bills. Senator J. William Fulbright took a leading role in the Senate in getting the legislation up for a vote on July 2, 1946, just two days before the Philippines was scheduled to be granted its independence. *Congressional Record* (1946), 6919, 6933, 7458, 7775–7776.

80. It is important to note that Filipinos, Chinese, and Indians were granted naturalization rights on a piecemeal basis and that other Asian immigrants remained racially barred. Although Japanese were the focus of the blood-quantum provision, other groups such as Koreans, Burmese, and Polynesians also remained ineligible to citizenship. 60 Stat. 416–417.

81. The Bell Trade Act, passed a few months before in April 1946, had established a provision that allowed the small number of Filipinos who had legally resided in the continental United States during the war period (1941–1946) to resume residence in the United States as nonquota immigrants. Filipinos admitted to the Territory of Hawaii under the special labor exceptions contained in the Tydings-McDuffie Act were not eligible under this statute. 60 Stat. 148.

82. 59 Stat. 659; 60 Stat. 339; 61 Stat. 401; See also K. Wong, *Americans First: Chinese Americans and the Second World War* (Cambridge, MA: Harvard University Press, 2005); R. Takaki, *Double Victory: A Multicultural History of America in World War II* (Boston: Little, Brown, 2000).

83. P. Agbayani-Siewert and L. Revilla, "Filipino Americans," in *Asian Americans: Contemporary Trends and Issues*, edited by P. G. Min (Thousand Oaks, CA: Sage, 1995), 141.

84. The Filipino Inter-Community Organizations of the Western States was a large umbrella group that worked closely with the resident commissioner's office on civil rights issues. *Congressional Record* (1946), A3920.

85. The quota of one hundred per year was allocated to the Philippines in accordance with provisions established in the 1924 Immigration Act. The quota on immigration was passed on the same day (July 4, 1946) as the granting of Philippine independence. 60 Stat. 1352 (1946); 60 Stat. 1353 (1946).

86. American companies owned more than half the sugar mills in Cuba and pressured the Truman administration to protect their U.S. market share from Philippine sugar imports. *Foreign Relations* 8 (1946): 861–863.

87. Congressional leaders made it clear to Filipino officials that passage of a postwar economic-recovery bill, known as the Philippine Rehabilitation Act, which allocated $620 million war-reconstruction payments to the islands, was contingent on approval of the Bell Act. Both bills were passed on the same day, April 30, 1946. The Philippine legislature was in no position to reject the inequitable terms of the Bell Act, considering the war-ravaged state of the country and its need for reconstruction assistance from the United States. See 60 Stat. 152–154; 60 Stat. 128. S. Shalom, "Philippine Acceptance of the Bell Trade Act: A Study in Manipulatory Democracy," *Pacific Historical Review* 49 (August 1980): 499–517; See also *Foreign Relations* 8 (1946): 861–863, 871, 937.

88. The term *rescission* refers to the act of rescinding or retracting a previously allocated financial obligation or contract. The twelve thousand or so men who served in the Philippine Scouts were eligible for regular veterans benefits because they were an official branch of the U.S. armed forces. 60 Stat. 14 (1946); see also *Second Supplementary Surplus Appropriations Rescission Act,* 60 Stat. 221 (1946).

89. President Truman vetoed an early version of the Rescission bill but signed off on an amended version a few months later. He acknowledged that the legislation undercut previous promises made to Filipinos but recognized the will of Congress to externalize

costs of postwar rehabilitation to the Philippine government. Truman stated that the passage of the act did not "release the United States from its moral obligation to provide for the heroic Philippine veterans who sacrificed so much for the common cause during the war." *Congressional Record* (1946), A2859.

90. The GI Bill of Rights contained programs that provided for education and college-tuition benefits, home loans, unemployment allowances, and vocational training. The Mustering Out Bill offered transitional funding to veterans to help them readjust to civilian life. The U.S. government offered $200 million to assist with issues of back pay and other benefits promised to Philippine soldiers, but this payout was contingent on the Philippine government dropping all future claims to benefits or rights promised to Filipino soldiers during the war.

91. United States High Commissioner to the Philippine Islands, "Annual Report of United States High Commissioner to the Philippine Islands" (1947), 65. See also 59 Stat. 401 (1945). U.S.-based members of the First and Second Filipino Regiments were qualified for full benefits as members of the U.S. Army. Members of the Philippine Scouts were similarly eligible since they were an official branch of the American armed forces.

92. *Congressional Record* (1946), A1020–1021.

93. 61 Stat. 608 (1947); 62 Stat. 193 (1948); 63 Stat. 661 (1949).

94. Romulo succeeded J. M. Elizalde at the Philippine resident commissioner's office in 1945. He praised Truman for his initial veto of the Rescission Act but pressed sympathetic colleagues in the U.S. Congress for remedial legislation to restore benefits to Philippine veterans. *Congressional Record* (1946), A1020–1021, A2859–2860.

95. 56 Stat. 183; 59 Stat. 658.

96. Vice Consul George Ennis was given naturalization authority in the islands by the INS commissioner, but apparently this was aimed at alien soldiers stationed in the Philippines, not at Filipinos. This was part of a larger program that sent INS officials to various military posts across the globe to naturalize alien servicepersons. Approximately seven thousand Filipino soldiers were naturalized during the war at bases outside the Philippines (mostly in the United States). The INS likely assumed that Filipinos did not meet the residency requirements of the Nationality Act and were therefore ineligible for citizenship. It was Attorney General Clark's ruling a month later that Filipino veterans were eligible for citizenship under the act that caused the INS to intervene, in an effort to prevent the large-scale naturalization of Filipinos. *Naturalization of 68 Filipino War Veterans*, 406 F. Supp. 931 (1975); *Olegario v. United States*, 629 F. 2d 209 (1980); *INS v. Pangilinan*, 486 U.S. 875 (1988), 796 F. 2d 1091 (1986).

97. *Naturalization of 68 Filipino War Veterans*, 406. F. Supp. at 933–934.

98. Carusi never produced any evidence to support his claims that a Philippine official asked him to revoke Ennis's naturalization authority. The recruitment of Filipinos to Japan after the war was covered in 59 Stat. 543.

99. About four thousand Filipino veterans were naturalized in the four-month period between Phillips's appointment and the December 1946 deadline. This is a relatively small number, since more than two hundred thousand servicepersons were eligible. *INS v. Hibi*, 414 U.S. 5, 94 S. Ct. 19, 38 L. Ed. 2d 7 (1973).

100. Quoted in *Naturalization of 68 Filipino War Veterans*, 406 F. Supp. at 937; see also *INS v. Hibi*, 414 U.S. 5, 94 S. Ct. 19, 38 L. Ed. 2d, 7 (1973).

101. *INS v. Pangilinan*, 486 U.S. at 879.

102. Filipinos living in the United States faced obstacles to the acquisition of citizenship even after the war. In the case of *Viloria v. United States,* a Filipino who worked as a civilian employee of the U.S. Army during the war was denied naturalization in Hawaii when the INS claimed that he failed to meet the residency requirements for citizenship. Viloria had been assigned to work for the Army Corps of Engineers in Guam in May 1946, which technically meant that he had been "absent" from the United States. His initial application for naturalization in Hawaii was denied by an INS examiner, but the decision was later overturned in U.S. district court. 84 F. Supp. 584 (1949).

Bibliography

Abel, Emily. 2004. "Only the Best Class of Immigration: Public Health Policy toward Mexicans and Filipinos in Los Angeles, 1910–1940." *American Journal of Public Health* 94 (6): 932–939.

Agbayani-Siewert, Pauline, and Linda Revilla. 1995. "Filipino Americans." In *Asian Americans: Contemporary Trends and Issues*, edited by Pyong Gap Min. Thousand Oaks, CA: Sage.

Alcantara, Ruben. 1981. *Sakada: Filipino Adaptation in Hawaii*. New York: University Press of America.

———. 1987. "The 1920 Hawaii Plantation Strike." In *Festschrift in Honor of Dr. Marcelino Foronda, Jr.*, edited by Emerita S. Quito. Manila: De La Salle University Press.

Almaguer, Tomás. 1994. *Racial Fault Lines: The Historical Origins of White Supremacy in California*. Berkeley: University of California Press.

Anderson, Benedict. 1991. *Imagined Communities: Reflections on the Origin and Spread of Nationalism*. New York: Verso.

Anderson, Warwick. 2006. *Colonial Pathologies: American Tropical Medicine, Race, and Hygiene in the Philippines*. Durham, NC: Duke University Press.

Anthony, Donald. 1931. "Filipino Labor in Central California." *Sociology and Social Research* 16 (2): 149–156.

Armstrong, Z. *Notable Southern Families*. Chattanooga, TN: Lookout, 1918.

Austin O. P. 1902. "Problems of the Pacific: The Commerce of the Great Ocean." *National Geographic Magazine* 13 (8): 303–318.

Ayala, Cesar. 1999. *American Sugar Kingdom: The Plantation Economy of the Spanish Caribbean, 1898–1934*. Chapel Hill: University of North Carolina Press.

Azuma, Eichiro. 2005. *Between Two Empires: Race, History, and Transnationalism in Japanese America*. New York: Oxford University Press.

Baldoz, Rick. 2004. "Valorizing Racial Boundaries: Hegemony and Conflict in the Racialization of Filipino Migrant Labour." *Ethnic and Racial Studies* 27 (6): 969–986.

Beale, Howard. 1956. *Theodore Roosevelt and the Rise of America to World Power*. Baltimore: Johns Hopkins University Press.

Beechert, Edward. 1985. *Working in Hawaii: A Labor History*. Honolulu: University of Hawaii Press.

Bender, Thomas. 2006. *A Nation among Nations: America's Place in World History*. New York: Hill and Wang.

Beveridge, Albert. 1968. *The Meaning of the Times*. Freeport, NY: Books for Libraries Press. Originally published in 1908.

Blumer, Herbert. 2000. "The Future of the Color Line." In *The Selected Works of Herbert Blumer: A Public Philosophy for Mass Society*, edited by S. Lyman and A. Viditch, 208–222. Urbana: University of Illinois Press.

———. 2000. "Race Prejudice as Sense of Group Position." In *The Selected Works of Herbert Blumer: A Public Philosophy for Mass Society*, edited by S. Lyman and A. Viditch, 196–207. Urbana: University of Illinois Press.

Bogardus, Emory. 1929. "American Attitudes towards Filipinos." *Sociology and Social Research* 14 (1): 59–69.

———. 1929. "The Filipino Immigrant Problem." *Sociology and Social Research* 13 (5): 472–479.

———. 1932. "What Race Are Filipinos?" *Sociology and Social Research* 16 (1): 274–279.

———. 1936. "The Filipino Repatriation Movement in the United States." *Sociology and Social Research* 21 (1): 67–71.

Bonus, Rick. 2000. *Locating Filipino Americans: Ethnicity and the Cultural Production of Space*. Philadelphia: Temple University Press.

Bouve, Clement. 1912. *A Treatise on the Laws Governing the Exclusion and Expulsion of Aliens in the United States*. Washington, DC: John Byrne.

Bowler, Alida. 1932. "Social Hygiene in Racial Problems—The Filipino." *Journal of Social Hygiene* 18 (8): 452–456.

Brands, H. W. 1992. *Bound to Empire: The United States and the Philippines*. New York: Oxford University Press.

Brown, Richard Maxwell. 1975. *Strain of Violence: Historical Studies of American Violence and Vigilantism*. New York: Oxford University Press.

Bruinius, Harry. 2007. *Better for All the World: The Secret History of Forced Sterilization and America's Quest for Racial Purity*. New York: Vintage.

Buaken, Iris. 1945. "You Can't Marry a Filipino, Not If You Live in California." *Commonweal*, March 16, 535–537.

Buaken, Manuel. 1943. "Life in the Armed Forces." *New Republic* 100:278–279.

———. 1943. "Our Fighting Love of Freedom." *Asia and the Americas* 43 (6): 357– 359.

———. 1948. *I Have Lived with the American People*. Caldwell, ID: Caxton.

Bulosan, Carlos. 1943. "Freedom from Want." *Saturday Evening Post*, March 6, 12.

Burma, John. 1963. "Interethnic Marriage in Los Angeles, 1948–1959." *Social Forces* 42 (2): 156–165.

Burnett, Christina, and Burke Marshall. 2001. *Foreign in a Domestic Sense: Puerto Rico, American Expansion and the Constitution*. Durham, NC: Duke University Press.

Calata, Alexander. 2002. "The Role of Education in Americanizing Filipinos." In *Mixed Blessing: The Impact of the American Colonial Experience on Politics and Society in the Philippines*, edited by H. McFerson. Westport, CT: Greenwood.

California Department of Industrial Relations. 1930. *Facts about Filipino Immigration*. San Francisco: R&E Research Associates.

Catapusan, Benicio. 1938. "Filipino Intermarriage Problems in the United States." *Sociology and Social Research* 23 (3): 265–272.

Chalmers, David. 1987. *Hooded Americanism: The History of the Ku Klux Klan*. Durham, NC: Duke University Press.

Cheng, Lucie, and Edna Bonacich, eds. 1984. *Labor Immigration under Capitalism: Asian Workers in the United States before World War II*. Berkeley: University of California Press.

Choy, Catherine Ceniza. 2003. *Empire of Care: Nursing and Migration in Filipino American History*. Durham, NC: Duke University Press.

Clifford, Mary Dorita. 1969. "The Hawaiian Sugar Planter Association and Filipino Exclusion." In *The Filipino Exclusion Movement*, edited by J. M. Saniel, 11–29. Quezon City, Philippines: Institute for Asian Studies.

Coloma, Casiano. 1939. *A Study of the Filipino Repatriation Movement*. San Francisco: R&E Research Associates.

Commonwealth Club of California. 1929. "Filipino Immigration." *Transactions* 24 (7): 307–378.

Coudert, Frederic. 1903. "Our New Peoples: Citizens, Subjects, Nationals or Aliens." *Columbia Law Review* 3:13–32.

Cressey, Paul. 1932. *The Taxi-Dance Hall: A Sociological Study in Commercialized Recreation and Life*. Chicago: University of Chicago Press.

Curry, Charles. 1921. *Alien Land Laws and Alien Rights*. 67th Congress, 1st session, Doc. 89. Washington, DC: GPO.

Daniel, Cletus. 1981. *Bitter Harvest: A History of California Farmworkers*. Ithaca, NY: Cornell University Press.

De La Pedraja, Rene. 1992. *The Rise and Decline of U.S. Merchant Shipping in the Twentieth Century*. New York: Twayne.

Dewitt, Howard. 1976. *Anti-Filipino Movements in California: A History*. San Francisco: R&E Research Associates.

———. 1978. "The Filipino Labor Union: The Salinas Lettuce Strike of 1934." *Amerasia* 5 (2): 1–22.

Empeno, Henry. 1976. "Anti-Miscegenation Laws and the Filipino." In *Letters in Exile: An Introductory Reader on the History of Pilipinos in America*, edited by Jesse Quinsaat and UCLA Asian American Studies Center. Los Angeles: University of California Press.

España-Maram, Linda. 2006. *Creating Masculinity in Los Angeles's Little Manila: Working-Class Filipinos and Popular Culture in the United States*. New York: Columbia University Press.

Espiritu, Augusto. 2005. *Five Faces of Exile: The Nation and Filipino American Intellectuals*. Stanford, CA: Stanford University Press.

Espiritu, Yen Le. 1995. *Filipino American Lives*. Philadelphia: Temple University Press.

———. 2003. *Home Bound: Filipino American Lives across Cultures, Communities, and Countries*. Berkeley: University of California Press.

Fabros, Alex, Jr. 1996. "The Fight for Equality in the U.S. Armed Forces in World War II by Uncle Sam's Colored Soldiers." *Filipino American National Historical Society Journal* 4:42–48.

Feria, R. T. 1946. "War and the Status of Filipino Immigrants." *Sociology and Social Research* 31 (1): 48–53.

Fischer, Lloyd. 1953. *The Harvest Labor Market in California*. Cambridge, MA: Harvard University Press.

Foner, Eric. 1999. *The Story of American Freedom*. New York: Norton.

Forbes, W. Cameron. 1928. *The Philippine Islands*. 2 vols. Boston: Houghton Mifflin.

Ford, Nancy. 2001. *Americans All! Foreign-Born Soldiers in World War I*. College Station: Texas A&M Press.

Foster, Nellie. 1932. "Legal Status of Filipino Intermarriage in California." *Sociology and Social Research* 16:441–454.

Friday, Chris. 1995. *Organizing Asian American Labor: The Pacific Coast Canned-Salmon Industry.* Philadelphia: Temple University Press.

Friend, Theodore. 1965. *Between Two Empires: The Ordeal of the Philippines, 1929–1946.* New Haven, CT: Yale University Press.

Fujita-Rony, Dorothy. 2003. *American Workers, Colonial Power: Philippine Seattle and the Transpacific West, 1919–1941.* Berkeley: University of California Press.

Gannett, Henry. 1904. "The Philippine Islands and Their People." *National Geographic Magazine* 15 (3): 91–112.

Gilmore, Glenda. 2008. *Defying Dixie: The Radical Roots of Civil Rights, 1919–1950.* New York: Norton.

Glenn, Evelyn Nakano. 2002. *Unequal Freedom: How Race and Gender Shaped American Citizenship and Labor.* Cambridge, MA: Harvard University Press.

Go, Julian. 2004. "Racism and Colonialism: Meanings of Difference and Ruling Practices in America's Pacific Empire." *Qualitative Sociology* 27 (1): 35–58.

Goethe, C. M. 1931. "Filipino Immigration Viewed as Peril." *Current History* 34:353–354.

Golay, Frank. 1998. *Face of Empire: United States–Philippines Relations.* Manila: Ateneo de Manila University Press.

Goldstein, Robert. 2001. *Political Repression in Modern America: From 1870 to 1976.* Urbana: University of Illinois Press.

Gordon, Linda. 2001. *The Great Arizona Orphan Abduction.* Cambridge, MA: Harvard University Press.

Gusfield, Joseph. 1986. *The Symbolic Crusade: Status Politics and the American Temperance Movement.* Urbana: University of Illinois Press.

———. 1996. *Contested Meanings: The Construction of Alcohol Problems.* Madison: University of Wisconsin Press.

Hall, S., C. Critcher, T. Jefferson, J. N. Clarke, and B. Roberts. 1978. *Policing the Crisis: Mugging, the State and Law and Order.* New York: Holmes and Meier.

Haney López, Ian. 1996. *White by Law: The Legal Construction of Race.* New York: NYU Press.

Heap, Chad. 2009. *Slumming: Sexual and Racial Encounters in American Nightlife.* Chicago: University of Chicago Press.

Higham, John. 1963. *Strangers in the Land: Patterns of American Nativism, 1860–1925.* New Brunswick, NJ: Rutgers University Press.

Hing, Bill Ong. 1993. *Making and Remaking Asian America through Immigration Policy.* Stanford, CA: Stanford University Press.

Historical Statistics of the United States, 1789–1945. 1949. Washington, DC: GPO.

Hobsbawm, Eric. 1987. *The Age of Empire, 1875–1914.* New York: Vintage.

Hodes, Martha. 1999. *Sex, Love, Race: Crossing Boundaries in North American History.* New York: NYU Press.

Holt, Thomas. 2001. *The Problem of Race in the 21st Century.* Cambridge, MA: Harvard University Press.

Horsman, Reginald. 1981. *Race and Manifest Destiny: Origins of Racial Anglo-Saxonism.* Cambridge, MA: Harvard University Press.

Ichihashi, Yamato. 1932. *Japanese in the United States: A Critical Study of the Problems of Japanese Immigrants.* Stanford, CA: Stanford University Press.

Jacobson, Matthew F. 1998. *Whiteness of a Different Color: European Immigrants and the Alchemy of Race.* Cambridge, MA: Harvard University Press.

———. 2001. *Barbarian Virtues: The United States Encounters Foreign Peoples at Home and Abroad, 1876–1917*. New York: Hill and Wang.

Jamieson, Stuart. 1976. *Labor Unionism in American Agriculture*. New York: Arno.

Jelinek, Lawrence. 1982. *Harvest Empire: A History of California Agriculture*. San Francisco: Boyd and Fraser.

Jung, Moon-Kie. 2006. *Reworking Race: The Making of Hawaii's Interracial Working Class*. New York: Columbia University Press.

Kerkvliet, Melinda. 2003. *Unbending Cane: Pablo Manlapit, a Filipino Labor Leader in Hawaii*. Honolulu: University of Hawaii Press.

Klinker, Phillip, and Smith, Rogers. 1999. *The Unsteady March: The Rise and Decline of Racial Equality in America*. Chicago: University of Chicago Press.

Knight, George. 1940. "Nationality Act of 1940." *American Bar Association Journal* 26:938–940.

Koessler, Maximillian. 1946. "Subject, Citizen, National, and Permanent Allegiance." *Yale Law Review* 56:58–76.

Konvitz, Milton. 1946. *The Alien and the Asiatic in American Law*. Ithaca, NY: Cornell University Press.

Kramer, Paul. 2006. *The Blood of Government: Race, Empire, the United States, and the Philippines*. Chapel Hill: University of North Carolina Press.

Kraut, Alan. 1994. *Silent Travelers: Germs, Genes, and the Immigrant Menace*. New York: Basic Books.

Kryder, Daniel. 2000. *Divided Arsenal: Race and the American State during World War II*. Cambridge: Cambridge University Press.

Lafeber, Walter. 1998. *The New Empire: An Interpretation of American Expansion, 1860–1898*. Ithaca, NY: Cornell University Press.

Lasker, Bruno. 1931. *Filipino Immigration in the Continental United States and Hawaii*. Chicago: University of Chicago Press.

Lee, Erika. 2003. *At America's Gates: Chinese Immigration during the Exclusion Era*. Chapel Hill: University of North Carolina Press.

Lee, Shelley. 2011. *Claiming the Oriental Gateway: Prewar Seattle and Japanese America*. Philadelphia: Temple University Press.

Linn, Brian. 1999. *Guardians of Empire: The U.S. Army and the Pacific, 1902–1940*. Chapel Hill: University of North Carolina Press.

Lui, Mary Ting Yi. 2005. *The Chinatown Trunk Mystery: Murder, Miscegenation, and Other Dangerous Encounters in Turn-of-the-Century New York*. Princeton, NJ: Princeton University Press.

Maddox, Robert. 1992. *The United States and Word War II*. Boulder, CO: Westview.

Majka Linda, and Theo Majka. 1982. *Farmworkers, Agribusiness, and the State*. Philadelphia: Temple University Press.

Masson, Jack, and Donald Guimary. 1981. "Pilipinos and Unionization of the Alaskan Canned Salmon Industry." *Amerasia* 8 (2): 1–30.

May, Glenn. 1980. *Social Engineering in the Philippines*. Westport, CT: Greenwood.

McClatchy V. S. 1924. "Oriental Immigration in California." In *The Alien in Our Midst: Selling Out Birthright for a Mess of Pottage*, edited by M. Grant and C. S. Davison, 188–197. New York: Galton.

Macfarlane, P. 1913. "Japan in California." *Collier's*, June 17.

McGovney, Dudley. 1923. "Race Discrimination in Naturalization Law." *Iowa Law Bulletin* 8:129–161.

———. 1934. "Our Non-Citizen Nationals, Who Are They?" *California Law Review* 22:593–635.

McWilliams, Carey. 1935. "Exit the Filipino." *Nation* 116:265.

———. 1951. *Brothers under the Skin*. Rev. ed. Boston: Little, Brown.

———. 2000. *Factories in the Fields*. Berkeley: University of California Press. Originally published in 1939.

Melendy, H. Brett. 1977. *Asians in America: Filipinos, Koreans and East Indians*. Boston: Twayne.

Miller, Stuart C. 1984. *Benevolent Assimilation: The Conquest of the Philippines, 1899–1903*. New Haven, CT: Yale University Press.

Millett Allan, and Peter Maslowski. 1994. *For the Common Defense: A Military History of the United States*. New York: Free Press.

Mintz, Sidney. 1986. *Sweetness and Power: The Place of Sugar in Modern History*. New York: Penguin.

Mitchell, Don. 1996. *Lie of the Land: Migrant Workers in the California Landscape*. Minneapolis: University of Minnesota Press.

Molina, Natalia. 2006. *Fit to Be Citizens? Public Health in Los Angeles, 1879–1939*. Berkeley: University of California Press.

Moore, Elon. 1930. "Public Dance Halls in a Small City." *Sociology and Social Research* 14:260–262.

Moran, Rachel. 2001. *Interracial Intimacy: The Regulation of Race and Romance*. Chicago: University of Chicago Press.

Mumford, Kevin. 1997. *Interzones: Black/White Sex Districts in Chicago and New York in the Early Twentieth Century*. New York: Columbia University Press.

Myrdal, Gunnar. 1944. *An American Dilemma: The Negro Problem and American Democracy*. Vol. 2. New York: Harper and Row.

Ngai, Mae. 2004. *Impossible Subjects: Illegal Aliens and the Making of Modern America*. Princeton, NJ: Princeton University Press.

Nomura, Gail. 1986–1987. "Within the Law: The Establishment of Filipino Leasing Rights on the Yakima Indian Reservation." *Amerasia* 13:99–117.

Olin, Spencer. 1966. "European Immigrant and Oriental Alien: Acceptance and Rejection by the California Legislature of 1913." *Pacific Historical Review* 35 (3): 303–315.

Olmstead Alan, and Paul Rhode. "The Evolution of California Agriculture, 1850–2000." In *California Agriculture: Dimensions and Issues*, edited by Jerry Siebert. Berkeley, CA: Giannini Foundation of Agricultural Economics.

Omi, Michael, and Howard Winant. 1994. *Racial Formation in the United States: From the 1960s to the 1990s*. New York: Routledge.

Osumi, Megumi. 1982. "Asians and California's Anti-Miscegenation Laws." In *Asian and Pacific American Experiences: Women's Perspectives*, edited by Nobuya Tsuchida. Minneapolis: Asian/Pacific Learning Resource Center.

Panunzio, Constantine. 1942. "Intermarriage in Los Angeles, 1924–1933." *American Journal of Sociology* 47 (5): 690–701.

Parreñas, Rhacel. 1998. "White Trash Meets the Little Brown Monkeys." *Amerasia* 24 (4): 115–134.

Pascoe, Peggy. 1991. "Race, Gender and Intercultural Relations: The Case of Interracial Marriage." *Frontiers* 12 (1): 5–18.

————. 1996. "Miscegenation Law, Court Cases, and the Ideology of Race in Twentieth-Century America." *Journal of American History* 83 (1): 44–69.

————. 1999. "Race, Gender, and the Privileges of Property: On the Significance of Miscegenation Law in the U.S. West." In *Over the Edge: Remapping the American West*, edited by Valerie J. Matsumoto and Blake Allmendinger, 215–230. Berkeley: University of California Press.

————. 2009. *What Comes Naturally: Miscegenation Law and the Making of Race in America.* New York: Oxford University Press.

"Present-Day Immigration: With Special Reference to the Japanese." 1921. *Annals of the American Academy of American Political and Social Science* 93 (182): 13–54.

Prucha, Francis. 1986. *The Great Father: United States Government and American Indians.* Lincoln: University of Nebraska Press.

Rafael, Vincent. 2000. *White Love and Other Events in Filipino History.* Durham, NC: Duke University Press.

Reinecke, John. 1996. *The Filipino Piecemeal Strike of 1924–1925.* Honolulu: University of Hawaii Press.

Report of Governor C. C. Young's Fact Finding Committee, Mexicans in California. 1930. San Francisco: California State Printing Office.

Report to the Secretary of Interior by Alaska Governor. 1921. Washington, DC: GPO.

Reuter, Edward. 1931. *Race Mixture: Studies in Intermarriage and Miscegenation.* New York: McGraw-Hill.

Revilla, Linda. 1996. "'Pineapples, Hawayanos, and Loyal Americans: Local Boys in the First Filipino Infantry Regiment, U.S. Army." *Social Process in Hawaii* 37:57–73.

Rojo, Trinidad. 1937. "Social Maladjustment among Filipinos in the United States." *Sociology and Social Research* 21 (5): 447–457.

————. 1940. "An Appeal for U.S. Citizenship." *The Philippines Mail*, February 26, 1–2.

Rydell, Robert. 1984. *All the World's a Fair: Visions of Empire at American International Expositions, 1876–1916.* Chicago: University of Chicago Press.

Salyer, Lucy. 2004. "Baptism by Fire: Race, Military Service and U.S. Citizenship Policy, 1918–1935." *Journal of American History* 91 (3): 847–877.

Sanchez, George. 1993. *Becoming Mexican American: Ethnicity, Culture, and Identity in Chicano Los Angeles, 1900–1945.* New York: Oxford University Press.

Saniel, Josefa M., ed. 1967. *The Filipino Exclusion Movement, 1927–1935.* Quezon City, Philippines: Institute for Asian Studies.

Santos, Bienvenido. 1942. "Filipinos in War." *Far Eastern Survey* 11:249–250.

Sassen, Saskia. 1990. *The Mobility of Labor and Capital: A Study in International Investment and Labor Flows.* New York: Cambridge University Press.

Saxton, Alexander. 1971. *The Indispensable Enemy: Labor and the Anti-Chinese Movement in California.* Berkeley: University of California Press.

Scharrenberg, Paul. 1928. "Exclude the Filipinos." *Organized Labor* 29:57–59.

————. 1928. "Vital Issues Confronting the California Labor Movement." *Union Gazette*, March 31.

————. 1929. "The Philippine Problem: Attitude of American Labor toward Filipino Immigration and Philippine Independence." *Pacific Affairs* 2:49–54.

————. 1933. "Philippine Independence." *Seamen's Journal* 48 (April): 54–55.

————. 1933. "What Do Filipinos Want?" *Seamen's Journal* 48 (February): 22–23.

————. 1934. "Filipino Exclusion an Accomplished Fact." *San Francisco Labor Clarion*, April 13, 3.

————. 1939. "Filipinos Demand Special Privileges." *American Federationist* 46:1350–1353.

Shah, Nayan. 2001. *Contagious Divides: Epidemics and Race in San Francisco's Chinatown*. Berkeley: University of California Press.

Shalom, Stephen. 1980. "Philippine Acceptance of the Bell Trade Act: A Study in Manipulatory Democracy." *Pacific Historical Review* 49 (August): 499–517.

Sharma, Miriam. 1984. "Labor Migration and Class Formation among Filipinos in Hawaii, 1906–1946." In *Labor Immigration under Capitalism: Asian Workers in the United States before World War II*, edited by L. Cheng and E. Bonacich. Berkeley: University of California Press.

Smith, Rogers. 1999. *Civic Ideals: Conflicting Visions of Citizenship in U.S. History*. New Haven, CT: Yale University Press.

Starr, Kevin. 1996. *Endangered Dreams: The Great Depression in California*. New York: Oxford University Press.

State Board of Control of California. 1920. *California and the Oriental: Japanese, Chinese, and Hindus*. Sacramento: California State Printing Office.

Stavrianos, L. S. 1981. *Global Rift: The Third World Comes of Age*. New York: William Morrow.

Steiger, George. 1930. "The Filipinos as I Meet Them." *Organized Labor*, March 8, 6.

Stern, Alexandra. 2005. *Eugenic Nation: Faults and Frontiers of Better Breeding in Modern America*. Berkeley: University of California Press.

Stone, Geoffrey. 2004. *Perilous Times: Free Speech in Wartime; From the Sedition Act of 1798 to the War on Terrorism*. New York: Norton.

Takaki, Ronald. 1983. *Pau Hana: Plantation Life and Labor in Hawaii*. Honolulu: University of Hawaii Press.

————. 2000. *Double Victory: A Multicultural History of America in World War II*. Boston: Little, Brown.

Tchen, J. K. W. 1999. *New York before Chinatown: Orientalism and the Shaping of American Culture*. Baltimore: Johns Hopkins University Press.

Thompson, Lanny. 2002. "The Imperial Republic: A Comparison of the Insular Territories under U.S. Domination after 1898." *Pacific Historical Review* 71 (4): 535–574.

U.S. Bureau of Census. 1905. *Census of the Philippines Islands*. 4 vols. Washington, DC: GPO.

————. 1943. *Population Characteristics of Non-White Population by Race, 1940*. Washington, DC: GPO.

U.S. Bureau of Insular Affairs. 1901. *The People of the Philippines—Letter from the Secretary of War*. Washington, DC: GPO.

U.S. Commissioner General of Immigration. 1913. *Industrial Conditions in Hawaiian Islands*. Washington, DC: GPO.

U.S. Congress. 1930. *Exclusion of Immigration from the Philippine Islands*. House Committee on Immigration and Naturalization Hearings. 71st Congress, 2d session. Washington, DC: GPO.

————. 1930. *Immigration from Countries of Western Hemisphere*. House Committee on Immigration and Naturalization Hearings. 71st Congress, 2d session. Washington, DC: GPO.

————. 1932. *Independence for the Philippine Islands*. House Committee on Territories and Insular Affairs Hearings on HR 7233. 72d Congress, 1st session. Washington, DC: GPO.

———. 1933. *To Return Unemployed Filipinos to Philippine Islands*. House Committee on Immigration and Naturalization Hearings on HJ 549. 72d Congress, 2d session. Washington, DC: GPO.

———. 1944. *Naturalization of Filipinos*. House Committee on Immigration and Naturalization Hearings on HR 2012, 2776, 3633, 4003, 4229, and 4826. 78th Congress, 2d session. Washington, DC: GPO.

U.S. Department of Commerce and Labor 1906. *Bulletin of the Bureau of Labor*. Washington, DC: GPO.

U.S. Department of Justice. 1942. *Annual Report of Attorney General of the United States, 1941–1942*. Washington, DC: GPO.

———. 1947. *Administrative Decisions under Immigration and Nationality Laws*. Vol. 2. Washington, DC: GPO.

U.S. National Commission on Law Observance. 1931. *Report on Crime and the Foreign Born*. Washington, DC: GPO.

U.S. Philippine Commission. 1900. *Report of the Philippine Commission to the President*. 4 vols. Washington, DC: GPO.

———. 1912. *Report of the Philippine Commission to the Secretary of War, 1911*. Washington, DC: GPO.

U.S. Secretary of Labor. 1916. *Labor Conditions in Hawaii*. Washington, DC: GPO.

Vargas, Zaragosa. 2004. *Labor Rights Are Civil Rights: Mexican American Workers in Twentieth-Century America*. Princeton, NJ: Princeton University Press.

Volpp, Leti. 2000. "American Mestizo: Filipinos and Anti-Miscegenation Laws in California." *UC-Davis Law Review* 33:795–836.

Wade, Wyn Craig. 1998. *The Fiery Cross: The Ku Klux Klan in America*. New York: Oxford University Press.

Waldinger, Roger. 2003. "Foreigners Transformed: International Migration and the Making of a Divided People." *Diaspora* 12 (2): 247–272.

Wentworth, Edna. 1941. *Filipino Plantation Workers in Hawaii*. San Francisco: Institute of Pacific Relations.

Whitehead, James. 2004. *Completing the Union: Alaska, Hawaii, and the Battle for Statehood*. Albuquerque: University of New Mexico Press.

Williams, Walter. 1980. "United States Indian Policy and the Debate over Philippine Annexation: Implications for the Origins of American Imperialism." *Journal of American History* 66 (4): 810–831.

Wingo, James. 1942. "The First Filipino Regiment." *Asia and the Americas* 42 (6): 562–564.

Wong, K. Scott. 2005. *Americans First: Chinese Americans and the Second World War*. Cambridge, MA: Harvard University Press.

Woolard, James. 1975. "The Philippine Scouts: The Development of America's Colonial Army." Ph.D. diss., Ohio State University.

The World Almanac and Encyclopedia 1901. 1901. New York: Press Publishing.

Zolberg, Aristide. 2006. *A Nation by Design: Immigration Policy in the Fashioning of America*. Cambridge, MA: Harvard University Press.

Index

About the Author

RICK BALDOZ teaches in the Department of Sociology at Oberlin College.